BWB

④

BW B

Heads, Hides & Horns

Texas Christian University Press

Fort Worth

HEADS, HIDES & HORNS

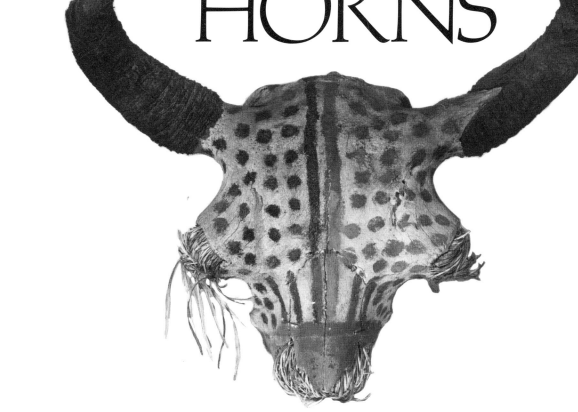

THE COMPLEAT BUFFALO BOOK

by LARRY BARSNESS

with a Foreword by

RON TYLER

Library of Congress Cataloging in Publication Data

Barsness, Larry.
  Heads, hides, and horns.

  Bibliography: p.
  Includes index.
    1. Bison, American. 2. West (U.S.)—Social
life and customs. 3. Indians of North America—
West (U.S.)—Food. I. Title.
F591.B277   1985   978   85-2606
ISBN 0-87565-008-2
ISBN 0-87565-017-1 (pbk).

Design and Production by WHITEHEAD & WHITEHEAD

With love,
to my wife Pat,
who encouraged and helped and shared

CONTENTS

FOREWORD

IN 1965, long before I came to the Amon Carter Museum as Curator of History, Mitchell A. Wilder, who himself had arrived on the scene only shortly before, conceived of an exhibition devoted to the bison in art. As director of the newly-opened Amon Carter Museum of Western Art, he was searching for good exhibitions on the American West—not just the obvious ones such as Charles M. Russell and Frederic Remington, whose paintings and sculpture the museum held in depth, but innovative shows that combined the disciplines of today's American Studies programs, which up to that point had been practiced in virtual exclusion of each other—and the bison offered a superb topic. This ubiquitous beast had fed and clothed and entertained Plains Indians for centuries and had inspired virtually every artist who reached the frontier. The buffalo had been written about extensively, but he had never been the subject of a well researched art exhibition.

Thousands of paintings, prints, photographs, sculptures, and artifacts were available, yet the bison exhibition remained little more than a dream until Wilder met Larry Barsness in the fall of 1968. In this extremely gifted writer, Wilder immediately recognized the talents necessary to combine history, myth, folklore, and fiction to tell the story of the buffalo. Barsness set to work the following year. Meanwhile I joined the Carter staff and began winnowing the immense amount of material that had been gathered for the exhibition, which was presented at the Amon Carter Museum, the Buffalo Bill Historical Center in Cody, Wyoming, the Glenbow Museum in Calgary, Alberta, and the Joslyn Art Museum in Omaha, Nebraska, in 1977 and 1978. Barsness was the author of a beautifully illustrated exhibition catalogue at that time, but scheduling, economics, and publishing eccentricities prevented inclusion of his full research.

Now, after years of additional study, Barsness has produced a factual yet highly readable account of the American bison. I am delighted to have been involved with the project and commend it to you as another example of the diverse and exotic American West, preserved forever in art and history—and now made available in this handsome format by the Texas Christian University Press.

Ron Tyler
Fort Worth

ACKNOWLEDGMENTS

ANY BOOK reaches completion because so many people helped the author—so many people that no author can thank each of them. Yet the wonderful thing to any author is people's interest in his project and desire to help. So to the dozens who talked with me—handed me pictures and newspaper clippings—thanks. I wish I could name you all.

I thank my associates at the University of Montana. Over the years some have read bits and pieces and made suggestions. Bill Farr found photos for me. Various people at the interlibrary loan desk searched out and obtained books and journals from all over the United States. The University of Montana Foundation granted money to visit the Conservation Center Library in Denver. And special thanks to Dale Johnson, Archivist at the Mansfield Library, who searched out letters and records even as the archives moved from one building to another.

Various people at the National Bison Range at Moiese, Montana helped the project along: Cy Young, Orville Kaschke, Joe Mazzoni and Victor "Babe" May shared their knowledge of the herd and took me to its out-of-the-way hideouts. I met Dr. Dale Lott there. He sent me his then-unpublished manuscript on buffalo sexual behavior.

Others outside of Montana also shared their time and knowledge: Mary Meagher, biologist in Yellowstone Park who knows so much about the park herd; Hugh Dempsey and his staff at the Glenbow-Alberta Foundation who piled one of their worktables high with buffalo material for me; Frank G. Roe, author of *The North American Buffalo*, who spent a day in Victoria, B.C. talking of buffalo over cups of tea; Peter Hassrick, director of The Buffalo Bill Historical Center, who showed me hundreds of buffalo pictures both at the Amon Carter Museum in Fort Worth and The Buffalo Bill Museum in Cody; Mrs. Roberta Wynne of the Denver Conservation Center Library, who organized my sifting of the American Bison Society papers there; Dr. George D. Coder who shared buffalo information; and Tom McHugh, author of *The Time of the Buffalo*, who stopped in Missoula to talk buffalo.

Eighty members of the National Buffalo Association, about half of the membership then, returned questionnaires I mailed to them. Their information contributed much to Chapter XXI. Hats off to them: fifty percent is an unusually high return of questionnaires.

And of course the support of the book by the Amon Carter Museum has added immeasurably. I wonder, in fact, if I would have researched and written all of those hours without knowing that Mitchell Wilder and his staff waited to help. It has been the warmest kind of relationship a writer could have. My thanks to Mitch, whose untimely death saddened us all, and to Sally, his wife. And thanks to Nancy Wynne, Librarian, and Margaret McLean, formerly Archivist; to Linda Austin, formerly Project Secretary, who discovered so many buffalo references; to Barbara Tyler, who started the project before she left for Canada; to Carol Roark, Assistant Curator of Photographs, who located countless photos and secured permission for their use in this book; and to all the rest of the expert staff who added their friendly help. To Ron Tyler, Assistant Director for Collections and Programs, who has gone the distance cheerfully and most helpfully, contributed ideas galore and wrote the book's fine foreword, my admiration and a big thank you.

The editing by Judy Alter at Texas Christian University Press has firmed the book. She and the press have worked hard to produce this well-designed book. Another thanks.

My children, Kristin and Eric, gave especial help, proofreading with me even as grade-schoolers.

Larry Barsness

INTRODUCTION

ORIGINALLY I meant this book to present only the story of the men who saved the buffalo, but as my research grew, so did the scope of the book. Its direction changed. I began writing about the relationship between buffalo and man on the North American continent, for this, it seemed to me, was the story that hadn't yet been completely told.

The grass-eating North American buffalo both led man to the North American continent, and then, by feeding him, clothing him, and housing him, made it possible for him to live there. The appearance of grass on the recently bared Bering Isthmus had attracted grasseaters, the musk-ox, the tapir, the giant ground sloth—and the buffalo—to the isthmus and to the grassy continent beyond. Man followed where the grasseaters went, especially such sizeable and easily hunted grasseaters: each kill provided food for many days.

Although some people on the new continent raised crops and others fished or hunted deer and smaller animals, many of the people who arrived here hunted amongst the plenty of the buffalo herds.

The buffalo population increased to millions, filling the Great Plains, spilling over into eastern forests and northern Mexican desert; the Great Plains tribes who depended on these buffalo lived surrounded by the beasts. Over thousands of years a buffalo culture developed among these tribes. They understood the buffalo's ways and respected them; they emulated his traits; they worshipped him (and the sun) as givers of life. Much that they did each day was related to their knowledge of and reverence for the buffalo.

When European white man arrived on the continent, the buffalo in turn affected his imagination: he imagined riches from the buffalo leather sold in Europe, he imagined owning herds of buffalo. He accomplished neither, but he lived on buffalo meat as he explored the continent. Later, as he began to farm, he raised cash grain crops but ate buffalo meat rather than raising cattle. And he tried to cross this native bovine with the bovines he had imported.

But when buffalo hooves trampled crops, when his eternal rubbing brought down newly-set telegraph poles, when his herds stopped railway trains, these men began to think of him as pest rather than life-giver. And when the plains Indians, fighting against the reservation system, fed upon the buffalo as they fought off federal troops, the United States government came to see the beast as a pest also. It saw to it that the herds were all but wiped out. Free Indians became reservation Indians.

Then, the few hundreds of buffalo remaining again captured the acquisitive imagination of the white man. Showmen exhibited buffalo, schemers captured calves and started commercial herds, brokers sold commercial buffalo to butcher shops for Christmas— and to Indian tribes that could raise the money to buy buffalo to renew buffalo ritual in their lives.

Also, the dwindling numbers of buffalo captured a different aspect of man's imagination—a totally new aspect in the relationship between man and animal— an idea of saving the buffalo species from extinction. This idea so captured the imagination of Americans that, even today, eighty years later, the question I'm most often asked is, "Do you think the buffalo is really safe from extinction?"

So that's what this book tells of: man and buffalo in North America.

My years with the buffalo have changed the way I look at my home country. As I ride through it I look at hillsides, and, where brush on a sunny slope grows in bunches, I see old buffalo wallows. My eyes follow cattle trails knowing that many of them are trails first scuffed out by buffalo. A gully with raw cutbanks I suspect began as a steep buffalo trail. The signs tell me I'm in buffalo country, but I see no buffalo.

Larry Barsness
Missoula, Montana

Heads, Hides & Horns

". . . the earth is covered with their Horns."
FATHER HENNEPIN

*"For three or four days the soil has been absolutely manured
with the dung of buffalo."*
SIR GEORGE SIMPSON

*". . . you might travel for days and weeks and not see
one of them. But their tracks were
everywhere."*
REV. DR. JOHN MCDOUGALL

O NE MORNING in July 1966, a lone buffalo bull grazed near the highway on the mountain between Virginia City and Ennis, Montana, unmindful of the click of camera shutters or the rustle of hesitant tourists getting in and out of automobiles. Nor did his tail rise and kink at carloads of miners and cowboys and storeowners and the rest of us, come up from the towns below. After awhile he crossed the highway, stopping on it just long enough to pose for the picture that appeared in Virginia City's weekly newspaper, *The Madisonian*, showing him astraddle the center line. He was a bachelor bull, alone in the way of bachelor bulls for ever and ever, roaming a range which 100 years ago had held so many buffalo that the valleys below stank of them. Today he roamed the thousands of acres of forest, unaware in his typical bachelor solitude that he was one of the few buffalo on earth—and lucky to be here at that, a curiosity. Big, tough, sure that nothing could harm him, he fled from men in nylon sport shirts no more than he had from early Spaniards in iron breastplates ("they remained quiet and did not flee," reported one of the Conquistadores).

Undoubtedly he belonged in Yellowstone Park, but just like his great-grandparents he grazed where he pleased, moving unpredictably from range to range across wide expanses of country and showing up where least expected.

Later in the day the bull moved along the ridge as sure of himself as if he still owned the millions of acres from which he had been dispossessed.

Something about the cry "Buffalo nigh!" always has pulled men out for a look-see. One Sunday in 1835, in the country south of the Tetons, the cry stole a congregation of mountain men from the Reverend Samuel Parker's preaching. And such a cry startled greenhorns along the Platte into realizing that those brown shapes they saw ahead in a valley were buffalo, not brown bushes. It brought '49ers tumbling out of Conestoga wagons for a go at a buffalo run. The same cry had brought us, miner and storekeeper, tourist and cowboy, actor and reporter, to gawk at a real, live, wild buffalo on the highway.

A gawk at a live buffalo was what every pilgrim of '49 and '63 wanted, but often the herds grazed far from the wagon trails, avoiding white guns. They were either hidden by Indian buffalo herders or wandering erratically into the wind. Nary a buffalo in buffalo land, but a man could see the buffalo lived there— buffalo sign filled the country.

The herds marked their territory with trails, thousands of them, some shallow traces, some eight-to ten-inch trenches, others "so deep that the animal's sides would rub the embankments." Millions of buffalo in thousands of years, buffalo feeding in the hills, walking down slopes to valley water, and crossing ridges in search of new pasture, produced trail crossing trail. They abandoned deep ones for shallow new ones until the paths led in any direction a man might go. They created mazes that frustrated prairie travelers. As Henry Kelsey, wandering Canadian plains in 1691, wrote, "by reason of so many beaten paths w[hich] y[e] Buffillo makes we lost y[e] track."[1] One hundred fifty years later, Zebulon Pike, when lost on the plains, tried to follow the trail of Spaniards, who, he felt, had good guides and would know where to find wood and water, but he lost their trail, it "being so much blended with the traces of the buffalo," and couldn't find it again "owing to the many buffalo roads."[2] An Oregon-bound emigrant of the 1850s wrote, "It is astonishing to see the ground stamped, worn, hoofed & trod upon by these old fellows."[3] Often, a wagon train traveling west along the Platte was forced to stop and repair wheels loosened by the constant thumping from crossing buffalo trails leading out of the river toward grass in the hills. Emigrants who had been forewarned would stow away extra tire irons and felloes to repair this damage from buffalo trails.[4]

But sometimes the trails were more help than hindrance. Buffalo had nosed into most every place a man wanted to go. If he wanted to ride through seemingly impenetrable canebrake in bottoms east of the Mississippi, he usually found a buffalo trail going his way. Mountain men like Zenas Leonard, weak and fighting deep snow, came upon trails broken for them by the buffalo (and were further saved when they shot the buffalo who had made the trails). Traders on the snow-drifted Canadian prairie saved their horses' strength by following the winding buffalo paths. Indians dragged travois in the convenient trails. Wagons followed paths beaten wide through the wilderness. Artist George Catlin, riding alone and chartless across the plains, did as many other wanderers: he looked to cross rivers where a buffalo trail broke steep cutbank into a slope his horse could manage.[5] Sometimes these travelers found buffalo hooves had squished such a crossing into quagmire, though at other times they had pounded it pavement-hard; often a hoped-for spring had been worked "into a loblolly of mud."

Trails led out of creek bottoms toward feeding grounds, forking, curlycueing across the grass in patterns as erratic as the whimsies of the beast. As many as twenty paths together crossed benches and saddles, going over them a couple of feet apart "like old corn rows but not so wide." (Men still run upon such trails in these low crossing places.) Father Hennepin noted, "Their ways are as beaten as our great Roads, and no Herb grows therein."[6] The trails eroded hillsides, left ridges barren and washing away, made gullies down steep coulees and clay cutbanks. In wet weather 200 buffalo would wear an instant muddy trail in one crossing of a meadow. Where the buffalo fed, men found footprints "cloven, and bigger than the feete of Camels" running "in all directions"; where the tracks lay thick, men found soil so "absolutely manured with dung of buffalo" it appeared as "a stallyard." Some places were covered with hundreds of skeletons, horns, and rotting carcasses.

Between the trails, tufts of buffalo hair fluttered amongst the grass; bits of it waved in the breeze from thorn-apple spikes and from lodgepole bark, a Spanish moss of the sagebrush country. If a man found a red squirrel's nest or a bird's nest he likely found it lined with buffalo hair.

Sign of elk, deer, antelope also imprinted itself on the land, but the prairie traveler's journal mostly noted buffalo sign. Like the beast itself, the quantity of sign outdid anything a woodsman or hunter had seen before . . . an animal bigger than an ox wandering seemingly as thick as the prairie dog, the pigeon, or the mosquito.

Buffalo dimpled the range with thousands of wallows, shallow dusty saucers horned and pawed in the bunch grass. At sunset and sunrise, when the wallows threw long, crescent shadows, the landscape looked pocked like the moon. These hollows stood brimful of rainwater in the spring, the "innumerable ponds which bespeckle the plains, and kept us at least well supplied with water," but by May were "thick and yellow with buffalo offal"—watering holes for buffalo only; buffalo could stomach anything. In late spring such manure and moisture produced a rank growth of grass, circular growths all about the prairie. By midsummer they dried completely, the grass disappeared under wallowings, and the soil became sifted by constant horning and pawing.

Although a man could easily pile the soft soil of the ubiquitous buffalo wallow into a hasty breastwork for protection from Indian attack, the wallows usually proved a nuisance. They forced wagons to wind amongst them, and, in the buffalo chase, caused steeplechase jumps across or wild springings to the side. And the homesteader found some of them almost impossible to plow because "down in the bottom of each of them wallows was a thick alkali deposit . . . the only way Father could handle them wallows when it came to farming was to haul in wagonloads of sand and dump them in to sort of loosen the ground up."[7] (Homesteaders were still plowing around buffalo wallows in Montana in 1910.)[8] In barren sand spots wallows grew to cover an acre or more.

Wet, spring months filled prairie swales with water, creating large ponds which filled with tall June grass—hay lakes, old-timers called them. Each seemed a green oasis until a man walked between stinking, brown buffalo carcasses and scattered white bones, a flotsam ringing the shore, the remnants of the old and sick—the weak—who had died or been wolf-killed. Buffalo drank and wallowed here in the spring and caked themselves with mud; when they moved they left behind a hummocky, boggy place, a nasty place to cross, another place for a man to detour . . . but a sanctuary for birds and amphibious wild life (pelicans waded them, evidently in search of food).

"The trees, also, furnished *their* evidence and every low limb was worn by the Buffaloe, while scratching his skin, after coming out of his mud or sand bath,"[9] wrote a tenderfoot, wide-eyed about buffalo doings; but such doings could make experienced North-West Company fur trader Alexander Henry (the elder) equally wide-eyed: "Buffalo have ravaged this small island; nothing remains but the large elms and oaks, whose bark has been polished to the height of the buffalo by their perpetual rubbing. Brush and grass are not to be seen in this little wood."[10]

A man walking near buffalo had to watch his step as in a cattle yard because of the dung. But on last year's grazing ground the droppings sometimes dried "hard as a clamshell," reached the color of a weathered cardboard carton, and became an odorless, papery disc, about 12 inches in diameter, drilled by hundreds of tiny insect holes. It made a perch for meadowlarks to sing from; it made a home for beetles and flies.

As everyone knows, buffalo chips burned: somewhat after six months drying but very well indeed after a full year or more. They were a traditional fuel; Coronado had found Indians enjoying such fires.

These chips were the "bois de vache," often the only "wood" available. Forty-niners on the Platte traveling one 160-mile section on the Oregon Trail found "no place in the whole distance where timber enough could be got on ten miles square to fence ten acres" but chips enough lay about "sufficient for any to cook by."[11] When a wagonmaster decided on a stopping place he searched first for a chip and water supply.

Men walking beside their lumbering Conestoga wagons drew "their ramrods, not to ram home cartridges but to stick it through the largest chip they could find and string them on . . . like so many pancakes." When a ramrod filled, a man slid the cakes into one of the chip sacks that swung underneath the wagon bed, out of the reach of a sudden shower.[12] Children ran extra miles gathering them, men gathered the "scutters" from where they hung on grass or sagebrush; they used sleeping blankets as chip hods. Women out for a stroll returned to the wagons with aprons full of the nasty burnables . . . all the nastier for the insects which scuttled about on the underside when a person picked one up. (The chips made homes for millions of insects. And burrowing owls, nesting in prairie dog holes, used the material to line their nests.) At first a woman hated to touch the things while cooking. She began by handling the chips with two sticks, progressed to a rag, then to a corner of the apron until, as a seasoned chip handler, "Now it is out of the bread, into the chips and back again—and not even a dust of the hands!"[13]

Expert chip users (one became expert in one crossing of the plains—perhaps three hundred chip fires) claimed the chip made a better fire than the dead cottonwood that they occasionally found, for it "ignited quickly; a mass of them made solid but almost transparent coals, which glowed with intense heat."[14] A wonderful fuel, they claimed, that hardened every year until a man found it difficult to cut its surface with a knife, a fuel that the "snows of winter" didn't change and the spring rains dampened only a sixteenth of an inch or so. Others, less smitten by the plains, wrote, "Our Buffalo Chips are of no account when it rains, and but little when dry. . . ." They gathered chips "before it began to rain."[15] Lucky men found "some scrawly timber . . . good . . . after nothing but buffalo chips to burn for three nights."[16] Alexander Henry, after trying to barbecue buffalo steak in the smudge of wet chips, decided he wanted no more "buffalo dung steaks."[17] Major Stephen H. Long's 1819 expedition to the Rockies experienced a cloudburst that washed "cow dung" into the water hole and turned it mustard color; they boiled meat in this effluent, creating a soup with the gagging flavor of a cowyard.[18]

Some men threw on buffalo tallow to make the buffalo chip burn—"a rather hard matter that the Buffalo should furnish the meat and then the fuel to cook it."

"Wagons Through the Train." Frederic Remington, *Century Magazine*, April 1902.
Courtesy Amon Carter Museum, Fort Worth, Texas.

Without the tallow, a fire of chips was small comfort against the cold, but chips heaped up under ribs on a spit during the night cooked breakfast, often making a morning fire unnecessary.

Mountain men tossed buffalo liver directly on the burning dung and popped it in their mouths when done, pausing only to dust off the thickest of the manure ash. Or if a hunk of roast rib snatched from the spit burned fingers, they would pop it onto a chip as a makeshift plate. A common joke on the plains was that steak cooked over buffalo chips needed no pepper.

Coronado's men, fearful of losing themselves on the bare plains, piled "heapes of oxe-dung" to blaze the trail. A man having to sleep on the snowy prairie arranged buffalo chips in layers to insulate himself from the ground (and threw a buffalo robe over himself). Homesteaders burned them in their soddies for winter heat; Father Gregory Mengarini at St. Mary's Mission, plagued with mosquitoes, drove them from his cabin with a buffalo chip smudge. Marksmen piled them up as gun rests. The buffalo chip was almost as handy as the buffalo himself.

In some spots on the grassland men found big, mysterious rings of verdant grass that they laid to buffalo doings. Not gouged out like the wallows, these looked like the mushroom-inspired rings called fairy rings (and many undoubtedly were), so they too became fairy rings. Some men claimed that buffalo bulls, trudging around calves and cows to protect them from the wolves, had scuffed out the rings in which later the grass grew tall—one man swore he'd seen bulls trudging in such a circle around calves. In 1956 another man, observing old, horseshoe-shaped fairy rings on sidehills, reasoned that "The calf if born on a side hill, the cow would face the wolf which would stay on the upper side and try to make a downhill run to get the calf. The cow would make the half circle run and back until it wore a deep rut."[19] Other men thought the cows, bedded down in a circle about the calves, dropped seeds from their shaggy manes which later sprouted to form the rings.[20] Some Indians laid the rings to the wear caused by dances of the buffalo, large circles caused by large buffalo, small circles by small buffalo;[21] some white men laid the rings to the wear caused by dancing Indians.[22] Iowa pioneers were sure that buffalo standing in a ring with their heads together stamped their feet until the grass wore away, allowing weeds to grow up.[23] And Dewey Soper, a Canadian biologist, thought the fairy rings on the Wood Buffalo range in Canada came about through the "normal action of parents circling about and licking the calf during its first three or four rather helpless days."[24] None of these explanations seem as good as the one given in the 1830s by George Catlin for the non-fungous rings. He surmised the rank, circular growth occurred in old wallows that had filled partially with "vegetable deposits" and soil.[25]

Buffalo changed the grasslands as no other beast: they made trails down hillsides into deep, eroded trenches, they bared the ridges even as their droppings fertilized them (certainly any favorite place of theirs became well-fertilized as well as denuded). They smashed down the alder and quaking aspen; they often denuded areas of grass (one buffalo eats as much as two elk or four deer).[26] Men continually ran across places where the grass "was eaten to the earth, as if the place had been devastated by locusts." Journal after journal complains of such a shortage: "The grass would be rather long were it not for the buffalo," "our horses are starving," "they ate up all the grass, it looked as though fire had burned the prairies . . . I lost all my cattle," "the teams began to grow weak and thin in flesh." The herds ate themselves out of forage: "The front herds swallow every herb and leaf. The rear masses now get nothing and they die like the forests strewn by the summer thunder."[27] A large herd moved likewise through water holes, leaving no water for horses; even if water remained, likely as not a man had to chuck rocks at buffalo to drive them out of the water.[28] But the erratic herds moved continually and travelers soon found that "Outside the buffalo runs, the grass was fine" and the water untouched.

To the Indian, also, buffalo meant hazard and nuisance. Corn raisers had to live outside of buffalo country to keep their fields beyond the range of the trampling herds. Indians living in buffalo country worried about buffalo trying to graze within the tipi circle or the occasional snorting bull who charged into camp. Sometimes, rather than staging a hunt for them, they could kill the animals grazing amongst the lodges.[29] Sometimes a buffalo would dodge into a tipi and the

men would shoot "him down from the opening to the top."[30] Once a bull entered a tipi in the middle of the night, snapped the lodge poles and carried the lodge skin with him off into the darkness where the former occupants could see it dimly "careening about the corral as if it were endowed with life . . . dancing round and round, a fiendish dance to a step of its own."[31] Grandparents had to watch that children playing away from the tipis might not fall into the path of a moving herd. Boys guarding the horse herd had to stop any horse from wandering off with buffalo nuisances, as horses loved to do.

Indian and white alike watched buffalo to read signs of disturbance. If a man cautiously topped a rise only to see a herd on the move, he paused to determine if other men moved in the dust cloud behind the herd. Or that dead buffalo—how long ago had it died? How had it died? If arrows were imbedded in it, what hands had nocked and feathered them? If someone had scooped out the brains . . . Good: a hunting party bringing hides and brains for tanning; no warring party would take brains. If a herd avoided a watering place, what danger lay there? Why did that herd run downwind? Were those faraway shapes monocolored

A homesteader's wife gathers the only prairie fuel. *Courtesy Amon Carter Museum, Fort Worth, Texas.*

like buffalo or varicolored like horses—horses and men? And were those buffalo out there or . . . time and again squaws screamed and men grabbed for arrows, all from mistaking a buffalo herd on a distant ridge for enemy; yet if monocolored and buffalo-shaped, hunters had best be wary. Raiding warriors sometimes tricked hunters by hiding in a herd under a buffalo skin. The practiced eye often hesitated to decide if it saw buffalo with hump, horse with rider, or man on foot. Or, in the shimmering distance, the eye might mistake a herd for a clump of trees—legs for trunks, humps for foliage; one man saw them looking "like piles erected to bridge the plain."

Buffalo sometimes seemed the saviors of the plains. Men crawled into buffalo carcasses to escape the blizzard. Some slept snug and warm, others lay awake through a long night listening to wolf teeth tearing at the meat all about them. Others, legend says, awoke to find the pliable carcass of last night now frozen stiff, making a prison of ribs and backbone, and died before a thaw could release them. A green hide, rolled into for the night, sometimes froze and also "boxed in" a man. However, to a starving man, buffalo seemed a blessing. John Bozeman and friend, robbed of everything by Crows, avoided starving by killing an old, blind bull with a hunting knife fastened to a long pole. Zenas Leonard, Zebulon Pike and other western wanderers all wrote of surviving on buffalo meat (although sometimes, before a man could butcher, he had to wave his coat to shoo away curious live buffalo gathered about the carcass). Yet, inexperienced Peter Koch, needing meat in January 1870, saw lots of buffalo, but he couldn't kill a one.[32]

White men lost themselves in the madness of the buffalo chase and wandered until starved, or killed, or rescued. Railway engineers braked their trains to a stop rather than risk stalling the cars in a collision with buffalo bodies. (Yarns have it that herds occasionally pushed cars from the tracks.) Men driving yoked oxen had to jump from the wagon and run for it when buffalo bulls attacked their team. Small prairie settlements awoke to gardens mangled and fences downed by buffalo night visitors. At forts buffalo wandering about the parade ground sometimes proved a nuisance.[33]

The buffalo experience equaled the Western experience, and, earlier, it had equaled the Eastern experience as well. Men in Kentucky had found salt licks so trampled that water no longer ran from them. Men in Pennsylvania had had haystacks devoured, even cabins knocked down by these pests. (In Canada haystacks had to be moved into a fort to keep buffalo from devouring them.)

Moreover, the beasts offered such easy living—steaks and roasts for the butchering—most eighteenth-century Kentuckians living west of the mountains ate meat instead of bread. They could make do with a tiny clearing of garden patch. Their failure to clear the forest because they were hunting buffalo held back the progress of agriculture for 100 years, until the buffalo was extirpated about 1794.[34]

Such freedom from want also made the frontier settler impatient with the constraints of government and community. Most everywhere on the continent the availability of buffalo meat slowed down progress. Spanish emigrants in Texas followed the buffalo rather than the plow until Governor Cordero ordered that each man had to cultivate land.[35] Settlers of the Red River Colony in Canada cared little for "rich homesteads so long as buffalo could be found . . . so long as we could get buffalo within three hundred miles we would prefer buffalo steaks to barley-meal. . . ."[36] The presence of buffalo on the Kansas plains retarded the introduction of cattle there. The homesteader ate free buffalo meat and spent his money for plows and seed.

The Indian himself preferred hunting buffalo to farming. With the coming of the horse (and the pressure of white settlement), several agricultural tribes moved onto the plains and gave up the corn harvest for the buffalo harvest.

Seeds caught in shaggy buffalo pelts were carried from Milk River to Musselshell River, from the Canadian to the Arkansas. The buffalo distributed them as the wind did for the flying seed carriers of the cottonwoods. Then, buffalo chips fertilized the soil the seeds had dropped on.

Wherever buffalo congregated, their droppings, their urine, their musky smell, their stagnant wallows, their rotting dead left an odor on the wind. A branch of the Jefferson River, a headwater of the Missouri, the Indians called the Passamari—the Stinking-water—because the place smelled so of buffalo.

Buffalo smell disappeared soon after the buffalo disappeared; first his smell, then his thousands of footprints and his tufts of hair. His chips disappeared next and then his bones. Underbrush sprang up again in cottonwood groves, canebrake resprouted about the salt licks. The tall grasses of the eastern prairie edged west a ways and spread a little in the shortgrass prairie—until cattle grazing removed them again. Wallows became grassy hollows. Grass grew in myriad trails.

"The Tourists' Trip Across the Plains." *Courtesy Amon Carter Museum, Fort Worth, Texas.*

We, on the hill above Virginia City, had seen old eternal buffalo wandering, satisfying his 100,000-year wanderlust, a wildness no government hay could feed out of him. We, in our gathering here, were kin to the Frenchmen of Gallipolis, Ohio, in 1795. Resident Monsieur Duteil, coming upon buffalo near the town's outskirts, fired without aiming at any particular bison and *voilà*! he killed one and scampered back to town with the news. The windfall brought on a Gallic celebration, music, wine, parading, dancing in the streets—and feasting on Monsieur Le Bison.[37] On Ennis hill we faced on foot the original roarer of the West and wondered if we could outrace him should that tail come up and he charge us. We stood as if we were Spanish Conquistadores . . . or '49ers . . . or literary sightseers, as anxious to tell of our buffalo experience as, say, Captain Vicente de Zaldívar. He, sent to search for the "cattle" Governor Juan de Oñate hoped to raise on a hacienda in New Mexico, saw his first buffalo in 1598 near the Pecos River and wrote, "Its shape and form are so marvelous and laughable or frightful, that the more one sees it the more one desires to see it, and no one could be so melancholy that if he were to see it a hundred times a day he could keep from laughing heartily as many times, or could fail to marvel at the sight of so ferocious an animal."[38] Not that any of us on the hill laughed. But we looked over that hump, that shaggy mane, those sloping hindquarters with similar delight, and we marveled at those curling horns and those wild eyes, and later told anyone who'd listen, the same as those who saw buffalo in the 1800s. "There is a mixture of the awful and the comic in the look of these huge animals, as they bear their great bulk forwards . . ."[39] said Washington Irving (four pages earlier he'd described buffalo aspect as "most diabolical"). "Nothing

Indian and frontiersman racing to kill buffalo. Notice the expression on the animals' faces. *Courtesy National Archives, Washington, D.C.*

can be more revolting, more terrific, than a front view of an old bull buffalo . . . a dirty drunkard beard . . . altogether the appearance and expression of some four-legged devil . . ."[40] wrote another prairie sightseer.

If ever animal inspired man to write, the buffalo did. Antelope, elk, deer, rattlesnake, prairie dog, sage hen—these often went undescribed in the journals of prairie travelers, but few men crossed the prairie without having a go at buffalo description.

The early Spaniards tried to picture him in simile. Fernando del Bosque's diary described "the hips and haunches . . . like those of a hog . . . at the knees . . . to the shoulder there is much bristle-like hair, like he-goats . . . they gaze at people like wild hogs, with hair abristle. They are of the size of cattle."[41] Francisco López de Gomara's account reveals "a horse-

mane upon their backbone," a tufted, lion-like tail plus a camel-like hump.[42] Pedro de Castañeda, with Coronado, also tried comparing buffalo to other animals: "Their beard is like that of goats . . . on the anterior portion of the body a frizzled hair like sheep's wool; it is very fine upon the croup, and sleek like a lion's mane . . . They always change their hair in May, and at this season they really resemble lions . . . they change it as adders do their skin . . . Their tail is very short, and terminates in a great tuft. When they run they carry it in the air like scorpions. When quite young they are tawny, and resemble our calves . . ."[43]

Later, other European explorers of the new continent mentioned seeing *buffes*, but this term as much referred to the buff leather that a beast might provide as it did to the beast—as much to elk or moose as to buffalo. And it's hard to tell from an occasional description just what animal was seen. David Ingram, who walked from Mexico to St. John's River about 1570, wrote, "great plentye of Buffes . . . wth are Beastes as bigge as twoe Oxen in length almost twentye foote, havinge longe eares like a bludde hownde wth long heares about there eares, ther hornes be Crooked like Rames hornes, ther eyes blacke, there heares longe blacke, rough and hagged as a Goate, the Hydes of these Beastes are solde verye deare."[44]

The most accurate part of this description, "Hydes . . . solde verye deare," fascinated European fortune hunters. Spaniards looking for New World fortune kept their eyes open for Cabeza de Vaca's "cattle." Coronado, interviewing the chiefs of the pueblo of Pecos, queried one much about the cattle in his land. What did they look like? One couldn't tell from the matted hides brought as gifts. A young chief brought forth one of his men; there on his skin Coronado saw a likeness of a cow painted. The General sent Captain

Alvarado and twenty-one men to size up the prospects of the real animal.

Spaniards thought the animal monstrous at first glance, but a second glance showed them his similarity to marketable cattle. Some Spaniards called him *Vacas jorobadas*, hump-backed cow, and some called him *cibola* as had Cabeza de Vaca—although more interesting to them than the name was the explorer's notation that the people of buffalo country "send great stores of hides into the Countrie," or another man's idea, "Indeed, there is profit in the cattle ready to the hand, from the quantity of them, which is as great as one could imagine . . ."[45] Profit was the gleam in the Spaniard's eye, whether from the gold in the supposed coffers of Quivira or from the free cattle in sight. Captain Zaldívar said that not a man in his command expected to own less than 10,000 of the leather-bearing wild animals.[46] Reports sent to the King of Spain emphasized the wealth in cattle. One overexuberant subject went so far as to ship the King

One of the first paintings of a buffalo herd, rendered by Titian Ramsay Peale, who accompanied Major Stephen Long's expedition, 1819–1820. *Courtesy Amon Carter Museum, Fort Worth, Texas.*

two buffalo bulls and four cows as a gift. Only a cow and a bull survived the voyage to surprise and—somewhat—please His Majesty. He instructed the giver to refrain from sending animals in the future.[47]

The French too saw a buffalo more as a commodity than as a wild animal, and thought of him as "ownerless." Although some Frenchmen at first called him by the ancient Algonquin name, *piskiou*, they soon called him *Le Boeuf*, *Le Boeuf sauvage*, Islinois cattle, or *Vaches sauvages*. Englishmen also saw him as an ox and knew that "their flesh [was] good foode, their hides good lether, their fleeces very useful . . ." They sometimes referred to him by the biblical "kine," but more often by buffe, or buf. Later he came by such English language names as Prairie Beeves, Shag-haired Oxen, Wild Ox and Cattle (it once meant wealth).[48] But the name De Soto had given in 1544 to the beast he'd never seen[49]—buffalo—came into common usage only after it appeared in Mark Catesby's *Natural History of Carolina* in 1754,[50] and then perhaps only as an interpolation of the *buffalo* and *buffilo* which writers for some reason had begun using about 1700.

And so the beast garnered his rolling name to go with his rolling gait; the same name as for the wild cow seen in India and Africa, although this wild cow of the New World shared only the characteristics that made all of these members of the family *Bovidae*.

About 1700 Frenchmen began calling the beast *Le Bison* perhaps because he looked so much like the European animal, *Bison bonasus*; they hit upon the scientific name for him, but he's buffalo to Canadians and Americans, and buffalo he remains here.

We still hear the expression "He sure had him buffaloed," meaning "bluffed"; it's about the only remnant of buffalo imagery except for "high-tailed it," which might refer to deer or antelope. But apt buffalo phrases arose to the lips of those surrounded by buffalo and buffalo doings. Prairie adventurer and novelist George Ruxton wrote of an Indian who was stabbed eight times before he died: "As much life in him as a buffalo bull." A hide hunter laconically called a human corpse "dead as a buffalo chip."

A mountain man's speech filled with buffalo metaphor, the most common image in his life. He called the animal, "buffler"; to him "a buffalo" meant a buffalo robe. When he said "robe season" he meant a cold spell; "old bull thrower" referred not to a liar but to his rifle. If he said "make meat" he referred either to running buffalo for the kill or drying buffalo meat—but he might say "running meat" to mean chasing buffalo (he might also go out to "kill some meat"). To

A woodcut done by an artist who relied on descriptions of the buffalo by adventurers returned to Europe. From Francisco López de Gomara, *La historia general de Las Indias*, 1554. *Courtesy DeGolyer Library, Southern Methodist University, Dallas, Texas.*

"Boeuf de la Nouvelle France." Copied from the Louis Hennepin drawing. *Courtesy Amon Carter Museum, Fort Worth, Texas.*

make this chase he had to "raise the herd"—put it into a full run. As he butchered he ate raw, body-warm liver over which he had dripped "buffalo cider"—bitter buffalo gall. If he went without buffalo meat for a few days he became "grease hungry."

He saw a running buffalo as "humping himself" and so coined the phrase. He saw not only a herd of buf-

Although buffalo differ a lot in looks, none of them carry a monkey face. "The Buffalo." 18th Century. *Courtesy Glenbow Museum, Calgary, Alberta.*

This same head of hair was worn by a buffalo sold at auction in Missoula, Montana in the 1970s. *Courtesy Amon Carter Museum, Fort Worth, Texas.*

falo but also a drove, a gang, or a band. And he saw half-breed buffalo, king buffalo, medicine buffalo, mongrel buffalo and razor buffalo. If he knocked a buffalo down in one clean shot, he "threw him in his tracks" but he might prefer to shoot to make him "pump blood."

If he needed analogy or simile, the mountain man as often as not used the buffalo; he might describe a man as "a big feller with hair frizzed out like an old buffler's just afore sheddin' time." Another man's hair "was matted and long—all over jist like a blind bull" and he was "lookin' like a sick buffler in the eye." When a mountain man felt brave he felt "as brave as a buffler in the spring," but when he fled "I ran as ef a wounded buffler was raisin' my shirt with his horns." And in telling a yarn of monsters, he described horrible dogs as having heads "bigger an' a buffler's in summer" (a buffler's head looks larger in the summer when he's shed most body hair). He swore to the truth of such a yarn by saying, "an' ef it aint fact, he doesn't know 'fat cow' from 'poor bull.'"

Buffalo images came into our language as names for things. We have the buffalo bean or plum, the buffalo bur (the sandbur—which made millions of journeys caught in buffalo wool), buffalo nut (the water chestnut, its black two-horned fruit looking like a buffalo's head), buffalo grass and buffalo clover and the buffalo bush with its reddish-orange buffalo berry, tart and delicious in buffalo-berry jelly.

But men also saw the buffalo as an ugly pest who fouled water, destroyed hay stacks and trampled down fields. In such an image Confederates called those who backed the Union "buffaloes," a sneer at the anti-slavery platform adopted in Buffalo, New York, in 1848, as well as a sneer at the black man, often called a "buffalo" because of his black skin and curly hair. After the war, black troops fighting Indians out west became Buffalo Soldiers, a derogatory name belied by their courageous performance of duty. And occasionally on the western frontier a fat woman was called a buffalo.

While to us the infinitive "to buffalo" might mean to bluff or to frighten off as well as cheat or bamboozle, to a plains Indian "to buffalo" meant to go ahunting of the buffalo (the French-Canadian said "Courir la vache"). These Indians also saw much of the world in buffalo terms. The Crows measured big trees as one-robe, two-robe or three-robe trees—however many robes would stretch about a trunk; likewise they spoke of tipis as twelve-robe or fifteen-robe tipis, indicating how many robes sewed together created each one. They used the term "Drop his robe"—simi-

lar to our "Died with his boots on"—to mean a man who had died where he stood.

Indians dreamed of the buffalo, prayed to him, told myths about him, made a sign for him—forefingers crooked inwards, like his horns—drew magic symbols of him. They had special names for various buffalo: they might call a year-old calf, "Fluffed hair one," a two-year old, "Blunt Horns" or "Two Teeth" because of his two teeth, and a mature bull, "Horns Not Cracked." When they rode into a herd to hunt for hides to make robes they looked for "Small Built Ones." Cows with a short forelock were called "Mourning-cows"—Indian women cut their hair short in mourning.

Most of all, Indians hoped a vision of buffalo would come to give big medicine to their lives. Men took on such names as White Bull, Buffalo Hump, Bull Tongue, Bull Could Not Rise Up, and Buffalo Chip; a woman might be called Buffalo Wallow Woman. They preferred buffalo meat to all other meat; they scorned the white man's beef until forced by hunger to eat it. The Blackfeet called only buffalo meat "real food"—*nitaniwaksim*. If a man returning to camp said, "The camp doesn't smell too good," he meant he smelled no buffalo meat cooking.

The Sioux (and others) kept a calendar of the years by naming the winter for its outstanding event and drawing symbolic representation of it on a tanned skin. In the old days, as often as not, they drew symbols of buffalo plenty or buffalo oddity, for these broke the placid life of the winter camp. Dried meat hanging from a drying rack denoted the good winter, 1845–46. A tipi with tracks near it symbolized the winter that buffalo stood among the tipis, 1861–62. A strange drawing with a human figure silhouetted inside it reminded the tribes of the winter "a buffalo cow was killed . . . and an old woman found in her belly," 1850–51.

Battiste Good (Brown Hat), a Brulé Dakota, also kept records. Using five colors and a paper drawing book, he drew suns flaming with corollas of symbolic tipis; each sun's face he covered with symbolic drawings of important winters. The drawings begin with a symbolic buffalo and sacred pipe to denote the period 901–930 A.D., when, the Sioux said, the buffalo was first given to them. The drawing for 1631–1700 symbolically shows the first killing of buffalo by Sioux on horseback about 1700: a man tied to a horse managed to kill a buffalo after the tribe had surrounded a herd by pitching its lodges about it. Battiste's calendar drawings depict the winter of 1702–3, "the camped-cutting-the-ice-through-winter"—wavelines for the ice, four blue buffalo heads to represent the 1000 buffalo the Sioux drove onto the ice to fall through, freeze fast, die, and furnish frozen meat all winter; a man wearing snowshoes and aiming an arrow at a buffalo head recalled the "wore-snowshoes winter" of 1719–20 in which many buffalo were killed mired in deep snow. . . .[51]

Each Indian year was made up of moons, a complete moon cycle often named for buffalo relationships such as fat buffalo moon, thin buffalo moon; moon of much buffalo hair, moon of hair gone, and the like.

But none of us, Indian or white, think "Brave as a buffalo" or "Kinky as a bull with his tail raised" anymore. He's not even become a cliche as have the sly fox or the brave lion. But he truly used to symbolize exploration, chance unlimited, power, new horizons. A westering man might so ache to see buffalo that he would record in his journal "at noon I saw the buffalo wallows for the first time."[52] Today the buffalo's gone from the back of the nickel—the "buffalo head" it was called—as well as the $10.00 bill. One no longer sees Buffalo Brand lard or Buffalo Brand shoes. Few would understand the term "buffalo cripple," used at the Fort Hays hospital to denote an injured hide hunter.[53] Insurance companies no longer choose the buffalo as a symbol almost as strong as Gibraltar. Although it's now the fashion for ranchers to collect buffalo as an ornament to their range (a profitable ornament when sold to the specialty food market), the hump-backed beast no longer creates symbols that grip men's minds. He may be part of our jumble of Western Myth—the Indian-cowboy thing—but this image is like the hero's white hat, a parody of the older West.

Battiste Good, a Brulé Sioux, often used a drawing of a buffalo to symbolize an era or a winter "count." Garrick Mallery, "Picture Writing of the American Indians," 1893.

*"Taking up some handfuls of soil, they said that the
animals were just as numerous as the grains of sand . . ."*
HERNÁN GALLEGOS

*"These buffalo seemed to knock all the water out of
the river when they'd plunge in headlong
to swim across."*
GEORGE BROWN

TODAY MOST of us liken all buffalo to the bull stamped on the back of the old buffalo nickel—see one buffalo you've seen 'em all; in the zoo, cow or bull, we can't tell which, we see only that some are bigger than others and that they all have humps and horns. But the frontiersman, who pushed through thousands of buffalo humps higher than his horse's back, could tell cows from bulls even at a distance: the bull's larger size, his bushier, longer pelage—especially his front pantaloons—his higher hump, thicker neck and heavier beard gave him away. The frontiersman could identify beaver buffalo and scabby buffalo, blue buffalo, and sometimes albino buffalo; he saw mean buffalo, scared buffalo, fat buffalo, lean buffalo; he saw hornless buffalo, and crumple-horned buffalo, and one-horned buffalo. Just when he'd found that "Bufalow are so tame they come almost in to camp,"[1] just when he'd come to expect all buffalo to give way to him, he'd meet up with one who, tail up and head down, charged him, demanded that he give way. A million buffalo meant a million individualities.

Frontiersmen became buffalo "experts." They saw differences between the buffalo on the prairies and those in the Rocky Mountains. Those in the Rockies, shy woodland animals, seemed larger (some said smaller, they were wrong) and blacker than the plains animal; they called these "mountain bison" but called the plains variety "buffler" or "buffs." The first explorers of the far north, near Great Slave Lake, saw big and black buffalo similar to mountain bison. This northern buffalo also seemed shyer than the prairie buffalo, for he used trees and brush to screen himself from view (as did the mountain buffalo). And he was nowhere near as docile as the prairie buffalo; he was "quite as wary and difficult to hunt as the moose."[2] You didn't ride amongst herds of him, more likely as you rode you listened to the crash of him disappearing, and as to hunting him, "When they have been once fired at, a second shot can seldom be got."[3] All men agreed that this northern buffalo in November looked blacker than the usual raisin-brown prairie buffalo, that his horns seemed more slender, and that he stood inches higher at the hump. About 1845 this biggest of the modern buffalo came to be known as the "wood buffalo." Now, some zoologists believe that perhaps the wood buffalo had earlier drifted south as far as Nevada and New Mexico[4] and became known as mountain bison there. The two are the same buffalo.

East of the Mississippi old-timers claimed that buffalo in Pennsylvania had grown larger and had developed a darker pelage than the plains animal. Zoologists

14

grown bull, killed fat" at 1800 pounds: 800 pounds of meat for his men, 1000 pounds of bones, hide and offal.[13] Henry Helgeson, who butchered more than 3224 government buffalo, said the biggest one he ever saw stood six feet eight inches at the hump.[14] Today we weigh them. At the National Bison Range, eight-and-a-half year old bulls average 1650 pounds and many weigh 2000 pounds. Cows weigh 600 to 800 pounds less and stand four-and-a-half to five-and-a-half feet at the hump. They carry less mane and appear much more frail—even their horns are slender.

Probably, all grazing animals ate alongside buffalo only as buffalo allowed. Today, on government ranges, if a buffalo grazes too close, elk move nervously away; occasionally a baby buffalo scares a big bull elk from a favorite pasturing place, and buffalo groups chase elk from hay feeding lots or from summer pasture.[15] The elk, moose, antelope and deer, competing for scarce grass, undoubtedly gave way to them in the old days. Buffalo once gored twenty-some horses, competing with them for winter range.[16] (Yet, on the western frontier, when not competing, stray horses and mules were often found "feeding with Buffaloa" and wagon trains kept losing cattle in the buffalo herds).

The cowbird befriends him, spending hours perched on a buffalo's back, often several spacing themselves along his spine like swallows on a telephone line, resting between flights to catch the insects buzzing about him. They live so much on a buffalo back that the Indians claimed they nested in the warmth of the shaggy hump; actually they lay eggs in other bird's nests, but in winter do warm their feet in the deep pelage. Sometimes they seem to ride out a storm on a buffalo's back.[17] Starlings, blackbirds and redwings also perch about the herd, attracted no doubt by the insects the animals carry or flush out of the grass.

In the day of the buffalo, wolves, now nearly extinct, hung about watching for signs of weakness amongst the old, or for glimpses of the strayed calf, yet they often ran through the herds unmolested and played about the waterholes as if they too were herd members. Buffalo paid so little attention to wolves about them that the Indian hunters crept into the herd covered with wolf skins. Only cows with young calves and the old or sick paid them much mind; prime bulls knew no wolf wanted to risk a crushed skull from a kick, or a skewered gut from those horns (horns that could, according to one tale, shred a

Usually, as here, wolves attacked mature buffalo only when they were in trouble.
"Wolves Attacking Buffalo." W. M. Cary, n.d. *Courtesy Glenbow Museum, Calgary, Alberta.*

17

pocket handkerchief on the ground). Healthy buffalo are a match for any wolf pack. Wolves in Canada's Wood Buffalo Park had trouble killing two stub-horn yearling calves: they chased them a day to exhaust them before killing only one.[18]

Either buffalo couldn't see very well or laid more importance on herd reaction to danger than on seeing danger for themselves. Hunters always came at him from the leeward, for a buffalo smelled danger sooner than he saw it; he grazed into the wind, sniffing it. As Captain Meriwether Lewis noted, "you may see ten or a douzen, herds of buffaloe distinctly scattered and many miles distant yet . . . traveling in one direction . . ."[19] As the wind changed, a grazing herd turned to face into it, sometimes boxing the compass in a single afternoon. A herd might turn at a right angle rather than cross the scent of a wagon train. Alexander Henry told of seeing large herds stop to smell the spoor left by a man walking through the grass, follow his trail, horning the earth, bellowing, until a brave one jumped the smell and all followed.[20] And if a herd smelled man, it might stampede downwind, back the way it had come, guided by neither sight nor smell. Sometimes this mad downwind stampede ran a herd close to hunters on the lee, danger that a more seeing animal would have noted and avoided.

Their eyes, "more wide-angled and mobile than those of domestic cattle," might determine horse from horse and rider at about a mile, yet they might miss nearby, stationary objects. This allows a man to sneak close by, moving when they graze, freezing when they look up.[21] Perhaps, in historic times, eyes meant little to this herd animal because he walked in an engulfing cloud of dust whenever the herd marched. In such dust a nose meant more than eyes in detecting danger. Perhaps also the mass of head wool sometimes obscured their sight, in spite of wide-angled eyes. Whatever the reason, most men agreed the buffalo depended on his nose more than his eyes.

Gregarious as a buffalo makes a good simile. The urge to join the group led them to attempt infiltrating the cattle herds trailing wagon trains bound for Oregon. Special riders had to shoo them off.[22] The great cattle drives north from Texas often contained a few buffalo drifting along just for the company.[23]

A buffalo feeds in early morning and late afternoon when the others feed; he lies down and chews his cud between times, when the others chew. Like his cousin, the domestic cow, the buffalo often moves to water in single file, having decided he's thirsty because some herd member, the leader for the nonce, has decided

that now is the time to be thirsty (sometimes the *day* to be thirsty, for in cool weather buffalo may have drunk only every other day—some say every three days). In the time of their millions the group moved sedately, single-file until water-smell filled their nostrils; then they often broke for it on the run, hit the creek and "seemed to knock all the water out," so eager to drink that those in back often shoved the leaders across the stream: "when I get to the water I run," sang the Blackfeet of the buffalo.[24] But they drank together, and afterward most followed the leader back to pasture.

In the past, buffalo lived most of their lives in small herds, twenty to 300 animals in the group, coming together in larger herds through the attractions of the summer rut. Today, as in the past, cows and bulls live pretty much separately from October to May, although during these months scatterings of the opposite sex graze within either group. Bulls, because of their independent nature, often stand at the edges of any mixed herd, from which arose the legend that they act as sentinels. Of course, because of this position they may well first note danger, but not purposely.

Cows tend toward more gregariousness than bulls. They move within a sizeable group throughout the year: in the past men have seen a cow "group" extend from horizon to horizon. Their calves, one, sometimes two and even three years old, stay with the cows and swell the numbers of their group. The bulls come and go, enter the cow group now and then; wandering together, they group themselves in smaller herds— seldom over twenty members. Some seem to live all alone, but actually wander in and out of the herd at will—not driven out as previously believed of "bachelor bulls." Yet even in their aloofness, most bulls remain loosely gregarious, wandering together somewhat.

From afar a man can tell a bull herd: the bulls scatter themselves more and eat singly and move about little; the cows bunch more to protect the calves and they move about considerably: they lie awhile, ruminating, but soon need to wallow; after a bit, up again to wander and feed, then another good lie down, then another wallow . . .

In his own group a buffalo lives under the dominance of older, larger animals and dominates smaller, younger animals, but the pattern of dominance appears to shift continually. Leadership may change whenever the herd moves, as the notion to move and to lead strikes an individual, although most often a few special cows lead. An animal establishes this leadership by heading off, then looking back to test for followers. If others come, he leads; if not, he returns.

At about eight years, when a bull reaches his prime, he will achieve his greatest success in the dominance pattern, by fighting if necessary, but usually by bluffing. He finds his place in the group by dominating smaller bulls, cows and equal bulls less adept at fighting. A cow also establishes her dominance by force, but perhaps by less actual fighting, more by threats and shoves. She dominates the smaller males in her group as well as other cows, but often has to submit to the larger three-year-old bulls yet with her group.

Every individual in the group knows well who dominates him and whom he dominates—no continual fighting takes place, just a giving away by lesser animals as animals higher in the hierarchy approach, except for a calf, who takes on the dominance order of his mother but establishes his own place in the calf group after four months. A lowly animal may derive some dominance by associating with a dominant animal. The lesser animal moves from a good feeding spot or hastens out of a choice wallow when a dominant animal approaches or lays his chin on the other's rump as a signal of dominance. He walks through the deep snow around a leader stopped and blocking the trail.

Although buffalo organize socially according to dominance, in an emergency the first member to notice the danger takes over the leadership; the rest follow no matter what their dominance status. Thus the lowliest may lead the stampede.

Buffalo sometimes even attack as a group: they have moved elk off choice pasture in this way. A group of wood buffalo advanced step by threatening step toward a Wood Buffalo Park warden, acting in offensive concert until the last ticklish moment, when they all wheeled and dashed away.[25]

Even a calf only three weeks old takes up with a calf group and spends much of his day in it; if he can't find his mother for a time, he returns to the calf group for solace: he even forces his mother into joining a "maternity club"—the mothers of his playmates.

At a year old he's a spike bull—his horns as straight as spikes—and he likely has a bosom buddy; the two of them feed together, race each other, butt each other's spikes about in mock battle; day by day he seldom ranges far from the other's side. And although other herd groups roam nearby, he still stays in his mother's group, a predominately cow group, a loose group that may lose or gain members as those nearby feed and intermingle.

When he's four years old, about the time his sperm becomes fertile and his horns attain the mature curve, he'll quit running with the cows and move with the bulls. Here he must accept the dominance of older, tougher bulls and lose any power which his three-year-old size had given him in the cow group. Now he has to give up a choice wallow or an easy place to drink if an old boy chooses it. But he's part of a loose group.

Erratic as a buffalo also makes a good simile. For one thing, although they might charge full speed at a man, they seldom carry out their bluff. Captain Meriwether Lewis, "to give them some amusement," called the bluff of three bulls charging directly at him by altering his direction to go toward them. At one hundred yards away they stopped, looked, and retreated.[26] Foot hunters claimed it was easy to outrun this erratic charge of nearby buffalo.[27] But most everyone remained wary of cow with calf; she might charge more seriously.

In the past, buffalo moved seasonally, often in large numbers, as well as moving locally looking for new pasture. Sometimes they appeared as though by magic during the night: "Next morning that plain, which had been vacant the whole day before, was filled with scattered herds of buffalo"[28]; sometimes a man heard them coming: "a low murmuring sound as of wind in the tops of pine trees . . could it be the buzzing of a bumblebee? . . . now becomes a roar . . . ."[29]

No man knew what locality might please them any one year. The Musselshell, which they loved, might see them several seasons and then see them not at all for several seasons. During summer months they might seek high, breezy places away from insects, and thus seem, to men following rivers, to have deserted the country. One man rode from Manitoba to Rocky Mountain House, good buffalo country, and saw not a buffalo—only chips from other seasons. The Pawnee once came off the plains discouraged by a bad winter hunt only to find buffalo thick near their villages.

In the fall buffalo moved toward a place of good winter feeding and protection from storms—usually wooded land, perhaps in a local mild climate. They moved haphazardly, those near the Rockies stopping sometimes in mountain valleys to eat flag grass growing on bottoms behind broken beaver dams, following no set trail, no yearly route, not so much a migration as a general shifting toward places they knew. Buffalo that had summered along the Milk River might meander 200 miles north into the Bow River country of Alberta; here they would enjoy the prairie sunshine

Buffalo in snow. *Courtesy Carl Davaz*, Missoulian, *Missoula, Montana.*

and the balmy days of the chinook. Buffalo of other high plains might move into the protection of mountains where they could root snow for grass or, in the worst weather, browse on willow; they fed more poorly in the mountains than when on the prairies, but they lived far from the reach of Indian arrows as well as the prairie blizzard. They might move back and forth from mountains to prairie as the winter weather changed. Some plains buffalo wintered in the cover of the cottonwood bottoms. Those buffalo on the Arkansas and the Canadian Rivers sometimes moved south a ways to winter on the Staked Plains or along the Pecos; they made perhaps the only definite southerly wintering movement in all of buffalo land. Yet even these cannot be called migration. Instead they are erratic absences, for these herds might not return north to the Canadian come spring, but wander elsewhere.

In April, when the bare patches of greening grass appeared on sunny hilltops between snowpacked coulees, the buffalo moved again, sniffing into the spring wind, moving toward agreeable smells, in whatever whimsical way overtook them but always into the wind.

The buffalo moved, that was his life. He moved erratically in hopes of running across better pasture. Sometimes he failed: Charles Goodnight, the famous Texas rancher, in 1867 rode upon a hundred mile stretch of starved carcasses—with grass just over the divide; a young girl on the Oregon Trail complained to her diary, "I was very sick all day in consequence of taking the scent of dead buffalo. There is a great many dies of poverty."[30] Each day buffalo wandered two miles or so eating, but home didn't mean coulees and streams in a twenty-five mile diameter as it might to a deer; it meant ridges and bottoms and bluffs for hundreds of miles in any direction.

If buffalo had moved more predictably, no mountain man need ever have unsqueamishly eaten grasshopper or rattlesnake saying "Meat's meat." At any time, he could have found a "migration route" and slaughtered meat. Instead he often watched every sign, followed every lead only to "move along hungry and sulk, the theme of conversation being the well-remembered merits of good buffalo meat." At these times not even the famed Red River hunters filled their meat carts.

When erratic buffalo wandered and a man saw not a single buffalo in weeks of travel, what greenhorn could believe farfetched stories of buffalo as thick as gnats? Or tales of buffalo passing camp "ten abreast" at "a long lope . . . for about four hours"?

Yet only by telling tales could a frontiersman convey to the greenhorn the numbers of buffalo he had seen. "We counted the buffaloes by the hour instead of trying to determine how many were in the herd," said a hide hunter from Montana's high country. "It was impossible to count them, so we stood and kept track of the hours a herd required to pass a given point."[31] One such herd took five days to pass a given point and was figured at four million head.[32]

Men saw such numbers of buffalo they feared no one back home would believe: Pedro de Castañeda wrote only because witnesses still lived; another Spaniard wrote, "it might be considered a falsehood . . . according to the judgment of all of us who were in any army, nearly every day . . . as many cattle came out as are to be found in the largest ranches of New Spain."[33] Years later a man marched the 210 miles from Fort Benton to Sun River constantly surrounded by buffalo; a "reliable young man" told of waiting three days between Fort Benton and Milk River for a herd to cross. He claimed that once it was gone he crossed the trail and found it eighteen miles wide, with "that whole distance being trod to finest dust to the depth of six inches."[34]

Lewis and Clark observed "buffalo in such multitudes that we cannot exaggerate in saying that in a single glance we saw three thousand of them."[35] Less cautious observers claimed "We Cold see at one time ten thousand Buffelow,"[36] or, at a single "coup d'oiel," 50,000 buffalo.[37] And Horace Greeley estimated, on his famous cross-country stagecoach trip, "I know a million is a great many, but I am confident we saw that number yesterday . . . [they] could not have stood on ten square miles."[38]

Many travelers shied away from giving figures, preferring to tell what they'd observed and let the reader conjure up the figures. Thus Thomas Farnham wrote that when traveling along the Arkansas fifteen miles a day, and able to see for fifteen miles on each side of the trail, in three days he'd seen about 1350 square miles of land entirely covered with buffalo.[39] If we use Colonel Dodge's estimate that buffalo in immense herds stood at about twenty animals per acre,[40] we find that Farnham would have seen a mind-boggling seventeen million buffalo in three days. If we reduce this number by 75 percent, he would have seen about four million buffalo in three days. Equally mind-boggling were the observations of a Canadian rancher who noted that 23,000 cattle occupied only a corner of a valley he had once seen filled with buffalo.[41] The Indians themselves said of the buffalo, "The country was one robe." Similarly, a white man said, "The ground seemed to be covered with a brown mantle of fur."[42] Yet their numbers disappointed one young man's expectations—immense numbers were in sight but he could "see the ground in many places."[43]

Although the herds stood "in such immense num-

bers as to defy computation," Ernest Thompson Seton, the Canadian naturalist, had a try at computing their overall numbers. In 1906 he estimated that since twenty-four million cattle and horses then lived on 750,000 square miles of fenced plains (about half of the plains available to buffalo) then surely forty million buffalo could have lived here. He estimated that another thirty million could have lived on the 500,000 square miles of the prairies—they would support these many buffalo per acre. And he estimated that only five million animals could have lived in the one million square miles of forests of the East. This gave him a total of about seventy-five million buffalo living in North America in primitive times; he conservatively lowered this to fifty or sixty million. As a population that expanded, he argued, at about five percent a year until Columbus arrived, they might have come, Seton thought, to the point of overcrowding.[44] Others believe that their enormous natural losses kept them from outgrowing their food supply. And Tom McHugh disagreed with Seton's figures. Using the "carrying capacity" of the 1,250,000 square miles of grassland available to buffalo as twenty-five acres per buffalo, he arrived at an estimate of thirty-two million here and two million living in bordering areas.[45] This seems the best estimate yet.

When the Spaniards explored north of the Rio Grande in the middle of the sixteenth century, they found buffalo. When, soon after, other Spaniards landed on the Florida peninsula and moved inland, they came upon some buffalo. When still other Spaniards came to the mouth of the Mississippi and the coast of Texas, they too found buffalo. In fact the only early Spaniards who saw and ate no buffalo were those who settled on the Pacific coast of California: buffalo of the high plains had been turned back by the barren Sierra Mountains and Mojave Desert, by intensive hunting, or by "late" arrival on the plains (they'd not had time to expand their range to that point).

The Dutch found buffalo along the Niagara; the Scotch found them along the Cumberland. Spanish De Soto heard of them being in Georgia country and French La Salle noted them along the Mississippi. Americans Lewis and Clark found them all along the Missouri, but not at all along the Columbia.

Buffalo filled the continent from the Great Slave Lake south to the Rio Grande and, in scatterings, a little below it. Perhaps in Mexico they had made it to the Pacific going through Sinaloa, perhaps a few once had wandered all the way to Nicaragua.[46] On the Pacific side of the Rockies they fed along the Clark's Fork of the Columbia, the Bitterroot and the Flathead, ranging as far west as the Pend d'Oreille region, and on into eastern Washington until the people there acquired the horse. Then hunting held them back and eventually destroyed them.[47] No barrier of food or terrain existed to stop them. Buffalo found easy access to the Columbia headwaters from the Missouri headwaters up Divide Creek and down Silver Bow Creek over an almost prairie-like Continental Divide. Thus they should have filled the Oregon and Washington plains between the Rockies and Cascades, yet only a few scattered skeletons have been found in eastern Washington and fewer still in southern Oregon and northeast California. Herds did graze along the Pacific-bound Salmon River and a ways along the upper Snake and Humboldt Rivers, having crossed the Divide on other easy passes but perhaps only when chased across by the white man's incursions.[48]

Buffalo filled the country from the Rocky Mountains to just east of the Mississippi. They lived in fewer numbers from there almost to the Atlantic Ocean, although they may have arrived in this country only a few hundred years before the first white man: the mound builders knew no buffalo, and the buffalo bones deposited in Big Bone Lick, Kentucky, "indicate an exceedingly recent arrival." Perhaps they only crossed the Mississippi after the year 1000 A.D.[49] Perhaps they felt less attracted to the east of the Mississippi country because, like cattle, they need one-seventh protein in their diet, which only the prairie and high plains grasses provided—1,250,000 square miles of it. They seem to have avoided entirely the country north of the Great Lakes but to have occupied most of the mountain country of the Atlantic seaboard.

They filled less of the country soon after the white man arrived. As early as the 1600s La Salle was complaining of the rapid disappearance of buffalo because of hunters poaching on his franchise in Ouisconsin (Wisconsin).

Where the prairie ends, at the top of the vast expanse of grass, before the tundra of the far north begins, grow willow bushes and fir trees, a cover for rolling hills above marshy, brushy bottoms, an almost impassable country blockaded further by lakes and rivers. This is the country loved by the wood buffalo or mountain buffalo, too shy to reveal himself on the barren prairies, happy behind the fir thickets of the concealing arctic jungle.

The wood buffalo's shyness came not from runtiness: he outweighed the prairie buffalo a few hundred pounds and his hump rose an inch or so higher. Yet for all his larger mass, even the old hunters saw that he was more skittish than his relative.

Today, in Wood Buffalo Park, he runs so from the scent of man that biologists who wish to observe him and wardens who wish to count him have had to make do mostly with glimpses of disappearing bodies. And like the prairie animal, the wood buffalo is erratic. He may run or he may block a trail. Wardens in Wood Buffalo Park have learned to relinquish the right-of-way to a bull in a trail, for although he may cannonade away over sapling and brush like a bear startled out of a huckleberry patch, he may charge. The charge might about-face, becoming a bluff just like the prairie buffalo's, but it's a bluff few men would want to call. Yet sometimes a man may walk up close to bulls and watch them as long as he needs. Erratic.

These northern buffalo seem not to meet in giant herds during the rut—perhaps the forest thickets separate one rutting group from another. But the rutting uproar (which begins in August rather than June or July) surrounds men moving through the woods; the rut creates pandemonium in the forest depths: scores of fights shake the thickets, but men glimpse the bodies only briefly through openings in the cover; bulls break across clearing in blind, pell-mell charges only to crash into concealing brush again; nighttime rampages keep men awake and sometimes arouse them to stand guard over tents and horses. Consequently, the northern rut seems more hazardous to man than the prairie rut. The bulls stand athwart trails rather than move aside as do the prairie animals. The mating hunt through curtaining trees seems to enrage them, unlike the mating hunt of their relatives who can see at a quarter mile what their rivals are up to.

During the rest of the year the northern herds seem more clanlike than those on the prairies. Bulls reportedly live with cows and calves during all seasons, the bulls perhaps remaining close by even during calving. Nor do bulls and cows separate into such distinct herds as do the prairie species—as far as observers can tell. Certainly the herds cluster in smaller groups than prairie herds, as if limited bits of pasture limit herd size. Environment has wrought significant differences, so much so that, exactly opposite the prairie buffalo, the wood buffalo seems to live together in larger groups in the winter than in the summer. And he seems to wander far less—one herd swam the Athabasca River, liked the new range, and has never returned. Nor have herds wandered far enough to discover the good food in the northeast portion of the park: they range within only 1500 square miles of the total 6900 square miles. [50]

Otherwise these wood buffalo live much as prairie buffalo. They wallow, choosing loose, barren, sandy soil for easy rooting; they rub near wallows, destroying willow copses, breaking down and uprooting saplings; they create hundreds of trails through brush and trees. Bachelor bulls roam the woods confidently, seeming to have lost the shyness that they had in the herds.

A casual observer can see one distinctive difference in the woods-dwelling buffalo: his beard is shorter, he wears it off in the brush.

Buffalo fecundity coupled with a long breeding life may have made for buffalo dominance through numbers. Almost every cow on the continent dropped a calf each year—although cows suckling calves sometimes tended to miss pregnancy. (Today in protected herds the fertility rate approaches 90 percent.) Perhaps 15 million new buffalo arrived each year in the days before the white man.

Buffalo live twenty-five to forty years in captive herds. Wild buffalo undoubtedly died a little earlier, the victims of wolf attack when weak, but the species tends toward longevity . . . one yarn spinner said he'd seen them so old their horns "had decayed and dropped off."

And buffalo remain fertile in old age. Some of Texan Charles Goodnight's cows bred until they reached thirty-five;[51] a government employee once butchered a wet 28-year-old cow carrying a calf.[52] Fecundity carried over into old age helped the buffalo increase his numbers.

And it made up for the more than 50 percent loss in each year's calf crop, which meant about seven-and-a-half million small dead carcasses annually. Late blizzards laid low herds of them, high water along the Missouri drowned them, sweeping their bodies to lodge wherever receding waters left them (Audubon's party one night slept on "a low island covered with dead Buffalo calves, creating a most unpleasant atmosphere to breathe").[53] Calves often made the mistake of adopting any non-buffalo foster parent who happened along, even a man or a horse (calves of domestic cattle will make the same mistake). One adopted Meriwether Lewis, out for an evening walk. It dogged his heels until he regained his canoe and paddled off.[54] Other calves followed less disinterested men, who encouraged them to tag along all the way to camp to make a veal stew; Alexander Henry's men brought such innocents to the fort daily. Indians brought little stragglers to camp for their children to play with and,

when the playing was done, butchered them. Sometimes the children killed them with their own bows and arrows. And undoubtedly, any calf, away from mother's protection, unable to keep up with man or horse, became dinner for wolves.

Mother usually protected him, but not always. If she found herself hard-pressed by pursuers, she sometimes deserted him, running off to leave him to the wolves. Meriwether Lewis observed, "The cows only defend their young as long as they are able to keep up with the herd, and seldom return any distance in search of them."[55] If a calf found he couldn't climb a bluff the herd had ascended, his mother would watch a while as he scrabbled at the cutbank, but then she would turn and follow the others. Men who wanted to begin a buffalo herd found it easy to gain a nucleus by driving a herd through rough country and picking up the calves that couldn't follow.

Luckily for buffalo survival, calves could pretty well keep up with the herd. Once a newborn calf traveled twenty-two miles by road in a herd being moved, traveled back home again with his mother that night (cross-country in deep snow) and was herded back the twenty-two miles the next day—about sixty-six miles before he was three days old.[56] And their speed and endurance increased rapidly: the William Hornaday expedition in 1886 chased a five-month-old calf fifteen miles, using a series of three fresh horses to run him down.

The careless cow often swam her calf into spring flood waters too strong for it and clambered out on the far bank without it. Hundreds of other calves died from falling through thin and melting spring ice, disappeared to appear again in an ice-free ripple far below, drowned, then floated downstream to join dozens of brown buffalo carcasses that punctuated the river bank.

Bulls and cows, too, filed out onto rotten March ice only to fall through and drown. Each spring, during the days of the breakup, thousands of buffalo carcasses floated down western rivers, a continuous line of brown floes. One year on the Qu' Appelle, trader John McDonnell counted 7360 of them drifting past before he quit counting;[57] Alexander Henry saw "drowned buffalo drift down the river day and night," and while traveling one May the stench from drowned buffalo was so great he couldn't eat his supper[58]; Maximilian, Prince of Wied, on his Missouri River trip of 1833, heard reports of complete dams formed of buffalo bodies,[59] dams which, others have claimed, caught silt to form islands.

These drownings make buffalo appear poor swim-

Prairie fire. Alligators, bicycles, lions—and buffalo? *Courtesy National Archives, Washington, D.C.*

mers, yet accounts of riverboat travelers up the Missouri abound with descriptions of them swimming this river, many of them "often struck by the wheels." Passengers lassooed swimming buffalo. They swam "so close together . . . as to make it look rather inconvenient"; they hung low in the water, just the top of heads and an occasional hump visible. In such style they paddled about in lakes and crossed the Republican, the Arkansas and the Missouri, traveling where they pleased. Yet in the spring, four or five buffalo at a time, finding themselves adrift on a floe, would stick with it and ride to whatever crackup lay ahead, rather than swim a river they'd swum before.

They learned nothing from numberless watery accidents. They rushed into swift waters to be swept over waterfalls. Grizzly bears hung around the Great Falls of the Missouri to feed on carcasses so killed. In midwinter, crossing rivers on the ice, they would "rush in a dense crowd to one place; the ice gives way. . . ." In March 1866, 1000 buffalo fell through the ice of the South Saskatchewan River, but did not drown; they were frozen in and starved.[60]

Other accidents also did in numbers of buffalo. Prairie fire left herds with "the hair singed off; even the skin in many places is shriveled up and terribly burned, and their eyes are swollen and closed fast . . . staggering about, sometimes running afoul of a large stone, at other times tumbling down hill and falling into creeks. . . . In one spot we found a whole herd lying dead."[61] Sometimes entire groups mired themselves in boggy mud and died in mass starvation or were eaten alive by wolves or bears. But, mostly, falling through ice did them in. Each spring the stench from carcasses snagged on river banks polluted the spring air, and rotting meat polluted the spring freshet. Today Canadian wildlife experts conclude that drownings are "far more cataclysmic" to the buffalo of Wood Buffalo Park than they had formerly thought.[62]

The buffalo's remarkable adaptability has always contributed to his family strength at all seasons of the year. He survived −50° winters and howling prairie blizzards. He also withstood summer drouth. If he had to endure several waterless days, he kept his strength and found it in him to race ten miles downwind to the water he could smell. He found prickly pear juice to sustain him when he had nothing else to drink, and he could drink the filth of his manure-and-urine-saturated wallow without upset.

The family lost few members to illness; buffalo seemingly lived somewhat beyond the reach of epidemic. Indian calendars reveal a terrible pestilence in 1825, when the buffalo were afflicted with the disease known as "whistlers," a time when "Six Lakotas [Sioux] Died of eating a diseased buffalo." (The plague evidently raged from 1820 to 1830.) This epizootic wiped out all cloven-hoofed animals from "the headwaters of the Blue across the salt basin toward the Platte," creating a dead land which not even the coyote, wolf or magpie entered to feed on the carrion.

"Herd of Buffalo Fleeing from Prairie Fire." M. Straus, 1888. *Courtesy Amon Carter Museum, Fort Worth, Texas.*

Buffalo trails stood out on the prairie from afar, distinctly edged by carcasses.[63] But buffalo seemingly suffered few such epidemics. Supposedly they developed brucellosis only after contact with domestic cattle; most herds today are vaccinated against it. And numerous herds today have contracted tuberculosis, perhaps again only after contact with domestic herds. External parasites such as lice, mites and ticks live in the hair, but hardly decrease their vitality. This is also the case with the internal parasites, larvae, flukes, lungworms and the like that have been found in carcasses.[64] Occasionally, however, a severe infestation can cause death or so weaken an animal as to make him susceptible to the bacterial infections.

Nor did ordinary accidents stop him: a dangling broken leg healed, broken ribs healed, bullet and arrow wounds scarred over. Not even the .50 caliber Sharps killed him for sure. Zebulon Pike's party, shooting lesser weapons, put nineteen balls into one buffalo before he died. Once a .30/06 bullet, fired from thirty feet against a bull's forehead and hairy mop, merely flattened.[65] Others have used other large bullets with the same results.

Buffalo also adapted to varying altitude. They lived at sea level, on the high plains, in the high mountains. They were seen in the geyser country of the Yellowstone; their bones have been picked up above an altitude of 10,000 feet, one wood buffalo skull at 11,500 feet.[66] Nor did rough country bother a buffalo. In spite of his bulk, in spite of the spread of his cloven

hoofs—an imprint in a marsh looks the size of a rhinoceros foot—he is about as sure-footed as a mountain sheep. Full grown animals scaled towering cutbanks along the Missouri—in places "they had leaped down bare ledges three or four feet in height with nothing but ledges of rock for a landing place."[67] They escaped horsemen in country too broken for horses' hooves to follow. More recently a herd escaped a new interior pasture at the Moiese Bison Range by scaling an unfenced talus slide which, it had been supposed, would have shut off one end of the pasture. Buffalo have always climbed, seemingly because they enjoy it (why else would they arrive above timberline where there's scant food?). If they tumbled, they protected their feet: of 3224 buffalo butchered on government ranges, not one showed a crippled foot.[68]

This sure-footedness in such an awkward-looking animal created a surprising defense when closely chased—an ability to switch ends while running. Buffalo Jones claimed a cow he was chasing "stiffened her forelegs threw her hinder parts around in the air, and, using her front legs as a pivot, reversed ends in a second."[69] (Forty years later a South Dakota smart aleck, chasing a buffalo in an automobile, discovered the same thing when the buffalo swapped ends and "put the auto out of business.")[70] And immigrant Noah Brooks wrote of seeing buffalo, while running away from a wagon train, "drop into a wallow while on a keen run, roll over and over two or three times, and skip to his feet . . with the nimbleness of a kitten."[71]

(He seems to be one of the few men who ever saw a buffalo "roll over"; most observers say their hump prevents it.)

Buffalo look slow, but, running singly, they can reach thirty to thirty-five miles an hour, though they're slower in the herd. The smaller cows easily outdistance the ponderously loping bulls. The buffalo has four gaits: the walk, the trot, the bound and the gallop. His bounding, an uncommon quadruped gait in which he extends all four legs simultaneously, he holds in common with some deer and gazelles. He uses it to move away fast when startled.[72]

Most everyone agreed the buffalo *could* outdo almost any horse. A man writing about herds in eighteenth-century Georgia noted that "though They are a very heavy beast, They will out Run a Horse and Quite Tire him . . ."[73] As Colonel Dodge put it, the buffalo has "more bottom" than the horse. Cowboy Charles Norris laid its endurance to the fact that "They pawed with one low side and after awhile changed to the other,"[74] a view similar to that of cowboy Clark Stocking, who claimed when a herd had run half a mile or more, "They changed both front feet to one side . . . to rest them."[75] Folklore. Buffalo move their feet in the usual quadruped running patterns—like a horse. They simply have more stamina.

A fast cow in rough country has to be chased by riders with a series of fresh horses. One of the last cows in Montana, wanted as a specimen by the Hornaday Smithsonian Expedition, ran twenty-five miles and wore out several horses before she could be killed.[76] Each year during the roundup at the Moiese Bison Range several fleet beasts outrun all of the lathering horses and hide out in the willows of Mission Creek ("Old Creek Bottom" has never been forced into the corral). Since these buffalo cannot be run through the chutes, they are counted as they are seen from afar.

Not only can this hulk of a beast run faster than expected, it can also jump far higher than any animal of his weight and proportion should. Old Sikes, a cantankerous bull of the Goodnight herd, corralled after a long chase, jumped the six-foot enclosure during the night, and on his way back to where he'd been found jumped all the fences in his way.[77] Today the Department of the Interior recommends that buffalo fences be at least seven feet high, but ranchers near Yellowstone Park tell of one park escapee who made it over a ten-foot gate. So agile is a buffalo that, from lying on his chest, legs folded, he can pop onto all four feet at once, "as if propelled by a huge spring."

The buffalo: agile . . . reasonably fast . . . long-lived . . . able to go without water . . . able to forage anywhere most any time . . . fertile for years . . . big . . . gregarious . . . he was made to win the West.

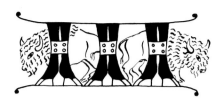

". . . the mind simply boggles at the idea that the Amerind,
armed only with spears, killed off everything in sight . . .
The mammoth was a grazing animal,
and while he declined another grazing animal seems
to have been doing very well.
He was the bison . . ."
LOUIS A. BRENNAN

MAN AND BUFFALO have shared much of the North American continent since man first crossed the Bering Isthmus during one of the last intra-glaciations of the Wisconsin age, about 25,000, perhaps 40,000, years ago. This paleo man—Llano man, archeologists call him—found a tundra-covered land bridge where water now stands. When millions of gallons of ocean water became entrapped in the great ice fields, the oceans receded until the floor of the Bering Sea was revealed, vegetated, and occupied by Arctic mammals such as the musk-ox and the big bison, creating a land called Beringea.

About this time, man underwent a population explosion brought about by the covering of the earth by grasslands and the subsequent proliferation of grass-eating mammals, animals who converted grass protein into quantities of flesh protein that fed men better than ever. Pushed perhaps by their own expanding numbers and pulled from hunting camp to hunting camp by the good living provided by the big mammals, Asians passed through what Loren Eiseley has called "the cold filter" of the Bering Arctic. In these northlands they found a hunter's paradise—just one bison would provide meals for several weeks for the skilled hunting band.[1]

These bands, carrying fine spears tipped with knife-sharp, stone projectile heads, left Beringea to move from kill to kill, traveling the land extending from Point Barrow to Mackenzie Bay. At this bay they discovered the great Mackenzie River flowing out of the south along a corridor between the ice sheets. Down its great trench led innumerable game trails, some of them scuffed out by giant bison. These trails brought men south to the edge of the grasslands of North America, the Great Plains, a land filled with big mammals.

The hunters found the Great Plains almost as they are today: a vast grassy expanse, drained by myriad small streams flowing into the larger eastward flowing rivers, the Saskatchewan, the Missouri, the Platte, the Arkansas and the Red—waterways lined with trees and bushes, storm-shelter for animals and men alike. On these plains grew, even as today, the high-protein grama grass, buffalo grass and needle grass, short grasses and bunch grasses that furnish good summer feed and also cure on the stem to lock in all of their nourishment for good winter feed. The highly nutritious soils of this temperate region made for lush growth that could support thousands of buffalo and other large animals. Due to the humidity and coolness brought on by the nearby ice fields, more moisture fell than now falls; men and animals found many more ponds and bogs than exist today.

Men moved down the eastern edge of the Rockies exploring the river courses to the east, but also moving south, always south, hunting the buffalo and other mammals. The Missouri River drainage gave passage to the Rockies to the west. Following this river to its headwaters, then following the Jefferson and the Beaverhead, animals and men could move over plain-like passages across the Continental Divide, then wander south to the shores of huge Lake Bonneville, a watery grassland later to recede into desert and the Great Salt Lake. Or they could wander west over the Divide on another easy plain onto the upper tributaries of the Columbia and out to the Pacific Coast. Other wandering groups ignored the Missouri and continued moving south on the high plains, eventually crossing the southwest desert (dry even then), into jungle, on across the isthmus of Panama and south to the bottom of South America, filling two continents with men who followed the grass eaters. But those who fed on the big mammals remained on the high plains and became the spear hunters supreme.

The newly arrived high plains dweller found many mammals who had lived here 20,000 years or more, since the previous intra-glaciation period, temperate-region mammals such as the tapir and giant sloth who had been able to cross Beringea during the warm period. Now the colder, tundra-covered land was suitable only for crossing by north-adapted animals—and man. The plains also contained quantities of the native mammals, the camel and horse, as well as an early bison who may have crossed Beringea with the tapir and sloth.

These hunters preyed on all of these large mammals. They killed many a mammoth, driving the fourteen-foot-high, red, elephant-like beast into swamps to mire him and spear him in the guts or mount his back and jab a spear between the atlas vertebra and the base of the skull. The smaller camel and horse fell to his spears as did the giant ground sloth, tapir and big bison. Very likely this bison attracted the hunters more than the smaller bison because just then he outnumbered the smaller one.

Then, about 6000 years ago, all of these large mammals died out—all except the smaller bison; either they died out or became extinct from man's over-hunting . . . or the smaller bison may have hurried the extinction of those other big mammals who competed for grass with him. For if early bison's habits were like those of today's buffalo, he could well have survived ecological changes that killed other mammals. Extremes of temperature would faze him little; he could live in the heat along the Rio Grande or in the cold about the Slave Lakes. If snows lay deep he could find the grass underneath. If a favorite pasture dried out, he could digest brush or cactus or move to a higher, moister elevation.

If, during a drouth, competition between sloth and buffalo became acute, the bison herd, wickedly horned, moving in a phalanx similar to that they use to chase elk from pasture today, could well have moved the sloth off wanted grass, starving him. Or, bison herds, if they ranged in the numbers of the later buffalo, may well have swallowed up the grass first and starved other grass eaters, just as they often chewed the prairie bare during historic times. And the bison perhaps adapted to changing conditions: possibly competition with other ungulates had made him smaller than his ancestors; he undoubtedly needed less grass, unlike the mammoth who failed to shrink to fit a decreasing food supply.

Although there were plenty of bison for carnivores to eat, the dire wolf and the sabre-toothed tiger also disappeared. Likely they found it discouraging to face, daily, the bison's formidable horns and powerful hooves, just as in historic times no grizzly bear or mountain lion preyed upon the buffalo for daily food.

Only man could kill him daily: paleontologists have found more bison bones than other prehistoric animal bones in twenty-seven of thirty-five important archeological sites, sites that somewhat reveal man's life here from about 15,000 to 5000 B.C.[2]

When man had drifted as far east and south as Florida, he may have found a few enormous *Bison latifrons* living in certain refugia, descendants either of the earliest bison immigrants from the Holarctic, *Bison priscus*, or a later emigrant direct from Asia. Earlier, *latifrons* had traveled as far as central Mexico, perhaps to Nicaragua, and from coast to coast, moving where he wished for he met no horned cattle to compete with him (as did the bison of Eurasia). He lived south of the ice for a glacial age, kept from spreading north again by the ice.

Paleontologists agree that the evidence from various digs points to the early arrival and longtime residence of *B. latifrons* across temperate North America, but they may disagree as to his origin (and the evolution of other species). For one thing, in examining prehistoric bison bones, they find tremendous variation in horn size.

Paleontologists have long interpreted the relationships of fossil bison by analyzing male skulls found in various digs in North America. (Skulls make up the most of the remains of prehistoric bison; few complete fossil skeletons exist. Male skulls predominate perhaps because bulls have always been more easily hunted than cows.) Although the scientists mostly agree on *latifrons* and other major prehistoric bison as species, as well as the time of their evolving and residence, they interpret the message of the various skulls and horns in differing ways too numerous for complete presentation here.

In general, three major theories have developed. All three try to account for the differences in skeletal remains, especially a shrinkage in total size from early bison to late bison. And the theories try to establish what line of descent led to today's buffalo.

One theory states that early bison arrived in North America in "successive waves"—the first wave that of *Bison latifrons*, a descendant of ancient *Bison priscus* (the Steppe wisent), a Holarctic species, then living in the Asian Arctic. *Latifrons* came here about 600,000 to 700,000 years ago. Other species followed later, in other waves, these scientists believe, smaller bison with smaller horns than *Bison latifrons* (whose horns spread seven feet and whose mass would have equaled two of our *Bison bison*).

According to this theory, one of these smaller bison, *Bison alleni*, fathered a species, *Bison antiquus*, the bison who lived on the Great Plains throughout the Wisconsin ice age (125,000 to 25,000 B.C.) and became man's main bison prey after his arrival here.

Further waves of bison came out of Asia and crossed Beringea, according to this theory, one of which, *Bison occidentalis*, became the immediate ancestor of our modern buffalo.[3]

A second theory holds that since the horns and skeletons of recent bison are smaller than those of the more ancient animals, the bison genus in North America began to shrink some 50,000 years ago or so—that the subgenera and species tended to develop in smaller and curlier-horned versions in a phylogenetic sequence.

A third theory differs with some of this. It holds that B. *latifrons* developed as North American stock, a descendant of B. *priscus* (the species that lived in the Arctic—Asian as well as North American), who had medium-sized horns. *Priscus* arrived in Beringea sometime in the middle Pleistocene, perhaps 700,000 years ago, at a time when Alaska was more Asian than North American. He probably came from old Asiatic stock, a descendant of *Leptobos*, the small ancestor of all bison, skeletons of which, two million years old,

have been found in China. He lived in the Alaskan Arctic from the Kansas epoch through the other ice epochs, except for a possible voyage to the southern plains during the late Yarmouth. Here he may have been cut off from the northern branch of the species by another advance of ice. This theory holds that during this ice epoch B. *latifrons* could have developed on the Great Plains from this southern B. *priscus* population and he, rather than B. *alleni*, fathered B. *antiquus*, early man's main bison prey.

This theory further holds that B. *latifrons* could, in part, have developed his seven-foot horns on the Great Plains for display and as an aggressive tool to compete with the larger, but unhorned Great Plains mammals, the mammoth, the giant sloth, the tapir and the small horse (who had been dominant until the bison's arrival), as well as to fight off such carnivore predators as the sabre-toothed tiger and the dire wolf. And, argues the theory, the increase in food on the Great Plains may also have contributed to the extra growth of horns: other bison species, those remaining far north and B. *antiquus* (descendant of big-horned *latifrons*), found no need for large horns. For one thing, as we have seen, they encountered no horned competition. And *antiquus* may have found his hairy mane, a heritage from the far north, adequate for display purpose (today's bison seem to rely on this excess frontal hair to increase the mass of their image: they stand in a semi-broadside position when confronting other bison).[4]

The three theories agree that B. *antiquus* thrived in temperate North America; he wandered from the Pacific Coast to the Atlantic, from the Missouri to central Mexico. Eventually he was joined, on the Great Plains only, by a bison from the Arctic bearing smallish, medium-sized horns, *Bison occidentalis*, who sired our modern species.

The European bison, the species *Bison bonasus*, the wisent, developed similarly. He also stems from B. *occidentalis* and looks remarkably like the North American bison except for his smaller head, which he holds higher, his legginess and overall slender appearance. He and *athabascae*, both woods-loving animals, seem more related to *occidentalis* than does B. *bison bison*, the plains dweller. About a thousand *bonasus* survive in state forests of Poland and Russia. Like our buffalo, he dwindled in number under the pressures of man— in fact Julius Caesar complained of his waste. He had all but disappeared by 1700.

Bison are ruminants—cud chewers; they regurgitate their food to rechew it. The genus itself, fossil and present, belongs to the family *Bovidae*, the *Bovini* part of it. He's an ox that carries fourteen pairs of ribs instead of the usual thirteen, develops a hump that is a growth of bone and meat on his vertebrae, grows long curly hair on his forequarters and head, has a broad moist muzzle and dangles a tail shorter than most of the family. He's closely related to cattle—his "post-cranial elements" can be easily confused with theirs and his blood is closely allied to theirs. Along with the musk-ox, he's also the member of the family with the peculiar musky odor. His skull looks different: it has more prominent eye sockets set farther apart than those of other cattle, a development that allows him vision to the rear around his mass of head hair. (In prehistoric bison this evolution may account for wider-placed eyes found in the hairier, Holarctic species.)

Our plains buffalo differs from all the other woods-loving cattle, for he, instead of feeding in the open only morning and evenings and spending other hours in the protection of the woods, stays mostly on the open plains and depends upon flight or a drawing closer together in the herd itself for protection.

"These wild cattle subsist in all seasons of the year."
LOUIS HENNEPIN

"It is surprising how the cows resist
the piercing N. wind, which at times blows with such
violence over the bleak plains . . .
that it cannot be faced; still these animals graze
in the open field."
ALEXANDER HENRY

L ET US stand behind an aspen growth on a bluff overlooking a grassy bottom and watch an imaginary buffalo herd. It's late April. Snow on the far sandstone bluffs seems to hang in earflaps down the dividing sandy washes. At this distance bunch grass clumps seem green sod grass. In the valley below, buffalo, just awake in the greying morning, start to feed; their grunts sound clear in the morning quiet. Immediately below us and across a riley stream, a cow noses a wobbly newborn calf, licks him and licks him. The wobbly thing takes a few "spider-like" steps, falls on his chin; she licks him. And when he's clean, he nuzzles, searching for her udder (it's small, probably a development against freezing damage). She ignores him, helps him not at all. She's watching a big raven pretending to feed nearby; she knows he might try to dine on the new calf's eyes. The calf finds the udder, he feeds. Nearby, grey wolves sit on haunches, aware of the new calf, but also aware of the cow's sharp horns. Now a cow over at the edge of the herd sees the newcomer by his mother's side and walks through the frost-covered grass to have a better look. The mother calmly watches her approach, lets her sniff and snuff the calf. Others of the herd, cows and young bulls alike, begin to amble that way. Soon mother and calf stand surrounded by the

curious, sniffing her, sniffing her calf, sniffing the bloody birthplace, satisfying their curiosity. After a while mother and calf move with the herd. The calf, only ninety minutes old, with a full belly, frisks about as if he found this place just right for baby buffalo. He bounds in a circle about his mother, but snuffles up close to her when others move too close, his little tail suddenly tucked between his legs in fright, like a puppy's.

It's April. The buffalo millions are being replenished, single calf by single calf—buffalo rarely bear twins. They are being replenished about one to one, heifer calf and bull calf.

In April, May and June the cows, still separate from the bulls, bear their calves, birthing sometimes within the herd, sometimes off alone. Cows with calves graze in the herd, pregnant cows group themselves a little apart, waiting, their approximately 275 days of gestation incomplete.

The yellow-ochre offspring, yellow but within a few weeks turned to cinnamon brown or the color of Black Hills gold, look like their cousins, the Guernseys—except for small, round ears and longer head. They're just as humpless; the hump will swell first at about three months and continue to shape for the next four or five years. Buffalo calves curl up in mama's shade just as their cousins; nuzzle the udder and butt it just as their cousins. But unlike these cousins, a calf comes at a wallow spot with buffalo instinct. His legs collapse at the knees to bring him down on his shin bones with his rump in the air, his hornless head sidles at the wallow as if to horn it up a bit, then down on shoulders and side to kick into a feeble quarter-roll; seemingly he can no more roll over now than later when his hump will prevent it.

Calves seem teddy-bearish through their color and those rounded, tuft-filled ears. From the side view the head is dog-like rather than calf-like; viewed from the front the long buffalo nose and the small ears seem polar-bear like. A composition of "divers animals."

In a month the dark horns just break the skin. By July comes a darkening under the throat; a moulting starts in August; baby hair begins to fall out, pushed from the skin it seems by the new, darker hair underneath; his face seems rubbed in charcoal, his neck looks unwashed. His hump grows. Come October he's buffalo-colored and somewhat buffalo-shaped, and he wears little black stubs of horns. His voice is changing; he grunts more nasally, as his elders.

He'll follow his mother, suckling, for seven to nine months before she weans him, and he may continue to follow after the next calf is born—cows have been seen followed by a calf, a yearling and a two-year-old—but usually, at one year old, he's on his own. In spite of her knack for losing her offspring, a cow finds her life controlled by the calf's wanderings, his stallings, his late starts. She hides him in the tall grass or bushes when she wants to feed unhampered, and there he stays although danger may step within a few feet of him. Usually, there he stays until she comes after him. She knows the spot exactly although she may have been driven far from it. Later on he may try to hide his bigger self, ostrich-fashion, head concealed in the grass, cinnamon rump jutting up and above it. A mother buffalo can usually find her own amongst the herd, sometimes seeming to recognize his grunt, other times seeming to recognize him by sighting him, singling him out with her supposedly poor eyesight, then relying on her nose in a good sniffing to assure herself that this one is hers. (Sometimes the system fails and the calf may starve.) Mother and calf grunt at each other, she to summon him, he to call for assistance, or, at times, just to reassure each other.

When the calf's a year old he'll weigh about 400 pounds and wear some longer hair on his forequarters, black hair beginning to be luxuriant. His horns will have grown to five inches and his legs to that gangly look. He's a doltish looking adolescent, mischief in his eyes, with a miniature but scraggly hump and a chin with almost no beard—all long legs and wild frolic. He's been able to outrun and outdodge most any pursuer for ten months.

In the spring buffalo look their mangiest, for now the long winter hair behind the mane loosens, pushed away from hide by the oncoming hair. First the hair on the lower neck, then between the forelegs, then the head and the woolly mane—the new hair entangled with the old. Next goes the shorter hair of the sides, back and hindquarters. In the spring, the bleached hair of a herd standing to the sunward reflects almost as if metal-covered—they are all brightness on the top and back, black shadow below. Patches of old hair mottle the sleek sides of new hair, like islands on a strange brown map; scraggly patches dangle from the belly and move in every breeze. Patches a foot square mark a trail, fluttering from sagebrush or lying lightly on the grass. A bull looks not so lordly now, for the rich dark browns and blacks of his mane have weathered into faded tans and tacky browns. He's like a sailing ship with tattered sails. To see one is to be at one with William Hornaday who felt "filled with the desire to assist nature by plucking off the flying streamers of old hair."

One has the notion to tell the old fellow to groom himself, and of course, that's exactly what he's doing. He rubs on whatever is handy to rid himself of this unsightly mess. He wallows in spring mud and summer dust, rubs against trees and boulders, but he may carry little patches of the obstinate stuff through the summer, and sometimes an occasional patch of last year's hair mottles October's lustrous pelage. The short hairs of his hindquarters expose his brown skin to sun and wind and insect bite; he wallows in mud perhaps to cool himself and coat himself as insect-protection. He may become a mud-grey bull, ugly, resembling not at all the magnificent lord of the prairies glamorized in paintings by Russell and Remington.

In late June and July the herds coalesce once more to mate. Sometime during this period the cow comes into heat for two days, but if not then impregnated another period occurs about three weeks later. A four-year-old joins the rut as eagerly as his elder, perhaps fathering a calf, although the older, heavier bulls, the seven- or eight-year-olds, usually tend the cows. But if an older bull finds himself too busy to tend a younger heifer, our four-year-old pushes forehead to forehead against the other young bulls to win her, although he'll probably not mate until he's five. Sometimes the young bulls try to keep a few small heifers for themselves, butting them and shouldering them away from joining the big crowd and the big bulls. Older bulls may ignore this, for once a bull comes upon a willing cow, he tends her monogamously, following her for several days if necessary, although he may leave her side briefly to join a fight (one of the eight or ten brief flurries of fighting during a day; they contest because on any one day the number of cows in heat adds up to less than the number of bulls).

A heifer usually mates during her fourth summer of the rut—at three years old. She (and all cows) like to be courted—seldom does she mate with a bull instantly upon his defeating others. Buffalo court in "tending relationship," the tending usually head to head rather than head to tail as in domestic cattle. If a cow repels a bull, he persists by standing and swinging his head toward her. He may put his chin on her rump, even attempt to mount her. He often signals his attempt to mount by emitting short panting sounds. Then she may try to dodge him or horn him off—not viciously, but hard—or run from him, dodging through the crowd causing a sudden game of chase that several bulls join, loping along, cutting off on a chord across the arc of her lead, playing a game that no one wins, for it stops suddenly and everyone goes back to restless milling, as nervous as salmon with the spawning urge on them. A cow accepts a bull at her pleasure; the mating bond is "essentially matriarchal," although she cannot mate with the bull of her choice if a dominant bull defeats him. Choice usually results in amatory licking of each other's fur for as long as ninety minutes before copulation. A cow may mate more than once during the rut, sometimes copulating on the run or in a fast walk, forcing the bull to run along with her on his two hind legs. The bond is exceedingly brief, rarely more than four to ten seconds (few men have seen the bond occur—which led to the myth that buffalo mate only at night). After the mating the successful bull stays by the cow's side defending her from bulls attracted by the copulation.

In the rutting crowd the young bull finds his bull voice, the bellow; it ranges from a "soft purring noise" to "a guttural growling roar" or "an extreme variation of the grunt"—the grunt being his natural voice (a herd sounds much like pigs grunting happily together); he may vary it to sound a threat or express delight while at play. He copies the bellow from his elders, unable at four years old to do more than echo higher, shorter, imitations of the grand noise of the big bulls, a noise that often continues as they eat, run or wallow. In the days of his millions a bull joined in on a chorus, answering any bellow until the joined bellows created one continuous roar, a cacophony that echoed for two or three miles across the hills. "Like the ocean beating upon a distant coast," said Francis Parkman. George Catlin's ear heard it as "the noise of distant thunder." Evidently buffalo ears hear in Catlin's way—at times they bellow in answer to low thunder rolls.

The young bull also learns to blast air through his nostrils in shorter and shorter snorts as he moves toward a cow group or threatens a rival, making a sound almost like steam emitting from a locomotive. And he may try bluffing by snorting and curling his upper lip and extending his neck as signs of his prowess. Or he stamps while approaching, to make a sound and, from the front, increase the display of his pantaloons. He learns to threaten. He tries the head-on threat: standing near another young bull, facing him, tail up, swinging his head in unison with him, down and across and back again—several minutes at a time. Or the broadside threat: a tail-down display of himself at ten to twenty-five feet from his opponent, parallel to him, sometimes accompanied by bellowing.[1]

The young bull learns to use wallowing as a signal of hostility toward a rival bull or as a "displacement activity" that substitutes for attack. During the rut a bull wallows far more frequently than a cow. He does as other bulls, paws the ground, sometimes horns it, urinates in it, rolls in it when he sights a rival, in a frenzy of wallowing unlike his habitual wallowing of other seasons. The sight of rivals brings him to horning and debarking trees as do his elders (at Moiese I saw one enraged bull tearing off mouthfulls of juniper branch to spit them on the ground).

In the old days, a matured calf wandered where he could, following any amatory adventure; his group of the winter had disintegrated; he belonged wholly to the mass, the dissemination of sperm amongst the cows his only concern. He might end up miles from his starting point, separated by hundreds of thousands of bodies from his buddy of last spring, out from under the familiar dominant bull, far from relatives. Thus, the buffalo mass stood in little danger of inbreeding.

After the end of the rut in August and September he found himself yearning for the company of bulls again, a year older, content until next July to be dominated, content until eight-years-old when he'll attempt to dominate.

The old bulls who now and then take it into their heads to stand aloof from the gregarious herd, frontiersmen called bachelor bulls, and rightly. They sometimes live alone, sometimes join another old misanthrope or two to ignore the starts and alarms of bunch life. Sometimes they alternate between herd life and bachelordom. Sometimes they return during the summer madness, but grumpily leave again. One such fellow has been seen walking away from the hurly-burly of the rut, on his way to a quieter watering place, stopping once to glance at the turmoil behind him and then trudging on. Frontiersmen claimed that such fellows took on their surly ways from being beaten in combat, cast out of the herd, perhaps because of age. But closer observers feel they choose partial bachelordom—"a misanthropic abnegation of society." Or perhaps they're exhausted. Age seems to play a part, but many quasi-bachelors are bulls in their prime.

Some bachelors want to mope unmolested; a trespasser in his secluded draw may bring his tail up, kinked. He waggles his head, paws, snorts, threatening that he means to charge. Other times he pays no attention to the trespasser—another erratic buffalo.

The fighting of the rut usually develops as a shoving match, matted forelock to matted forelock, horns locked in the traditional fighting hold, a hold designed to keep a rival's horns from making a flank attack. The lock forces heads low to the ground. Bulls strive to win by breaking the lock through powerful upward lunges, hoping to free their horns for a swift flank goring or, at the least, to unbalance their rival and push him into submission. The pushing, pawing action arouses screening swirls of dust, out of which the loser backs, on guard until out of range.

Forelock hair absorbs the shock of any short charge, but the occasional vicious fight may result in the curved horns, oilyblack and pointed, of the eight-year-old—sixteen inches long—hooking through the ribs into the lungs. A fullgrown bull can lift another bull on his horns; his full strength charge can crush ribs and break legs. No fights to tempt an aging bachelor or a young tyro.

Not that a bull has to fight if challenged. He can avoid it by retiring quietly when a threatening bull bellows at him or walks toward him stiffly stamping his forefeet or lunges at him. If he is attacked he can signal submission by backing away swinging his head back and forth in a "No!" Or he can drop his head to a grazing position and eat a few mouthfuls.[2]

During the rut a bull does most of his fighting and courting during daylight, but, unlike his usual self, he sleeps little at night; he splits the usual nighttime quiet of the prairies with his bellowing, unable to sleep in his need to answer any challenge. The quieter cows stay their own sleek selves, but the fat that the buffalo grass of May has put on the bull melts. He loses 100 to 200 pounds. He often stands in the blazing sun, on guard, while she loafs in the shade chewing her cud; at night he bellows while she rests. While she drinks, he stands off suitors, able to snatch only a few gulps for himself. At night while she lies down to sleep, he often stands. Just after dawn, when he normally eats, the sexual appetite comes on and he misses breakfast. And it comes again at dusk so that he misses supper. Luckily, the cured buffalo grass of October will put his winter fat on him quickly.

A hundred years ago, during the rut, buffalo moved more careless of attack than usual. A wagon train might drive through a gigantic coalition of herds yet disturb it little: "As we advanced along the trail, the droves would quietly separate to our right and left, leaving a lane along which we traveled with herds on each side of us. From an eminence, looking backward and forward, one could see that we were completely hemmed in before and behind; and the space left for us by the buffalo moved along with us."[3] Such an intrusion brought the bulls to tending their cows more closely, as if the strangers might inseminate the cows; the cows, who a few weeks before would have galloped away with their calves, now pretty much ignored the interlopers.

Buffalo reach their prime condition in late fall. Bulls, finished with the nervous continual movement of July and August, have regained their lost flesh and have sprouted the fine new pelage for the coming winter. Now a grand old bull's mane reaches six inches long, the tufts about his forelegs hang in a ten-inch fringe, his beard dangles down twelve inches, his tail whisks a nineteen-inch tuft. His hindquarters show new hair three inches long and growing. Trappers watched buffalo's new hair as a weather forecaster; the curlier-haired the buffalo the harder the winter, they believed. His fall pelt would make a grand robe, but the skin, two inches thick in places, is too awkward to tan; robe hunters looked for cow skins.

In the old days (and in larger herds today), by November, the bulls and cows had separated and wandered in small herds numbering fifty to 300—small herds separate from the other thousands of small herds of similar sex grazing a large area together. When northers blew, the bulls, sensible males, plodded deep into the nearby sheltering trees that they'd chosen as wintering places. But the cows and their calves could "resist the piercing north wind" and often grazed in the open. Only when the blizzard continued without let did the cows lead their calves away from the nourishing bunch grass, to huddle together in the trees and make do with bottom grass, or browse on willow leaves and cottonwood bark.

Buffalo moved about somewhat in winter just as in other seasons, but if the feed remained good they seemed content to remain where they'd established trails and knew the shelter (locally they might thunder off to a less-hunted pasture, kicking up enough snow dust to obscure them, but they tended to stay nearby). They favored certain wintering areas—the upper reaches of Beaverhead, the prairies along the Bow, the "mountain fastnesses about the headwaters of the Arkansas"—the "Bayou Salade" of Colorado—and many others. Buffalo wintering south of the Republican and the Arkansas found shelter from northers in wooded bottoms. Along the Mississippi River they moved to canebrakes and ate the young cane as winter feed. Farther east they found sheltered valleys with giant salt licks in the Appalachians. A local drought year might drive the herds from favorite spots—as would over-hunting—but, normally, they stayed where they found good feed.

A man found few buffalo along streams in winter,[4] for often they ate snow instead of drinking (in some places cleared the ground of it). Consequently they made few trips to water, saving hours each day; a good thing, for foraging through snow-cover slowed down feeding, and they fed only during the shortened winter daylight.

Probably few wild snow storms ever decimated the buffalo, although local storms may have killed local herds: the great South Dakota storms of the 1850s (especially the snows of 1852–53: thirty-eight inches of moisture in 1852 which Battiste Good pictured as "Deep snow used up horses winter") reputedly killed many buffalo.[5] And "many buffaloes" near the Salt Lake supposedly died in the great snowstorms of 1837.[6] In 1872, during a blizzard that stalled a Nebraska train, buffalo froze to death standing in its lee as passengers watched. But mature buffalo in their prime were built to withstand the blizzard; their deaths through it were rare enough to become the stuff of legend.

Buffalo Jones claimed the buffalo "king of the blizzard" because if caught in one, they nosed into it looking for shelter rather than turning and drifting aimlessly in the front of it as did cattle. This seems more of his folklore. A rancher who had gathered a herd from the wild in the 1880s found he had to put feed out when a storm approached to keep them from drifting—and even then he had to keep an eye on them.[7] Soldiers at Fort Dodge fired cannon during a blizzard to drive away drifting buffalo shoving against the walls.[8]

Although they seem to dislike deep snow and avoid it when they can, snow bothers them little. A twentieth-century observer of government buffalo herds claimed a buffalo lay down facing blowing snow, and he further claimed that lying there he put his nose in the long hair of the front legs so he could still breathe.[9] Buffalo use a back and up motion of beard mop and black snoot, brushing snow from the ground "like a razor back hog after artichokes" to find the cured grass. Sometimes, especially in crusted snow, they brush until nose-skin wears off to bloody flesh and they have to paw at it. As a buffalo forages he sometimes digs through four and five feet of snow to get at the grass below (calves completely disappear in the hole dug by mother). In snow a foot or so deep they root individual eating holes until it looks as if pitted by small shell fire, or snowplow a long, narrow trench exposing a strip of cropped grass. Yet a buffalo likes a warm spot in winter as well as any animal: one old bull starved on the warm, grassless sinter slope of a Yellowstone Park geyser, seemingly because he wouldn't go back into deep snow again. Wintering buffalo sleep late of a morning, sometimes dozing until eight o'clock; in summer they arise before dawn. They nap but few afternoons, unlike their summer practice.

Within their local wintering ground, buffalo avoid large patches of drifted snow by traveling through a maze of trails. In deep snow, they make trails carefully; where the snow trail leads they follow: once a cow followed Alexander Henry's "meat trail" right into the fort where the dogs held her at bay until a shot killed her. At another time thousands of them poured past his fort as his hunters fired into them; they altered their course not at all, "the first roads beaten in the snow were followed by those in the rear."[10] They can buck new trails through drifts to escape danger, but this wears them out quickly; they rest frequently, their progress is slow.

In the old days, February found them only a little less sleek than November unless unusual snowfall had forced them "to fast for days together." But in March and April they gaunted: "many are so weak that if they lie down they cannot rise." James Willard Schultz put their sudden gaunting to the change from eating snow to drinking water again;[11] more likely they needed new green grass to replace old pastures now eaten off. In April and May, after the cows birthed, they gaunted further. Early spring was not the time to feed on buffalo; then was the season when Indian and white alike complained of chewing tough meat. It was a bad hunting time also because bull herds had become increasingly wary, and cow herds with calves to care for were also flighty. And the scarcity of grass kept them always on the move. Some hunters claimed the thinner they became, the warier they seemed.

"... *hunting bands of considerable size and impressive social organization were supporting themselves on the Great Plains some 8,500 years ago.*"

JOE BEN WHEAT

THE SUPREME pre-historic bison hunter, Folsom man, followed his prey about 9000 years ago. Archeological finds of his kills indicate that man had grown more adept at bison hunting after the passing of the larger mammals. Building on the cooperative hunting skills that preying upon the large mammals had brought him, he began to drive the buffalo, trapping them in box canyons, sometimes miring them there. The first authenticated find of man-made projectile points *in situ* with the bones of *Bison antiquus* (*figginsi*) occurred in a box canyon and former marsh near Folsom, New Mexico (thus the name given to the kind of projectile point discovered there, Folsom point, and to the hunter who made them). Possibly Folsom man had learned from the wounded buffalo himself just how to trap him: a buffalo's first desire when wounded is to separate himself from the herd and hide in a remote ravine. Here, trailing Paleo hunters would find that the wounded animal could neither run from a spear throw nor charge effectively. An experienced hunter would soon realize he could bring unwounded animals to such a place for an easy kill; he needed only to drive them there. And Folsom man must have driven bison into a box canyon as easily as a barefoot farm boy, centuries later, brought his bossies to the barn at milking time.

Herding buffalo to a chosen spot depends not upon speed but upon bison savvy. Men walking behind a herd, staying hidden, showing themselves only now and then at a distance move a herd nervously but slowly along. A glimpse of such men moving to their right brings the herd leaders slanting to the right, following the deep-lying propensity of all buffalo (and some other game animals) to cut across in front of anything moving forward on a flank. A wisp of smoke, just a tang of it from a bit of burning dried grass, drifting downwind, moves a herd slowly away from the smell. Little advantage lies in running the animals; they are herded easily by men moving slowly on foot. (Today, on a ranch in Wyoming, buffalo herders on foot round up the buffalo.) Surely a skilled Folsom hunter could herd the cattle-like herds to any killing ground he chose—walking them, not running them.

He could also walk a bunch to near a jump-off and scare it into running over the edge, a mass kill providing meat and robes for everyone. One such kill in Colorado, "some 8500 years ago," unearthed in 1957, resulted in 193 dead—a harvest of about 75,000 pounds of meat. The evidence of the bone strata indicates that not only had people cooperated in a systematized hunt, they had developed a system of butchering to care for the tons of meat. The existence of a system would indicate they must have made many

Pre-historic hunters, on foot, knowing all of the buffalo's habits, could easily drive him
into such a cul-de-sac, close enough for a spear throw. *Courtesy National Park Service.*

such harvests, for it implies lots of practice at butchering by a highly successful foot-hunting buffalo society. This group probably encompassed about 150 people, the number necessary to manage such a drive and to care for the meat. These people had, as one might expect, removed the best meat first, even as did the later, historic people. They first opened the buffalo down his spine in order to remove the hump meat, the forelegs and the innards: the forelegs were consistently found at the bottom of each pile of severed bones. Next they took the pelvic girdle and the hind legs, then, last, the least desirable neck and skull.[1] All in all the evidence left by this group of foot-hunters shows ease of food gathering—this one kill might have fed them on "fresh" meat for twenty-three days and on dried meat for another thirty days. A successful drive every two months would have sufficed— if they had no dogs to feed.

And, between drives, they could kill buffalo in many other ways: Throwing a spear while the animal drowsily chewed its cud. Moving into the herd under the cover of the whooshing prairie wind. Taking advantage of buffalo's typical carelessness when summer bugs tormented him or when the rutting fever was

upon him. Moving animals into deep snow to jab them at spear length. Sneaking into the herd covered by a wolf skin or buffalo hide. Lying in a buffalo trail stained in disguising mud to await those going to water.

Folsom man had excellent killing tools. He killed many bison not only because of his hunting skills but also because of his skill in flaking points. He learned to pressure-flake his bluntly curved, snub-nosed "Folsom point" to an edge that pierced hide and flesh nearly as well as does the finest steel.[2] So well did it kill bison that men saw no need for any other projectile point for two thousand years: Folsom points accompany most finds of ancient bison bones.

A man who understood buffalo nature could kill buffalo pretty much as he chose. And surely he had at times, as did later buffalo hunters, to drive pesky buffalo out of camp rather than hunt them.

Once the other great mammals had disappeared, the buffalo made possible man's life on the Great Plains, a good life more than likely, although a nomadic one. He made his home in small, collapsible, transportable buffalo-skin tipis. He learned to cook in

"Taking the Hump Rib." Alfred Jacob Miller. *Courtesy Amon Carter Museum, Fort Worth, Texas.*

skins by dropping in hot rocks; carrying water in buffalo stomachs, he needed no bulky, breakable pottery. He preserved his abundance of meat by drying it. He slept in the coziness of the buffalo robe (undoubtedly he used it: buffalo skeletons he left are tailless—gone with the taking of the hide). He trudged about the vastness carrying his totables on his back and camped in hundreds of places, but left scarcely a trace of kitchen midden to mark his camps, for he stayed so briefly and toted no heavy buffalo bones from killing ground to camp—only meat.

He followed where the easy buffalo life led. Although he subsisted by foot hunting, the abundance of buffalo meat meant that he lived better than other foot hunters—one buffalo fed more mouths than did one deer. Thus buffalo hunters could band together in larger groups than could deer hunters or rabbit hunters, and larger groups could winter together. Buffalo-hunting groups had more protection through mutual defense, more companionship through shared living.

The hunting life could well have left him, as it does some hunters in today's primitive hunting societies, "an unconscionable" amount of time during the day for napping. His life following the herds offered much:

first, the hilarity of big feasting and entertaining when tons of meat had fallen; second, the excitement of the hunt and the kill, the roaming unfettered over the plains, as at home one place as another, continual variety; third, the slower rhythms of lying about camp, lazing in the spring sun or toasting near the autumn campfire with absolutely nothing to do; fourth, the satisfactions of handwork, the flaking of a point, the fashioning of a bow or the tanning of hide. Likely he divided his time as do some modern "subsistence" hunters of big African game: about a third hunting, a third visiting and a third entertaining;[3] he did not, as does modern "civilized" man, "stand sentenced to a life of hard labor"; undoubtedly he, like today's bushman, lived well and found "hunting and gathering . . . a persistent and well-adapted way of life." Perhaps more so because of the ease of taking buffalo.

These hunters' lives were short no doubt, perhaps about twenty years to a generation; their population increased little over thousands of years; they made little technical progress except to invent or copy the bow and arrow and the atlatl (a stick to notch into a spear for swifter flight). Perhaps they saw no need for progress; like men of primitive tribes today, their lives were complete and extra time turned into extra idleness—sleeping, feasting, visiting, entertaining. Drought might keep the herds away, but they could fast as well as feast; they knew the herds grazed somewhere and would be found.

This foot hunter domesticated the dog—perhaps early enough to have fed it scraps of mammoth meat. He used it to drag a travois, to carry a pack, and to hunt.

Ever on the move, a buffalo hunter undoubtedly saw more wonders than the stay-at-home deer stalker, mice catcher, or salmon netter. He trudged along near geyser and sinkhole, found obsidian cliff and pipestone deposit, knew the best places to camp. He followed interesting streams, remembered pleasant lakes. As most seasoned travelers do, he learned a bit about the ways of other people. He learned to trade his soft robes for whatever trinkets others might offer, to trade meat for corn. He grew a little accustomed to putting up with ways of life differing from his own.

For thousands of years this Paleo man chose to live on the high plains. He lived as the luckiest of foot hunters, surrounded by great herds of placid bovines, animals that required little of the hunter in the way of tracking, trap building, snaring, stalking, long range accurate shooting or investment of time. Probably he couldn't have lived on the high plains without the buffalo to feed him. As Alexander Ross, fur trader and explorer once said of later life there, the buffalo was "the only inducement to the plains."

During times of great drought on the plains, especially the great droughts of 8000 to 6000 B.C. and of 12,000 B.C. when large sections of the plains became uninhabitable, the buffalo probably retired to high moist places such as the Yellowstone headwaters country, or moved east to wetter places along the Mississippi and beyond it. Some peoples of the plains followed the buffalo to the high moist country to continue their nomadic buffalo-hunting life, others perhaps moved down the easterly wending plains rivers to farm in the moister Mississippi Valley and occasionally hunt buffalo.

When the wet years returned, some of these peoples returned to the plains. Those who had retreated east moved back by traveling west along the Platte, the Republican, the Missouri and the Yellowstone, planting their corn in the protection of the fertile bottoms, living in log houses covered with mounds of earth or in caves. Each autumn they left these secure villages to tent among the herds in search of buffalo meat for the coming winter. On the Powder River about 4500 years ago such men killed buffalo with spears driven by atlatls; on the Yellowstone some 2000 years ago (about the time of Christ) such men drove buffalo over cliffs; along the Yellowstone about 1600 years ago such men used the bow and arrow to kill buffalo.[4] These people, like the people along the Republican, planted their corn in the bottom land wherever they found loose patches of soil, little patches sometimes as much as five or ten miles from the village, the only ground free enough of sod to be stirred by their buffalo scapula hoes.[5] When dry years came they retreated downstream a ways again, only to return with the onset of wet years, pushed upstream perhaps by pressures of other peoples as well as lured back by buffalo wealth.

Scattered over the high plains that lie close to the Rockies lived a more nomadic man. He had probably followed the buffalo to the mountainous, moist country during drought years, and back to the high plains during wet years. He most likely lived continuously in the West as a buffalo hunter. As anthropologist Leslie White said, "Today's available evidence, ethnographic as well as archeologic . . . makes it clear that the Plains were not nearly as difficult of human occupation as has long been supposed."[6] Especially, we might add, because of the buffalo.

About forty years after Columbus's first voyage to America, the Spaniard Cabeza de Vaca and crewmates became stranded on the coast of today's Texas. Cabeza de Vaca and three mates, wandering westward in search of Christians, somewhere on the Pecos River came upon buffalo hunters and became the first Europeans to see buffalo (probably Cortez did not see one in Montezuma's zoo as heretofore supposed)[7] and to eat their meat. He thought the meat "finer and fatter than that of this country [Spain]" (it'd been a long time since he'd tasted beef). In the buffalo hunter he and his mates found kindly people who made great festivities over their arrival, who gave them "blankets of skin" and made "houses" for their reception rather than throwing lumps of mud at them, beating them, enslaving them or putting "arrows to our hearts, saying they were inclined to kill us" as had other peoples. They found these generous people seated in their houses, their faces toward the wall, a pile of their possessions in the center from which they presented blankets of skin and other things—"they had nothing they did not bestow." Cabeza de Vaca, in a book he wrote later about his adventures, judged the friendly buffalo

Buffalo rarely paid this much attention to wolves in their midst—the reason for the success of this disguise in hunting. "Buffalo Hunt, Under the White Wolf Skin." George Catlin. *Courtesy Amon Carter Museum, Fort Worth, Texas.*

hunters as "the finest persons of any people we saw, of the greatest activity and strength, who best understood us and intelligently answered our inquiries." The buffalo hunters treated them so well he entitled the chapter about them "The fashion of receiving us changes."[8]

A few years later the expedition of Francisco Vázquez de Coronado also ran into buffalo hunters along the Pecos (called the Rio de las Vacas by the Spanish because of the numbers of buffalo they saw). Similarly, Coronado found them more hospitable than the Indians they had dealt with heretofore. Pedro de Castañeda, a soldier of the expedition, remembered that the buffalo hunters "did nothing unusual when they saw our army except to come out of their tents to look at us, after which they came to talk with the advance guard, and asked who we were." No running in hysteria from unfamiliar horses, no flights of arrows, no threats; a people adept at meeting strangers, so used to it, they had developed a sign language through which "they made themselves understood so well that there was no need of an interpreter." Castañeda found them intelligent, a description he used for no other peoples on the route. The Spaniards visited these people only

two days, for such people, living "like Arabs," took their "tents made of the tanned skins of cows" and moved on to be "near the cows."

In the next day or so the Spaniards came upon more roaming bands of "Querechos" (Apaches) living among an incredible "great number of cows."

Toward the end of his narrative Castañeda again mentioned the buffalo hunters—the Querechos and also the Teyas, both buffalo hunters, speaking different languages but related in life style and dependence upon the buffalo. He remembered them warmly and called them "kind people" and "faithful friends."[9]

The free and independent buffalo hunter of the Pecos and the Staked Plains, worldly and traveled, had received the Spaniards with a hospitality born out of a life that brought them into many unfamiliar camps; they knew they needn't fight strangers just because they talked unintelligibly and dressed outlandishly—unless the strangers tried to frighten off or kill their buffalo: buffalo-hunting Querechos and Teyas often fought. (Later, buffalo hunters learned to distrust Spaniards and to fight them.)

These native hunters killed buffalo for their hides, tanned them and transported them to settlements to the south, settlements built far from the herds so buffalo might not trample or eat the growing corn. Here the hunters wintered. These settlements relied upon the buffalo hunters to bring them hides and meat in exchange for corn and blankets. The hunters traveled back and forth in the midst of enormous dog trains—sometimes as many as 500 dog-drawn travois to a train. A comical sight to Spaniards were the scores of dogs, head clamped between women's knees, being packed for a trip. The dogs traveled, tied one after the other in a long string, snarling as they worked, but moving along steadily as if they were under rein. They'd been castrated to make them into plodding oxen.

The Querechos, who originally had traveled south from the tundra buffalo country of the Far North, traveling south through Bayou Salade buffalo country, to cactus buffalo country, as well as the Teyas, who had come from the farms of the Southeast, were fine foot hunters. The Spanish described their ability: "They kill them at the first shot with the greatest skill, while ambushed in brush blinds made at the watering places,"[10] or, "a good shot for a musket,"[11] after seeing a Teya put an arrow completely through a bull's shoulders. Men and women alike used the bow and arrow dextrously.

These foot hunters killed enough buffalo to distribute "a vast number of hides into the interior country," according to Cabeza de Vaca. In fact, buffalo hunters so loaded him down with "a store of robes of cowhide," he had enough to give many to Christian Indians he met later on.[12] Not only did the buffalo hunters have hides to spare: the corn-growing pueblo dwellers along the Rio Grande made gifts of hides so freely, they obviously had stores of robes for the giving.[13] Most everywhere the Spanish went they found hides brought in by the expert foot hunters, and received gifts of hides (if such gifts were not forthcoming they soon began to confiscate them).

Nomads, hunting on foot, had filled the country with their trade robes. From what Pedro de Castañeda could tell "a good deal more" people followed the herds than lived in the settlements.[14] Likewise, Conquistador Zaldívar noted "the Indians are numerous in all that land,"[15] and Fray Alonso de Benavides wrote of a "great deal of slaughtering to sustain innumerable Indians."[16] Thousands of people had come to these temperate plains to live as nomads. They found the life lucrative, for they wandered near settlements that wanted meat and hides. They found the life good, for they rarely wanted food, clothing or shelter.

Later European explorers, invading the interior of the new country from the east, following the Mississippi, also found foot hunters killing buffalo.

In the seventeenth century, Sioux foot hunters in Minnesota so impressed French fur trader Pierre Esprit Radisson with their ability to run down buffalo that he named them "the nation of beef."[17] In the eighteenth century, an Illinois Indian group were found to kill more than 2000 buffalo a year—enough to feed a village of 400 people one year if they used all of the animal.[18] Father Binneteau, a Jesuit missionary, noted that such Illinois men hunted only now and then and spent most of their time playing and singing; he concluded "They are all gentlemen."[19] Buffalo had continued to bring leisure to the foot hunter.

In the 1600s, Father Louis Hennepin, chaplain for LaSalle and leader of the first expedition on the upper Mississippi, found the Miamis making a buffalo hunt on foot each fall, moving into the herds "with their whole families to go hunting wild Bulls." They killed such great numbers he was amazed that the herds could still multiply. He watched the Indians drive forty or fifty buffalo into the water and there kill them. He saw them "set fire to the grass everywhere around these animals, except some passage which they leave on purpose, and where they take post with their bows and arrows. The buffalo, seeking to escape the fire, are thus compelled to pass near these Indians, who sometimes kill as many as a hundred and twenty in a day, all of which they distribute according to the wants of the families . . ."[20]

He was watching foot hunters who could help themselves to buffalo meat almost anytime they needed it. One hundred twenty dead buffalo dress into at least 50,000 pounds of meat plus edible entrails, enough to feed one hunter twenty-five years—most of his life, if he ate an average of six pounds a day. A buffalo hunter needed about 2200 pounds of buffalo meat to feed him one year—about five buffalo—five of the most easily hunted quadrupeds ever to fall prey to a hunter. Father Hennepin noted that the Miamis who drove the forty or fifty buffalo into the water took only the tongues and the best parts;[21] hardly the harvest of people worried about chasing down their next meal on foot.

He found people who had established strict hunt rules. He told of sitting in a tipi on the Mississippi feasting with Indians when suddenly the tipi filled with angry warriors from up river seeking to punish hunters here who had disturbed the buffalo herds and ruined their hunt.

Other men far up the Missouri and the Platte, along all of the streams pouring into the Mississippi out of the west, and men on the northern and southern plains, hunted buffalo—semi-nomadic buffalo hunters, who part of the year still followed the herds, or men who spent all year amongst them. They moved about the prairies with their tipis and their belongings piled on travois pulled by dogs. These Indian dogs chased gophers, dug out mice; if a wolf trotted too close to camp: "in ten seconds all that will remain of him will be skin." These dogs, big enough to pull travois, domesticated and required to stay about camp, needed half as much meat as a man (sometimes more: much later, on the Canadian prairie six men and twenty-four sled dogs "finished" a buffalo in one overnight stay).[22] Foot hunters had to kill a lot of buffalo just to feed their dogs.

The hunting strategies of these fifteenth and sixteenth-century buffalo hunters, seen through the few reports of explorers, appear almost unchanged in the reports of the nineteenth-century explorers who traveled buffalo country. What becomes apparent in either sixteenth or nineteenth-century accounts is the ability of the Indian to herd buffalo, to move buffalo when he needed them and where he needed them. The ability was implied in a North-West Company trader's statement: "They have invented so many methods for the destruction of animals that they stand in no need of ammunition to provide a sufficiency for these purposes . . ."[23]

The buffalo hunters "invented" none of these many methods; they resemble all of the ways hunting societies everywhere take animals. Applied to the buffalo these methods worked extremely well because of his cowlike placidity and his gregariousness.

The ancient method of the surround, a drive accomplished by all the people of a village encircling a group of animals, worked well—so well that sometimes a village could set up a tipi circle around buffalo before the animals saw their danger. A Cheyenne legend tells of two old men who learned through a dream how, by waving eagle wings, to entrance a buffalo herd so that it would follow them into the tipi circle where the people killed it.[24]

More usual was the foot surround of the kind that Henry Kelsey, explorer for the Hudson's Bay Company, saw in 1691: "Now ye manner of their hunting these Beast on ye Barren Ground is where they see a great parcel of them together they surround them with men wch done they gather themselves into a smaller

Compasse Keeping ye Beast still in ye middle & so shooting Ym till they break out at some place or other and so get away from ym."[25]

The surround meant that any large group of people could kill buffalo where they found them; it served to bring down twenty to forty buffalo; it required nothing other than agile people, wise in buffalo ways, expert in shooting bow and arrow.

The surround brought the hunter to where he could put the arrow instantaneously and exactly where he wanted it and with the force necessary to penetrate the buffalo rib cage. He needed to take no distant random shots at the hulk of the target before him, although he'd practiced until he could, at seventy-five yards, put his arrows everytime where he wanted them. As a boy his bow and arrow took the place of the lasso of Mexican boys or the slingshots of American boys. He shot constantly, practiced on rolled or tossed buffalo chips or any other handy targets: two little Kaw boys, watched by a trader, shot loose an arrow lodged in a tree, shot a woodpecker out of a tree, stuck his bill in the bark and shot "until he was used up."[26] Blackfeet boys learned to shoot by playing a game in which one boy dragged a piece of meat at the end of a rawhide while other boys shot at it. Sometimes the boy stopped, pawed like a buffalo and swung the meat in a circle about his head while his friends shot at it.[27]

The foot hunter had learned to work close to his enormous prey: "So expert are the natives, that they will take the arrows out of them when they are foaming and raging with pain & tearing the ground up with their feet & horns until they fall down."[28] The foot hunter absorbed this through living amongst buffalo grazing backyard close. And he'd followed the hunt since before he could remember, chased the calves, eaten the bloody gut and raw meat until his little belly ached (the night after a hunt, children wailed in many tipis: their bellies hurt from gorging buffalo hunt goodies, just as do bellies of modern tots from gorging county fair goodies).

In addition to surrounding the buffalo, foot hunters drove animals into a pound, the easier to shoot arrows into them at point-blank range. In the 1500s Cabeza de Vaca found the Apaches forcing buffalo "into certain inclosures or toiles"; almost 300 years later Lewis and Clark found Missouri River Indians harvesting buffalo in the same way. It was a favorite method for catching lots of buffalo although it often meant the work of piling logs in a circle sometimes 100 feet across. A pound occasionally was temporary; a village set it up near buffalo and drove just these buffalo into it. But often a successful pound might be used all winter.

If buffalo came from the south, the people made the mouth of the pound to the north, knowing that startled buffalo ran back along the way they had come. Often they built behind a gentle rise to hide the enclosure. They usually built the pound from logs or poles as a freestanding corral, but they might also clear a circular area in a grove of trees, except for the medicine tree in the center and the stumps left to hinder the buffalo's running. They attached brush and poles to the circumferential trees to form the corral, and sometimes erected impaling pieces jutting inward. Or, if in a hurry, they could improvise by throwing up a makeshift corral of travois poles. Or, in the winter on Canadian prairies, they were said to have piled buffalo bones or frozen buffalo carcasses into corrals. Sometimes they constructed scarecrows on the walls. They often laid a corduroy ramp leading up to a slight drop-off. When, in freezing weather, this had been spread with moist chips, few buffalo could clamber back across the icy logs.

A V-shaped fence of poles led from the pound's entrance, making a short fence to funnel buffalo into the pound; then, for about one and one half miles beyond these legs, occasional heaps of chips, rocks, or roots marked a lane to guide the buffalo. Sometimes several lanes led into a pound from different directions.

The pound built, the time for the expert, the decoyer to bring in the buffalo, had arrived. He went out toward them, studied the lie of the land and the positioning of the buffalo, smoked his pipe, thought out his plan. If the buffalo had scattered themselves over the plain, he lit a fire in a handful of grass, making a smidgin of smoke that soon drifted to the noses of the buffalo and bunched them. Or he might show himself briefly along the top of a ridge with the same effect. (As he worked, the villagers took places along the legs of the V leading to the trap, or hid behind rock, brush or buffalo chip piles.) If the buffalo had already bunched themselves, his smoke might move the herd right into the V and onward toward the pound. Other times he had to decoy the buffalo into the V. Then, disguising himself under a buffalo robe, he went out into sight of the herd and there tried to entice them into the pound by imitating the cry of a calf or by bellowing or by shaking his robe—anything to gain the attention and arouse the curiosity of the animals nearest him (buffalo, especially bulls, seem compelled to investigate anything unusual). He often worked in

pre-dawn greyness when they would have difficulty seeing. If he could excite the few closest animals into coming toward him, the others nearby would follow, and then others. Slowly and carefully he moved toward the pound, easing along so as not to startle them into flight and make him a laughingstock. Not only would he then lose his reputation but also he might make the pound unlucky, unfit to use, and thus waste all of the work and ceremony put into it. But practiced decoyers, by covering their faces and imitating animal movement, easily deceived the herds.

As soon as the decoyer had come into the corral and the leaders of the herd had advanced far enough into the trap that they couldn't escape, the "watching waiters" began to close in behind the herd from the V wings, sending it scampering ahead. The decoyer ran for cover. If he had time he dashed to the medicine tree, suspended there his buffalo robe, then jumped out of the pound just as the herd and the whooping, robe-waving crowd arrived.

When the last buffalo leaped from the jump-off, a solid line of men, robes pulled over their heads, moved into the twenty-foot opening, to stand stockstill, blocking it. Upon this movement the crowd ceased yelling and flapping robes for fear of sending the buffalo careening through the corral wall. Soon the thump of running hooves in there stopped. Then the puffing and blowing of the herd was broken by the first zing of a bowman's arrow, the start of the kill. When the last adult buffalo had died, the boys entered the pound to fight and kill the calves. When they had done, the carcasses were apportioned by a chief to all of those present, those who had fluttered robes receiving the same portion as he who had decoyed, although he might receive special gifts.

If the herds had been found grazing far from the pound, a herder, an aide to the decoyer, would have gone for them, ten, twenty, as far as fifty miles away, to work them toward the pound, again using smoke and available wind, or showing himself at strategic moments, or running at top speed to turn the herd when necessary, or sitting for hours to wait for a "convenient season." At night he might nudge them along by slapping his robe on the ground to startle them into movement. When the herder had brought the herd close, the decoyer took over.

An advantage to the pound was that it little disturbed other nearby herds: an expert herder found the group he wanted, bunched it and brought only it to the pound; the buffalo beyond heard nothing, smelled nothing, saw nothing; unknowing, they stayed nearby until their turn came. With luck a village could use

Men and buffalo in a pound. The decoyer has scrambled up a pole, the "medicine tree." "Buffalo Hunting near Fort Carlton." Paul Kane. *Courtesy Royal Ontario Museum, Toronto.*

Buffalo over cliff. *Natural History*, January–February 1932. *Courtesy Amon Carter Museum, Fort Worth, Texas.*

Buffalo being run toward cliff. *Natural History*, January–February 1932. *Courtesy Amon Carter Museum, Fort Worth, Texas.*

one pound all winter (Blackfeet then tore it apart for firewood; Cree didn't, believing this would bring on a storm). As fur trader Duncan M'Gillivray said, "Of all the methods which the Indians have devised for the destruction of this useful animal—the Pound is the most successful."[29] The Cree and the Assiniboine were especially adept at this impounding. They depended on it extensively even after the advent of the horse—and never became horsemen equal to the riders of the more southern lands because of this dependence.

The drive over cliff edge has become the most well-known of the various bison drives because of the paintings produced by melodramatic illustrators of the West: end over end, through the air, tumble buffalo from a cliff seemingly hundreds of feet high. But usually the cliff was just a drop-off that might kill, stun, or injure the huge beast, not mangle him—although

the higher the drop, the larger the kill, and the fewer arrows shot. Especially was this drive meant to put the stunned beast at easy arrow shot. Occasionally he fell into a natural *cul de sac*, a box canyon or coulee wash-out, but, usually, especially at the bottom of a small drop-off, some sort of corral kept him penned—a corral sometimes substantial, but oftentimes fashioned of poles similar to lodge poles, crossing each other in lattice-like fashion, the empty areas filled with brush, posts (if any) supported by rock piles rather than post holes, the whole inclining inward. Alexander Henry sneered at such contrivances: "So much do these people abhor work that, to avoid the trouble of making proper pounds, they seek some precipice along the bank of the river, to which they extend their ranks and drive buffalo headlong over it."[30] (It's likely trader Henry felt peevish about these drives because they kept Indians away from fur trapping.)

Thousands of buffalo tumbled into piskins (a Blackfeet word for such impounding places meaning "deep-blood kettle") since villages used the same spot for many harvests. For one thing, this minimized the labor of constructing lanes, removing obstacles and the like;[31] for another thing, many jumps lay in a naturally good spot for a drive: one Canadian jump was used for about 1600 years.[32] Fifteen hundred arrowheads have come out of the archeological diggings at Emigrant jump, Montana, and at Sun River jump buffalo remains several feet thick cover five acres, an estimated 25,000 tons.[33] This weight would account for 2,500,000 dead buffalo, if calculated at the traditional estimate of twenty pounds weight to each dried buffalo skeleton.[34] A more likely calculation might set 100 pounds of debris per animal and account for 500,000 animals. Whatever the figure, this jump, over a long period of years, killed a lot of buffalo. And the varied density of bone finds indicates it probably killed the most buffalo in late prehistoric times.[35]

The piskin often lay at the lower end of a long valley, a natural and easy place to run, preferably one that lay with the prevailing wind and thus foiled buffalo sense of smell. (Any place drop-offs occurred, hunters were liable to make animal drives: bison jumps have been discovered in Illinois and North Carolina).[36] In Montana, the Missouri River drainage provides many such natural drop-offs. At least twenty-four pre-historic drive sites lie near the Sun, Madison, Teton and Marias Rivers, only a portion of Montana's total, jumps that contain "no objects of metal and no materials suggesting contact with the horse."[37] Some men suspect buffalo population increased abruptly some 2000 years ago, and the use of piskins increased correspondingly until the coming of the horse.[38]

A piskin on the Big Hole River in Montana is the culmination of a valley two or three miles long at a jump-off of not more than forty or fifty feet into the river valley. For a mile or so back from cliff edge occasional piles of flat rock about two feet high still mark the V that guided the buffalo to death, even as in impounding. Piles of brush or piles of chips may also have marked the V, each pile about forty steps apart, each providing a hiding place for a person awaiting the passing of the herd, although each person probably actually hid under his buffalo robe, for the small rock or chip piles offered almost no hiding place or protection. Sagebrush and bushes often were piled upside down to give a strange, perhaps manlike appearance to increase the apparent numbers, as well as to increase the illusion of a fence. Some peoples called these "dead men." A V often stood about 100 steps

wide at its apex and 1000 steps wide at its mouth. Sometimes a line of "fist-sized" rocks marked it. If snow had fallen, the people might lay a line of buffalo chips between the rock piles making a guide that the buffalo seemed to follow. Often several lanes led to the drop-off to make choice possible according to wind direction or herd location.

This kind of harvest demanded that the village move near to the piskin and the buffalo be herded to the neighborhood, for, as in impounding, the caller (decoyer) needed herds within one to ten miles to work with. The caller, a man of big medicine, decided the day of the kill, directed every preparatory move and ceremony. If a village had no one so skilled, they asked a caller of a friendly village to help, paid him for it, called him the greatest man in all of the villages, addressed him as "Bringer of Plenty" rather than by his name, feasted him, carried out his ceremonies meticulously, built a new piskin if he felt he needed it.

On the day of the hunt, the caller, again often working in the pre-dawn half-light, enticed the herd into the trap in much the way as did the decoyer into the pound. When the herd had begun to run and had all but caught him, he might disappear for awhile, to leave them milling uncertainly, only to reappear and entice them again. Each hidden person waved his robe, perhaps burned sweet grass both as ritual and as nose-tickler, and perhaps shot small-pointed arrows into the mass to sting it into further confusion.[39] As the caller brought the herd to cliff edge he ducked into a pre-selected hiding place, safe, he hoped, from the animals that tumbled over him pawing at air for footing.

Since the pound and the piskin were primarily cold weather pursuits, the cold held down the decay of flesh, but both Alexander Henry and Duncan M'Gillivray complained of the smell of the pounds they visited. Likewise, Lewis and Clark, at the mouth of the Judith River, complained of the horrible stench from carcasses at a piskin they passed—but it was May 26. Such decay eventually made as much telltale odor as campfires; no herd would approach such a stink. Charred bones found at the Emigrant jump in Montana indicate people may have burned offal to clear up the stink.[40]

The pound and the piskin wasted animals, not only from the immense amounts of their innards, which could not be preserved by drying, but also from the bulls who died needlessly, for only cows were cut up, since no woman could tan the thick, heavy bull hide into a robe, and no man would eat tough bull meat if cow meat came his way. Only wolves, bears and dogs ate the fallen bulls in the piskin and the pound. Some peoples built holes into corrals to allow the dogs at this meat—a mistake, for the gorged dogs lay about, not even bothering to bark at strangers. Perhaps only fifty percent of the dead animals became human food: Conspicuous Consumption.

The foot hunter brought down buffalo through many other methods than the drives. Hunters decoyed buffalo by mimicking the bleating of a calf, swam beside them and stabbed them (a difficult kill for only the head remained out of water), crawled amongst them wearing buffalo hides or "a cap with long ears," ambushed them in coulees, chased them by dog, enticed them with salt, took advantage of their preoccupation during the rut, caught them napping, brought them down as they trotted past day after day bound for no one knew where, startled them into fleeing toward hunters, searched out hiding calves or enticed calves to follow them.

Winter was the best hunting time. Men easily ambushed buffalo coming single file down deep, snowy trails. And deep, crusted snow impeded a buffalo's flight; men on snowshoes could run as fast as he. Often, as a storm approached, men lay in wait at the sheltering woods they knew the buffalo would seek. And when deep snow made decoying and driving herds unsuccessful (mostly pound and piskin were used in late fall and early winter), men on snowshoes hazed

buffalo into the deep-drifted coulees, mired them, and, while their dogs worried them, drove arrows into them point-blank, speared them or even stabbed them. They knew of especially good coulees and drove groups into the usual drifts as regularly as they used established piskins, using now one side of the coulee now another—on whichever side the drifts grew. Some plains Indians found this hunting more successful than the pound or the piskin. Sir William Butler, Canadian explorer, saw Indians kill eighty buffalo in a day this way.[41]

One group of Canadian Indians would build little snow huts for a mile or so along a buffalo trail. A hunter stood in each hut with bow and arrow while friends shooed a herd down this gauntlet. The snow huts seemingly masked the human scent from buffalo.[42] The Mandans, armed with bow and arrow, drove into herds on light sledges drawn by dogs. The dogs so loved the hunt no driver could hold them back once they saw the herd.

If no snow fell and lakes lay frozen and bare, hunters hazed the buffalo onto the ice where any charge, any fancy whirling on forelegs brought them crashing down, struggling to get up, easy victims once again.

Following a winter hunt, women needed to dry no meat; it kept well in a snowbank. Winter meant buffalo plenty as long as the herds stayed by—and their tendency was to do so.

"Acquisition of the horse . . . gave a last colorful
fillip to a mode of life old when
the first Conquistadores set foot
on the Great Plains."
WEDEL

"As an intensifier of original plains traits,
the horse presents its
strongest claim."
WISSLER

WHEN WE think of buffalo we picture horsed Indians riding carefree amidst loping buffalo, drawing taut the bowstring, releasing the arrow into the buffalo's flank, galloping on to another buffalo—the Indian we've seen so often in movies, the horsed Indian. Yet, when the buffalo disappeared in the 1880s, most buffalo-hunting Indians had been hunting them on horseback less than 150 years.

The horse came to the Indian from the Spanish herds in Mexico, from the enormous remudas necessary to operate the stock-raising haciendas that sprang up all across nothern Mexico. At first the Spanish governors decreed that no Indian could learn to ride a horse; they knew the part their horse had played in the Conquest: "After God, we owe the victory to the horses," said Hernando Cortez. The Spanish tried to keep the natives fearful of this *tequane*, this monster, warned them against the ferocious horses that might kill and eat them. Only Spaniards were to ride herd on the cattle of the haciendas.

But cattle increased faster than did Spaniards, and soon the conquistadores found their herds too big for them to care for alone. If the wealth of New Spain was to fill coffers, Indians had to ride horses, ranchers had to put their Mexican help in the saddle, raise the servile peon to an independent vaquero. And the re-

mudas continued to grow; a hacienda found it needed about twenty horses for every rider; luckily, horse breeding had boomed to the south, and Spanish horses flooded into northern Mexico to supply the need.

Soon puddles of horses dribbled farther north, across the Rio Grande. In the sixteenth and seventeenth centuries southern Mexico had to send horses by the thousands to the northern haciendas to replace those flowing north illegally. Then the Pueblo revolt of 1680 drove the Spaniards out of New Mexico and forced them to leave their horses behind, prey for the raiding buffalo hunters, Apaches and others. Thousands of horses came into the hands of buffalo-hunting Indians.[1]

The horse revolution spread north and east across the grasslands in about a century after the Pueblo revolt. By 1754 Antony Hendry saw wild horses on the Canadian prairie and commented on the frequency of horse dung. He had expected to find Blackfeet hunting buffalo on horseback and he did.[2] By 1770–1780 most of the plains tribes rode horseback, so commonly by 1800 that a woods Indian assumed Alexander Henry a Sioux because he'd ridden up on a horse.

The fastest and strongest of horses Indians learned to train as buffalo chasers. In the brief span of years he rode the horse, the American Indian became one of the finest equestrians in history.

Dogs the buffalo people still had knee deep (a visit to a camp meant fighting off a horde of dogs). They continued to use pack dogs through the nineteenth century, even though an occasional rabbit-chase scattered spoons and kettles throughout the sagebrush and once lost a baby completely. In a rare winter move, pack horses broke trail for pack dogs.

With dogs, five or six miles had been a good day's journey; with the horse, ten, fifteen or even twenty miles could be traversed. The tribes now could insure better winters by carrying more pemmican and dried meat, seek out better camping grounds, escape from danger more easily. In the spring the horse carried people through the mud and melting snow to follow the buffalo who had begun to leave their winter shelter. At any season, riding rested their feet. And the horse swam while they rode or floated by his side clinging to his mane. The horse toted the aged and sick; carried toddlers in a "tray shaped basket or hoop, latticed with hide thongs." Mothers rode and dangled baby's cradleboard from the saddle. Any traveling done before on foot, the Indian now did on horseback. The horse suited nomadic needs exactly.

Yet the horse little changed the part-time buffalo hunting habits of those tribes that lived in fixed villages. The Mandan used the horse for hunting buffalo but continued to live part-time in permanent villages. They became horse traders who sometimes traded too many and found themselves with not enough horses for the hunt. The Kickapoo moved into buffalo territory, used the horse for hunting, but lived in one place. The Pawnee, too, stayed in their villages except for their winter hunts (although their caches for grain storage became smaller after 1800, perhaps because they now relied more upon buffalo meat).[3]

Nor did the more nomadic tribes need to move continually to keep themselves in buffalo meat. Only six, perhaps eight, moves a season sufficed for some tribes (although the Blackfeet were known to move so often their travois poles wore short). Often a big camp could remain stationary for weeks, the hunters using the horse to commute from camp to temporary hunting sites. The buffalo stood nearby as quietly as dairy cattle, the hunters bothering only the herds selected for the kill.[4] Such hunters also could live in big summer encampments because the horse allowed them to search out herds and to bring back enough meat to feed thousands.

A man and wife came to depend upon at least five horses to move them, a horse to carry the tipi, a horse to pull tipi poles, a horse for meat and goods, and two horses to ride. But this left them short a buffalo horse

for the buffalo hunt, and without it they'd remain always a poor, five-horse family. A family of eight needed ten horses to survive, an old person needed two.[5]

Others had too many horses. A rich chief might own 300 of them—he may have become a chief because of his horse wealth. Blackfeet averaged fifteen horses per lodge; the horse-rich Crow more: one village of 300 lodges found itself encumbered with 9000 to 10,000 horses, more than they needed for transportation and hunting, a daily bother and worry, a herd that each winter had to be sent to Wind River to feed.[6] Such a surplus meant that the camp crier more often announced "We move today, the grass is short." The horse's need for grass may have forced as much nomadism as did the erratic perambulation of the buffalo.

Horsed buffalo hunters skirmished more than formerly because they trespassed more upon the hunting country of neighbors—the Nez Perce for instance could cross the Rockies to raid the buffalo herds of the Blackfeet. And, when tribes stole the horses of another tribe, friction arose. The Crow and Blackfeet continually fought over horses, and the Crow, not as expert warriors but more clever as horse thieves, became the richer in horses. Further friction amongst horsed tribes occurred because one of the methods of warfare became the capturing or killing of an enemy's buffalo herds. Thus the Osage, traveling with Zebulon Pike through the Kans' hunting ground, tried to "destroy all the game they possibly could,"[7] and the Crow, with General Crook, after destroying without using a number of buffalo, explained, "better kill buffalo than have him feed the Sioux."[8] (Later, the United States said much the same thing regarding all the tribes.)

Useful as the hunters found the horse for nomadic living, they found him even more useful to enhance their age-old ability to move buffalo when and where they needed them—to herd buffalo: "Their mastery of 'herd psychology' of the buffalo was so complete that they could not only slay a herd at once, but herd after herd in a spot of their own choosing."[9] An ability, we might say, to handle the wild buffalo herds as neatly as cowboys later handled the near-wild Longhorn herds. Cattle savvy the cowboys had, buffalo savvy the Indians had.

Frontier accounts abound in incidents of horsed Indians herding buffalo. They early adapted horse-riding to herding: in 1772 Matthew Cocking noted of the Blackfeet, "they set off in the Evening: and drive the Cattle all night . . . They are well-mounted."[10] A

A disguise that enabled mounted men to enter a herd unnoticed. "Indians Simulating Buffalo." Frederic Remington, 1908. *Courtesy The Toledo Museum of Art, Toledo, Ohio.*

century later hide hunter Norbert Welsh wrote of a visit to an Indian camp: "The Chief and an Indian went from tent to tent collecting tobacco, tea and sugar to give to the scout. He was a fast rider who was going out to ride all night, and to locate and herd the buffalo in the direction of the pound. The man was an expert at herding buffalo."[11] And Lieutenant G. K. Warren, surveying the Black Hills in 1857, found the Minaconjou "actually herding the animals" while they waited for the pelts to become prime enough for a hunt, holding them from drifting into enemy territory.[12] Indians in Wyoming asked Morton Frewen's outfit to shoot some buffalo for them, since they had run out of ammunition (he doesn't explain why they couldn't use arrows). The whites said "if they would move their herd so as to cross our trail the next day at the same hour about seven miles higher up from where we were then in camp, we would oblige . . . Sure enough the next day the herd appeared in three or four long lines . . . The Indians were moving the herds very gently; no noise but just showing themselves in the distance down wind." The whites killed ten buffalo for them.[13] Artist Paul Kane, hunting with the Métis in Canada, "fell in with one of the hunters coolly driving a wounded buffalo before him." Kane asked him why not shoot him. The man replied, not "until he got him close to the lodges, as it would save

the trouble of bringing a cart for meat." Later, he killed him "within two hundred yards of the tents."[14] Hunters in the Southwest reported Mexicans often drove buffalo to their settlements before killing them.[15] Indians near a Dakota lake held buffalo nearby until it froze over, then drove them onto the ice and surrounded them.[16]

Handling of buffalo had become not so much wild animal hunting as rounding up and butchering of private herds—something of which frontier Judge A. McG. Bede meant in a letter recalling the buffalo of the Sioux in South Dakota—"They were the semicattle of the Sioux, their property upon which they relied for a living."[17]

The horsed Indian also engaged in the ancient impounding and piskin methods, using the horse to find more herds and quickly bring them in, moving the animals and chasing down escaping animals so expertly, butchering so quickly that no wounded excited animals could run amongst other herds and frighten them.

Just as of old, when all was ready the people took their places along the V, the caller approached the herd on horseback and, at about 150 yards, he lay on the horse's back under his robe and bleated like a buffalo calf. The buffalo followed the mounted caller into

Mounted Indians chasing a herd into a pound, a technique learned when they hunted on foot. "A Buffalo Pound." Paul Kane. *Courtesy Royal Ontario Museum, Toronto.*

the piskin just as before they'd followed the caller afoot. Another more exciting method stampeded the herd into the wings and over the drop into the piskin.

Horsemen also took part in the ancient surround—although often on the morning of the surround about a third of the men in camp joined in minus a horse—some had had no luck in catching one up that morning, others had no horse capable of chasing buffalo. The hunters surrounded the chosen herd, footmen with guns downwind of it, horsemen with bows and arrows slowly riding to circle it upwind. When the horsemen noticed restlessness in the herd they galloped their ponies to finish the circle about it, then, shooting arrows and yelling, drove the animals toward the footmen, who fired into them, throwing them back in confusion against those animals behind who were fleeing the arrows of the horsemen. "A surround party of 80 to 100 persons will in this way kill from 100 to 500 buffalo in the course of an hour," wrote Edwin Denig, factor at Fort Union.[18]

This horsed surround meant closing with frightened animals in a melee of footmen, horsemen and galloping buffalo. Artist George Catlin saw it first hand, painted it, and also wrote about it:

. . . these noble animals . . . becoming infuriated with deadly wounds in their sides, erected their shaggy manes over their blood-shot eyes and furiously plunged forward at the sides of their assailant's horses, sometimes goring them to death at a lunge, and putting the dismounted riders to flight for their lives; sometimes their dense crowd was opened, and the blinded horsemen, too intent on their prey amidst the cloud of dust, were hemmed and wedged in amidst the crowding beasts, over whose backs they were obliged to leap for security, leaving their horses to the fate that might await them . . . some who were closely pursued by the bulls, wheeled suddenly around and snatching the part of a buffalo robe from around their waists, threw it over the horns and the eyes of the infuriated beast, and darting by its side drove the arrow or the lance to its heart.[19]

All this in eye-blinding dust, on a plain pocked with hoof-catching prairie dog holes, riding 800-pound ponies in the shadow of 1800-pound buffalo.

As buffalo hunting tribes acquired the horse, they came even more than before to regard as their own those buffalo that grazed upon hunting grounds they claimed and now could effectually patrol and protect. They came to regard land within certain boundaries as their hunting ground to hold inviolate against all other hunters: the Minaconjou prevented Lt. G. K. Warren from traveling on their lands to complete the survey in the Black Hills;[20] the Pawnee held up for several days the group in which Marcus Whitman traveled, rather than let it proceed through the herds and frighten the buffalo; Jacob Fowler found that the Arapaho would furnish "plenty of the beast of buffelow meet at a low Rate bu do not Wish us to Hunt them our Selves."[21] (Somewhat a commentary upon the white man's poor shooting as well as the Indian's territorial rights; Indians knew they themselves could bring down more buffalo than the white, with far less disturbance of the herds.)

Various tribes developed "boundary lines established by treaty . . . marked usually by natural topographic features," or, if no natural feature stood out, by boulders carried in buffalo hides to the boundary line. If the Omaha, following "their" buffalo herd, needed to follow it into Pawnee land, they asked Pawnee permission and agreed to adhere to Pawnee rules.[22] Fur trappers tried to buy permission to trap beaver, but if they couldn't, as with the Blackfeet, they poached, and sometimes lost their scalps.

As horseback hunts became larger, as the horsed Indian became even more of a one-crop, single harvest hunter, his hunts had to succeed lest he starve or freeze. He had to make sure that nearby buffalo served the most people, that no one disturbed them by individual hunting, especially in the summer when larger groups of people came together in somewhat permanent camps for protection from enemies and to join seasonal rituals and festivities. These hunts provided fresh meat for the present and a supply of almost hairless hides for new tipi skins. They differed from the fall hunts meant to provide quantities of meat and robes for the coming winter. To avoid hunts ruined by careless or greedy people, most buffalo tribes carried out traditional, strict, summer hunt rules, rules that the foot hunters had devised, but now, because of the horse and its speed, more important than ever. They enforced the rules through special groups, the "soldiers"—each of the men's societies, which, as its turn came, blackened faces as a sign of authority. Each so-

Here the Indian uses the horse in the same ancient killing technique he devised in his foot-hunting days—the surround. "Buffalo Hunt—Surround." George Catlin. *Courtesy Amon Carter Museum, Fort Worth, Texas.*

ciety competed to provide a standard for efficiency in government and to bring honor on their group. Often a tribe held council after the winter hunt to decide on laws for the coming summer hunt and the group to enforce them. Other tribes varied the duties throughout the year.

Scouts went out to find a herd for slaughter, a herd possibly a day or more march away. Just as ocean fishermen look for schools of fish amongst the rolling waves, they scanned the plains for birds soaring above the herds, giving away buffalo hidden by the rolling hills. If they found buffalo (some swore to the truth of this by a laying of hand on a buffalo chip) and if the chiefs decided to hunt this herd, the scouts designated the direction of the hunt and led the group, but the soldiers took over control of the march to the herd. The march was orderly, although hunting groups forayed to pick off small buffalo bands passed up by the leading scouts or to herd them toward the main band.[23]

Under the summer-hunt rules people understood that even if they lived in a few lodges apart from the main group, they weren't to hunt within six to ten miles of the big encampment. Furthermore, people understood that once the tribes had decided on a hunt, no person, white or Indian, could hunt and disturb the herd. If the herds grazed close by, the soldiers told owners of barking dogs to shut them up (they once took hatchets away from noisy fort woodcutters). Even men tracking runaway horses could not follow toward the herd. Shooting of firearms or loud talking might bring reprimand. The soldiers might break an offender's gun, or fine him a horse if he'd wandered too near the herds; beat him, kill his horse, rip up his clothes, if he'd hunted unlawfully; club him back if he'd pushed forward of the starting line before a hunt; kill him if he'd frightened the herds away through his crime.[24] The Ogalalas once killed a horseman and his horse for going amongst the whites, for fear the white man smell might disturb the buffalo.[25] Such strictness helped to avoid bloody intra-group battles over who frightened away the buffalo.

Soldiers also protected the herd from indiscriminate hunting during the spring calving season to avoid disturbing the cows who might seek less hectic feeding grounds. They not only protected the herds from their own people but also from unfriendly tribes that might attempt to run them off or poach them. And soldiers enforced the boundaries of the surround, watched to see no hunter chased off too far, for enemies often saw the dust, heard the rifle shots of the surround, and lay in wait for the stray excited hunter to wander into

ambush. Kiowa soldiers beat hunters who exceeded the boundary of the hunt.[26]

Since everyone believed a big kill depended on the performance of hunt rituals as much as on speed of the horse or skill of the hunter, those in charge of the hunt also oversaw these. They saw to it that the hunters approached the herd solemnly, slowly. The Omaha stopped the slow procession four times to smoke and pray, interludes that subdued excitement and focused thoughts upon the ritual kill. Although writers tell of Indians yelling during the chase, George Bird Grinnell thought it would be as "fitting to write of a farmer as yelling in the excitement of plowing or of milking his cows" as to write of a Cheyenne warrior whooping in the buffalo chase. Perhaps such silence arose amongst such pandemonium so that the single shout would be heard: The Omaha shouted only to let others know they'd dispatched their animal[27]—bloody froth had appeared at his nostrils and mouth although he still ran. Following the kill, amongst the Blackfeet, "no one cheered the hunters or spoke, nor laughed. It was too solemn a moment . . ." An Indian buffalo slaughter had almost no resemblance to a similar slaughter by whites.

Following the hunt, the soldiers made sure hunters properly sacrificed the first game killed. Pawnees took the carcass to a sacred lodge to perform secret rites, then removed it to the southeast corner of camp, cremated it, creating a sacred smoke in which all grasped for handfuls to rub onto the body. Assiniboines cut up the carcass and gave it to the crows, magpies and wolves, saying, "I give you this that I may always be able to kill and feed the wolves, that I may be successful in war."[28]

The white man's gun arrived amongst the tribes with the horse, and also upset the traditional ways of living and brought power to those who obtained it first. Thus in the north the Cree and Assiniboine, living east of the Blackfeet, traded with the whites earlier than they, obtained guns and were able to drive them west. But when the Blackfeet got the gun and then got the horse from the Shoshone before the Cree and Assiniboine, they took whatever buffalo territory appealed to them—Cree or Assiniboine or Kutenai— and drove the Shoshone south out of buffalo land. The southern buffalo hunters, although they had the Spanish horse early, had no guns, for the Spanish allowed no Indian trade in firearms. And, since the French along the Mississippi traded in guns, the tribes there, the Pawnee, the Comanche and the Sioux also became powers. So the Shoshone and the Utes, far

George Catlin loved to paint the Indian at risk. Here, as in his painting of the surround, he shows trick bareback riding on both buffalo and horse. *Courtesy Amon Carter Museum, Fort Worth, Texas.*

from the traders in guns, lost their influence, their land, their buffalo.

Many Indians west of the Mississippi used flintlock muskets manufactured in England. These old muzzle loaders had a five-eighths inch bore in a barrel two and a half to three and a half feet long. They dropped buffalo pretty well up to a hundred yard range. When the buffalo hunter became mounted he filed off this long barrel, halving it for easier use on the gallop— just as he'd made his bows about three feet shorter than he'd used for foot hunting.

Indians found they could shoot more often with the bow than with the muzzleloader which they had to load with powder and ball for each shot. They could, by holding some arrows in the bow hand—point down, feathers and notch up—in one minute "ride three hundred yards and discharge twenty arrows." Whether or not each of the twenty would find a target in a running buffalo is doubtful. If a man discharged all twenty at buffalo, he had to make them account for five beasts: four to kill a buffalo was his allowance, more disgraced him, only one made him renowned.[29] If he put a single arrow through the animal he gained more renown, although the arrow may have left such a clean hole that the buffalo galloped away. He preferred the bow for a long time. White Cloud said the Sioux could handle the bow with certainty, but the

trade gun they found unsteady on horseback and liable to shoot over the animal.[30] Plenty-Coups said, "The bow was the best of weapons for running the buffalo. Even the old-time white men, who had only the muzzle-loading guns, were quick to adopt the bow and arrow in running buffalo."[31]

Indians tried to drive an arrow "forward and downward through the buffalo's paunch" rather than trying for the musket's bony target behind the shoulder blade "a few inches above the brisket." (Occasionally a mounted gun-hunter preferred the target "at or near the ear.") Often the kill was surer with the arrow, for the galloping of the wounded animal vibrated it, cutting him to pieces deep inside. And the hunting arrow, with its special large head, opened a gash; the gun made a clean hole. A tough old buffalo could stand half-a-dozen bullet holes blown in him and live; many a buffalo carcass gave up several old lead balls embedded in its meat.

Occasionally riders used the lasso to nab buffalo: Sitting Bull's warriors in Canada, bereft of ammunition, did so. They also contrived spears from knives lashed to poles. Hunters had always used the lance during the chase, but usually only after a beast already carried an arrow or two. Amongst the Kans, only chiefs could use the lance, which they thrust "again and again through the liver or heart." The "common

Indian" used the smoothbore musket (never the rifle, for the sharp crack of the discharge, and especially the whining zing of the bullet they thought of as magic). The poorer ones of the tribe still used the bow. Probably the lance, bow and smoothbore brought down an equal number of buffalo,[32] but the lance, according to a hide hunter, meant "jab, jab, jab, until the poor critter toppled from loss of blood and cuts to his vital organs."[33]

The Blackfeet, Cheyenne and other tribes rarely used guns for the horse chase, because the musket report scared animals away, while the silent bow revealed nothing of the hunter's presence. The Assiniboine prohibited the use of the gun in the chase. Sometimes when they obtained guns, they gave them away.[34]

For another thing, Indians preferred the bow to the musket for the hunt because it used no powder and ball, and they needed powder and ball, which only traders could supply, to survive in warfare. If they should use it up at hunting they would be at the mercy of any roving band of gun-carrying warriors. The gun suited the Indian idea of warfare—shoot without bringing yourself into range; muskets made much fighting a standoff at about 100 yards distance. As Denig said, "the possession of firearms had unquestionably promoted war. . . . It . . . facilitates waylaying and killing their enemies, a matter of which they are remarkably fond, and could not be well accomplished with arrows, lances, etc., without equal danger to both parties. Guns and ammunition are considered the soul of warfare, more so than of the chase."[35]

A man could repair the bow himself; the gun he likely had to take to the fort. Arrows he could make, shot and powder he had to purchase. He could retrieve arrows from the carcasses to be used over again; only now and then could he prize out a lead ball. Furthermore, arrows were interchangeable; a man with a bow could use his neighbor's arrows, but oftentimes in an Indian camp one man's ammunition would not fit his neighbor's gun. Thus in a skirmish any one man out of ammunition might seriously deplete firepower. Better to use bow and arrows for hunting, save powder and lead for war. Furthermore, the arrow killed quietly; it was good to use while traveling and hunting in enemy country. Then, too, the use of the gun in the hunt depended upon the availability of powder and ball or shells. Camped close to a fort the Indian might use his gun—after all, he received at least twenty balls and appropriate powder for each buffalo carcass he provided to the fort. Or use might depend upon tribal edict. Or upon wealth, the man of standing

conspicuously consuming white man's goods, an unluckier man using the bow.

Some of the objection to the smoothbore disappeared after some hunter, white or Indian, overcame the slow shooting of the musket when he found out how to load the gun fairly quickly while galloping. "A Wisconsin Youth in Montana" described the process wonderfully, although at second hand:

> . . . the untutored savage had devised a method for converting his crude flintlock trade-gun into a rapid-fire weapon by an ingenious but simple process. In order that the long, clumsy musket might be used in one hand, the barrel was filed off, reducing its length nearly one-half. The stock was similarly amputated and the result might be called an immense, clumsy horse-pistol. To avoid the necessity of opening the pan and priming it at every shot the touch-hole was reamed out to a generous size. With horse at full gallop the possessor of this remarkable weapon poured into the muzzle an unmeasured charge of powder, and upon this haphazard explosive he spat, from a supply carried in his mouth, one large, round, leaden ball, which fitted so loosely in the generous bore of the musket that it settled into place without aid of a ramrod. The gun was carried muzzle up during all this performance and until the moment of discharge, and primed itself through the enlarged touch-hole. Thus prepared, the Indian hunter had only to urge his horse to the approved position alongside the running buffalo, when the weapon was pointed and discharged in one motion. There could be no possibility of missing, but there was an ever-present chance that the gun might burst.[36]

Many hunters bore scars on face and hands—or had lost a hand—because they'd held the gun at the horizontal before firing, allowing "air to intervene between the powder and lead to cause an explosion and splinter the barrel." Extreme cold or a powder overload caused explosions and splintering and may have caused as much shortening of the barrel as deliberate cutting.

The fastest hunters could fire these flintlock guns and reload them about twelve to fourteen times a mile, faster than the percussion cap gun, slower than the bow, but certainly fast enough for any buffalo hunt.

Only the repeating rifle or the revolver could equal the swiftness of the Indian's arrow shooting—but the guns held fewer projectiles. A man told of seeing an Indian put five to ten arrows into the air before the first arrow hit the ground. Another saw "such rapidity that one long stream of them seems to be cleaving the

"The Buffalo Hunt." Note the musket upraised until the moment of firing to keep the ball from rolling down the barrel. *Courtesy Amon Carter Museum, Fort Worth, Texas.*

air." They saw exceptional shooters, but most Indians fired fast enough to always have one arrow in the air. Thus the swiftness of the Colt revolver's shooting amazed the bow and arrow expert not at all, as Josiah Gregg, traveling the Santa Fe Trail, discovered. He emptied his new Colt rapidly for the edification of a Comanche chief, whereupon the chief picked up his bow and fired arrows with the same rapidity. This chief had before demonstrated a bowman's accuracy with an offhand shot that trajected an arrow to drop behind a prairie dog's mound and pierce the mostly hidden dog.[37]

Yet the coming of the breech-loading rifle switched Indian allegiance from the bow to the gun. Plenty-Coups couldn't rest until he had one—gave "ten finely dressed robes" for it and "laid my bow away forever," for after using the new gun "the bow seemed only a plaything," and, encased in the new cartridge, his powder was always dry.[38] But most plains tribes continued to hunt buffalo with both the cheap, hand-crafted bow and the gun right up until the end of the buffalo.

Horses, as did the pound, brought animals within arrow range. But also, horses had to be guarded as a supply of meat as well as buffalo chasers. A tribe that went into the winter owning 5000 horses could see enough meat on the hoof to insure survival until spring if buffalo hunting should turn bad. Horses increased a hunter's chances of bringing in buffalo meat, for if the herds wandered, he might find them. Horses made the tribes less dependent upon dried meat as winter emergency rations. Horses equalled the Indian's insurance.

*"Your saddles bind
The buffalo,
Half a day,
We will hunt."*
(CALL SUNG BY SIOUX CRIERS)

*". . . he was on his way to the Comanche country
to have another tumble among
the Buffaloes."*
THE MORNING STAR,
HOUSTON, TEXAS,
APRIL 10, 1845

AS THE COMING of the horse improved many of the old ways of living for the buffalo hunters, so it gave special importance to the man with the best horses. Also, the horseback chase of buffalo gave these buffalo hunters a way of hunting lethargic buffalo that brought excitement to it, excitement so fulfilling it became addictive. The horseback chase combined the qualities of the horse race and the hunt. It pitted rider against rider and horse against horse. The successful rider gained prestige for his killing skill. And he felt the satisfaction of having trained and ridden a fast horse, a strong, fast horse, one that could catch up with running buffalo . . . his common horse wouldn't do.

In the chase the hunter deliberately put the buffalo to running; he wanted him to run, had no use for him standing still. He came up to a herd from the leeward, as in all buffalo hunting, working as close to it as covering brush, hills or coulees would allow; he put his horse into a gallop the minute the herd broke, just as in a surround, but now no foot hunters—men without horses—stood beyond the herd to turn it. This was a test of horse speed against buffalo speed. The idea was to get into the herd from the flank (it tended to split away from hunters coming into it from the rear) and get into it fast so as to bring down a cow

or two before their fleetness put them out front, left the hunter behind amongst the lumbering bulls. Each hunter attempted to select a cow and ride beside her long enough to put an arrow into her gut—two or three if necessary—then, when blood frothed at nose and mouth, crying to others to waste no arrows here and dashing to another cow, killed as many as possible before herd escaped or horse gave out.

The kill from the chase often totalled less than from the earlier piskin drive or foot surround, but in the chase the take of meat became less important— the sport was the thing. The Blackfeet knew that "our far-back fathers soon found . . . nothing so exciting, so satisfying as the running of a herd of buffalo with a fast, well-trained elk-dog,"[1] and the Sioux found it "one of their most valued amusements." James Willard Schultz rode many hunts with the Blackfeet, and spoke for them: "Oh, how we loved it all: the thunderous pounding and rattling of thousands of hooves; the sharp odor of the sage they crushed; the accuracy of our shooting; the quick response of our trained horses to our directing hands. Always the run was over all too soon."[2]

So it was with all the tribes that mastered the horse, although they conducted the chase as ritual, just as in other buffalo harvests, with dancing beforehand and a medicine man accompanying the riders to the herd.

For Blackfeet hunters, the chase was "an old clothes affair": leggings, breechcloth and shirt, nothing fancy for they shed most of their clothing just before riding into the herd, a process Charlie Russell saw as similar to "a lot of schoolboys going in swimming." But their medicine man was resplendent. On one chase he wore elk-skin clothing decorated with colorful animal pictures and on his head "a gaudy dress of eagle feathers." He carried a medicine stick four feet long "decked with eagle feathers, otter skins and scalps"; a shield emblazoned with a green buffalo hung at his back. He rode a pony painted "in all colors and at his fore-top hung a wisp of buffalo tail and some weeds, which are considered good luck."

As the men undressed, the medicine man brought out his pipe, filled it with willow bark mixed with tobacco, offered it to the four points of the compass, then lit it with the fire he carried in a smouldering buffalo chip (a chip would "hold fire many hours"). He sat cross-legged and smoked as the men mounted, "at each draft made a noise like that of a man eating soup." He prayed for them in a loud voice, while they rode toward the herd, talking kindly to their horses, telling them not to be afraid of the buffalo, to run well and bring in lots of meat.[3]

The buffalo had a chance in the chase because few horses could keep up with him. The moment the buffalo spied mounted men "the whole extent of the country, as far as the eye could reach, became perfectly animate with living objects, fleeing and scampering in every direction. From the surrounding valleys sprang up numerous herds of these animals which had hitherto been unobserved."[4] The chase had to start close enough to a herd that the horses galloped only five or six minutes before overtaking the buffalo, otherwise they failed to reach them. A man had to choose almost immediately which of the many bunches to follow (the experienced Indian chose the small herd headed for the direction of his camp so the meat would fall closer to home). Once into the bunch a man had to choose and kill quickly, for most horses fell behind the frightened herd in a mile or so. And some horses seemed not to want to keep up; the noise and the musky smell that hung in the air turned them away. And, on moist days, the stinging clods, hoof-thrown against the horses, pelted them, covered them with mud, and turned back all but the most eager of them.[5]

For such a chase a man needed a special horse, a horse larger than the usual Indian pony, a horse trained to bring his rider within six to fifteen feet of this musky-smelling, snorting monster, to stay with her until knee pressure signaled the shots had met their mark—although some impatient horses gave a man just so much time at a cow's side and then went on, signal or not—to swing away from the slashing horns as each arrow penetrated, and to catch up with the next fat cow on signal. Each rider had to learn to pick good meat, or other hunters would laugh at his choice and "remind . . . [him] . . . of it at gatherings"; some swore that the horse could pick out the fatness a prime cow showed at the roots of the tail as well as could the rider. A man often rode without a hand being laid to rein or halter, for hands must be free to nock arrows and draw bowstring or reload single-shot fusil and fire.

As a prospective buffalo horse, a man selected a three- or four-year-old, usually a male, that showed speed, sure-footedness and spirit. If the untrained horse bolted in his first chase, his owner later forced him as near a dead buffalo as possible, tied him to the horns to accustom him to the sight and smell. If he then proved to have courage in succeeding chases, a man continued his training. (A Comanche also trained him as a sentinel to signal danger to him as he butchered a lone kill—ears waving meant buffalo or coyote close, ears pricked forward, man.)

This was the horse a man expected his wife to show loving care to: a rubdown following the chase, grass pulled for him alone when lowlier horses had little or none, cottonwood bark peeled for him when snow lay deep—a diet that might cause his hair to fall out but kept him alive. A man sometimes dashed cold water on this horse morning and evening to toughen him, just as he daily rubbed his own fingers in sand or snow to keep them limber for the bow. This horse he staked out close to the tipi to keep him safe from enemy raiders, might even sleep with his arm serving as picket pin so that an unusual movement could awaken him.

A man rode this horse only in the chase. He led him to the chase, mounted him at the last moment, for the animal would need every ounce of his strength. And a good mount, rested and needing exercise, expended it willingly, recklessly: he delighted "in the pleasures of the chase and is so animated at the sight of a Band of animals that he can scarcely be restrained from pursuing them."[6] He seldom needed whipping. His first bound might take him twenty-one feet toward the herd. The fastest buffalo horse at Fort Union invariably nipped his rider on the leg if he tried to check the pace. A buffalo horse, left behind because his master had read bad signs and refused to hunt, sometimes broke his tethers, joined the hunt riderless, and might, as did the experienced buffalo horses purchased by Lewis and Clark, surround a herd, doing their job without guidance as expertly as city milk horses on their routes did theirs. A man could always tell a seasoned buffalo horse. The grunting and bellowing of the herd in rut or the whiff of buffalo musk on the wind scared him not at all—he pricked up his ears, eager for a run; the green horse hung at the camp end of his tether rope, anxious to be near companionship and away from the wildness.

Perhaps only one tipi in ten owned a really good buffalo horse, even though a village might own many horses, for most horses were too runty to keep up with a herd. Also, enemies tended to steal the buffalo horse. Stealing such a horse from an enemy meant reducing his meat harvest—a blow at his supply lines, as well as gaining a horse trained for and experienced in the hunt. And a man could count extra coup for the extra danger involved: common horses grazed away from the village, stealing a buffalo horse meant creeping into the village to where he stood tethered.

In addition to chasing buffalo in the big hunts a man could use a buffalo horse to chase down an animal or two for his household. This small hunt, the day-by-day bringing of meat, made the horse valuable to the Indian, for it saved the hours of walking in search of animals and it brought more of the meat home and from farther distances than back-packing.

A man with a good buffalo horse brought in lots of meat. He saw to it that fresh meat filled many pots, that many people shared his good fortune. Some of them pitched their tipis near his, helped him in his butchering, looked to him for leadership. A man with a good buffalo horse could become a chief, for he could feed a lot of dependents. And in the big tribal hunts, if he had good days when the buffalo lined up just right and his arrows were found in several animals, he became a big name in camp. And he could enlarge his name by racing his horse and winning—everyone loved to gamble. A fast horse that won bets for friends could further his popularity.

A buffalo horse seldom came up for trade. For one thing a trade meant losing that which a man loved as much as his family. And for another thing a man had to think of his people before he traded: the loss of a good buffalo horse meant the loss of gambling winnings and loss of meat for all. A horse-rich man might trade his buffalo horse, but a horse-poor one, seldom. A man might loan his horse to a friend who had no fast, trained horse, a loan for a portion of meat (some owners demanded half), but trade it, no.

The power a man could obtain through the chase,

the excitement of the chase and the satisfaction from owning and showing off such a horse soon drove out the older methods of buffalo hunting.

The horse-rich tribes neglected the surround; eventually they seemed unable to plan it and carry it off. When the Flatheads, traveling on the upper Beaverhead with trapper John Work, needed meat badly, they planned a surround but ended up trying to chase the animals.

The southern Blackfeet neglected the piskin: the young men no longer aspired to be buffalo callers; they wanted to ride in the chase. No man wanted to stand with the women on the sidelines waving a buffalo robe when he might be enjoying the fun and winning fame on the back of a buffalo horse: "every one is crazy about horses. Our warriors, young and old, think only about going to war and taking horses."[7] Eventually the cliff drops remained unvisited except at times when a village had lost, through accident or horse thieves, too many horses to stage a chase. The southern Blackfeet used the piskins last about 1857; the northern, poorer horsemen, about 1870.

The loss of these ancient hunting methods made all of the people too dependent upon a few horses and their riders, especially when in some camps so few men had horses capable of chasing buffalo. And in northern winters, when deep snow covered grass, even these horses weakened: in 1831–32, trapper John Work searched the Beaverhead drainage with the Flatheads for herds upon which to survive. He wrote of starving horses on October 5, 1831, and did "not raise camp" on November 22 so as to allow the horses to feed. Five days later he camped in a bad defensive situation, but "could not find grass in a better." On December 1 he wrote "our horses are very lean and few of them able to catch buffalo now." Four days later "all hands employed themselves cutting grass to give the horses in the night while tied up, which is a great service to them." But not enough of a service, for on December 7, "Some of the people in pursuit of buffalo, but with little success. The most of our runners are so weak that they cannot come up with the buffalo. The ground is so slippery that the horses are afraid." February 7, 1832, "the horses . . . are living so bare that few of them can catch the buffalo." February 23, "The horses are so lean and feeble that few of them can easily catch buffalo." In March they pursued buffalo "but scarcely a horse either of ours or the Indians could come up with them."[8]

The usual rider only killed an average of two to three animals in each chase; a man who killed eighteen in one hunt became a Blackfeet legend. Thus, some chases produced few carcasses. The Fort Sarpy journal in August 1856 notes "Crows run Buffalos again making three runs this day—killing in all about 80 cows some very fat"—a "great number of Crows" were in on the hunt. Two days later in another run they killed only twenty.[9] With the horse, Indians could make more drives and thus increase the total animals killed. Yet these repetitive hunts fatigued the horses until some days they ran not as well as other days; at the beginning of the fall hunt the horses were fat and the dogs lean; at the end the horses were lean and the dogs fat.[10] Horse fatigue decreased the efficiency of the chase.

The horseback chase involved fewer hunters than the older method—perhaps another reason for its popularity; it quickly brought in meat without the necessity of finding many people to wave hides. A chase took only twenty or thirty Indians, variously armed; a surround took eighty to one hundred men. Also, the horseback chase was more selective than the older methods; the hunter attempted to choose and shoot only fat cows; bulls escaped. Thus the chase left less meat to rot—but perhaps the herds thinned as rapidly, for selective destruction of cows meant fewer cows to bear calves each spring.

In spite of its drawbacks, the chase became increasingly useful to the Indian, as the white man, moving into Indian country, kept the herds disturbed, making a quiet, selective surround, pound or piskin difficult. The spooked herds had to be chased—and the more they were chased the more they spooked; they ran from man more often than in the days of the conquistador when they ran not at all. As the herds thinned under white and red hunting, the Indian had to take to the chase more often.

As the white trapper invaded the plains, Indians taught him to chase the buffalo and loaned him buffalo horses to ride. Early fur trappers became as addicted to the chase as their hosts and would trade their traps and possibles to a man willing to trade a horse that ran with the best of them. The price shot up. In Canada in the early nineteenth century a common horse could be "purchased for a gun, which costs no more than twenty-one shillings" yet the buffalo horse couldn't "be purchased with ten, the comparative value of which exceeds the property of any native."[11] A priceless white buffalo hide might purchase a buffalo horse from the Hidatsas or Gros Ventres. As late as 1870 a good buffalo runner sold for $100 to $250 cash,[12] more than most other horses in the United States but worth it to the man depending on

buffalo meat: F. A. Chardon, trader at Ft. Clark on the Missouri complained—with buffalo in all directions—"I'm sorry to say that I have no good Horse that is able to catch them, so that we are obliged to eat poor Bull Meat—."[13]

Chardon could have ridden a slow horse to a herd and then stalked it on foot; it was the chase he missed. Something about this race infected a man. Even a beginner on his second run caught the disease: "I was like a madman . . . I was so carried away by the fury of the chase that . . . I wound up ahead of the herd, as I continued to shout and throw myself about on my horse like a madman."[14]

The exhilarations of the chase made addicts out of serious artists and sober scientists. George Catlin discovered it drowned his prudence although "both horse and rider often seemed rushing on to destruction, as if it were mere pastime and amusement . . . I have often *waked* (as it were) out of the delirium of the chase . . . through which I had passed as though a delightful dream, where to have died would have been but to have remained, riding on."[15] Scientists Thomas Nuttall, John Kirk Townsend, and John James Audubon each came west as observers not as bloodthirsty sportsmen, but each rode into the excitement of the chase just as wantonly as less scientific travelers. Audubon's party, on the Missouri, intended only to try the chase once, but like the first drink the Temperance people of the day bewailed, one buffalo chase led to another and to consequent remorse: "We now regretted having destroyed these noble beasts for no earthly reason but to gratify a sanguinary disposition which appears to be inherent in our natures. We had no means of carrying home the meat and after cutting out the tongues we wended our way back to camp, completely disgusted with ourselves and with the conduct of all white men who come to this country."[16]

The chase slightly favored the buffalo—a way of hunting the beast which made it somewhat a sport rather than a slaughter—although its slaughterhouse aspects disgusted many men: one of a company of gold seekers found it not much of a sport, for he saw the buffalo as "a large unwieldy animal, easily overtaken or easily killed by still hunting; in fact, to me hunting them has few charms. It seems too much like barnyard slaughter."[17]

Most all buffalo chasers had troubles in the dust kicked up by the buffalo, "a cloud of dust so dense that none of the detail can be distinguished." It formed mud in the nostrils and mouth and created a terrible thirst. Charlie Russell, the cowboy artist, riding in the dust of a Blackfeet hunt, lost sight entirely of Indians and buffalo, knew he was among them only by "the rattle of the hoofs, and the shooting and yelling of the Indians."[18] Yet a rider was supposed to pick out a good cow and take out after her specifically; often it would seem he had to take out after the animal that first appeared through the haze. John Fremont wrote that he first saw buffalo when within only thirty feet of them. Francis Parkman had the same experience: "I could see nothing but a cloud of dust before me . . . In a moment I was in the midst of the cloud, half-suffocated by dust . . . Very soon a long dark mass became visible, looming through the dust." George Bird Grinnell hunted the beasts in dust so thick that "to see the ground was impossible."[19] Undoubtedly on moist days or in small chases, where the hooves raised less dust, it was true that "the quality of the animals spoke the true hunter. Many men could kill, but not many could pick," but in dusty, big chases a hunter might have to shoot whatever meat he could see, not whatever meat he could pick.

James Willard Schultz came back to a Blackfeet camp from a buffalo chase to find the women wailing "young Arrow Maker had been killed, his horse disembowelled, Two Bows had been thrown and his leg was broken." Ely Moore, New York greenhorn, hunted with the Miamis in 1854 on the day Jimmie Squirrel had the calf of his leg torn off by a bull horn—a thrust which also disembowelled his horse. Crow warrior Buffalo Not Kill Him was gored by a buffalo bull and recovered, but Bear Dung was sent sprawling to the ground where a bull gored him to death. Because of this ever-present danger, a rider often made a ritual stop before the hunt at the painted bull's head to ask the buffalo to refrain from goring him. More practically, in the buffalo chase a long lariat dangled behind each horse, a lifeline to grab in case one landed amidst the herd. One of the first things an Indian buffalo horse learned was never to step on a dangling rope. Not so the white man's horse. Charlie Russell's horse stepped on the line dragging from Sleeping Thunder's horse and pitched Russell's friend into the herd. Luckily Russell made it near enough to kill an attacking bull.[20]

Yet white plainsmen might pooh-pooh the danger from buffalo in the breakneck ride, saying "There is more accidents happen in running buffalo by riders getting frightened and suddenly checking their horses than any other way." And George Bird Grinnell believed Indians in the chase more often injured themselves from falling on whip stocks, arrows, bows and guns than from buffalo action—a man needed little skill to join in the chase, he said.

The saying was, "Any man who can ride a horse and keep his head can chase buffalo." But if so, a lot of men, come to the frontier, could do neither. Henry L. Ellsworth, traveling with the Washington Irving party as Indian Commissioner making a study of the country west of Arkansas, found he had difficulty:

> The Rangers had positive orders in the morning to march in a line and not break ranks for any cause . . . We soon saw 3 large Buffaloe . . . Buffaloe! Buffaloe! Buffaloe look at them—there they go—
> Forgetful of all the commands given them, 20 Rangers broke from the rangers at once—8 or 10 fired at the Buffaloe who now began to run up hill—Mr. Irving started with his new horse & pistols—I caught the flame of pursuit and spurred up my poney . . . into the thick bushes & vines, and coming to the ravine neither the horse nor myself noticed it and *down he fell* with *his neck under him*—I need not say I was off beside him—my gun went into the ground & the barrels were filled with mud 6 inches—I though[t] my poor horse had finished his journey, by breaking his neck—I pulled out his head, He jumped and gr[o]aned [?] a few times—then shook himelf, and let me get on—Others were as bad off as myself, and some much worse—One ranger was thrown against a tree his rifle dashed in pieces, and his horse ran away with the wild Buffaloe; so that he never was found—among all that pursued—none overtook the Buffaloe some who boasted of the fleetness of their horses, were so far outdistanced, that they never ventured again, on the same chase—I was thankful having escaped any injury, and resolved that I would never pursue Buffaloe again, especially on my horse—[21]

Further danger arose because shots whizzed close to riders. (Before the charge into the herd Indian elders warned the less experienced not to shoot each other; whites often had no such elders.) Commissioner Ellsworth also experienced this: ". . . so anxious were the rangers to fire at the Buffaloe that seemingly a hundred guns were fired at once. The balls *whistled* by me, on every side and I have not yet been in more danger, than at this moment from the bullets of the Rangers."[22] Because of such danger, some U.S. Army officers, called upon to take visitors on a chase, let them ride along but sometimes disarmed them to avoid typical accidents:[23] yet General Custer once lowered his revolver and blew out the brains of his wife's horse. A greenhorn raised his and blew off his own hat. Greenhorn J. A. Kanouse, a lawyer from

Newark, held his revolver above his head, lowered it for a branch, rested it on his shoulder where it fired, luckily missing him but setting his coat on fire. He jumped from his horse to dowse the fire and his horse ran off.[24] In every greenhorn hunt horses ran away when the rider jumped off, often to aim a long shot at the buffalo his horse couldn't or wouldn't catch. An experienced hunter kept his revolver in his belt until alongside the cow, then removed it, lowered his shooting arm, cocked the gun as he raised it and shot with little aim as the muzzle came up. And even this some men sneered at. One hide hunter said he occasionally shot his revolver at a buffalo, but "always when I wanted to show off and be a hero in somebody's eyes."[25]

The eagerness of the buffalo horse accounted for some danger. He tended to push into the thickest of the herd following a cow until his rider discovered no avenue leading out of such a press; a rider extricated himself by gradually slackening the pace; some men claimed they had to ride this way for a half hour before freeing themselves. Expert hunters felt that, if the horse should fall, one should stay with it, for the buffalo would swerve around it and save the man from being trampled.

Another part of the danger, to Indians at least, came from their love of teasing a wounded beast following the chase, deliberately wounding him to make him attack. They carried spears as much to tease him as to kill him. Once they goaded a bull to attack they rode around and about him, fluttering bits of red rag at him and yelling, dodging his charges, sinking their spears into him, lassoing him to throw him down. When his strength had gone, when he bristled like a porcupine with arrows and bled from dozens of spear thrusts, the bravest men would dismount and seize him by the tail and jerk him about. The buffalo fought until the last, bravely, wholeheartedly, if madly and with little plan, charging at any likely target, sometimes dashing into a nearby stream to cool off for a moment, charging out again when his tormentors came near. They admired his bravery under torture—teased him to bring it out. Trappers loved this torment also; the hairbreadth 'scape was part of their derring-do.

Now that the tribe depended upon fewer men to feed it, now that each person no longer helped equally to provision the tribe as he had done in the foot surround or the drive to piskin and pound, now that a few men, the owners of fast, skilled horses, did the killing, new problems of meat division arose. Just as the good stalker in the days before the horse had claim to any animal he killed, so the horseback chaser came to feel he had some claim to any buffalo dead from his arrows. But the whole tribe had to be fed.

Most everyone should have been too happy to quarrel. The hunters sang their victory song, the people gorged. They drank raw blood, nibbled on bits of raw stomach and raw cow's nose. Buffalo blood streaked even the children; some men bathed in it. Blood dripped down horses' sides; bloody dogs stood belly deep in offal. It would seem no one engulfed in buffalo meat had reason to fight, but squabbling arose: George Catlin, watching the Mandans after a surround, was "continually amused . . . by the clamorous contentions that arose, and generally ended, in desperate combats; both amongst the dogs and the women, who seemed alike tenacious of their local and recently acquired rights; and disposed to settle their claims by 'tooth and nail.'"[26]

If anything the horseback chase might have caused less squabbling than the horseback surround, for the carcasses lay strung out over rolling hill and coulee, at the bottom of arroyo, in the middle of a willow thicket—butcherers often worked out of sight of each other.

The same rules of division applied to dividing animals fallen in the surround or in the chase. Typically, the skin might be set aside and on it be piled the arrow that killed the beast along with the four best pieces of meat. If more than one man's arrow had entered the animal, the killing arrow received the hide, the liver and one side of the animal, the second likely killing arrow the other side, and a third arrow the brisket and some other parts. The usual rule of division amongst the Assiniboine, for instance, was to give the killer the tongue, the hide and the four best pieces of meat; whoever skinned the animal acquired all the rest of the beast. In some tribes all the hunter demanded was the robe; the meat belonged to those who cut it up and hauled it home.

Hunters using the gun sometimes tried to establish claim by loading a certain number of shot to produce a countable pattern as theirs alone. Any hunter had many ways of establishing claim. Not all buffalo looked alike to him; he might have noticed a split horn or a peculiar color patch, an unusual hair growth or a strange expression. Or he remembered a certain rock or a scrawny sage brush and knew where his buffalo lay. Or he dropped a piece of clothing near each kill. Or he kept track of how many animals should be his by counting—not the animals he hit, but the shots he missed. None of these methods should have taxed his memory at an average of only two kills per chase.

Tribes had a further check on claims of buffalo killed—they gathered the tongue of each dead bull, calf and cow to complete an accurate tally (and because they provided such fine eating). Perhaps the tally was the reason some tribes dropped all tongues at the doorway of the soldiers' lodge; surely the soldiers could eat only a few of the tongues rendered them, especially since people also dropped off choice hump pieces for them.

The chase tended to string out over rolling hill and coulee until the hunter lost sight of his kill. As he rode in the distance, the men who had no buffalo horses and the women (those who belonged to a hunter's household or no) began skinning his kill, working so quickly that often much of this work was done by the time the hunter rode back. Even though he might be quite aware of the animals he had downed, those eager for meat may have already stolen it. Such stealing became so common that an Indian saying was "The slow horses get all the buffalo."[27]

*"What the coca-nut is to the East Indian,
and the plantain and the calabash
to various tribes of Africans, such is the 'boss' to the
carnivorous son of
America."*
SIR RICHARD BURTON

WHEN GENERAL Alfred Sully and his troops destroyed 400 lodges in a Sioux village in 1863, they discovered among the charred lodgepoles about 500,000 pounds of *dried* meats.[1] This would make, at the usual one and a half pounds of dried meat per day per person, a seventy day food supply for these 4800 people, an equivalent to one and a half million pounds of fresh meat; about 3500 buffalo carcasses would have gone into the making of it. In Montana's Judith Basin, army scouts at an abandoned, Blackfeet-razed Nez Perce camp ran upon "tons of dried and partly dried meat lying around"; they ate breakfast from the "big pile" of meat before destroying it.[2] Such quantities of dried buffalo meat came the way of most buffalo tribes. Each November they fell upon the herds to gather meat for February and March, the Nez Perce once socking away so much of it they seemed to "have thought the winter was going to last about 99 years."[3]

On the buffalo range the Indians ate three to five pounds of fresh meat per person per day.[4] Their surplus of food prevented "all fear of want, a fear which is incessantly present to the Indians of the north."[5] So much meat meant they were seldom out of food, although day by day eating of dried food instead of fresh red meat made them complain of starving,[6] an attitude seen in trapper John Work saying his traveling companions, the Flatheads, were faring "but indifferently having only dry meat . . ."[7]

Buffalo surplus meant that on many days the buffalo Indian could, instead of hunting, train his buffalo horse, reglue his bow, braid a bridle, make arrowheads, take care of his trappings. And he yet had time for long afternoons of the stick game: guessing in which hand a man of an opposing team held small polished bone. Like today's wheat farmer, he worked the harvests but had many weeks relatively free.

Women too had time to play. They wove but little cloth, threw no pottery, planted and tended no corn patches, did little fancy cooking. Once they had the white man's metal pot, they boiled meat all day long; when someone grew hungry, he dipped into the pot. Boiled meat was Indian fare. They made up for such monotony by feasting and giving feasts; here they ate roasted gut and barbecued ribs, a change from the everlasting, boiled, unsalted soup.

Women gambled in their free time just as the men. They sat in on the stick game. Or played their own favorite, the plum-stone game, casting eight polished plum stones marked variously, much as dice, to make a count. Or they gambled trying to catch a tiny loop of beads on the end of a kind of knitting needle. They played a host of other games and spent much free time swimming and riding.

Both men and women spent days performing the great ceremonies of the year, the "Sun Dance," the tobacco planting ritual, the Medicine Hat ceremony. They spent hours attending meetings of their societies, performing the buffalo dances, telling tales of exploits. As Wooden Leg remarked, "We had but to kill and eat. As I now think back upon those days, it seems that no people in the world ever were any richer than we were."[8] And Tom LeForge, a white man who lived as a Crow amongst Crows, recalled, "Oh it was a great life . . . At all times I had ample leisure for lazy loafing and dreaming and visiting."[9]

Each autumn, folds of thin-sliced meat hung drying on pole racks under the crisp autumn sun, a good fly-free time of year, moisture-free to boot. Indian summer, a time of big hunts, days when 50,000 or 100,000 pounds of meat needed butchering and 200 hides needed saving before dark, lest during the night wolves ruin the meat and mangle the hides. A job that took all hands—man and wife could cut up a buffalo in about an hour. As of old, they severed the meat from the bones to reduce the weight to be carried back to camp. Such butchering white men called "Indian fashion" and complained that it "may do on the prairies but a good deal of meat is lost in this manner" (left on the bones). They preferred theirs "cut up after a Christian fashion . . . good roasting pieces."[10] Back at camp, women sliced the big hunks into long strips as thin as one-fourth inch. These the women of some tribes braided before hanging on drying poles, others plaited strips into a mat, others just dangled them from the poles as cut. Tongues, split lengthwise, also dried in the sun or smoked on racks over fires.

Each night the women took the meat off the racks and piled it on the ground, covered the pile with a buffalo robe and trod it to squeeze blood out of it. The next morning they hung the meat back on the racks again (someone must have kept the dogs from it during the night), hung so as to vary the place that touched the pole—spots that touched the rack continuously would spoil. Magpies raided the drying racks and had to be shooed away; so did mischievous boys called magpies who tried to make off with some meat, a traditional stealing game that prepared them for the stealth useful in stealing horses. If the meat survived such raids for a week or so, it was ready. Just before it became brittle, the women folded it and packed it in parfleches (rawhide containers) for transportation. It

would keep about a year, then the fat became rancid and the meat tasteless.

Some of the meat they dried by smoking—fire dried. It became known to us as jerky (from the Spanish *charqui*). It might dry in a day or so by forcing, but most palates preferred it slow dried. The fast dry did for quick camp curing. While on the march the strips of meat could cure when tied to travois parcels; there the sun could work on them as the village moved.

Father Hennepin ate the dried meat of the buffalo people along the Mississippi and found it prepared so well that "it keeps above four Months without breeding any Corruption: and it looks then so fresh, that one would think it was newly kill'd."[11] But some people only put up with it, found it "as hard and tough as sole leather, but . . . good stuff after it had softened between two rocks."[12] Other men only found it palatable stewed—if one threw away the first water in order to remove the dirt (all of that trampling under a buffalo robe was bound to pick up something). And even stewed it had "a 'faraway' taste which continually reminds one of hoof and horns."[13] But old mountain man and fur trader Bill Sublette, retired and living in St. Louis, craved the smoked stuff and pemmican so much he sent up Missouri each year for a batch of it.

The tribes made pemmican from dried meat (often using the poorer neck meat) if they wanted to preserve meat more surely. Dried meat could be ruined by damp and mold, pemmican could be ruined only by fire, for it consisted of dried meat pounded into bits, over which melted buffalo tallow and marrow was poured.

For the best pemmican, the Blackfeet used only the best and leanest of the meat—the hams, loin and shoulder. When this had sun-dried on the racks, the women built two quaking aspen fires and further dried the strips by throwing them on one fire until it smoked too greasily and then on another fire, back and forth, without scorching them, until they seemed brittle enough for pounding. This they did on a buffalo-skin threshing floor, using a flail similar to the old-fashioned farmer's threshing flail—a flopping, heavy stick fastened to a longer handle. Some flailed while others melted tallow; tallow from cows' udders for the best pemmican (white tallow came from calves, yellow from older animals; the Osages preserved it by putting bits of slippery elm bark and twigs into it). Other women prepared the pemmican bags, sometimes unborn-calf skin, sometimes two pieces of bull hide sewed together. Into these they poured the meat

Women dressing a hide. Racks of dry buffalo meat near the tipis. George Catlin.
Courtesy Buffalo Bill Historical Center, Cody, Wyoming.

and tallow, about fifty pounds of dried meat to forty pounds of tallow,[14] stirring the mixture to spread the meat particles and to remove air bubbles. Or sometimes they bagged the mixture layer by layer. When it had cooled a bit, the women sewed the top, laid it down and jumped on it to force more bubbles out of it. The bag weighed from ninety to one hundred ten pounds; it had taken the lean meat of two to three buffalo cows to fill it. If the cooks had chokecherries or service berries available, they often mixed these into the tallow, making, some said, "a delicious food, which was extremely nutritious"; a pound of pemmican had the food value of five pounds of meat. People ate pemmican as it came from the sack or boiled it in water.

Both jerky and pemmican made food not only for bad times when the scouts found no buffalo and winter times when the blizzard blew, but also they made nutritious cold rations for the warrior and horse-stealer, rations for traveling near the enemy camp when the smoke from a fire would reveal whereabouts. Its dehydration saved space: a handful crumbled, thrown in boiling water, swelled like beans.

Indian and frontiersman liked to eat parts of the buffalo uncooked but warm—warm from body heat just after the kill. They liked to drink the warm blood, liked more to gash the udder of a cow and drink the mingled warm blood and warm milk, liked even more to gash open the stomach of a suckling calf and drink the curdled mother's milk therein. They also mixed warm blood with warm brains, dripped warm gall on warm liver; they stripped the warm partly-digested contents of the upper intestines into their open mouths, ate bits of warm raw kidneys and kidney tallow. One wonders if this craving for vitamin-filled innards arose naturally from days of eating vitaminless boiled food and dried meat.

Big feasts in camp celebrated the hunt. Each successful hunter paraded about the tipi circle calling out invitations to eat with him. Guests ducked into tipi after tipi, ate at each feast to show their courtesy, ate until they vomited to eat some more. They ate baked, boiled or smoke-dried tongue, calves' heads baked in hot embers, dried kidney fat mixed and pounded with dried corn, and Blood Clot Soup—about a quart of blood to a quart of water and brought to a boil in a skin bag by dropping in hot stones.

The back fat, stripped off the back bone from shoulder blade to last rib and smoked, made a delicacy offered to any guest—a sign of welcome. A piece of this fresh off the buffalo "about as thick as one's hand" might weigh from five to eleven pounds. To prepare it the women dipped it in hot grease and then smoked it for twelve hours; so treated, it kept indefinitely. French trappers named it *depouille* which other trappers pronounced depuyer; any of them would pay the equivalent of a dollar a pound for it. No meal seemed complete without it; at Fort Sarpy, if it wasn't on the table, guests and help alike fussed until it appeared.[15]

Depouille was the bread of buffalo hunters' society, marrow fat boiled out of buffalo bone made its butter. But marrow was a luxury, a product of a big kill near camp, for only twelve pounds of it boiled out of the bones of one animal, and hunters rarely brought home heavy bones from a distant kill. This rare delicacy old folks liked to keep to themselves; Grandma sometimes told youngsters not to eat it or their teeth would come out—and showed her gums to prove it. Poured into distended buffalo bladders and cooled it had "the appearance, and very nearly the flavor, of the richest yellow butter."

Unborn calf cooked in the liquor of the womb made a feast delicacy, as did milkweed buds boiled with buffalo meat. Liver, spread with marrow and roasted on coals, as well as tripe, boiled or roasted, tempted palates. Sometimes the cooks covered roasted meat with a sauce made from wild honey, water and tallow. The Cheyennes saved the scrapings from inside the hides, poured boiling water over them, stirred the pulpy mass to produce a dish which tasted like boiled potatoes. Sometimes they added chokecherries for fancy flavor. All men liked *boudins*—wilderness sausage—the section of small intestine, often turned inside out to put the fat inside, stuffed with tenderloin and kidney suet or backfat, boiled a bit, then toasted before the fire.

Special feasts came from meat holes, small, waist-deep barbecue pits, filled with alternate layers of chokecherry boughs and buffalo roast, heated by a bottom layer of white-hot rocks, the whole covered with a buffalo paunch and hide. Atop the pit a fire burned all night, insulated from the covering hide by a layer of gravel: "Next morning when we opened the hole to feast, even the birds of the plains were made hungry by the smell of the cooked meat."

The Mandans and Arickaras yearned for a strange delicacy—the meat of drowned buffalo. Their villages, on the banks of the Missouri, overlooked the annual spring flotilla of buffalo carcasses. When the ice floes moved, every eye watched for the first floating, putrid body so that the village might miss none of the feasting, a time of "high spirits, anxiously waiting for the drowned Buffalo to pass." They paddled out on ice cakes and bull boats and towed the carcasses to shore, where everyone gorged on raw flesh so putrified they could eat it with horn spoons. A bad spring which brought no cargo of rotting flesh cast the Mandans into gloom. Some winters they couldn't wait for spring; then they piled snow over a buffalo carcass, left the gut unopened in order to putrify the meat. Or they drowned a few by chasing them onto thin ice, retrieved the carcasses, and left them "for some time to take flavor."

Buffalo people ate most parts of the animal although some refused to eat the thymus gland: they thought of it as a remnant of human flesh stuck in the throat of the last mythological buffalo to eat human flesh. And some people believed they shouldn't eat the heart; they left it to perpetuate the species. No people milked the cows; the thought of drinking milk revolted some of them, except while butchering.

Buffalo hunters gorged at feasts, ate what was at hand, worried not about tomorrow, sure that their hunting skill would bring more meat to camp even though bellies might shrink a little before fresh meat filled them again. Some men ate ten to fifteen pounds of meat in a night's feasting.

Between hunts, everyone ate everyday. Any tipi was open to any hungry passerby; he came, ate what he wished and left, following custom. Even in time of shortage each person received meat; a Blackfeet chief, for instance, rationed equal portions of meat to each head of a family—no matter how large the family.

We read accounts of hungry, wintering Indians, but this hunger often arose not because they could find no buffalo, but because they wouldn't hunt, preferring to grow gaunt rather than break camp in the cold to find a herd. And some came upon hard times not through buffalo shortage but through smallpox killing the best hunters. But usually when snow blew, dried meat supplies sufficed. And, since snow kept everyone from riding in war or horsestealing parties, winter, between hunts, was a fallow time. Hides from the fall hunt often lay stacked beside tipis, frozen stiff, unworkable until spring sun made them pliable. Mending chores, arrow-making chores, clothes-making chores could fill but few of the long winter hours. Feasting, gambling, religious duties, discussions and storytelling kept campfires glowing through tipi skin until long after dark; winter mornings were times for sleeping late, for lazing. A winter camp surrounded by snowdrifts felt little danger from raiders except during a prolonged chinook.

Spring meant earlier rising, meant robe making for the women, using hides now thawed, meant the first move to follow the buffalo. The tongue hungered for fat cow but the cows were wary and often bull meat filled the pot, sometimes varied with the veal of new born calf. Luckily, by late May, when the toothgrass bloomed, bull meat tasted the best it would all year. Meat was plentiful.

This time of year a camp moved often, heading for favorite camp grounds, places they'd named, here for a boy's prank, there for a topographical feature or an unusual happening, places they looked forward to because of pleasant memories or good water or natural beauty. If they followed a moving herd, they saw no reason to put up all the tipis for just overnight; friends shared a tipi or some people slept under the stars. If a night rainstorm doused the tipis, better to stay camped until they dried—a wet tipi overloaded a travois. A pleasant trip, journeying through the spring countryside.

Summer days saw the great gatherings of the Plains Indians such as the one that Jacob Fowler came upon: an Arapaho and "Chean" village of 900 lodges, each lodge holding twelve to twenty people[16]—an average, say, of sixteen, for a total of 14,400. These gatherings of Indians together coincided with the great gatherings of buffalo in the rut, the times when buffalo humps seemed to fill all of the space between a man and a horizon. Cows had begun to fatten after birthing; the massed animals ran but little from men; buffalo meat came campward every day. It had to: the camp of 14,400 people and their dogs would eat about 144 buffalo a day, 57,600 pounds of meat, assuming they mostly harvested cows at an average of 400 pounds of edible meat per animal[17]—an average of an animal a day brought down by each of the 100 hunters possessing good horses.

Summer saw the great rituals of horse stealing and resultant warfare: the rituals that buffalo plenty made time for. A man could afford to leave off hunting to go raiding; his family would eat well on buffalo provender: Blackfeet historian Returns With Plenty told of Miah, about to try for Cutthroat scalps and horses, who left it to his brothers-in-law to care for his wives. When he returned he found the women had been "well-supplied with meat."[18] A horse-stealing party or war party could travel miles with no need to burden itself with food for the expedition; it fed on buffalo. And if it found no buffalo, as did a Cree party on a raid into Snake country, it turned about: bellies were empty, the medicine for the expedition had become poor.

Each warrior killed fresh meat as he journeyed on a raid, but he carried a big parfleche of dried meat and some *depouille* with him for the days of closing on the enemy camp. He cached some of it close by before the raid; he wore a small pouch of it at his waist during the raid to carry him towards home if he couldn't retrieve his cache. It would do until he killed fresh meat.

Only gatherings of large numbers, gatherings that pooled warriors and food, could afford such war games, such prolonged absences from home. And such gatherings depended on a gigantic food supply, the buffalo.

Just as Coronado in the 1500s found the Apaches trading hides to the Pueblos, the La Vérendrye brothers, in the 1700s, found the buffalo tribes coming to Mandan villages to trade for corn. And Sergeant Gass, with Lewis and Clark in the 1800s, found people of "the Dog nation" trading surplus meat and robes to "Rickarees" for surplus corn and beans.[19] Soft, pliable, cozy robes—for warm cloaks and soft bedding, painstakingly fleshed and tanned—went for as much corn as the market would allow.

The buffalo hunters themselves used quantities of robes. During the day some of these lay rolled and stacked out of the way under tipi edge; at night, unrolled, they provided soft beds which held out the cold of any blizzard. Most buffalo Indians wore a buffalo robe summer and winter, often going naked under it. These were cow robes, hair left on, leather tanned to a white and decorated in color design, most often worn painted side out, clutched together from within. A well-dressed Indian might demand two new ones a year; thus he had two for sale to traders each year, more if an industrious wife prepared them for the painting. A man might paint his own robe or arrange to have one of the camp's robe painters do it for him, a man or woman: a man if he wanted schematic but realistic paintings of his exploits, a woman if he wanted schematic, symbolic paintings. Among the Comanche, an "hour-glass" figure often occupied the center of the robe, a stylized, geometric representation of the buffalo. Usually the painting on robes recorded the wearer's deeds in battle and hunt. The artists used paint brushes of soft, spongy buffalo bone—humerus or knee cap. Following the painting, a wife cut a fringe at the bottom of the robe and further decorated it with porcupine needles, then rubbed in white clay to give it its soft whiteness. From the deck of an approaching river boat, Indians on shore, in their whitish robes, looked like ghosts standing in the shadows of the trees.

Usually a woman had split the hide in half in skinning, a cut down the spine and another down the belly. She might further slice a wide belt of hide from hump and spine regions of these halves to rid herself of this difficult thick hide; she used it for other things. If she bothered to skin a bull, she sometimes left the thick hide over the hump on the carcass.

To prepare a half buffalo hide she first hung it by one corner from a post and removed the bits of flesh and subcutaneous tissue that clung to the skin by hacking at it with a toothed tool—about a half day's labor. Next she spread it on the ground, and standing on it, she thinned it, using an adze-like tool edged with flint or iron, which she changed or sharpened as it dulled. She removed about a third of the hide's thickness in another half day's labor.

This initial preparation done, the cleaned hide could be tanned with the hair on as for a robe, tanned after the hair had been removed (following a soaking in lye from ashes) as for tipi skins and other leather items, or left as untanned rawhide as for parfleches (the folded and laced rawhide boxes) and other containers, and for thongs, which, wound green around stone heads and wooden handles, shrank as they dried, to bind the two fast. The rawhide fastened around hooves made good horse shoes. It also made various kinds of useful lines to be used singly or braided. Green hides covered willow-framed, circular bull boats—the hair side in—and shrank to fit. To make thick, tough shield-leather, a woman alternately smoked and soaked bull hide, using a slow fire for the smoking.

To tan a robe, after it had been fleshed and scraped, a woman sprinkled a little melted grease over the skin and suspended it a few hours over a small fire, then she smeared it with a paste of boiled brains or liver mixed with grass, roots or bark. It could now be dried and preserved in such a mixture and finished later. Since this shrank it, she next pegged it to stretch it,

Blackfeet woman wearing tanned buffalo hide in the usual way—tanned side out. *Courtesy University of Montana Archives, Missoula.*

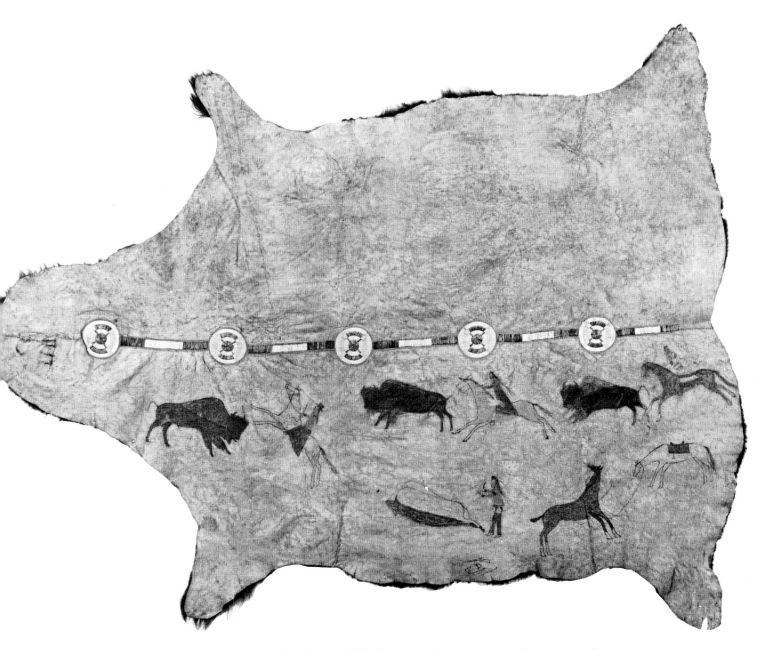

A Shoshone-decorated buffalo robe. Probably the naturalistic painting is by a man and the geometric quill work by a woman. *Courtesy Buffalo Bill Historical Center, Cody, Wyoming.*

then washed and scraped the stretched hide until it turned white. Then she slowly heated it again over a fire and rubbed it with a pumice rock or spongy shoulder bone until about half dry, when she began the final operation—drawing it back and forth through a loop of a rope tied at each end to a lodgepole, or over a post top, rubbing it and heating it, sometimes smoking it if she wanted yellow leather instead of white, until dry and soft. She could produce brown or grayed leather by the smoke from various roots and barks.

When she had readied the two halves she cut the pegging holes from the edges and sewed the two together. The robe was ready for painting if to be worn, or ready for bed, floor, or willow backrest.[20] It weighed about ten pounds, thirty to forty pounds less than when green.

If a woman tanned continuously, rather than at her convenience, she could tan a robe in about three days, making "the skin just as soft and durable as our leather dressers do in 6 months," creating a leather

"Squaws Curing Hides." Theodore Davis, *Harper's Magazine*, January 1869. *Courtesy Amon Carter Museum, Fort Worth, Texas.*

that might be soaked and dried repeatedly without stiffening. Three-day robes sometimes meant robes done for the robe trade; personal robes might be kept moist for ten days during the process and rubbed across the pole many more times.

The women cleaned these family robes with white clay, rubbed in and brushed off when dry, or rubbed them clean with porous rock or bone. The Crow, Cheyenne and Sioux women made the robes most admired by whites; for one thing they had hides of northern buffalo to work with, hides that developed a more luxuriant growth of hair.

Tipi skins came from old, thin cows killed in the summer when the new hair was short and easy to remove. After soaking the hide a woman removed this hair by striking at its roots with a rock, chipping it off without pitting the hide, and by scraping. The women who would live in the new tipi tanned the skins, but the intricate cutting—as many as thirty-five large and small pieces out of eighteen to twenty-five whole skins—often became the task of a woman specially known for her craft. Neighbors joined in on the sewing much like in our old-fashioned quilting bees; everyone working together could make a new tipi in one day. They sewed with buffalo sinew from along the spine that they'd removed, scraped, softened by

soaking and rubbing between hands, then repeatedly stripped to create a tough thread; even later it proved more serviceable than trader's cotton or hemp: a sinew had about ten times the strength of a similar cotton thread. As a needle they used a sharp bone splinter or a buffalo-berry thorn.

The new tipi in place, the women tore the old one apart and saved the pieces for clothing, the smoke-saturated top pieces used especially for moccasin soles. A new tipi a year marked the good tipiwife; an industrious village shone with new, white tipis.

The Crow told a tale of a mythical woman whose husband demanded she tan a robe in one day. A typical fairy tale character, she cried instead of going to work, but animals pitied her and helped her. Beavers and badgers pegged her hide; rats, moles, mice, ants, bees and flies dried and scraped it; a skunk, beavers and badgers helped to soften it; the porcupine gave its quills. And the robe was done on time.[21]

The American Indian, deluged with buffalo manna, found thousands of original uses for it.

He was born on it—what nicer maternity couch than the softness of the robe? And immediately after birth he was dusted in a powder of buffalo chip and fine clay or puffball, wrapped in a layer of hair from

72

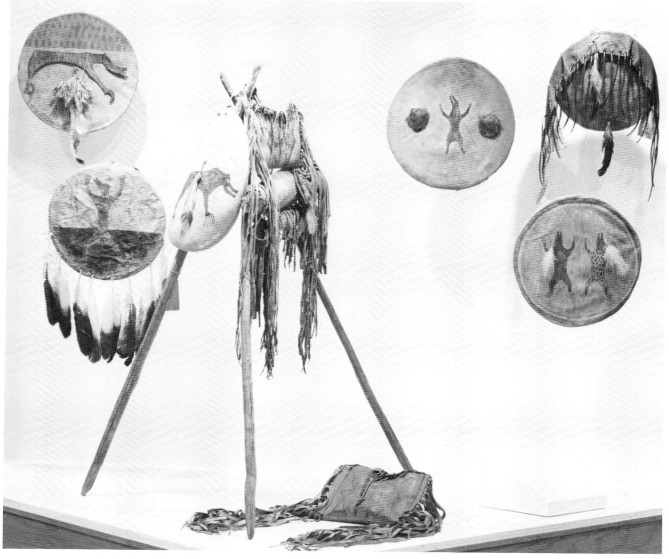

Display of bullhide shields (left to right): Crow, c. 1870, Sioux, c. 1875, Crow, c. 1860, Hidatsa, c. 1875, Hidatsa, c. 1885, Sioux, c. 1880. *Courtesy Buffalo Bill Historical Center, Cody, Wyoming.*

the buffalo's head, then in a tanned calf-skin and laid on a piece of stiff rawhide. Shredded buffalo chip made up his diapers.

As a child he spun tops made from horn tips on the ice, or threw yearling horns attached to long sticks to make them slide. He slid down hills on sleds improvised from buffalo briskets tied to shape with the neck cords, or on some backbone and ribs or piece of buffalo hide. He took turns being tossed in a robe. He rolled, kicked and tossed balls made of buffalo skin stuffed with buffalo hair. He spun buffalo ankle bones on sinew—bull roarers—to fill long, winter, tipi-bound evenings. He could annoy elders with various bone rattles. And he piled up, used as targets, tossed about and flung at other children a lot of buffalo chips.

As a young man he went a-courting in a fancy buffalo robe pulled up to cover his head. To prove his ability to provide, he took his lady out to the buffalo herd and downed, for her own robe, the buffalo she chose; she proved her ability as wife in the tanning of it. They both rode saddles padded with buffalo leather stuffed with buffalo hair, and they used as saddle-blanket a calf-skin. They both spent hours brushing their long black hair with a rough buffalo tongue scorched to hardness or a porcupine tail. Likely they both greased their hair with back fat, sometimes greasing their bodies as well. He twisted or glued buffalo hair into his own hair until it reached to the ground; she sometimes wore false tresses also. In the hide-covered sweat bath each used the fluffy tail to expunge water onto the hot stones to raise steam.

73

Indians crossing the Missouri in "Bull Boats." Charles Graham, *Frank Leslie's Illustrated Newspaper*, May 4, 1878. *Courtesy The Library Company of Philadelphia.*

In everyday life each would find a myriad of uses for buffalo products. Stiff, untanned hides made good windbreaks and sunshades. Bones made handles, or, when drilled, made arrow straighteners. They made admirable splints for broken human bones—put on green and allowed to tighten around the break. Whitened shoulder blades made slates for pictographic messages. Some bows were fashioned from ribs, and bow strings from the large tendon below the shoulder blade. A hoof left on a leg bone made a good mallet. Horns made up into various spoons and cups, arrowheads, clothing decoration, club heads—innumerable objects. The paunch and pericardium made good water containers but were extremely perishable; the first duty of women after the hunt, even before caring for the meat, was to fill these with hot tallow and preserve them in shaped holes in the ground until needed. In use a paunch hung from a lodgepole. Squeezing its sides brought water to the top for drinking. Most tribes cooked in the paunch held upright on sticks, boiling the contents by slipping in heated rocks.

Long hairs from between the horns braided into usable ropes, although horsehair was "much stronger." A buffalo-scalp bridle, wiry and light, had the advantage of being easily held in the teeth while swimming next to one's mount. Hair bracelets were common and hair made warm insulation when stuffed inside an oversize moccasin. Warm boots and caps were fashioned from hide, hair side in.

A buffalo Indian, like the Armour Company with the hog, used everything from the buffalo but the grunt. His corpse continued the use: it was shrouded in a robe.

The availability of buffalo discouraged tribes in buffalo country from practicing agriculture; in fact, tribes such as the Crow and Cheyenne had given up farming to become buffalo hunters. Buffalo tribes had plenty to eat, suffered no vitamin deficiency because they ate all of the innards, and, whatever variety of diet they craved, they satisfied by using the numerous wild berries, roots, greens and seeds of the grasslands. Even east of the Mississippi, the buffalo's numbers, although not as great as west of it, may have hindered the development of agriculture by providing an easier way of living, one that kept the peoples happy with subsistence agriculture.

The plains Indian depended too much upon the buffalo: although he seemed the most wealthy and most independent of hunting peoples, he was also the least diversified—his entire social and economic order depended upon plenty of buffalo. Consequently when bad weather kept the buffalo away, when accident or war destroyed the dried meat supply, or when white man's disease killed off hunters, many buffalo peoples, having forgotten how to fish, unskillful as trappers, suffered more privation than people such as the Cree who trapped and fished as well as hunted buffalo. Following the destruction of the buffalo in the 1880s the Pueblos, the Kwakiutls, the northern Crees maintained their way of life; the prairie tribes—without food, without robes, skins and sinew, without buffalo ceremony and ritual—disintegrated.

"Do not let your spirit touch my spirit to do me harm."
PRAYER TO BUFFALO

A BUFFALO INDIAN often arose before dawn to watch the greatness of the coming light, the first graying, the pale blue followed by the pink clouds; these pulled behind them the sun, forced it once more into the sky; pale morning light each day brought forth—*created*—the sun. The Indian prayed his morning prayer to the sun, the giver of life, the giver of buffalo to man.

But, likely as not, outside his tipi the evening before, he had cast a buffalo stone on the ground to foretell tomorrow's luck. Buffalo power and sun power intertwined to make good medicine.

The man with a buffalo stone knew buffalo would fall to his arrows and rain would erase his tracks in front of pursuing enemies. At night, in the glow of the tipi fire, he told once more how he came by his lucky, buffalo-shaped amulet (pebble or fossil).

He had heard it singing, he said, singing a song that his ears recognized as no bird song, the magical sound a buffalo rock sang. He had slid off his horse to search about the grass bunches for the singer. But although he'd searched until dark, sniffing for the odor such a rock emitted, he found no humped buffalo-shaped pebble, no curled ammonite. He'd ridden toward home thinking he'd heard a bird song, not a rock song. Then he'd almost bumped into a grey, ghostly

buffalo in the dusk, and he knew him for a sign. Early next morning he'd ridden back. There, almost on the spot where his moccasin had first stepped, lay his curled stone. Big Medicine. A male rock—see how it's wrapped—definitely a male. Once he had wrapped male and female buffalo rock together and they had produced little buffalo rock offspring—but everyone did that with buffalo rocks. Everyone had seen the care he took of it, greasing it with castoreum, wrapping it in leather; everyone had seen his many horses, his big tipi, his good wives; everyone had seen him cast his rock to learn the good days to hunt, the bad days to war, had heard his prayers to it, knew he wore it on his successful horse raids.

A fossil, a pebble, curved buffalo-like, held buffalo power; a stone, carved buffalo-shape, held buffalo power. A rock, jutting hump-shaped above the grass, held buffalo power; any hunter riding nigh knew to drop an offering at it: an eagle feather, a bit of clothing, a bead, an animal skin, a bit of pemmican. Anything to acquire a little of the rock's power.

For buffalo were magic. Some believed they had the power, after being eaten, to reflesh themselves and live again.

No man had ever scanned a land full to the horizon circle with antelope, with deer or jackrabbit, as

Oftentimes a Plains Indian carried, for good medicine, an uncarved stone in which he saw a buffalo shape. *Courtesy Provincial Museum and Archives of Alberta.*

he had with buffalo. Although a prairie dog town stretched for miles and teemed with bodies (the estimated five billions of prairie dogs on the plains outnumbered the estimated thirty to sixty millions of buffalo), only buffalo numbers filled the hunter's dreams; prairie dogs, like sparrows, seemed boy's prey. Also, lakes and rivers teemed with trout and bass, but gathering fish to a Blackfeet was downright revolting—he'd eat none of it.

On the Pacific Coast, salmon filled the Columbia and the Frazer, but fish had little of the magical appeal that the buffalo did. On the Atlantic seashore, shellfish, like dropped acorns, lay scattered thick for the gathering, and alewives choked the streams, but no magical clam or godlike fish filled men's concepts of life and the supernatural.

No danger lay in these plentiful foods as lay in the chanced sudden reviving of a half-dead buffalo bull under the skinner's knife, no danger to give a harvester pride in taking such a monster. No sensuous pleasure of hands dipped into warm entrails came from these cold bloods. Nor did these plenties provide as much for a good life as did the buffalo. A man wore no fish skins, nor lived in clam shells, nor sewed with ligaments from fish or clam.

Algonquin tribes of the north experienced a "demiurge" toward a symbolic Great Hare (which perhaps, as buffalo tribes, they transferred to the buffalo). And deer hunters came to revere the deer, but entire deer

herds seldom pushed themselves into bow range, nor did deer herds surround the deer hunter day and night moving within sight and hearing as did the buffalo. No deer herds had to be chased away from tipis. Buffalo at a waterhole had little of the deer's take a step or two, look around, drink a swallow or two, freeze in watchfulness, bolt at a twig snap, that made deer such unsure prey.

The buffalo had early come to mean something more to man than meat to eat, skin and sinew for clothes and shelter, bones for clubs or earth tampers. At a prehistoric site near Cody, Wyoming, where 180 fossil bison were found, the hunters had removed the tops of the skulls and the horns and carried them away, as if for ceremonial use (they're not scattered nearby as if the butchers had opened a cranial hole to scoop out the brains for hide tanning). Occasional ancient bison bones carry inscribings, whether decorative or ceremonial no one knows; other bones have seemingly been purposely split, whether ceremonially or for marrow, no one knows.[1] Buffalo and buffalo ceremony seem to have gone together early in the culture of the buffalo hunter.

The buffalo herds gave a way of life to the buffalo hunters, a vision of existence developed through their nomadic following of buffalo and their use of buffalo for food, clothing, shelter and implements. Theirs was the Plains culture.

The tribes involved in Plains culture used the skin-covered tipi, the travois pulled by dog and horse, depended much upon the buffalo chip as fuel, ate jerky and pemmican; they developed a plains-wide sign language to converse with other groups. The buffalo tribes engaged in ritualistic warfare. Common to most of the tribes was the counting of coup: a greater honor could come to a warrior from touching an enemy than from killing him. The use of a police force to govern their marches and their hunts was common to all. They were ritualistic peoples who used smoking ceremonies, used the buffalo chip as a sacred item to swear on, or as a ritualistic mix on top of a pipeful of tobacco, or as a pipe rest to assure the pipe touched not the earth, or an altar or a sacred mound. Most of these tribes performed the Sun Dance as a most important ritual of the summer gatherings and shared the great reverence for the sun as the giver of life. They were similar in the use of the vision quest by the young men as a means of finding a ritualistic and symbolistic center to their lives, in the use of sweathouse ceremonies, in a belief in the ritualistic magic of the numeral four, in uses of magic buffalo protection—the buffalo stone, decorations of buffalo hair, horn and other parts. Most tribes thought of the hereafter as a place where life and the hunting of buffalo went on as in the here and now.

Some of these things infiltrated the old plains culture (the culture that the Spaniards observed in the Querechos) from the eastern Iroquoian and Algonquin cultures as these peoples infiltrated the Plains: the policing of hunts, the counting of coup, the vision quest may have come into Plains culture with these tribes. But the great beliefs in the magic of the buffalo, the desire for his protection, the rituals designed to assure good luck in hunting and continued buffalo plenty, as well as the customs necessary to the buffalo hunt and the nomadic life, developed with peoples who for a long time had lived among and followed the herds.

Although people wandered amongst the buffalo on the high plateaus near the Rockies from the late Paleolithic to modern times, no remnants of their language existed in the tribes found there by the Europeans. Those Apaches found on the plains by the Spaniards seemed acculturated to the plains and buffalo ecology, but their language is related to the Athabaskan of the far north; they had moved south to desert lands, had not descended from ancient buffalo hunters here. The Kiowas of southern Kansas also lived on the plains pre-historically, either a continuation of an age-old residency or an emigration from parts unknown (their language relates to Pueblan

groups). The Blackfeet and Arapaho-Gros Ventres were old occupants of the northern plains but had come from the eastern woodlands, pushed there by the Cree. The Pawnee, the Kiowa-Apache and the eastern Shoshoneans also had come to live the buffalo life by the time of the Spaniards. All of these had moved to the plains from the fringes; none seem to have sprung from the ancient nomadic hunters of the high plateau.

The Cheyennes and other latecomers to the buffalo life adopted the nomad life and buffalo economy. The old timers taught them how to hunt and ride, how to tan robes and make tipis; and as they learned this, the newcomers assimilated much of their teachers' mythology and embellished their own beliefs to fit the new life style. All of them who lived amongst the herds developed differing buffalo mythologies, although they all looked upon the buffalo as a gift from the sun (to the Kiowa the buffalo stood as the sun personified). The sun, the giver of life, had made the special gift of the buffalo to chosen people that they might live in plenty. Perhaps not a direct gift, but a gift provided by supernatural human beings:

The Cheyennes said buffalo came from a wonderful sack: Wihio (Great Spirit) stopped overnight in the tipi of a man who had a big sack hanging from a lodge pole. This man had plenty meat drying about his lodge, but no game grazed nearby. Wihio was very curious about the sack. That night while the man slept he stole it. He carried it far, far off, carried it until he had to sleep. But when he awoke he was back in the man's lodge, stretched out in his bed-place, his head resting on the sack.

"What are you doing with my sack?" asked the man.

"You've been so nice I thought I'd carry it for you," said Wihio.

The man said not a word, but tied the sack back on the lodge pole. Wihio wanted that sack; he puzzled how to get it. Then he found out that the man was frightened of geese. So he pretended to leave, but that night he sneaked back into the tipi in the shape of a goose. The man ran off into the night, but he took his sack with him. Wihio followed, and in his goose shape frightened the man one, two, three times. The fourth, the magical time, the man dropped the sack and ran off calling out, "I can only open the sack four times."

When Wihio returned to his lodge, he opened the sack and a buffalo bull ran out. He could see the heads of buffalo cows in the sack, so he quickly tied it. He killed the buffalo and ate well. When the meat was gone, he let another buffalo out of the sack and killed it. He let another one out the third time he needed meat and another one the fourth time. But the fifth time he opened the sack all of the buffalo rushed out, trampled him and his family to death and scattered north, south, east and west. And that's where all of the buffalo came from. So said the Cheyenne. But the Cheyenne also tell of two boys releasing the buffalo from a magical spring. And another story of theirs tells of Ehyophstah, the yellow-haired woman, whose influence brought the buffalo to them, but whose later disobedience lost them.

When the Comanches told of the first coming of the buffalo, they said: An old woman and her young cousin had had all of the buffalo penned. Coyote came to the Indians and together they planned to free them. They put a little animal out where the young cousin would find it and take it home as a pet; there it would release the buffalo according to Coyote's instruction. The suspicious old woman refused two pets, saying, "Everything on earth is a no good schemer"; but she gave in to the young cousin's wishes for a third animal. That night it howled, scaring the buffalo into breaking down their pens and coming to live on earth. So said the Comanche.

The Blackfeet tribes had still a different magical tale about this: A long time ago a man and his wife and son owned all of the buffalo. The people prayed to Old Man, saying, "The buffalo and antelope are gone. Help us or we will die." Old Man heard them, and, taking a young man with him, went to find the buffalo. By and by they came to the lone lodge of the man who kept the buffalo, whereupon Old Man changed himself into a little dog and his friend changed into a rootdigger (a stick used by Indian women to dig roots). The woman found the stick, the little boy found the dog. Each kept the find, though the man objected. The next day when the woman and the boy went to dig roots they walked near a buffalo cow standing in the mouth of a cave. Instantly the stick and the dog darted into the cave, found all of the buffalo and drove them out, themselves riding out hidden in the long hair of the last buffalo bull. So said the Blackfeet.

A Crow story tells of a race of giants who ate no buffalo but used them as horses, who held their noses as men cooked and ate "stinking" buffalo, giants who gave to four men buffalo they had kept in a hole in the ground. Many tribes believed all the buffalo came from and disappeared now and then into a hole in the ground. Why else would the plains hold thousands

one day and none the next? Northern tribes located the buffalo home under a Canadian lake. Some tribes believed herds came out of the south, moved north never to return.

Most of the buffalo-hunting tribes also told tales of the early time when the question arose whether buffalo should eat man-flesh or man eat buffalo-flesh. In those days, before man had weapons, buffalo had killed and eaten many men (leading to the Cheyenne belief that the buffalo's thymus gland was a remnant of jerked man-flesh stuck in the throat of the last buffalo to eat man-flesh). The Blackfeet believed that when Old Man, the Maker of People, saw his Blackfeet dead and torn to pieces by the buffalo, he pitied them, and showed them how to make the bow. When next the buffalo chased them saying "Saiyah, there is some more of our food," the Blackfeet killed buffalo. Old Man gave them flint knives to cut up buffalo and showed them how to make fire and cook. The buffalo had become man food. The Cheyenne told of a great foot race that decided who was to eat flesh and who was to eat grass. A Cheyenne man won the race against all of the animals (with the help of a magpie). The old men buffalo told him, "From now on everything will be done by the outcome of this race. You are on top now, above every animal and everything in the world. All we animals can do is supply the things you will use from us." When men became the eaters of buffalo flesh they also became users of buffalo hide: a supernatural woman put poles together, tanned hides, showed how to sew them together and cover the poles to make a tipi.

The buffalo came to be the chief animal spirit (to the Cree he was The Master Spirit of Food—the giver of all). The buffalo made the greatest medicine of all the animals, greater than that of the bear, or the raven or the wolf . . . although all were the friends of man. Bear smelled, heard and saw well, and he could cure himself; he traveled quickly and fought fiercely. Raven spotted game at long distances; he helped man by flying in the direction of game. Wolf hunted craftily, stole upon his prey, attacked savagely, endured the long chase; people liked to see him out in the sagebrush traveling parallel with them as they moved camp, for he meant good luck in hunting.

All of the animals had superhuman powers and if pleaded to might reward a man with some of these attributes. A man who had adorned his shield with eagle feathers might acquire the swiftness and courage of that bird; owl feathers might give a man the power to move silently and see in the dark. For animals could do many things better than men: fly, swim, stay out in the blizzard, run, smell, fight, dig—each had his own special powers that men needed.

The buffalo, the biggest animal, made the greatest medicine—he and the grizzly bear. His size, his numbers, his endurance outdid that of other animals. He could kill any man—yet he ran when hunted; he could outfight any other animal—yet he gave his body to men. He was big medicine. If buffalo lay dead from the hunt, they must be thanked for giving up their lives, lest the great buffalo spirit be offended. Perhaps a robe left behind might thank them for so many dying that man might live.

A man who wanted power hoped for a vision of an animal by which he might acquire some of its power, for he interpreted such a vision to mean that the animal favored him. As a young man he quested for such a vision to start a direction for his life; as an older man he quested for new guidance. Each quested by going to some lonely and dangerous place to lie for a magic four days, choosing perhaps a cliff ledge or a much-used buffalo trail, a butte top or the base of a pictograph panel on a cliff. Here he fasted and thirsted, smoked his pipe occasionally (a Crow might whack off a finger to give to the sun). He lay in the heat of the sun and the cold of the moon; some men chose to lie two days on one side and two days on the other. Stomach shrank, tongue parched, muscles cramped— and visions came; dreams while asleep, hallucinations while awake. A passing animal seemed to speak or toss its head in a significant way. Stompings in the brush, howlings or snortings took on meanings. His eyes and ears picked up the slightest animal movement, magnified it into significance. He prayed for animal appearance: a rabbit would do; a fox or a beaver also; a wolf or a bear or a raven would reassure him. A buffalo would give him confidence that his would be a good life. Once his dream had come, he reached for his medicine pipe to smoke while he interpreted what he must understand from his protector.

Yet he need not dream of a buffalo to be able to call upon buffalo protection. A wolf-person or bear-person also prayed to buffalo, asked them to run on level land only, to choose no rough country upon which horses might stumble in the chase and injure riders. Any man's sweat lodge faced an ancient, dried buffalo skull. When he emerged after purification, he smoked to it and asked the buffalo to be plentiful, asked it to flesh itself once more and join the herds. Here in this low, willow-frame hut, sealed and darkened by buffalo hide coverings, he had purified himself in four sweatings in steam. Now he would face the sun and the great buffalo spirit.

Any buffalo thing might bring a man good medicine. If a man thought of fighting enemies, he looked in a cup of badger and buffalo blood. If in it he saw an enemy scalp, he daubed on his war paint; if he saw himself scalped, he put his paints away. Or he looked in the blood at his reflection. If his face seemed old and wrinkled, he would live to an old age; if hair fell down over his image, he would die a natural death. If he fell ill, buffalo parts and special rituals performed by men known as Buffalo Doctors might cure him. A peculiar horn, or a lopped ear or a bobbed tail on a buffalo kill might mean good luck. So might a rare spotted hide or a curly-haired hide; or the smooth round ball found sometimes in a buffalo's stomach. A man might purify himself by dragging about camp buffalo skulls tied by thongs to slits cut in his back. A man could gain buffalo power by carrying his arrows in a quiver made of buffalo-calf skin. To appease the buffalo, he might, after eating, present a bowlful of meat to a buffalo skull saying, "Eat that." If a man swam poorly he could tie some buffalo gut, grease and bladder to a stick and set it afloat in a stream, saying "This is to enable me to cross without accident, let no wind blow, nor pain take me in crossing." If a crossing place looked threatening to a Crow, he dropped an offering of fat buffalo meat into the water—if it sank something might go wrong in the fording.

A man might gain buffalo power by the luck of killing a rare white buffalo. These, men said, were the chiefs of the buffalo: other buffalo respected them, for they stayed away from where they grazed, gave them room to themselves. The rare jet-black buffalo, black even as a calf, also made big medicine—but not as much as the white buffalo.

Many tribes venerated the white buffalo, and some tribes, having killed a white animal, left it unskinned to rot where it lay, only counting coup upon it. Other tribes nervously skinned it. A Piegan, Medicine Weasel, having killed one and promised the tongue and robe to the sun, "trembled so, that he could not use his knife, and some of our party took off the hide for him, and cut out the tongue, he standing over them all the time and begging them to be careful, to make no gashes, for they were doing the work for the Sun."[2] Some tribes brought the hide to camp to be consecrated by a renowned warrior and a medicine man and to be tanned by certain consecrated women. Although worshippers might count coup on a white buffalo kill and take the hide, the carcass often lay unused or perhaps only a kidney eaten, for eating such flesh made one's hair turn prematurely grey. The Crow offered the hide to the sun in a sunrise ceremony and prayed to it. During this ceremony each person came forward to touch the hide, to partake a bit of its power.

Some tribes saw nothing sacred in white hides; they saved them as valuable items to trade to the tribes that did or to the white man who valued its curiosity or to the trader who saw profit in it. Francois Chardon at Fort Clark on the Missouri sold a white robe to the Mandans for thirty robes and two horses.[3]

The brown buffalo bull often wandered about mud-caked to a clay grey. This change of color came to symbolize his powerful nature; men daubed mud over their bodies, greyed themselves to gain the muddy bull's power. The mud-caked, grey-colored bull may also have peopled the legends of ghost buffalo, a monster of the night plains.

Another buffalo monster filled Indian legend, the double-toothed bull, he who grew double incisors in both his upper and lower jaw. Small and humpless, with short horns and short snout, he came into camps stealthily and ate people. But he came once too often to a Shoshone camp: they killed him and he's not been seen since. A band of Arapahoes venerated a "petrified buffalo," perfectly preserved, they said, near Fort Hall. The Blackfeet told of a giant buffalo that lived along the Missouri—so big that the river's water couldn't cover his hump. And, according to "Joway" Indian tradition, a high isolated rock on the left bank of the Missouri was the petrified remnant of buffalo dung deposited by a similar giant buffalo.

Mythical buffalo had human weaknesses, such as gullibility: Old Man and Fox had tried all the ways of killing four Bulls, but no success. At last Old Man plucked all the hair from Fox but for a tuft at the end of his tail and sent him running and tumbling past the Bulls. When the Bulls saw this, they began to laugh—and they laughed themselves to death. And another time: Coyote challenged Buffalo to a race. Coyote chose a place near a cliff; Buffalo stupidly raced over its brink; Coyote ate him.

Buffalo were born, they suckled, they copulated, they bore children, they suffered old age, they died. Buffalo fought, bled, starved, drowned, froze. Buffalo were afraid, buffalo were brave. Buffalo swam, walked,

and ran. Man and buffalo shared the water and the land. They shared life.

Storytellers told of buffalo who shed their shaggy hump and cloven feet, their horns, to walk upright as men. They told of bulls who married girls, of men who married or copulated with heifers. Offspring from such couplings might look and behave like men, or like buffalo, or change back and forth from four-legged to two-legged, hairy to almost hairless.

The Crow told a story of a man and heifer marriage: A man married a buffalo cow. She turned into a beautiful woman. She said, "I don't care if you beat me, but don't ever call me names." All was well. They had a son. Then one day the man forgot and said, "You look like a ghost." That night she went back to the buffalo and she took the son with her. The man, sad for what he'd done and lonesome for his wife and son, went among the herds, crying. At last his son, now a calf, saw him and ran up to him saying, "Don't cry. Tomorrow when a lot of calves run by, if you can pick out your own son they'll let you have me. When I run by I'll shake my left ear so you can know me." The next day the calves ran by, the calf-son shook his left ear and the man chose him. He still wanted his wife. His calf-son said, "Tomorrow when the cows run by you'll have to choose your wife or the bulls will trample you. I'll play with my mother in the wallow and smear her tail and legs with mud. Then you'll know her." The next day the man chose the muddy-tailed cow. "You may take them back," said the bulls. The man took them back; they became human. And the man didn't call her names ever again.

Another Crow story is of an unmarried mother who put her baby in a buffalo wallow: Seven bulls discovered him. They decided to keep him and gave him to one of their number, Crazy Buffalo, because such a child just suited him. They made him a bow and arrow and taught him to shoot. In winter he lay warm in the thickest hair of his friends. One day other buffalo killed his seven friends, but even so these others befriended the boy, taking care of him and giving him of their teeth and fine robes. Finally they sent the boy back to his own tribe where he became a mighty buffalo hunter who always took care to protect the seven bulls who'd befriended him (they'd come alive). And when he married, his son could become a calf and change back to being a boy again as he wished. When he was older, his father took him to be raised by the buffalo that he might learn all of their lore.

When a man had a specific animal's power he was a person-bear, or a person-rabbit, or a person-buffalo. A

Pipe carved in graystone by an unknown Sioux. *Courtesy Amon Carter Museum, Fort Worth, Texas.*

person-buffalo might believe he could feel a buffalo kicking inside of him. When his neighbor, person-wolf, saw him come out of the tipi, he saw a person-buffalo who seemed to him a little humped and shaggy. When person-buffalo noticed person-wolf standing there next door, he saw something of his fangs and tail.

When the herds wandered afar, when no ear cocked down a badger hole heard a faraway hoof rumble, when scouts found no buffalo, then everyone knew the buffalo had returned underground, using the hole through which they'd first appeared, and that he must help to enchant the herds into returning.

Many tribes used buffalo skulls to attract a herd. Some laid out on a knoll a medicine charm circle of skulls twenty feet or so in diameter, a large skull in the center, the others all pointed nose toward it, decorated with paint. To attract buffalo the Comanche might ring a camp with old skulls pointing toward it. A Crow medicine man pointed campward just one skull, sang all that night; six buffalo stood nearby in the morning, more the next morning; when the tribe had killed enough meat, he turned the head; the buffalo came no more.

Some peoples played a hoop game to entice buffalo. The Arikara believed in the power of an oblong parfleche stuffed with seven gourds plus the remains of local birds—the "birdcase." Carrying a whole buffalo carcass (minus head and entrails) to the birdcase a magical four times could assure a man he'd never want for buffalo. On high rimrocks the Assiniboines piled rocks into a cairn surmounted by a buffalo skull to attract the herds. The Blackfeet built pyramids of elk horns and buffalo horns, each passerby throwing on another horn.

Some Indian buffalo hunters specialized in charming the buffalo into coming nearby, having found the specialty in dreams. One man dreamt of a man with a rattle who could bring buffalo. The dream man instructed him to make a similar rattle, to paint buffalo tracks on his tipi, to bellow in imitation of a bull, a cow and a calf, to sing the dream song and to roll in the mud like a bull. He did, and "next morning the whole plain was covered with buffalo." The famous Pawnee, Carrying Mother, could command escaping buffalo to return by waving a flag from a nearby hilltop; he fed multitudes from one magic little piece of buffalo meat and changed buffalo chips into pounded meat and pemmican by covering them with his robe.

The Mandans, who feared they might encounter Sioux if they ventured far from their permanent sod and log villages, preferred to dance back the buffalo. They devised many varieties of rituals to enchant them.

When young scouts reported buffalo, but yet at a distance, a buffalo dance began, performed by dancers each wearing a buffalo head and carrying a bow or lance. They danced incessantly, day and night, shaking rattles, singing and yelling, ten or fifteen dancers at a time, others watching, waiting to dance when these men tired. The dance ceased when the buffalo appeared. Since the dancers might perform for days, even weeks—time enough for the herds to wander close—the dancing always brought buffalo.

The Mandans depended upon many other magical ceremonies to bring the buffalo to them and to insure successful hunting. All plains tribes similarly danced and performed buffalo-attracting ceremonies.

All tribes honored the sun, the buffalo, and other mystical things in the annual Sun Dance, the chief ceremony of the summer. Through the ceremony the buffalo people expected the sun to do something for them and for all people: give them long life, good health, success in the hunt, many horses, many buffalo, much grass and much rainfall.

The ceremony took at least four days of midsummer. It came about because someone had vowed to sponsor the ceremony: a woman promised it to the sun if her sick child was cured, a man offered it if his life was spared, a person sponsored it because of a dream. Such a sponsor took on much responsibility. The sun had heard the vows; should accident or miscarriage of ritual mar the ceremonies, the sun had rejected the sponsor's claims to purity. All would scorn that one.

Much buffalo ritual filled this ceremony. Usually a sponsor saw to the gathering of tongues and backfat for the rituals; the eating of buffalo flesh from a ritually killed bull took place in most such ceremonies—chewing of backfat, the tasting of a bit of sanctified tongue, a ritual similar to Christian eating of bread and drinking of wine. Painted buffalo skulls, symbolizing the earth, made altars. Buffalo chips made a sacred pile to count coup upon. Buffalo robes, made sacred by some peoples through symbolically spitting upon five times, were worn; other robes were sliced in ritual to make consecrated belts and consecrated thongs for tying together the poles of the medicine lodge. Perhaps a buffalo effigy tied to the center pole hung there until ceremonially shot down.

The Sun Dance ceremonies practiced by the Sioux, the Arapaho and others early on the plains, were copied by latecoming tribes—more than copied: changed and added to so that each ceremony varied in detail of ritual.

Other Indian ritual used the medicine inherent in buffalo parts. The dried skull found itself used as an altar, in the sweat house ceremony and corn festivals, as a pillow for a vision seeker; the eating of bits of the tongue and the eating of heart gave men strength, the eating of the liver strong eyesight. Parts of the buffalo repeated in symbol brought power: the feathered tail of the Crow "war bonnet" represents the buffalo backbone. The Mandans kept tails and teeth in sacred bundles. The Pawnees kept sacred buffalo scapulae to use in their corn dance. At the end of this dance, hunting luck could be foretold by examining the dance ground: if many buffalo hairs lay about, many buffalo would graze nearby. Other signs could foretell buffalo whereabouts: a walking-stick insect squeezed and asked where to find buffalo would walk toward them; a horned toad asked the same question ran toward them.

Many ceremonies or rituals used the buffalo chip. A Crow village, seeing its scouts coming in howling like wolves and kicking the ever handy buffalo chips ahead of them, knew they had sighted enemies. A Cheyenne used a chip as a pipe rest. Some men refused all pipes but those which used powdered chip atop their tobacco as tinder. A Crow Indian kept a chip in his sacred bundle—a chip at least fifty years old; once a year he opened the bundle, sprinkled bits of the chip in the fire and talked to the smoke. An old medicine man purified his medicine bundles, if they had been knocked to the ground, in the smoke of a chip fire on which he sprinkled sweet grass. A Crow shaman used a broken buffalo chip to conjure buffalo into coming close. He made buffalo tracks all about the swept floor of his tipi, placed the broken chip in one, and on it placed a buffalo-shaped rock, and smeared the rock with grease. He said, "Buffalo are coming, bid the men drive them here." The buffalo came; the men drove them over a cliff.

Buffalo could bestow favors upon men—they gave of their own kind that people might eat, might tell in a dream the location of a herd. Some people thought that in such tellings only the buffalo bull talked—but talked to men or women, although buffalo were usually thought of as associated with men; smaller animals such as the otter, swan, owl and squirrel were

"Sun dance" worshippers revered the buffalo as much as the sun. A Sioux chief, Short Bull, painted these. *Courtesy American Museum of Natural History.*

A painted skull, stuffed with sweet grass, used in religious ceremonies. *Courtesy Museum of the American Indian, Heye Foundation.*

associated with women. To Humped Buffalo, a Crow, worried over a wound, a dream buffalo communicated only by opening his mouth to show his toothless gums; Humped Buffalo knew by this he would live to be a toothless old man, and worried no more over his wound. Buffalo became his medicine, he became "heavy and slow in battle," he wouldn't run away no matter what happened. Buffalo of the olden days had told men how to cook buffalo meat and how to prepare buffalo hides, and a magical buffalo head had arisen out of a lake to give instructions for making a buffalo shield.

Buffalo, the center of life, controlled the destinies of men and earth. The Skidi Pawnee held that the father of all buffalo stood at a north gate "where the heavens touch the earth"; each year he shed some of his hairs—the world will end when all the hair has dropped.

Old Man once decided man's fate by a buffalo chip: A long time ago, when Old Man made the first people, he gave them strong bodies. No one sickened for a long time. Then one day a child grew sick and each day he grew paler and thinner; nothing—no herbs, no prayers—improved his color or bestirred him. At last his mother, a somewhat foolish woman, went to Old Man for help. He took her down to the creek and pointed to a rock and a buffalo chip.

"I will throw one of these into the water," he said. "If what I throw floats, your child will live and all persons will live forever. If what I throw sinks, your child will die and all persons will die when their time comes. You choose what I shall throw."

The foolish woman thought for a long time. At last she chose the stone. Old Man threw it into the water. It sank, dooming her child and all men to die.

The Mandan, like many Plains tribes, decked themselves in buffalo parts to perform special dances. "Men of the Mandan Buffalo Bull Society," watercolor and pencil sketch by Karl Bodmer. *Courtesy The InterNorth Art Foundation, Joslyn Art Museum, Omaha, Nebraska.*

*". . . there was not a single thing in the trader's stock
that was not an unnecessary article of luxury
to the Indian."*
TRADER JAMES WILLARD SCHULTZ

THE FUR TRADERS of seventeenth- and eighteenth-century Canada sought to exploit the riches of a remote wilderness, a wilderness crisscrossed with navigable streams that teemed with fur-bearing animals (especially beaver) and populated with natives who saw no "value" in the animal skins they wore, but who could be taught to value them; natives who knew not the luxuries of iron tools, sweetenings, stimulants and alcohol, but who could be taught to value them also.

In the seventeenth and early eighteenth centuries, French voyageurs canoed up streams, found portages, and mapped the beginnings of a fur empire extending through the Great Lakes to Lake Winnipeg, spurred into exploration by the possible 75-fold profit in trading with simple Indians: furs that cost two livres in gewgaws in the outback trading room sold for perhaps 150 livres in the Paris Salon.

When the beaver near the Great Lakes disappeared, trade moved to north of Lake Winnipeg. Then, as the beaver thinned again, Frenchman La Vérendrye and sons set up posts near the Saskatchewan in 1748. Likewise, in 1774, the Hudson's Bay Company, heretofore dependent on Indians traveling to them, moved to the midwestern Saskatchewan prairies, and then, by 1800, to the Athabasca, in sight of the Rockies. To reach these posts both French and English traders depended upon the native voyageur— the French and Indian mixed-blood who spoke the tongues along the way, who knew the customs, who could build the "thin Birch rind Canoe" that stretched "eight fathoms long, and one and a half wide," and could carry "as much as an India Ships Long boat and draws little water, and so light that two men can carry one several miles with ease." These at first carried 2000 pounds of goods and crew but eventually some carried 8000-pound loads. (A big load was a necessity, for often one's license to trade allowed only five canoeloads of goods to go up river.)

To compete with the British, the French had established portages and trails northwest from Lake Superior and had provisioned the route as well, keeping pace pretty well with the British. Then the fall of Montreal to the British in 1760 and the 1763 Treaty of Paris gave them control of the streams, made British subjects out of French trader, Indian trapper and their offspring, the French-Canadian voyageur. French buffalo now became English buffalo.

Travel to the Saskatchewan and Athabasca Rivers sent men across lands as trackless as the seas crossed by British ships bringing home the riches of the East Indies trade. Sailors' food took up valuable space in

"Meeting the Boats and Inland Trains." *Harper's Monthly*, June 1879. *Courtesy The Library Company of Philadelphia.*

"Making a Portage." *Harper's Monthly*, June 1879. *Courtesy The Library Company of Philadelphia.*

holds of India boats, space that might otherwise contain pepper or cinnamon; space was even more valuable in Canada's canoes. Dry sea bread did for sailors; what space-saving food might canoeists eat? How might canoes paddle upstream into the wilderness, gunnel deep by weight of beads, knives and rum, then drift home again almost awash with baled furs, and yet carry food for the many paddlers?

The French had already shown how. In the country west of Lake Winnipeg, they had traveled through immense buffalo herds; consequently they had eaten better than at home. Montreal entrepreneurs, discovering that voyageurs, trappers and clerks worked happily when fed cheaply on buffalo meat, had begun trading with the natives for pemmican and other buffalo provisions as well as furs. Their voyageurs working west of Lake Winnipeg fed on fresh buffalo meat and pemmican; east of the lake worked the "pork-eaters," those voyageurs who fed on cargo-saving dried corn mixed with buffalo or hog fat. Because of such

food, canoe loads comprised eighty percent trading goods: sixty packages of merchandise at ninety to one hundred pounds, provisions to one thousand pounds and eight crewmen with allowable baggage of forty pounds each.[1]

The French had shipped pemmican to forts along the way to feed men en route. But they had shipped it so haphazardly that the eastern voyageur sometimes ate rich buffalo broth of pemmican, sometimes ate corn and grease drippings, sometimes tried to trade for food along the way, sometimes chewed moccasins for the glue in them, sometimes ate the moss from rocks, and sometimes went hungry.

The Englishmen of the Hudson's Bay Company worked out a better system for the Athabascan trade, a necessity if their canoes were to make it from Edmonton House at the foot of the Rockies to meet the York boats at Methye Portage on the Clearwater River and back, a round trip of more than a thousand miles between May and August. Captain Clark, helping

Lewis keep an eye on the British fur trade, recognized this dependence: "Without such resource [buffalo] these voyageurs would frequently be stratened for provisions, as the country through which they pass is but scantily supplied with game, and the rappidity with which they are compelled to travel in order to reach their winter stations, would leave them but a little leasure to surch for food while on their voyage."[2] The British filled provision depots with pemmican—seven or eight tons of the stuff to a depot, about 400 "pieces" of pemmican and dried meat. Similarly, the upstart North-West Company (an amalgamation of many independent fur traders organized by Montreal Scotsmen to improve the transportation of goods—but primarily organized to establish posts to gather buffalo meat and distribute it)[3] stockpiled pemmican and grease at Cumberland House, at the junction of the English River and the Saskatchewan, and at Fort Alexander, on the mouth of the Winnipeg. At the depots, crews unloaded pemmican and jerky from makeshift buffalo-skin boats, food stored to await their hurried return voyage to the western posts.

John McDonald of Garth, one such traveler, described the buffalo harvesting method:

> We took while we got the buffaloes enough to last us when we would get none—viz. from the Prairies to the Strong Woods, Lakes & Rivers where there are only a chance Deer or a Black Bear—plenty of fish—if time was given to catch them & nets prepared. We got all safe to Cumberland Depot, Deposited the Pemican etc. safe for the Northern Departments where nothing of the kind can be much procured. This is the usual way of supply; care was taken if possible to procure a sufficient quantum to enable all the Brigades to proceed without loss of time & all encouragement given the Indians to supply us as want of Provisions would prevent progress & stop the Trade . . . a second supply also came from Red River . . .[4]

Back east, Hudson's Bay men at Prince of Wales Fort had to kill more than 200 partridges a day to survive, sometimes as many as 90,000 partridges a season. And company men around Hudson's Bay who fed on a diet of fish became weak and developed scurvy; not true of men in the West who fed on buffalo—pemmican and fresh meat.[5]

Not that pemmican delighted the tongue and made a man ask for more, more. A voyageur would trade his share of company pemmican back to the Indians for fresh meat any time he could—so often, in fact, that the Hudson's Bay Company forbade it. Voyageurs also occasionally chose to buy fat dog meat rather than swallow the lean buffalo meat brought in during early fall. Few people ate pemmican by choice. Canadian Captain W. F. Butler found "nothing else in the world that bears to it the slightest resemblance . . . [It] can be eaten, provided the appetite be sharp and there is nothing else to be had."[6] Even the Indians who invented it often complained when they had to eat it, and the mixed-blood Métis, like many who ate it, "suffered habitually from dyspepsia."[7] One of its big advantages—a man could eat it without cooking it—improved its taste not at all.

Tasty it isn't; nourishing it is. Voyageurs who would eat eight to twelve pounds of fresh buffalo meat a day found a pound and a half of detested pemmican plenty. Like space food and C rations it carries a lot of energy for its weight and bulk, but would dismay diners at a Sunday dinner table.

Not only did pemmican equal three or four times the food value of fresh meat but also the stuff seemed nigh imperishable: taureaux, ninety-pound bags of it, remained perfectly edible after a summer of lying in a damp warehouse. Taureaux left uneaten at one fort grew shiny from repeated transshipment to other forts and grew years old in their travels; fifty-year-old pemmican survived to be consumed. And a taureau took up little room since it often only filled an unborn calf's skin or a cow's stomach. It "had the solidity and weight of a rock" and made a small packet for tucking into a canoe or toting, one on each shoulder, at a portage.

Such a compact and nutritious food seemed perfection to the men directing the fur companies, for it filled the need of saving space to fill with gewgaws, upstream, and furs, downstream: the 540 pounds of pemmican consumed in sixty days by each six-man crew made up only a fifth of each 2500-pound western river canoe load. Men in London and Montreal saw the fur trade as resting upon the hump of the buffalo.

The North-West Company's "Lower Red River Department" in the years 1800 to 1808 produced 1125 taureaux of pemmican (about 110,000 pounds), plus some tons of grease, tongues, humps and beat meat; the "Saskatchewan district" supplied another 200 tons; one half of the company's expenses came from the outlay to provision and pay their voyageurs.[8] Likewise, the Bay Company from 1839 to 1842 spent five thousand pounds for buffalo products alone;[9] a warehouse in Edmonton was "stacked to the roof" with taureaux of pemmican. Both companies shared buffalo products when one or the other was short.[10]

On the prairies a company factor stood ready to barter for fresh meat, especially in July and August when the brigade, just arrived up river with a new supply of goods for the winter's trading, needed the help of all hands to construct a new fort, and its provisions were skimpy.[11]

And in order that the dried beat meat brought in by Indians remain untouched, saved to manufacture pemmican for travel, employees at a trading fort did little more from September to January than hunt buffalo to feed themselves. Often thirty or forty people, their dogs plus scores of Indian visitors depended on this meat. A brigade at the Pembina River Post of the North-West Company, seventeen men, ten women and fourteen children plus forty-five dogs, ate 147 buffalo (about 60,000 pounds) in nine months,[12] five and a half pounds per person per day (plus scraps for the dogs), four buffalo carcasses a week.

Alexander Henry of the North-West Company, forted up on the Vermilion River in 1809 with a company of 130 to feed, put his hunters in a tent out among the herds to shoot buffalo. (Most hunters killed for a royalty per head of four shillings, one and three-quarter pence plus a tot of liquor.)[13] Then, that the carcasses might not spoil or be torn by wolves, Henry demanded "quart de loge": each man at the fort required to put twenty carcasses "on a stage" away from harm, care for them and haul them to the fort, as well as to save twenty hides to make twenty pemmican bags (the green hide shrank around the meat, compressing it). From September to January, Henry worried that prairie fire might drive away the herds, complained about his hunters, jotted progress in his journal.[14]

On January 31, 1810, four and a half months since the buffalo harvesting had begun, Henry noted the end of the slaughter: "Laid meat in the icehouse—550 thighs and 380 shoulders." This meat in the icehouse (the *glaciere*) his men would eat now and during the spring when cows were calving and bulls too poor to eat, and the men, too busy to hunt, made ready for the coming voyage. When Henry embarked in May, those left behind, Indians and "mongeurs de lard," the indentured laborers whom the company abandoned each summer, might feast on some of this until it thawed and ruined. In 1810 Henry left behind "about 400 limbs of buffalo, still frozen," about two-fifths of his harvest.

Men had dug the *glaciere*, a huge pit, and lined it with ice blocks cemented together by water poured between the cracks. Then they had piled in quartered buffalo carcasses, skin and all, until these filled the pit, then covered them with straw and a shed roof against the spring sun.

This completed, they were free to coast on homemade sleds down icy river banks, wrapped in the arms of giggling Indian girls, to drink and quarrel until embarkation time neared. Then they turned to pressing skins into bales, mixing beat meat with grease to make pemmican, constructing willow frames "nearly in the shape of a canoe" on which they stretched buffalo hide, hair side inside, to make extra canoes capable of transporting furs and buffalo products—capable as long as once a day they dried in the sun or over a fire, and as long as used only for floating with the current.

The fur trader, moving into buffalo land on the western Saskatchewan, found peoples who, unlike the eastern Indians, saw little advantage in trading. The Blackfeet, during Antony Hendry's visit in 1754, had refused to travel east through fisheater land to trade with the English. They and other buffalo peoples needed little of traders' goods. Robes kept them warmer than blankets, last season's tipi cut up into all manner of necessities, arrows slaughtered ample buffalo. They'd never killed small animals much, not needing them; consequently traders such as Alexander Henry, the elder, found them little interested in trapping small fur-bearers: "They [the Assiniboine] continued with us . . . selling their skins and provisions for trinkets. It is not in this manner that the Northern Indians dispose of the harvest of the chase. With them the principal purchases are the necessaries; but, the Osinipoilles are less dependent on our merchandise. The wild ox alone supplies them with everything which they are accustomed to want."[15] (One must remember that many of these Indians gathered buffalo products without the aid of the horse.) The Blackfeet—the Bloods and Siksikas and most Piegans—disdained to chill their bones wading in icy mountain water to set beaver traps; they stood off from trading skins. The Cree and Assiniboine, once beaver trappers of the eastern woods, forced westward as they trapped out eastern beaver country, moved into the prairie amongst the herds and changed; they learned to hunt buffalo and found a "principal occupation" in "making pounded meat and grease, which they barter."

When the tribes slew buffalo, and buffalo products flowed into the storerooms, they were "good hunters who stay in the strong woods." When they were bad, when they ignored attractive offers for fresh meat, when they failed to come in with either meat or furs, then the trader wrote in his journal of bad Indians and lazy Indians, saying, "They have been lying at the buf-

"The Balance of Trade." *Harper's Monthly*, June 1879.
Courtesy The Library Company of Philadelphia.

falo pound all the winter and neither have procured furs or provisions,"[16] or they "amuse themselves driving Buffalo into a Pound—a very unfavorable circumstance for our returns,"[17] or they had gone "toward the Red Berry hills where they will pass the winter eating buffalo, and not killing a good skin the whole season."[18] Then journals complained "we have made sixty bags of pemmican and there is not a grain of pounded meat in the house and not much fat . . . no prospect of any coming in . . . the Indians say that the provisions was so plenty here last year that they was turned out of the houses with their provisions and they are determined to make us go on scanty allowance this year."[19] They were bad Indians, indeed, those who refused to hunt the buffalo or trap furs for the trader.

But illegal liquor brought them to the traders sooner or later as surely as it had eastern tribes. The seduction of western tribes by alcohol proceeded rapidly. The English began building forts in the West in 1774. By 1794, Duncan M'Gillivray observed of the Blackfeet trading at the North-West Company's Fort George: "The love of rum is their first inducement to industry, they undergo every hardship and fatigue to procure a Skinfull of this delicious beverage, and when a Nation becomes addicted to drinking, it affords a strong presumption that they will soon become excellent hunters."[20]

By 1810, when the traders had been amongst the buffalo tribes sixty-six years, the tribes on the North Saskatchewan, trading with Alexander Henry, mostly killed buffalo to exchange for drink. He got men drunk in exchange for beat meat and pemmican—and sneered at them. His journal reveals constant Indian drunkenness: the Crees "were going and coming all day trading and begging liquor. Those fellows are great drunkards," and "The liquor I sent on the 15th nearly occasioned murder among them," and "The Sarcees were drinking all night and very troublesome; one of them climbed over the stockade, and I could not avoid using him ill." A quiet evening at the post meant "only Dumont's wife was drunk."

The fur companies tried to protect their buffalo supply by discouraging others from coming in to buffalo land. They rumored their trapping lands unfit for settlement. They had reason: wherever settlers stopped they soon killed off neighboring buffalo.

Consequently, in 1812, when Lord Selkirk of the Hudson's Bay Company brought to Canada a number of Scots, forced out of sheep-growing at home, and settled them in the Red River Valley, he seemed to the North-West Company (as well as to some of his Hudson's Bay Company partners) to have taken the step that would kill the fur trade. When Sir Alexander Mackenzie of the North-West Company heard of these proposals to settle buffalo country he said, "Such settlements struck at the roots of the North-West Company."[21]

The Pemmican War resulted.

To the North-West Company, Selkirk's charity looked suspiciously like a Hudson's Bay Company move to cut them off from buffalo products, for his Red River settlement lay across their path of pemmican supply—between buffalo country and the Great Lakes. To forestall colonization, they tried to prejudice the British Parliament against it, avowing in newspapers that the valley resembled a "Cimmerian desert of primeval solitudes." But the colonization was granted and "Assiniboia," the name Selkirk chose for

"Trade-Room, Hudson Bay Company's Fort, in the Plain Country." *Harper's Monthly*, June 1879.
Courtesy The Library Company of Philadelphia.

the settlement, was formed. Soon came the first blow to the North-West Company.

In 1814, Miles McDonnel, Governor of Assiniboia, forbade export of buffalo provision "for one twelve-month" from Assiniboia. His reason: North-West fur brigades ate well while the colonists went hungry, yet "the ordinary resources derived from the Buffaloe . . . are not deemed more than adequate for the requisite supply."[22]

But that winter the Governor blundered when he forbade the native Métis to run buffalo. The North-West Company made use of this to play on these natives' economic fears and got them to run buffalo in defiance of the colony and its governor; the Métis went further—they prevented the colony's settlers from running buffalo, causing some hardship.

In the spring of 1815 the North-West Company induced a number of settlers to desert the colony and bring their military field pieces with them. On June 15th the Company attacked those who remained, broke into the fort, trampled the grain fields, chased the residents downriver and set fire to their houses.

Lord Selkirk's colony seemed defeated—over pemmican supply.

But new Swiss settlers, former mercenary soldiers for Britain, arrived—unarmed until Selkirk smuggled U.S. arms to them. With their aid he captured the North-West's Fort William, arrested its principal officers, and seized considerable arms and gunpowder. From here, during the winter of 1816–17, he deployed detachments to take North-West forts Fond du Lac, Lac la Pluie and Douglas. In the spring many of his mercenaries moved to Assiniboia with him and settled there under an arrangement to provide defense for the colony. Now no one could attack it successfully.

The Pemmican War ended, but peace between the Hudson's Bay Company and the North-West Company came only after the repeated incursions of the Bay Company into the Athabascan country, countered by suicidally violent attacks from the North-West Company, brought the latter to near bankruptcy. It was forced to merge with the Hudson's Bay Company and share the rapidly thinning buffalo herds.

In the United States no such fur company hysteria arose over settlers' right to buffalo. American Missouri River companies worried little about settlers encroaching on buffalo land, for few farmers settled on the upper Missouri during fur days. Earlier settlers had moved into eastern Iowa, Kansas and Nebraska, land mostly cleared of buffalo.

When, about 1830, city men in Europe and the United States quit buying the beaver hat (felt hats made from the soft, under hair of the beaver), the beaver trappers' heyday ended in the United States. But buffalo robes began to sell well in the East. American fur trade changed. South of the Canadian border, the Missouri River companies, especially the American Fur Company, decreased trading for beaver plews and increased trading in buffalo robes. Traders found that robes, which heretofore had sold as a novelty, a few at a time (only 850 came down the Missouri in 1803), could now be shipped thousands at a time. By 1815, robes shipped down the Missouri each year totaled 26,000.[23]

North of the border, robe trade increased only slightly as beaver trade declined; the Hudson's Bay Company lacked the Missouri's swift, non-portage transportation and its steamboats, and thus could not profitably carry robes to market. In 1810 only ten robes came out of the "Lower Red River Outfit"; the same district sent out only 214 robes from 1801 to 1810.[24] Yet Manuel Lisa, on the Missouri at that time, in only one year shipped downstream 15,000 robes.

The Canadian fur companies needed far more men gathering provisions and transporting furs than did the American companies. Consequently they carried to market only the smaller furs that brought the highest prices. Drawing upon the diverse fur animals of the Arctic, the Bay Company continued to think of the buffalo as a food supply rather than as a major source of peltry.

The 1832 journal of Fort Pierre on the Missouri shows the burgeoning of the American robe trade. Entries for April 6 and 9 record the arrival of seven skin canoes containing probably 3500 robes, 500 robes to a canoe; May 2, ninety-odd packs of robes arrived (900 robes—ten to a pack); June 17, the keel boat *Male Twin* and four bateaux left for St. Louis with 1400 packs of robes (some of these boats, sixty-five feet long with an eleven-foot beam, could carry twelve tons of cargo plus crew and supplies); June 24, the steamer *Yellowstone* went downstream with 1410 packs of robes (the American Fur Company had her built especially for the trade); July 11, four bateaux headed for St. Louis with 355 packs of robes and 10,230 pounds of beaver skins, intending to pick up another 120 or 130 packs of robes at "Yancton." Robes now outdid plews in volume. In 1835, Fort Clark sent 203 packs of buffalo robes down the Missouri against only eleven packs of beaver plews; in 1836, 302 packs of robes, four packs of plews; in 1837, 320 packs of robes, five of plews.[25]

More than 140 trader's forts appeared along the Missouri and Yellowstone drainage to gather the thousands of robes. Such a number of forts was necessary because of the trader's dependence upon the Indian bands to gather and *process* the hides; the Indian tanning that made the robes valuable in the East made American traders as dependent as Canadian traders upon the Indian. Earlier, in the United States, the gathering of the beaver pelt had depended mostly upon the mountain men, the skilled white trappers. These white hunters could have killed the thousands of buffalo to produce the hides, but only Indian women could produce the robes from them.

Of especial value were the painted robes, decorated for wearing apparel; they brought three or four times the price of ordinary robes. But the price of a robe was anything a trader could get for it, although certain standard values supposedly attached themselves to it, values that varied from time to time and place to place. In 1716, James Knight at York Factory, writing to "The Honorable Governor and Committee of Adventurers of England," let them know that the good northern buffalo robes sold for about nine or ten shillings a robe (they "cost . . . dear" because the Indians had brought them 300 miles on their backs); the poorer southern robes sold for about half as much.[26] A century later, in Canada, a robe traded for a fathom of tobacco (three-quarters of a pound), or two horn combs, or twenty charges of powder and ball, or sold for five shillings.[27] At about the same time robes sold for $5 each in West Virginia, but brought only the equivalent of $1 to $1.50 on the plains. In the 1830s along the Missouri, the demand for painted robes had driven the price up to $8 to $10—for inferior robes.[28] But in the 1840s, a pilgrim on the plains found "For a piece of chewing tobacco as big as a hand one could get a fine buffalo hide (robe)."[29] By the 1860s the standard ran: "10 cups of sugar makes one robe, 10 robes make one pony, 3 ponies make one tepee,"[30] but for a painted robe a man might pay $35. By the 1870s, at Fort Berthold, the price had fallen to three cups of sugar plus one of coffee for one robe.[31] In spite of such variation, on the Missouri the robe became the standard of exchange, its value fixed at an imaginary $3 each. In Canada the standard was the plew, equal to the one pound beaver skin (about sixty-seven cents).

Posts dealing in robes also sprang up along the Arkansas and the Republican, along the Platte and at stopping places along the Oregon and Santa Fe Trails. All of these depended upon buffalo meat for sustenance, the buffalo robe for trade.

According to most estimates, the total robes traded from these posts amounted to about 100,000 per year. Yet at one Missouri River post alone, Fort Clark, an average of 3000 robes were received and shipped down river each year from 1835 through 1838. Fort Pierre in 1832 sent 19,000 robes down river, and Fort Benton averaged 20,000 robes a season.[32] A total of 43,000 robes from only four posts (with perhaps some duplication). If we consider that Bent's Fort on the Arkansas also sent some 10,000 robes a year overland to the Mississippi, that other outfits brought wagonloads of robes east, that the Red River Métis illegally traded thousands of robes to St. Paul, then 100,000 robes per year for all trade seems too few. Especially when we know the American Fur Company alone sent 110,000 robes down to St. Louis in 1848,[33] and that in the years before the robe trade hit its peak, 1825 and 1828, New Orleans handled almost 200,000 robes a year; in 1827 and 1829, well over 100,000.[34]

American companies depended on no farflung gathering of buffalo provisions; each fort existed pretty much on its own, gathered or traded for its own buffalo, tightened its belt when buffalo disappeared. An American Fur Company fort, with no canoe voyages to support, relying on steamboats for supplies, needed fewer buffalo products. Unlike Alexander Henry and his compulsive hoarding of meat, a journal keeper at Fort Benton became "heartily tired of this meat business." He complained in January 1856 of "more arrivals of Gros Ventres with meat [beat?] meat—we do wish they'd stop it but it seems they will come with it notwithstanding all we can say." Next day Big Feather Blood arrived with "some meat of course," and the following day the writer complained again of the deluge of "meat meat meat."[35]

Fort Union needed about fifteen buffalo a week to survive, but stored little for emergency, although Kenneth McKenzie had used a *glaciere* there in the 1830s. But in 1852, when buffalo wintered far from the fort, causing sixty pounds per day of dried meat to disappear (for which a good market existed at Fort Pierre), Factor Edwin Denig felt no responsibility to feed his laborers; he sent them off into the snow to find buffalo and feed themselves.[36] He followed the precedent of F. A. Chardon at Fort Clark, who in 1836 had sent his hunters off "to make a living in The Prairies—or starve as fate May direct."[37] In the United States few *glacieres* provided for emergency needs.

American companies, unlike the Canadian companies, sold buffalo products in the East: dugouts gunnel deep with buffalo fat went to St. Louis for candles and soap. Barrels of salted tongues went also—in 1842 that city received 16,000 of them, so many an official complained "What are we to do with our Buf. Tongues." Four years later they had become "a cash article in St. Louis."[38] (A century earlier, 1726, a Canadian tongue merchant had floated a canoe load of tongues the length of the Mississippi River to sell for luxury prices in New Orleans). To preserve tongue on such a journey, he pickled it: "to a 19 Gal. Keg well-packed 1 Table Spoonful Salt Petre—of Tongue &—of Salt dry for Some Three Weeks Then put in a Weak pickle with the Salt Petre with 2# Sugar."[39] Often a trader tried to improve each tongue's appearance by painting it with molasses and water to give it a "dark smoky color."

But bales of robes folded ten together, to sell for eastern sleighing wraps and overcoats, became the staple American fur trade item.

American forts sometimes hired salaried Indian meat hunters, to make sure they brought in meat rather than just killing for the hide—which, along with the head, heart, stomach, stone and unborn calf, belonged to the hunter. In winter they killed buffalo one day, brought in meat the next. (They inflated bladders and set them on poles near the carcasses overnight to frighten off wolves.)

To American traders, as to their competitors to the north, the good Indian was the one who traded skins, robes and meat for less than their worth, and the bad Indian, those like the "Honcpapas," the "Se ah sap pas" and the "Etas epe chos" who refused to.

Meriwether Lewis discovered an abandoned Indian camp and knew it was Assiniboine by the hoops from rum kegs, "for no other nation who visit this part of the Missouri ever indulge themselves with spiritous liquor."[40] Captain Lewis had learned that the Crow and local Blackfeet then abstained, but the Cree and the Assiniboine exulted over the buffalo hunting skill that allowed them, their wives and tots to get drunk often.

For those willing to risk it, a keg of liquor packed into the very tipi circle assured good robe trade. Charles Larpenteur came through winter snows to a Cree village and set up post in a double lodge readied for him; he soon sent word he needed water "to make firewater . . . and before I was prepared to trade the lodge was full of Indians, loaded with robes, ready for the spree." That night "the whole camp was in a fearful uproar . . . By morning I had traded 150 fine robes." During the night, those with robes had traded them buying drinks for those without robes. And the price had held high, since most Indians traded at any asking price for goods brought to their camp, although usually they'd travel extra miles to trade at a post that offered the best price. Next day Larpenteur traded for fifty more robes; altogether he got 200 robes for five gallons of alcohol.[41] In a photograph he looks out at the world, trimmed curly sideburns curving to his chin, wide mouth, soulful eyes, stiff collar, string tie, white shirt front: the very model of the unctuous businessman.

Although Congress early banned the importation of liquor for Indian trade into the buffalo country, thousands of kegs made it, hidden inside bales of dry goods, concealed in flour barrels. For awhile Fort Union's Kenneth McKenzie distilled his own (sugar he imported, corn he got from the Mandans); discovery of his practice made one of the scandals of the fur trade and brought McKenzie tumbling from his throne as King of the Missouri—but stopped the plying of Indians with liquor not a whit.

Liquor peddling was the only inducement to trade according to George Catlin's seeming whitewash of the fur companies; prohibition of alcohol would, he

Buffalo Jones wearing a buffalo coat. Too heavy and too warm to work in, the buffalo coat warmed mostly those who had to sit in the cold—stagecoach drivers and the like. *Courtesy Amon Carter Museum, Fort Worth, Texas.*

said, result in "a complete annihilation of the Company's business and even greatly jeopardize the lives of the persons employed in it."[42] As early as Catlin's time some Indians had quit attacking traders because they were the only source of whiskey.

Forty years later along the Missouri, they still refrained from attacking those traders who kept a pailful of liquor behind the trading counter. Each trading Indian who entered James Willard Schultz's post got a free drink; he "always wanted to taste of the liquor before buying." But, Schultz admitted, "a few moments after one of these extremely haughty customers had taken a drink, his manner changed. He became quite affable and loquacious." No doubt he also traded less sensibly with drinks under his belt: twenty prime robes for a rifle that had cost the trader $15.00, or one robe for a quart of whiskey—"very weak," or a robe for twelve steel arrowheads (six cents' worth), or whatever. "There was certainly profit in the trade."[43] Some men filled the bottom of a tin half-pint cup with buffalo fat to reduce the liquor, already cut four or five times. Frontiersmen avoided diluted "Indian liquor"; they claimed a barrel of good whiskey could produce a hundred barrels of such dilution.

Trader Andrew Garcia, squatting on the Musselshell, bartered sugar for robes: ". . . buck gave me a robe and wanted sugar for it, but as sugar cost money out here, I only give him ten pounds. . . . Then another buck says, 'boys, this one is on me,' and he gave me another robe, for another shot of sugar for the gang."[44] A trader sometimes mixed white sand amongst sugar granules to cut his costs, or used false bottom whiskey cups. And as for his goods: "A fiery red calico dress, warranted to fit any bust . . . warranted to hold their color against everything but water"; and gewgaws: a cheap bracelet produced in the East at "five dollars a bushel" traded for three robes.[45]

In addition to liquor and sugar a trader needed to stock coffee and tobacco, always in demand, luxury items, just as calico and junk jewelry. The robe trade resulted in a kill of 200,000 to 300,000 buffalo a year, most killed to exchange for junk . . . a process similar to wasting raw materials to build snowmobiles and non-returnable cans.

The changes in Blackfeet style of living illustrate the demeaning influence of the robe trade on the buffalo hunters. When Canadian fur traders began offering powder and guns in exchange for buffalo robes, the hidden streak of acquisitiveness that other tribes had long ago discovered popped out in the Blackfeet. For one thing, they needed to trade for war guns to resist the Cree and the Assiniboine, who had used their British-made muskets to push them westward. Trapping beaver might demean a Blackfeet, yet he could kill buffalo for trade and continue to respect himself. Blackfeet-killed buffalo meat and robes began to move across the trading counters. And the guns that slid across in return, coupled with the newly-acquired horses, gave the Blackfeet the power to lay claim to all of the prime hunting lands along the Bow and upper Missouri. A claim built on buffalo trade, a power that came as lagniappe: hunting they loved, robes they had always produced.

The Blackfeet came to the posts as barterers experienced in inter-tribal trading; they knew a few trading tricks themselves. They learned that traders gave them poor prices for wolf skins traded alone, so they held them back until they had some valuable buffalo robes and then traded the two batches at once—demanding good prices for wolf skins or no trade. And, rather than bring in a few robes at a time and take what they could get, they learned to stack up 100 robes on a trader's floor—an amount to make him offer a price large enough to keep them from taking the whole pile to a rival. They also learned to fire the prairies around the fur trader's forts, making the buffalo move far away in search of grass, too far away for the fort hunters—thus making their own meat more valuable.

The Blackfeet became aware of the possibilities of becoming wealthy and powerful through the robe trade. They could trade robes for guns, and guns for horses, and horses for wives. A woman could dress maybe ten *good* robes a year; a man with two wives had only twenty robes a year for trade. Obviously, if a man meant to be wealthy, he needed more wives. He could trade his surplus horses for them, thus turning his idle capital into productive capital. Soon Blackfeet men acquired four—five—eight wives, each kept busy rubbing brains into cow hides. Such polygamy amongst many of the buffalo hunters horrified the early missionaries; they mistook the business arrangement between man and plural wives: "a brave regards his wife as a purchased commodity . . . that he may keep in as large numbers as he can afford to buy and support . . . He aims, to be sure, to have always apart a dainty one for his own private pleasure, but the others are for the most part working women—old maids or widows."[46] The new Blackfeet buffalo robe affluence was a boon to women who ordinarily would have had no man to look after them, who might starve during any extraordinary winter when no one would share with them.

A man who meant to have wealth from robes found his many women overcrowded the tipi: eight women and various offspring stretched out sleeping feet toward the fire left no room for guests or further wives. He demanded that his women build a larger tipi, cut more lodge poles, tan more leather to make an eighteen-skin tipi rather than a twelve-skin. The size of Blackfeet tipis grew.[47]

Each move toward wealth meant complication: his wives, same as all wives, demanded spending money; when the trader piled brass checks, each worth a dollar, on the counter in exchange for robes, they scooped up a few. He needed more horses to carry more wives and children, to drag larger, heavier tipi skins, the ever-mounting piles of robes, pemmican and jerky. So he stole horses and traded robes for horses until he stood tall in council as a big horse and hide man. His robe trade might bring an income of about $2000 a year,[48] more income than that of the average white man of the time (and he made this even as the trader cheated him).

But with the rise of the Missouri River robe trade, traditional Blackfeet abstinence there vanished. By the 1870s, the chase of easy wealth from the trading posts brought on debauchery. Perhaps eighty-eight Blackfeet died in the drunken brawls of 1871. From 1867 to 1873, an estimated twenty-five percent of Blackfeet deaths came through liquor.[49]

As the speed of robe production increased, robe quality deteriorated. Early in the trade an Indian woman produced perhaps ten robes a year, but by the 1850s, when Kurz was painting at Fort Union, he noted that a man taking three days to chip an arrowhead worked "a longer time than an Indian woman needs to prepare a buffalo hide." While at the fort, Kurz searched for a robe to suit him amongst all those coming in. He owned one gift robe, "hair as fine as silk; the under side like velvet," to use for comparison. Amongst 130 buffalo robes brought in by Rottentail's band of the Crow, formerly famous for robes, "I did not find among these great piles a single buffalo robe that satisfied me. On most of them I found the hair imperfect." Two weeks later, another 130 robes arrived, and he failed "to find one of the first quality." Again, when 400 arrived from McKenzie's post (from the Assiniboine) he found not one; although these were tanned in a "painstaking manner," he objected

to them because "the women, to save themselves trouble, cut out that part of the hide which, even on a cow's back, is very thick, and then sewed the two parts together." (Actually they usually removed this and used these hide strips to make beds, saddle blankets and the like.) Now and then, he observed, they worked so carelessly as to "sew together parts of hides that were taken from different animals, which produced a singular effect."[50]

Yet Kurz felt the women were right to carelessly tan robes intended for trade because "Fur traders pay more attention to quantity than quality. The bourgeoise sell thousands of buffalo robes in packs of 10 robes each. Salesmen first examine the packs and sort the robes, including in every assortment both at this trading post and in St. Louis at Choteau Jr. & Co., at least 1 robe of the best quality in every pack of 10. Sometimes, for the sake of the fine, curly hair, small hides of 1-year-old calves are sold for robes made of cowhides."[51] And sometimes "anything with hair on" found its way into the pack.

Two-day robes and robes sewed with mismatched pieces bespeak a deterioration of craftsmanship, of pride in work, that on the Missouri paralleled the withering sense of identity, the torpor, the alcoholism of the last days of the Plains Indians. Furthermore, white man's diseases, especially smallpox and tuberculosis, had reduced the tribes until only a few thousand remained. The robe trade declined in the '80s not only because of the vanishing of the buffalo, but also because of the vanishing of the Indian who produced the robes.

The buffalo herds thinned and the Hudson's Bay Company suffered. As early as 1859, Edmonton House, chief supplier of buffalo products, failed to keep up with the needs of its 3000 employees.[52]

By 1863, two observers noted hardly a winter but what the men endured "serious suffering from want of food." In 1864, a twenty-year-old boy, raised in the once buffalo-rich Red River country, joined a hunt going elsewhere because he'd never seen a buffalo. The company began farming in Saskatchewan to alleviate the food shortage. The price of buffalo grease went up, and it became so scarce as to keep the company from making pemmican. A few years later Edmonton House itself experienced famine and only Fort Pitt, farther west and south, could find buffalo for the brigades. Pemmican rose in price from two pence a pound in 1855 to a shilling a pound in 1868. By 1870 no pemmican supply came on the market; the buffalo were gone from the fur company's territory.[53] Then it sent letters across the international line; one came to James Willard Schultz pleading "The buffalo are gone. Send us as many tons of the stuff as you can for our trade." He passed the word to the Cree near his post on the Marias and "everything went that was meat—poor cows, old bulls, and perhaps crippled horses."[54] And the Métis farther south, on the Mussel-shell, made pemmican to trade to the Hudson's Bay Company[55] until the buffalo vanished.

The Cree cleared the Montana coulees of their very sustenance; the fur trade had made the independent red man into a scurvy market hunter—a man willing to trade his birthright. Even the conservative Black-feet had become hide hunters, willing to let carcasses rot, meat waste if robes could bring luxuries. In Crow camps men took to stealing hides left outside a neighbor's lodge. And the Blackfeet, too: Andrew Garcia took in robes knowing "No Injuns have robes to swap now unless he steals them on a raid. But that need not bother you, for most of the time you can never tell where an Indian robe comes from."[56]

Duncan M'Gillivray saw it right when he wrote "Those [Indians] who have the least intercourse with factories are the happiest."[57]

*"I'll take you where you don't need to hunt them,
just kill what you want
and chase the rest away."*

A.R. ROSS

"In my early consciousness the buffalo was a pest."

P.E. MCKILLIP

*"I would as soon think of shooting my neighbor's oxen as these
great, clumsy, harmless creatures."*

HORACE GREELEY

"God forgive us for such waste and save us from such ignorance."

JOHN MINTO

THE CRY of "Buffalo! Buffalo!" waked Lieutenant George Brewerton from his afternoon nap. Out he came from under a wagon along the Sante Fe trail "to take a first look at the mighty beasts of which I had heard so much." As the lone old bull humped himself out of sight, Brewerton grabbed his gun and took after him on foot. He wounded the bull, then killed it as it charged, then seated himself on the skeleton of another buffalo (there were skeletons most anyplace, bones of the millions killed since 1830) to wait until the buffalo seemed dead for good. He arose, tested the carcass for sign of life, drew his bowie knife—and for thirty minutes "labored . . . pulling, slashing, and hacking, right and left at the huge carcass . . . until I blunted the knife, lost my temper . . . it was a broiling day . . . and I, in a melting mood, was stretched alongside the stiffening buffalo, which I had killed but was unable to cut up . . . I was exactly in the position of the gentleman who won an elephant in a raffle . . . the lucky man didn't know what to do with him."[1] He finally hacked out "the lingual member" and sawed off the tail to prove he had *killed his buffalo.* The tongue he boiled but couldn't chew.

This is the Lieutenant Brewerton who said he "could never bear to interfere with the gambols" of

prairie dogs by shooting at them, "but that he enjoyed shooting at buffalo just to see them fall."

Better than the flip-over of a shooting gallery target, that fall: real blood gushing, a swaying, feet propped wide against it, then the topple, all movement disappearing in an instant. It lacked only the tink of bullet against metal target.

A pilgrim had to kill his buffalo as a part of his Western Experience or at least shoot, even at an impossible distance "just that I might say I had one shot at a buffalo." The killing made him a frontiersman, initiated him, made him one of a brotherhood as if he'd sledded across the Arctic Circle or sailed across the Equator. He'd heard buffalo, buffalo from the moment he started west. The old hands complained as they ate mutton from the sheep band trotting with them or longed for mouthfuls of buffalo between bites of antelope, venison or elk. He was like a sea voyager who "cannot long more for land than the traveler in that region for the buffalo; for only in the land of the buffalo is there comfort and superfluity. Anxiously the days are counted till one may expect the first buffalo. Every sign is investigated by which one may gauge their vicinity. Weight is attached even to dreams."[2] Antelope curiously stepping, sniffing the wind—sign of buffalo country ahead; elk grazing in the bottoms—sign of buffalo soon. Old, saucer-like wallows; old dried chips thick as at a cattleyard; cut-banks sloped, hoof-packed to water's edge; tufts of brown fluffy hair caught on hawthorn needles and strands wedged in the rough bark of cottonwood—such signs as these even a pilgrim could read. When the manure lay soft and brown, when sharp footprints shaped the mud, when the wind smelled of musk, old hands began to envision buffalo ribs dripping by the night fire. Suddenly a herd appeared: "Our first enthusiasm brought ruin to the careless herd; for twelve of them were immediately shot, and of most of them the tongue only was taken. The juicy, nourishing buffalo meat we all found more palatable than the lean flesh of the antelope."[3] The True Western Experience had begun: Buffalo Blood had been let. A man created ritual for the occasion: "This evening, about 5 o'clock, I felled a mighty bison to the earth. I placed my foot upon his neck of strength and looked around, but in vain, for some witnesses of my first great 'coup.' I thought myself larger than a dozen men. I tied little Blackhawk to his horns and danced upon his body, and made a fool of myself to my heart's content, then cut out his tongue and sat down to rest and moralize."[4]

The Western Experience continued until a tenderfoot could say, as did Lewis Henry Morgan, the anthropologist, "I have now seen and shot at buffalo until I am tired and quite satisfied."[5]

Sir Richard Burton, the English observer and translator of *The Arabian Nights*, crossing the American continent in 1860, met a British vice-consul who assumed that Burton traveled the United States only to try "his maiden hand upon buffalo." Burton wondered about a man whose brain could find nothing in America but bison shooting, although he admitted that the New York papers carried many notices of Britishers crossing the water to "enjoy the society" of the buffalo. Burton himself followed the example of countryman Charles Dickens, who refused an invitation from Choctaw Chief Pitchlynn to hunt buffalo, saying, "Supposing I went, I should not be likely to damage the buffaloes much."[6] But earlier visitors had not practiced such conservation.

In 1854, the most infamous of the titled buffalo slayers, Sir St. George Gore, moved onto the prairies with six wagons and twenty-one carts. One wagon carried his guns only. He slept in a brass bed set up for him in a linen tent; each morning his foot stepped out of the bed onto snug carpet instead of cold prairie grass. He killed 2000 buffalo, 1600 deer and elk, and 105 bears. He irritated the Indian Agent at Fort Union into writing, "What can I do against so large a number of men coming into a country like this so very remote from civilization, doing and acting as they please, nothing . . ."[7] Gore had aroused the Indians against himself; and because of his excesses an irritated Congress passed its first game protection law—mostly ignored.

Captain William Drummond Stewart of Scotland caught the buffalo-killing fever along the Platte in 1832. He rode and shot, drank and feasted to suit the finicky standards of mountain men and Indians alike. In 1843, now elevated to knighthood, he again visited the United States "to buffalo" along the Platte (and perhaps to spy for Her Majesty) with William Sublette and Robert Campbell, Rocky Mountain Fur Company men. On this trip he complained, "Our hunters brought in two fat cows . . . The Oregon people have run them nearly out of the country."[8] But those Oregon people in covered wagons behind him, who had to ride a day off the trail to find buffalo, blamed buffalo scarcity on "The presence of Sir William Stewart, with his pleasure party and fifty or sixty-five horses for the chase; who, while we were passing through buffalo country, constantly kept several days ahead of us—running, killing and driving the game out of our reach . . . cheap sport to them, but dear to us . . . if ever again an English or Scottish nobleman sees fit to look for pleasure in the Rocky Mountains while an emigrating party is passing over them, it will be prudent to place him in the rear, instead of the van."[9]

Of course the difficulty arose from the numbers of inexpert, brash buffalo plinkers traveling the great western emigrant trails, disturbing the herds wherever they went, making everyone unhappy, even a French-Canadian displaced along the Santa Fe Trail: "Mais sacré . . . les Americain, dey go to de Missouri frontier, de buffalo he ron to de montaigne; de trappare wid his dam fusil, he follow to de Bayou Salade, he ron again. Dans les Montaignes Espagnol, bang, bang! toute la journée! . . . go de sacré voleurs. De bison he leave, parceque des fusils scare im vara moche . . ."[10]

This kind of chase made for hard feelings between the wagon trains and the Indian, for the white man, passing through, saw it as a game, chased the herd today, to hell with tomorrow; the Indian saw it as an exciting ritual that harvested the animal with the least disturbance to the herds.

Old hands sarcastically asked greenhorns to save

The first buffalo caused great excitement in an emigrant train. *Harper's Weekly*, August 26, 1871. *Courtesy Amon Carter Museum, Fort Worth, Texas.*

"the horns, hoofs, etc.," said one greenhorn, "and agreed to eat them if we would kill a buffalo and bring them in." Also, old hands claimed "the first buffalo meat brought into camp would create a fight . . . ,"[11] for the greenhorn expected his every shot to fell a buff; usually several of them had their sights on the same beast, and, if it fell, each claimed his shot had done the job.

Yet, for all his bumbling, the greenhorn of the buffalo hunt might, in this barnyard-like slaughter, bring down the only trophy he could—bear, antelope, deer and elk often took more prowess than he possessed. His chances increased if he gave up the horseback chase and stalked the buffalo on foot. Such stalking frontiersmen scoffed at as pot hunting, a sure thing "if one does not find it too troublesome to creep on hands and knees often for a mile." A man tried to keep out of sight until he heard their teeth cropping grass, coming to almost point-blank range.

Although the greenhorn found the stalk with the high-powered rifle the safest, surest method, some danger existed from a wounded buffalo's charge. Hunters often stayed together to help stop it. Customarily, if a bull charged, all the hunters shot at his forelegs to shatter them. But the single hunter in the same predicament? . . . well . . . hunters at Fort Union solemnly told artist Rudolph Kurz to shoot a charging buffalo in the nose, "the shock will stop him for an instant." Or, if his gun was unloaded, the hunters, pokerfaced, instructed him to "prop it firmly on the ground, so that, in running, the beast will strike his head against it." To be done "only at times of extreme danger," they assured him.[12]

The buffalo became something of a plaything. Sometimes vicious play as in "had some sport with a buffalo bull which had two of his legs broken. Got him very mad by plaguing him," but usually of a more frivolous kind such as sneaking up on a band of buffalo drinking below a cutbank, giving a yell to startle them: "Such fun! They ran over one another, fell down in heaps, nearly drowned a lot of calves, etc. Just such another stampede as a man would probably never witness in a lifetime." Indian scalawags loved to chase a herd into camp; cowboys couldn't resist laying a rope on one. Charlie Russell chided cowboy friend Pat Tucker about the buffalo bull "you droped your loop on thirty-seven years ago. If I remember right he got one for foot through the loop and the hondue lay in front of his hump and judging from the way he traveled you and Bunky wasn't eaven a good rough look . . . you through of your dallyes and made him a preasant of you raw hide."[13]

Sometimes a man on a dare jumped on a hump for a wild ride. Skylarking cowboys roped and branded them: one old bull carried brands from each of the local ranches. Cowboys thought it a great prank to tie two together and turn them back into the herd. The favorite task of Texas cowboys was riding in the buffalo herds to retrieve truant Longhorns: a great time for wild pranks and chases.

But mostly men played shooting gallery with this huge plaything. Alexander Henry, who each winter husbanded his jerky and his pemmican for his voyageurs and each autumn worried until he'd filled his ice house with buffalo meat, wasted enormous quantities in other seasons. He shot grazing buffalo from his canoe for target practice, not deigning to paddle ashore for a tongue from the animals downed.

Other traders joined in the general buffalo shoot. John McDonald wrote of shooting hundreds of "Buffaloes and Deers & many grizle Bears" without need; one New Year's Day, four hunters in Zenas Leonard's camp killed ten buffalo and picked over the carcasses as one might cull potatoes, just to choose the best hump for the day's feasting.[14] Duncan M'Gillivray excused such wantonness to himself: "Hunting is the only amusement which this country affords . . . I am persuaded that violent exercise is very necessary for the preservation of the constitution."[15]

Early Spanish expeditions to the southern plains also wasted buffalo. Coronado killed 500 buffalo to provide his men and Indian followers on his return trip from "Quivira"—at least three-fourths of a buffalo per person, 75,000 pounds of dried meat.

Forty years later (1582), eight Spaniards, accompanying some "naked Indians . . . going to kill cattle for their food . . . killed with their arquebuses as many as forty cattle [16,000 pounds of meat], made jerked beef, and returned to the settlement."[16] A hundred years after this (1684), the sixteen men of the Mendoza-López expedition helped Indians slay, between March 16 and May 1, 4030 "beeves"—which number includes only those carcasses brought to camp, not those skinned in the field for their hide only, nor the many little calves brought to camp. And, during May, traveling with "only some families," the sixteen men and few Indians killed an additional 400 buffalo (175,000 pounds of meat), 225 killed in one day, 120 on another day.[17] If Spaniards and Indians had totalled 100 persons, they yet could have left 183,000 pounds of meat to rot.

Later, Americans on the western plains slaughtered buffalo partly because they lived amongst what they saw as swarming buffalo pests: a swarming of 1500-pound bodies that stank of musk and churned up dust until nostrils clogged and eyes smarted. A swarming that stopped wagons and horses and footmen, filled water holes with manure and urine, ate grass until horses gaunted from lack of food. A swarming onto army parade grounds that led to an order commanding those shooting at buffalo to "not fire in the direction of the Commanding Officer's quarters," that compelled an agent at a stage stop to kill to keep his mules from stampeding. A swarming in farmyards so thick that one man often "shot them from the walls of my corral, for my hogs to feed on." A swarming over campsites and between moving wagons that made a vicious dog welcome company on the Santa Fe Trail—the dog chased the buffalo off. "The pioneers . . . were in turn surprised, astounded and frequently dismayed by the tens of thousands of Buffalo they observed, avoided or escaped from."[18]

As did the Indian, the white man butchered the best meat from a buffalo without slitting his belly; if he had help, he rolled the carcass onto its stomach, if not he let it lie as it had fallen. He only needed to split the hide down the backbone from the head; he then pulled the skin down from the hump to the belly. Just behind the neck he removed the *petite bosse*, a hump on the back of the neck that when broiled tasted like marrow and was very nutritious; next came the *depouille*, the broad fat meat sometimes four inches thick along the spine from shoulder to tail; then the hump ribs, sometimes broken off with a foreleg used as a mallet; then the *fleece*, the flesh covering the ribs. Mostly these hunks of best meat sufficed—along with the tongue. The hunter removed it by cutting open the flesh under the jaw. Rarely did he fail to take it, not only for its wonderful flavor, almost like smoked beef tongue, but also as evidence of his hunting prowess (a tongue for him, horns for Caesar's Romans); he dared not boast without tongues to back it.

Sometimes a man on a dare would jump on a hump for a wild ride. Note mounted figure slightly right of center. *Courtesy Glenbow Museum, Calgary, Alberta.*

Often mountain men and Indians chopped through the ribs to retrieve the tenderloin, the tallow, the liver, the kidney and the fatty milk gut. This sampling of delicacies provided well over 100 pounds of meat; the other hundreds of pounds could rot.

After a long chase the livers were a delicacy, eaten raw sprinkled with juice from the bile. Old hands at the hunt, like Indians, usually ate the milk gut raw right at the kill, the chyme dripping down their chest; sometimes they roasted it in the coals for breakfast, swearing it tasted as if someone had stuffed white pudding into the gut. And sometimes they turned it inside out, stuffed the fatty, newly formed interior with tenderloin, tied both ends, roasted this sausage about twenty minutes, dropped it in boiling water for five minutes or so and ate it (or they did as the Indians, instead of turning it inside out, they stuffed the chopped meat in one end of the gut forcing the "original contents out the other"). Most frontiersmen and travelers called such sausage by its French name, *boudin*, and judged it a delight (with the possible exception of Sir Saint George Gore with his wagons of imported wines and provisions). The mountain men sometimes ate a *boudin*, beginning each at an opposite end of the greasy gut lying coiled "on a dirty apishamore . . . like . . . a huge snake," each trying "to gain a march" on his partner by bolting, whole, more yards of *boudin* than he, or, by a sudden jerk of the head, to withdraw "several yards" of gut from his neighbor's mouth and stomach.[19]

In spite of such gorging, the useable 400 to 600 pounds of carcass made more meat than a small party could keep, and more than it had time to cut and jerk, although some outfits stopped half days to smoke meat. Groups wasted meat unavoidably: five men decided to shoot no more game than necessary but had to shoot a buffalo a day, for they "could not encumber ourselves with unnecessary weight." Conversely, three or four men might eat a fat deer for their supper and breakfast—"in the morning . . . nothing but the bones left." Larger parties that could afford extra weight carried hunks of raw buffalo on the pack saddle; exposed to dry prairie air, it kept four or five days. And travelers in covered wagons tacked buffalo steaks together, "hanging them over their wagon covers outside. Gritty? Yes. But not worse than Platte water."[20] But most travelers wasted meat thoughtlessly: "kill'd 2 cows & one Bull took meat enough for a couple of meals," or ". . . every day we shot a fat cow, of which we took only the best pieces."

In part they wasted because they'd found the best pieces the only ones fit to eat: the stew meat of even a fat, three-year-old cow chewed up into a cold, greasy, gristly, unswallowable cud. This meat the Indian wisely dried, pounded and mixed to make pemmican. No other way does a man want to eat it, certainly not for a quick, broiled supper. And as for any cut of bull meat, "this was no good no not at all," forcing some pilgrims to "run their fingers down their throats" to relieve themselves; others found it "surprisingly elastic . . . a very clever imitation of Indian rubber. It recoiled from our teeth with a spring."

Occasional men said "very little does me" of either bull or cow, complained of poor buffalo veal, due, one man thought, to the paucity of the buffalo cow's milk and to the calf's continual running from wolves; he found the buffalo served at stage stations "a tough, dry, wooden fiber, only to be eaten under great provocation." Sir Richard Burton, who'd traveled the world enough to point out the similarity between the aroma of a stage station burning buffalo chips and a Hindu village burning cattle chips, who'd eaten many exotic meals, thought buffalo tasted good to plainsmen only because otherwise they had to eat lean antelope; to their boast that buffalo fat bothered their bellies none, he replied neither did tallow disturb the English ploughboy's stomach.[21]

Men who'd never eaten buffalo meat before, men like French Pierre Le Sueur and his followers, found themselves eating six pounds a day plus four bowls of broth although they, like all who changed to the strictly buffalo diet, seemed to sicken on it at first.[22] Many journals mention the "sickness amongst us"—a diarrhea possibly caused by alkali water rather than buffalo meat.

But most men disagreed with these dyspeptics—from an early Spaniard who wrote, "The flesh of these cattle is very good, and very much better than that of our cows," to Charles Dickens, who found the tongue "an exquisite dainty." Mountain men came a runnin', knives ready to spear a rib, at the call "hyars the doins, and hyar's the coon as savvys 'poor bull' from 'fat cow'; freeze onto it boys!" A pilgrim seeing western sights in 1834 agreed: "And is such meat really good? What a question to ask a hungry man! Ask a Catholic if he loves or believes in the Virgin Mary"; the Long expedition threw away elk or deer meat when it could get buffalo; a soldier of the Injun-fightin' Army remembered "that a cut from yearling and young dry cow buffalo was tender enough to absorb through a straw."[23]

Likewise, most Plains Indians seldom ate deer, elk or antelope—when they had buffalo. At first, on the reservation, when the U.S. government issued them beef, they gave it to their white neighbors and went off "to buffalo." Not until the buffalo disappeared did they raid the white man's cattle herds for the unsatisfying taste of his beef. Similarly, whites raised on buffalo meat found beef distasteful.

Passengers on western public conveyances adhered to the custom of the great shooting gallery of the West—plink it if it moves, especially if it's big and easy to hit. Along the Missouri River "Steamboat a'comin'" was signaled as much by gunshot as whistle, bell and chuff of stack. Passengers potshot at herds come to drink under the bluffs or at shaggy heads snorting above the water as buffalo swam the river. The captain winched a carcass or two out of the water—free meat for the dining salon—and the rest floated downstream. (Similarly, Mississippi River passengers shot down ducks with rifles, "rather a dull amusement since we could never get our game, but what can you do on ship except act silly?") The Northern Pacific railroad advertised that Montana passengers could "either from the window or platforms of the moving train . . . test the accuracy of their six-shooters by firing at the retreating herd." A Union Pacific passenger who had no gun could buy a souvenir tongue at the Cheyenne station; Harry Yount, later to become first gamekeeper of Yellowstone Park, sold hundreds to passengers at $1 each. Plinkers made Sunday excursions in response to placards in railroad stations "RAILWAY EXCURSION AND BUFFALO HUNT"— a round trip for $10 in country where "Buffaloes are so numerous they are shot from the cars nearly every day"; a gala outing, refreshments available, "Ample time for a grand Buffalo HUNT ON THE PLAINS."

Even church groups came to sponsor such excursions ("in the most elegant coaches drawn by the untiring horse of iron"), taking lah-dee-dah dudes westering. Dude E. N. Andrews joined such an outfit in Lawrence, Kansas—his contribution to a local church.

He and 300 other people, including a "correspondent" for *Frank Leslie's Illustrated Newspaper*, boarded the train on an October morning of 1868. That night the train stopped at Ellsworth where all, including the twenty-six ladies aboard, slept as best they could on the seats "with feet as high as our heads."

After they left Ellsworth the next morning, *Leslie's*

Shooting buffalo on the line of the Kansas Pacific Railroad. *Courtesy Amon Carter Museum, Fort Worth, Texas.*

Using live steam to move buffalo from the tracks. *Courtesy Union Pacific Railroad Museum Collection.*

"Brother Van Shooting Buffalo." Charles M. Russell. *Courtesy Montana Deaconess Hospital, Great Falls.*

man found "a slight difference in the size of the wood-piles" the only scenery, but dude Andrews and others

were on the *qui vive*, asking "Are there any buffalo about here . . . most of us had probably never seen a buffalo . . . I desired to see a buffalo . . . before the close of my mortal existence . . .

Leslie's man grew more excited after the herds appeared, and, after riding fifty miles beside animals beyond rifle range,

about twenty were discovered making for a curve in the road . . . Keeping his engine at a speed just sufficient to encourage them in their effort, the skillful engineer of the Seminole [the engine] threw down the gauntlet . . . In an instant a hundred car windows were thrown up, and the left of our train bristled with two hundred guns. The engine screamed and the spectators shouted . . . The mass were too quick for us, but three immense bulls were cut off . . . In the darkness of the evening they could scarcely be discerned, except by the flash of the guns . . . with a lurch and a bound they sprang across the track . . . In a flash our gunners were at the opposite side of the train . . . Two were seen to stagger and fall . . . "Down brakes" was whistled, and men, women, and

children tumbled from the train . . . Scarce a hundred yards from the train the largest one fell dead . . . Your correspondent, . . . tumbled over his wife and the drum, but was on the ground in a trice, just as the irrepressible Catts, of the Lawrence Band, mounted upon the ridge-pole of the buffalo's paunch . . . to disembowel his majesty was the work of but a few moments . . . a rope was attached to his horns, and two long files of men, with joined hands, and preceded by the band, playing Yankee Doodle, dragged him bodily to the front car and hoisted him aboard. We have christened him Maximilian. Captain Coombs is putting him through a course in embalming and when we reach home we propose to mount him on a dray and carry him in triumphal procession through the streets of the "historic city."

Back in Lawrence at 10:30 p.m. of the fourth day, Andrews thought such an outing better than a trip abroad "to enlarge the conceptions of creation, and to give the peculiar tonic of novelty . . . especially when for the first and perhaps the last time one finds himself among the princely buffalo."[24]

Only five years later passengers on the same Kansas line saw "few live ones . . . but whole catacombs of dead. For twenty miles in one place, the sight is aw-

"The Buffalo Hunt as It Really Was." Probably drawn by Henry Worrall. These cartoons accompanied a tongue-in-cheek account of the Russian Duke Alexis's hunt. *Frank Leslie's Illustrated Newspaper*, February 10, 1872. *Courtesy The Library Company of Philadelphia.*

ful . . . we saw many thousands of their carcasses." A railroad conductor, J. H. Hilton, recalling those days, said, "One could have journeyed more than 100 miles along the railroad right-of-way, without stepping off the carcass of a slaughtered bison."[25]

Killing buffalo also became a social outing—a fling—the thing to do. A Nebraska judge hunted in 1872 in silk hat and a "coat with long spike tails";

earlier, a Texas judge, a "very respectable and independent man," every summer took his children and a couple of black servants to the prairie where he "spent several months in killing buffaloes . . . for his own private amusement."[26] Such hunters brought cooks to fix meals of brown turkey, fresh buffalo stews and roasts, white bread and yellow butter—all served on white tablecloths.

Millionaires and European noblemen came from New York City to buffalo land, brand new gun under one arm, champagne bottle under the other, to make a brave safari amongst the herds and to bivouac amongst the cottonwood trees. These sometimes had a go at slaughtering under the shepherding of Buffalo Bill Cody (a "most excellent guide; but the fact that he can slaughter buffalo is by no means remarkable, since the American bison is dangerous only to amateurs") and oftentimes traveled as guests of the U.S. Army. Officers excused these luxuries and the company, a bracing change from the drabness of frontier post life, on the premise that these buffalo hunt maneuvers gave soldiers practice bivouacking.

The most publicized of these sorties occurred when the Grand Duke Alexis of Russia visited the United States in 1872 and participated in a festive buffalo hunt. General Phil Sheridan, General George A. Forsyth, General George A. Custer, and General Innis N. Palmer planned its strategy. Buffalo Bill Cody led the skirmishers. Glasses of champagne were drunk on the prairie after the Duke (or someone) made his first kill. Spotted Tail, a Sioux chief, provided entertainment—an Indian buffalo hunt, a mock Indian battle, and an evening "war dance." The kill of about ninety buffalo in two days made a nice celebration for the Duke's twenty-second birthday.

A man who butchered buffalo each day liked to tell of the unusual days when butchery had offered variety: the time one ball had felled two buffalo, or when, forted up against Indians, he shot a nearby bull in the liver that he might bleed slowly to fall almost within hand grasp, or when, alone in horse and buggy, he dropped enough stampeding buffalo to "split the herd" about him. To hear them tell it, all buffalo hunters— trappers, soldiers, voyageurs and hide hunters—shot like Deadeye Dicks, dropping buffalo after buffalo each with a single shot. But most plinkers had the shooting skill of Alexander Henry's voyageurs who shot from daybreak until 9 a.m. into buffalo passing within a few paces of the fort: the result of twelve guns shooting—three cows and one bull killed.[27]

But pipsqueak arguments about big heads, bodies dropped, lucky shots and the like brought about pipsqueak buffalo-killing contests. The most famous contest occurred (if it did) between Buffalo Bill Cody and Billy Comstock for the title Buffalo Bill—and a side bet of $500. Cody killed a total of sixty-nine in three

runs into three herds; Comstock killed forty-six. The Kansas Pacific mounted the heads and sent them about the country as advertising.

Another brutally inane contest took place because the boys on Frenchman's Creek said that, by God, Buffalo Curley (Jack McCall—who later murdered Wild Bill Hickok) could shoot more buffalo than Doc Carver. Curley believed 'em and challenged Doc to a $500 contest, so Carver got to make the rules: the most buffalo shot on one run was winner—and a man could shoot until his horse could no longer run.

Early on a frosty morning with snow and ice on the ground, trappers and wolf poisoners, hide hunters, Lieutenant Schwatka escorting the ladies from nearby Fort McPherson, and Indians come to watch the one kind of white man's play they understood, all disturbed the loneliness of Mud Springs.

In the early light a herd moved, stringing single file from feeding ground to water. When they had all plunged in to drink, an official fired a shot, the hunters and crew rode at them, seven men—the two contestants, the three officials (referee and two judges), plus two Indians to shoot red-feathered marking arrows into buffalo downed by Carver, blue-feathered into those by Curley.

The ladies found thrills enough that morning to make the early hour and cold feet worthwhile. Curley rode his horse to death, but lost to Carver who shot 160 animals (110 red arrows, fifty tails—so it is said). Curley lost his temper and swore he'd kill Carver, but the Doc got the drop on him; the Lieutenant interfered.[28] And so ended the gala day at Mud Springs— the ladies back to warm their toes, the Indians back to their buffaloless reservation, the hide hunters back to their hovels.

The buffalo lay there, freezing. They'd not rot until the spring sun warmed them and then the smell of chokecherry and wild rose blossom would mingle with their stench . . . these hundreds and other hundreds and more hundreds, to make a spring odor the plains knew too well, the odor from thousands of rotting buffalo carcasses.

By 1883 the plains became "desolate beyond their . . . desolation," for the placid herds had been fine company during the long treks through lonesome space.[29] Today, as we ride through the emptiness, we fail to realize it once seemed friendlier because the eye saw buffalo.

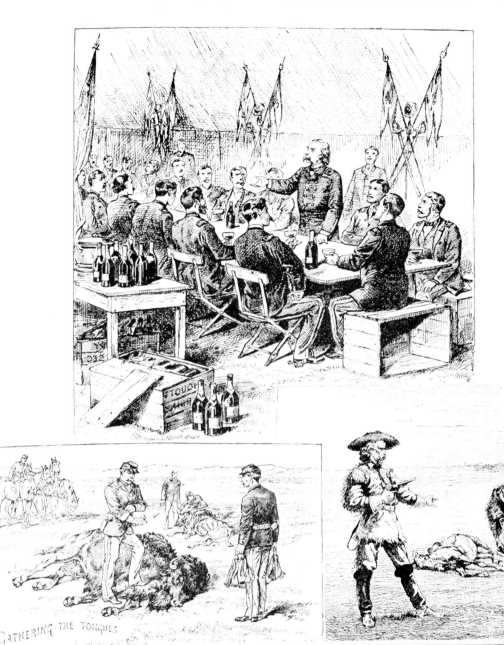

Clockwise from below: "A Buffalo Undecided as to an Attack on General Custer," by Frederic Remington. In the excitement of the chase, Custer, just as many a greenhorn, has shot his mount—his wife's horse.

"A Match Buffalo Hunt." A. Berghaus.

"Gathering and Counting the Tongues." A. Berghaus.

"Supper given by the Vanquished to the Victors of the Match Buffalo Hunt." A. Berghaus.

Illustrations from *Tenting on the Plains*, by Elizabeth Custer, 1889. *Courtesy Amon Carter Museum, Fort Worth, Texas.*

GATHERING THE TONGUES

109

Caricature of Buffalo Bill riding a buffalo. H. H. Cross. *Courtesy Buffalo Bill Historical Center, Cody, Wyoming.*

" 'Tis an awful sight.
Such a waste of the finest meat in the world!"
GRANVILLE STUART

"I was a business man.
And I had to learn a business man's way
of harvesting the buffalo crop."
FRANK MAYER

IN THE sixteenth century, Spaniards entered the buffalo hide business, killing the buffalo to skin him for leather. In the seventeenth century, the French explorer La Salle was granted the franchise on the buffalo leather business in Ouisconsin; he complained of other hide hunters who made inroads on "his" herds. In the eighteenth century, King Louis XIV of France granted a royal franchise to Sieur Charles Jucerau de St. Denis for a tannery business in buffalo hides on the Ohio River. Jucerau and 150 men traveled by boat from the New Mission of Kaskaskia, down the Mississippi, then across country on foot to the Ohio's "Grand Chain of Rocks." Here in 1703 they built oak tanning-vats and began slaughtering buffalo; by April 1704, they had killed 13,000 of them just for the hides and had infuriated nearby Indians by such waste of meat. In June the Indians attacked and killed everyone but Jucereau who somehow escaped. He buried some treasure, left his vats and hides to rot and made his way back to Kaskaskia, to die there before he could retrieve his treasure.[1]

In the early nineteenth century, as the North American population grew, the consumption of buffalo grew, for the development of railroads east of the Mississippi brought meat from Mississippi Valley herds to eastern butchers, as well as hides for eastern tanners. Although soft and spongy, the leather made up into good upholstery and wall covering, and fine buffers for machinery. By mid-nineteenth century, hunters had set up businesses along the emigrant trails west, to sell buffalo meat to the wagon trains. And Midwest settlers in need of quick cash could raid the herds and sell the meat locally "for more than our loss in taking the team off the grade-scraper for the time we were gone."[2]

The increased hunting—the continual disturbance of the herds by gunfire—made the Indian chase and surround difficult; this, coupled with the waste of meat, irritated Kansas Indians as much as it had Illinois Indians of Jucerau's time, and they, too, filled hunters with arrows. Consequently, at first, such Plains hide and meat hunting thrived mostly in the winter when the tribes were quiet.

Before the Civil War most of the western buffalo range had lain too far from eastern markets to make buffalo products profitable. (One man, much scoffed at, had proposed overcoming this by driving 1000 buffalo at a time eastward to the lower Missouri River, corraling them, then beefing them or sending them to the East in cattle cars.)

The demand for any kind of leather increased during the Civil War, and more white hunters entered the herds. After the war, the building of the Union Pacific up the Platte and the Kansas Pacific up the Arkansas (which split the western buffalo population into masses called the northern and southern herds) made possible the easy transportation of hides and meat to eastern markets and created new local markets. Hunters such as Buffalo Bill Cody furnished roasts and steaks to feed track layers—which monotonous diet they detested. And local citizens tended to buy cheap, tender buffalo meat rather than expensive, Texas trail beef, stringy and tough following a 500-mile walk north—the beef went to the profitable eastern market. By 1868 numbers of unemployed men from the East had come to the West to hunt buffalo commercially, and buyers had begun to develop gathering points and storage yards for hides.

Those hunters in the meat business took the hindquarters, some of the hump ribs and the tongue, but usually left the forequarters to rot. Often they sent as much bull meat as cow meat to eastern butcher shops, for the bull provided more meat per carcass and was much easier to kill. (Eastern customers, who brought home buffalo meat to discover they couldn't chew it, gave it a bad name.)

J. Wright Mooar, typical of men in the meat business, hunted near Buffalo City, Kansas, in 1870 (later Dodge City because Kansas had other Buffalo Cities). Only two years out of his eastern duds, he'd quit chopping firewood on contract when he discovered he could do better shooting buffalo.

European and American tanners had discovered how to make good leather from buffalo hides—leather for machinery belting, shoes—any of the uses cowhide filled. In 1870, a German firm ordered all the hides they could get from J. N. DuBois, a Kansas City hide dealer. In 1871, he sent circulars to the meat hunters' towns offering to buy summer hides as well as winter hides and telling how to care for them. The men who heeded his circulars made $1.75 per bull hide and $1.25 per cow hide; it proved better than selling only meat at 2¢ to 3¢ a pound, and a lot less trouble. Then, later in the year, an English firm ordered 500 hides through W. C. Lobenstein of Leavenworth: the British army had begun to wear more buffalo-leather accoutrements. J. Wright Mooar contracted to help fill the order.

The Indians bothered less than usual, since the Medicine Lodge Treaty of 1867 had given them exclusive hunting rights south of the Arkansas. Mooar had no trouble filling the order for 500 hides; in fact

he had fifty-seven left over. He sent them to his brother John, who was seeking his fortune in New York City.

At that time the leather merchants there had seen few flint hides: "A few untanned robes are sent to New York from Texas, but there is no particular price demanded or paid for them; in fact, I do not think that they are mentioned in the fur market";[3] they mostly knew the Indian-tanned robes shipped east by the Chouteau firm of St. Louis. New York tanners might have done something with Mooar's hides, but as the shaggy load trundled through the city on an open wagon, a Philadelphia tanner saw it and offered $3.50 a hide to experiment in tanning them. Brother John sold. The Philadelphia tanners soon wrote to him claiming they could tan buffalo hides for any leather use and requesting 2000 of them. Mooar quit his New York fortune-seeking to seek it amongst the Kansas herds with his brother.

Only the Chouteaus had made a fortune in buffalo products heretofore—by monopolizing the Missouri River robe trade. Few others had become rich by converting buffalo into product, although everyone on the frontier had fashioned buffalo things other than the traditional buffalo robe (they depended on Indians for it). The tough hide had wrapped canoe cargo and covered buried cache; it had, after being sliced into cord, tied bundles and lashed gear onto saddles or into wagon box; braided cord had lassoed animals; straps of rawhide had harnessed horses. Buffalo rawhide was to the wagon what baling wire was later on to the Model T—more: only the lashing of buffalo rawhide and wooden pegs held together French-Canadian Red River carts.

American commercial tanners had long manufactured a buffalo coat and a buffalo overshoe, a crude footgear worn hair inside that brought on "conflicting emotions—mortification at the ridiculous size of my combined footgear, big boots inside of huge overshoes, and supreme comfort derived from feet that were always warm."[4]

These clumsy overshoes and the big bundly buffalo overcoat were the winter wrappings of every stage driver in the West, as much a mark of his profession as the silk glove on the hand that handled the cold lines. And his passengers burrowed under buffalo robes—they furnished their own or otherwise nigh froze. And at night the experienced passenger substituted his own robe for the crawly, dirty thing the station agents "called a robe" and provided for "the dangerous 'bunks' of the stations." In fact any experienced frontiersman always carried his own robe. It made a waterproof cover in summer storm, as well as snow-proof cover in winter blizzard. And, legend says, although snow might pile on it, he, breathing through his rifle barrel, stayed snug.

Horns had their frontier uses; men hung their hats on horn hatracks; sometimes they propped their feet on horn-legged footrests while sitting uncomfortably in ingenious chairs with buffalo horn legs and Longhorn horn arms. And buffalo wool made up into cloth. Kentucky housewives had spun and woven it. Thrifty Mormon women on their trek west had gathered and spun the strands that decorated bushes along the way. Western trappers swabbed guns with this handy material. As the eastern market developed, meat and hide hunters cut off the beard and mop to sell at 15¢ a pound, a price that would hardly create a fortune.

In November 1872, John Mooar met brother J. Wright in Dodge City. J. Wright had been hunting buffalo close by—within an easy haul to the railroad and near enough town to reduce Indian worries. He'd sold 3000 pounds of meat at 3¢ a pound. John wanted to learn the ropes, so J. Wright hired him, their cousin Charles and another hand, each at $50 per month. At the end of a month, J. Wright, back in Dodge City, sold 20,000 pounds of short-cut buffalo hams at 2½ cents and 305 hides at $3.05 each. Half of the meat money went for freight, yet he made $250 on it and his hides brought $930 ($1180 for his month's work). He had made three or four times what wages would have brought him in an entire year, less only $150 paid his greenhorn help. John Mooar and cousin Charles each borrowed $250 from J. Wright to "enter the firm."

Behind them on Three-Mile Ridge, they had left 160,000 pounds of meat and entrails rotting. During this year, on the East Coast, poor city people starved to death. Nearby, troops sent to the Republican River to shoot buffalo to feed Kansas settlers, starving after a grasshopper plague, arrived after the hunters had used up the herds. The area around Dodge City became known as The Great Slaughter Pen.

In 1872, after the Sante Fe ran out of money and laid off hundreds of track layers, the Kansas plains filled with men—young men mostly, "hardly more than kids"—learning how to hide hunt. Just as in a gold rush, the "whole Western country went buffalo wild." Employed men quit jobs and small-business men sold out, restless Civil War veterans came west to hit the buffalo bonanza. They figured to kill a hundred buffalo a day at $3 apiece and make a profit of $200 per day, $6000 per month—three times the salary of the President of the United States.[5]

That first year, 10,000 to 20,000 men, somehow, even in their ignorance, managed to kill and skin enough buffalo to flood the market and drive down the price from $3.50 to $.25 a hide. This depression removed most of them from the hide hunting business, and the price went up, but only to $1.50 or $2.00 a hide. Just as in a gold rush some lucky greenhorns made it rich: one business group, having lost all of the stockholders' money, went to buffalo hunting, and, green though they were, recouped the losses.

Men went out in small groups. Those who shot well did the hunting—the hunters. Others learned to skin the carcass and butcher it—the skinners. Still others learned to care for the hides, to cure meat, to cook and to tend camp—the rustlers. Some learned by tagging along wherever experienced hunters led, just as pilgrim gold seekers had followed old prospectors. And, similarly, one of the things they learned was that a herd belonged to whatever party first located it, almost as a mining claim.

At first, hunters had tried to copy the ways of the Indian and free trapper—chase 'em on horseback. But these men were no "buffalo runners"; their hunting became known as "tail-shooting": shooting buffalo from behind as they rode. According to hide hunter Skelton Glenn, at the end of the day's hunt, buffalo carcasses "would be strung on the ground for a mile or more, from ten to fifteen yards apart, and in this way the skinner had so much territory to go over he couldn't make wages." Also, this way a skinner might miss a batch of carcasses. The hunter found he had to dismount to make money, but he always called himself a "buffalo runner" when he came to town. Men sneered at foot hunters.

He walked after the cussed things—"tail hunting" he called it, probably because he did more hunting than shooting: instead of riding to follow where the scampering herd led, he walked through the ravines it went around and cut it off as it came by. But often the carcasses he had shot lay on opposite sides of the long ravines. "The skinner and his wagon and team would have to travel to get in a day's work to make it profitable," said Glenn. In this walking hunt, the hunter crawled near the buffalo, shot, they ran off, stopped while he caught up with them. If they smelled him, they'd run and "not halt for a mile, and sometimes not for five," forcing the hunter to walk twenty-five miles

This kind of hide hunting was called tail hunting. S. E. Walley, 1877. *Courtesy Amon Carter Museum, Fort Worth, Texas.*

a day, leaving a sparse spoor of carcasses behind him. "This system was afterwards dubbed 'tenderfoot' hunting and did not often pay expenses for either hunter or skinner," Glenn claimed.[6] But hunter John Jacobs and partner John Poe using this very method on the Texas plains in 1876 brought in 6500 hides.

The hunters wanted the quantity of hides that the piskin and the surround had given the Indian, but manning such a drive would have meant divvying a few hides to each, Indian fashion, and cutting profits. They needed a new, efficient way of killing buffalo.

For one thing, they needed a better rifle. John Mooar appealed to the Sharps Rifle Company of Bridgeport, Connecticut, to modify one of its rifles especially for buffalo hunting, one that would pack a wallop but not depend on a large bullet that might drift in the constant Kansas wind—"much stronger than it was in Bridgeport."

Hunters had tried types of the "needle gun," but its paper-encased shell wasn't the best for tough, frontier, day-by-day use. And it seldom dropped a distant buffalo at first shot. The popular Henry and Spencer rifles likewise proved too light. These guns killed buffalo well enough for those who shot buffalo just to stake a big drunk. But fortune-seekers wanted a gun that "whether it hit the right place or not, it would make him sick," one that wasted little time for the hunter, piled bodies neatly for the skinner, proved efficient for the hide-producing team. Any gun did for floaters. Early on, the choice of gun divided the pros from the amateurs.

The amateur hunter irritated the pros—for the same reasons Indians hated them: they disturbed the herds and drove them off. The lumpishness of a hundred central Texas farmers out for meat so irritated one hide hunter, he arranged to give them all the meat they needed just to keep them out of the herds. And he arranged to send thirty to forty wagons of meat to Las Vegas, New Mexico Territory, to keep the ciboleros, Mexican horsed lancers of buffalo, from making their annual trek to the herds.

Usually the Mexicans arrived on the Texas plain in the fall, traveling in groups large enough to fight off Indians, sometimes one hundred carts and wagons traveling together and camping at night in a sprawl of ten acres or so. They carried only enough old flint-locks to battle Indians; to bring down buffalo they depended on ten-foot lances tipped with eighteen-inch razor-sharp blades or the bow and arrow.

They ran the buffalo in the usual chase or in a variation of the surround: the horsed lancer helped to put a herd to circling then rode at its circumference, spear-ing buffalo just behind the shoulder blade, keeping at it until his horse gave out or until he broke his spear. Charles Goodnight saw one mount at his camp and, in a 600-yard run, lance to death six bulls. An American hunter watched a party of ciboleros dash into a herd and kill sixteen in a few minutes.[7]

Americanos detested these horsed hunters even more than meat-hunting local farmers, for their running of the buffalo often broke up a hide hunter's herd. When one man lost his animals to such a stampede, at a cost of $150, he shot three horses out from under Mexican riders and discouraged the group into leaving his territory. Once, Skelton Glenn's outfit thought to go partners with Mexicans they met, hides to Glenn, meat to the horsemen, but "we soon saw that we could not get along together, their ways being so different from ours."[8]

The ciboleros stayed on the plains about six weeks. They slung the fresh meat over buffalo hide lines to dry in the sun. When dried they tossed it into carts and trampled it down to make room for more. They made a favorite dish from this dried, powdered meat mixed with chili and tallow and heated, a kind of Mexican instant pemmican. At the end of their hunt they rode back to the Pecos, an unusual and picturesque sight, familiar in the Southwest as far north as the Santa Fe Trail: men clothed all in leather except for a small, flat straw hat, holding tasseled lances upright and butted into a strap hanging from the saddle.

But Texans, harvesting only the hides, couldn't cotton to men who harvested only the meat and ruined valuable hides by spear slash. A rifle was the tool for hide hunting, and the Sharps Company had developed a suitable tool: a .50 caliber breech-loading rifle, same as they had been making but chambered for the new metallic cartridge rather than the old-fashioned paper or linen one. This cartridge used ninety to 100 grains of powder behind 473 grains of lead bullet, a bullet hollow-based to spread and keep accuracy as the barrel heated and encased in a paper patch to keep the bore from lead-fouling—or, because of the scarcity of paper in the wilds, in antelope buckskin stretched thin. A single-shot rifle, since the buffalo hunter had no use for a repeater. At more than one shot a minute a gun barrel heated until the rifle no longer threw an accurate pellet; eventually it warped. Yet a man could fire this blunderbuss ten times a minute in a short Indian skirmish. Few Indians closed with the Big 50 in an open skirmish; some of them called it "shoots today, kills tomorrow."

This gun, along with some Remington .50's and Springfield army model .45's, became the one for the

Texas hide hunters skinning their kill. *Courtesy Texas State Library Archives, Austin.*

professional hunter among the Kansas and, especially, the Texas herds, the gun of Jim Cator, Robert Parrack and Billy Dixon. The Big 50's did away with most of the Texas buffalo. Texas liked bigness even then.

Some Kansas hunters, the Colorado and Nebraska hunters and, later, the Montana, Wyoming and Dakotas hunters preferred another, later Sharps rifle, "a rifle to end all rifles," the .45 caliber shooting 380 to 550 grains of lead and 120 grains of powder. This was labeled "Sharps Old Reliable" and became known as "the Buffalo Sharps." It could put nine out of ten shots into a circle the size of a dinner plate at 400 yards and put four out of five shots into a silver dollar at 100 yards when shot from a prone rest using telescopic sights. (Many professional hide hunters used telescopic sights, although the usual hunter depended upon rear, peep sights.) The men who bragged that this Sharps could "cut a twelve-pound steak out of a buffalo at 1000 yards" overlooked the fact that at 1000 yards the bullet dropped sixty-two feet—any hit was mostly luck. It figured as the only rifle in the world to its lovers: "If my life depended on one shot from one

rifle and I could take my choice, I'd rather have my old 'Sharps Buff' in my hands than any other gun."[9]

With the Sharps, the "Pet of the Plains," buffalo hunters developed the standard method of killing for hides, a variation on the old Indian surround, the stand—it "surrounded" the herd with the Sharps's firepower rather than manpower.

A hunter trying for a stand looked for a herd of twenty to seventy animals located apart from nearby herds that might spook, and away from a water hole— some hunters felt they seemed restless near water. A hunter spent much of his day locating this herd, often riding out late in the afternoon to find tomorrow's shoot, rising before dawn to relocate it. Once he located such a herd, he walked toward it upwind (in a light wind he determined its direction by tossing a feather or dried grass), keeping behind hills if hills were there, then crawled as close as possible; within 200 yards he stood a good chance of spooking them. If he found them scattered, he might try to bunch them in a gully; it made for ease of killing and ease of skinning. Sighting from behind a covering bush or rock, he usually chose a cow he figured to be the "leader" of the herd, perhaps a standing animal rather than a reclining animal—not from his sportsmanship, but because no man could be sure of placing a shot accurately in the lazing buffalo. His best luck came, he thought, just as buffalo got up after a sleep.

A hunter had as his target the lungs, which lay behind "a circle as large as a cowboy's hat, just back of the shoulderblade," a different target than that of the sportsman stalker who aimed at the heart, which lay far lower in the rib cage, almost at the bottom of the chest profile. The hide hunter's shot into the lungs filled them with blood, and a slow death by strangulation came that created no stampede since it only caused the animal to "hump his back as if he had the colic and commence to mill and round in a slow walk," a gait that drew curious buffalo nearby to sniff the blood and follow it about. A heart-shot buffalo might gallop 200 yards before he dropped, scattering the herd in his panic. Some men figured a shot to the kidneys brought on more milling than a shot to the "lights." But, an occasional man favored the neck and heart, relying on the Sharps to knock 'em down and keep 'em down.

As the herd milled, the hunter shot, watching all movement closely, firing about once a minute, shooting those animals that began to move out from the herd, usually bulls or cows with calves. Most of the herd ignored the boom of the Big 50. Some hunters believed the usual prairie wind blowing from the herd to them drove some sound away, yet the herd also milled on windless days, and on those days the smoke from the black powder settled on the ground ahead, affording cover for a crawl even closer to the herd.

A man shot mostly cows because their hides sold for more money. He held his shots to one a minute for sake of his rifle barrel, cooling it and cleaning the residue of black powder from it every two or three shots by pouring water through it or running a water or urine-soaked rag through it; in winter he doused it in handfuls of snow; sometimes he alternated two guns. He held the herd "as well as the well-trained cowboy would hold his herd, only the hunter would use his gun. This was termed mesmerising the buffalo . . ." (a tenderfoot who passed to the windward side of a stand was likely to have a ball whistle past him—his smell would break the spell).

A hunter usually quit shooting when he'd downed all the carcasses his skinners could work that day— often he quit shooting before noon: "Killing more would waste buffalo, which wasn't important; it would also waste ammunition, which was."[10] He shot not only to kill efficiently but also to avoid creating a sieve-like hide from excess bullet holes—some buyers knocked two-bits off a dollar hide "depending on where the bullet holes were." Not only did he know he had to kill efficiently, he also knew "it was not always the best shot but the best hunter that succeeded, that is, the man who piled his buffalo in a pile so as to be more convenient for the skinner to get at."[11]

If he shot more than the skinners could skin by dark, they cursed him the next morning (unless a full moon had kept them working after sunset), for in warm weather the bodies had swelled during the night tightening the skin, creating a carcass the skinners hated and called "stinkers." Yet, difficult skinning or no, some outfits "often killed the buffalo the day before they were to be skinned." Occasionally the hide would bake on the animal in four or five hours of intense sunlight and "could not be removed from the carcass. Sometimes we would soften one that had been partially baked by pouring water on it. But such hides would always be weak where they were baked and would not possess full market value."[12] Leaving an unskinned carcass overnight also risked wolves mangling the hide. And, in the winter, on the northern plains, hides left overnight froze onto carcasses making skinning impossible; so, on a bitter day, if a hunter had killed a day's harvest but the herd still milled, he began shooting to cripple animals, knowing tomorrow would find the cripples gasping through frost-rimmed, bloody froth, their hides preserved warm and flexible for the skinner. On the other hand, if, at any season, a hunter had an exceptional stand going, he kept shooting to kill: he might shoot more than one hundred in a day and become a Frontier Figure—whether he could use the hides or not. Everyone knew of Tom Nickson who shot 120 in forty minutes, using two guns, letting one cool while he used the other. Furthermore, he'd killed 3200 buffalo in thirty-five days.

Many methods of taking the beasts arose, although each pro thought only one true method existed—his: Skelton Glenn pooh-poohed what he called tail hunting; J. Wright Mooar avowed no outfit ever had more than one hunter, but Seth Hathaway, who hunted both in Texas and Montana, remembered that in outfits of fifteen or twenty men "we would all shoot at the leader . . . the herd would stop momentarily and would give us a chance for more shooting . . . I have seen as many as 50 or 60 buffaloes dropped right in those first few minutes, within a radium of an acre or two."[13] But Hathaway avowed no man could hunt

The pictures show shooting a "stand" and killing the wounded.
R. Caton Woodville, *The Illustrated London News*, October 23,
1886. *Courtesy Amon Carter Museum, Fort Worth, Texas.*

buffalo alone, ignoring J. Wright Mooar and others who did.

Some expert hunters calculated to kill eight buffalo for every ten shots, but many experienced hunters averaged far less. Hunter Buck Wood shot sixteen buffalo with fifty-one shells. Hunter George Brown said he'd put one, maybe two bullets in a buffalo, then, "If that wasn't enough I'd put still another into him. I have often shot a buffalo ten or fifteen times before I got him . . . I have often shot two belts of cartridges away at one stand. Each one of those belts would hold forty-two cartridges."[14] Outfits could rarely afford such inept shooting: hand-loaded cartridges cost about 12½¢ each, store-bought about 25¢. Ten to fifteen shots might cost more than they'd make on the hide, since the holes cheapened the hide. Especially since Dr. Joel Allen, in his famous study of bison in the 1870s, estimated hide hunters only wounded one out of three animals they hit. Furthermore, Colonel Dodge estimated that, in 1872 and 1873, hides from only a fourth to a third of the dead ever reached market.

Some men shot from a sitting position, some from a kneeling position, some from a prone. Most rested the heavy gun on a forked stick or several sticks tied or a commercially produced folding "prong stick." Some men demanded a rest three feet high, figuring a rest closer to the ground caused the sound to magnify and disturb the herd. Some supported the rifle by lying on their back, resting the barrel on their feet and aiming at buffalo along the length of their body, head strapped into shooting position. Some men, shooting made-to-order guns with set-triggers, sandpapered their fingers until they bled to sensitize them to the exact touch.

Some men arose early in the morning to shoot, some preferred mid-morning after the herds had rested. Each had the same problem: "He must know his buffalo . . . Which of all that number was the leader . . . Where, then, must the bolt fall that would immediately down him and cause the others to gather around . . . ?" Most of all the hunter had to have luck; he somehow had to be where the buffalo were. No matter if he was "able to judge distances accurately; to make allowances for the direction and velocity of the wind, and the undulation of the prairie . . . to visualize the arc the bullet must describe . . . to land squarely on a vital spot of the selected animal";[15] if he wasn't where the buffalo roamed he made no money. And, often, he failed to achieve a stand.

Good hunters early learned to shoot lots of buffalo

when buffalo were nigh. Seth Hathaway's group spied "thousands upon thousands" feeding nearby late one afternoon. They concluded to go to camp, load cartridges and have at them early in the morning; at dawn they found only 200 roaming where the thousands had grazed. "For the next two or three days, hunt as we would, we did not see any more. Gardner kept the air blue with his swearing at himself for not shooting all he could the night we first saw them in such vast numbers."[16] They skinned out only twenty-eight carcasses.

The Mooars expected the buffalo to make them capitalists; they butchered when many others took hides only. They sold 62,000 pounds of meat at 7½¢ from the kill of the winter of 1876, an extra $4600 for the winter, more than enough to pay for the trouble. Frank Mayer, his last full year of hunting, made $4000 selling meat and heads, only $2000 on hides. Many other outfits planned to harvest the meat but "this plan was never generally carried out." Mayer in spite of the income found it "took too much time as well as work" and quit the whole hide-hunting shebang.

If an outfit butchered, it fell to the hunter to cut out the tongues—they had to come out before the ravens got them. Sometimes he also opened the carcass and removed the gut-tallow, but usually the skinner did this, since he also carved off the hindquarters and hump before completing the skinning.

Later, the camp rustler cut the buffalo thighs into three boneless pieces, ham-shaped and called hams, cured them in a hide tub and smoked them in a hide-covered smokehouse. The meat stayed curing and smoking for about six weeks, then the hams were stacked in a wagon and sooner or later driven to butcher shops or to boxcars headed east. Tongues especially rode the rails, hundreds of thousands of barrels of them; they were worth $8 or $9 a dozen, bringing the fanciest prices because they sold to fancy eastern hotels. Humps and hams sold well before Christmas, because many American families traditionally ate buffalo for Christmas dinner.

A typical, professional hide-hunting outfit employed a couple of skinners to follow each hunter, and a camp rustler or two to cook the meals, tend the hides, watch the meat vats, bestir the smokehouse fires, whit-

These are professional hunters, determined to run their camp as a business: note the tongues drying on the rack. George Robertson, 1874. *Courtesy Western History Collections, University of Oklahoma Library, Norman.*

tle pegs to peg down the hides, keep tabs on the numbers and kinds of hides credited to each hunter, guard the camp and help mold bullets for the days ahead—he rustled.

Six men made up the usual outfit but some numbered as high as sixteen, often too many to make money (although one sixteen-man outfit shot 28,000 buffalo in one summer). But many hunters had little idea of their expenditures or how much they'd come out ahead, they only knew they had a pocketful of money when the work was all done that spring. Hunter Frank Mayer, who kept books and hunted well, found he'd made but $125 a week profit on his outfit. He hunted full-time for six years, part-time for another three, which, he said, made him "the marathon dunce of the buffalo ranges," for most men kept at it only a couple of years. He figured he'd made $5000 clear in nine years; at that, others told him he'd made more than they.[17]

In some of the larger camps a hunter shot buffalo for a percentage of the hide price: when hides sold for $3 they made 25¢ a hide, but if hides sold at $1 he made only 5¢—about five to eight per cent of the price. If he owned the outfit, he gambled on price and hunting luck.

Good winter hides brought more than the poorer summer hides; a flooded market reduced prices. Furthermore, early in the hide boom the market paid $3 for cow hides, $2.50 for bull hides, and 75¢ to $1.50 for small heifer or spike bull hides (kip hides they called them) and 25¢ to 75¢ for calf hides—if on the market: calves were taken only by stray shots or when the orphan standing by its mother seemed about to start a stampede. Later in the hide boom, when farmers, bummers, hangers-on and all moved into the herds, the price fell and good hides sold for only $1 apiece, poorer ones for 40¢ to 60¢. Only "a remarkable good hunter" could then keep a buffalo outfit in the black, *if* he was followed by good skinners.

The skinners usually worked in pairs. Sometimes they made 5¢ less, per animal, than the hunters, but most often made 25¢ an animal or worked for $50 a month. In addition to skinning, they shot wounded beasts not yet down and calves who butted them while they skinned out their mothers.

Wyatt Earp claimed the organization of most hide-hunting outfits was unbusinesslike. The hunter foolishly paid for having hides skinned that he could have skinned himself, paying because tradition held that no hunter would stoop to skinning—"Touch a skinning knife? Not on your life!"

Also, Earp claimed the hunter usually bought his equipment and hired men on the assumption he'd kill a hundred buffalo a day and sell the hides and meat at about $2 to $5 an animal, whereas actually outfits averaged fifty animals a day and sold hides for about $1 to $2. Earp's most outlandish scheme was to do his shooting with a shotgun. He knew that although the Sharps killed some big stands, the average stand tended to stampede after thirty or forty animals had been killed. He figured the tractable buffalo would allow him within fifty yards of them, good shotgun range.

Later he claimed it worked just as he had planned: "My lowest score for a single stand was eighteen buffaloes, the highest, twenty-seven. As I never shot but one stand a day, that meant twenty to thirty-five dollars apiece for the skinner and myself." When the stand had been killed, Earp joined in the skinning and found out why the hunter's code forbade it—it was dirty, hard work. But he claimed it paid off. In April 1872 after selling his hides he had cleared more than $2500.[18]

Blood stiffened the skinner's canvas pants—canvas rather than buckskin that they might occasionally be washed. Dried blood matted his beard and streaked his hands and face, bits of buffalo wool clung to him here and there. He smelled and was a "paradise for hordes of nameless parasites." When he came to some ramshackle, hide-buying towns, he had to visit the barber shop, have his filthy clothes laundered before he was allowed to enter the rude, dirt-floored saloons. In rougher towns he came as he was and gambled for drinks by seeing who could catch the first louse.

On the prairies, hunters and skinners sat around flaming buffalo chip fires, flaming as chips never flamed, from gobs of buffalo tallow "as large as an ear of corn" thrown upon the fire, gobs cut from hunks the skinners had hacked from carcasses and sent campward, as much as 500 pounds of it in a hide wagon. It was their all-purpose grease: they ate it as butter (they cured it for eating by tossing it into a tree or over a rock for a few days), they greased guns and shells with it, and they greased wagons with it, as well as burning it. Sitting around its fire, yarning, they got drunk if a whiskey peddler had brought his wagon and barrels nearby. Relaxed times, for the hides from animals slain by noon were sometimes all in camp by early afternoon. Some days no herd did they see, days of lazing about, sharpening knives, molding bullets or riding cross county to visit nearby camps.

They ate well if they provided well. As little as possible did for the fly-by-nighters, perhaps just flour, salt and sugar—they tended to eat mostly buffalo.

Bacon and ham and dried fruits filled the grub boxes of the professionals, especially bacon. They said straight buffalo meat made the palate crave smoked salt meat. If skinners and hunters ever came close to revolt, it came not from living in swarms of flies, working in blood-stiffened stinking clothes, sniffing rotting offal, eating at catch-as-catch-can hours, and enduring freezing cold, but because the bacon was gone.

When the weather drove them to it, they slept under cover in tents, in cabins, in dugouts (sometimes creating a village of caves so unobtrusive that buffalo grazed in its limits) and in wikiups (some of spacious rooms hollowed out in dense hackberry thickets, with ceiling, walls and floor covered by hides—"snug" they called them).

In the 1880s, hunters living in the country between the Yellowstone and the Missouri, a country of winter blizzard or clear-sky, 50°-below "cold snap," went to cottonwood bottoms in September and built log cabins and corrals near where they knew the herds usually wintered (they wanted the full winter pelage on their hides). Others dug into cutbank or sidehill to create the typical cave—a "soddy." These northerners had more than buffalo chips to burn—scrub evergreen grew in every lee, lignite outcropped in many a cutbank. L. A. Huffman, frontier photographer and buffalo hunter, remembered "fellowship . . . by the light and warmth (of that) fire piled high with fat piney and crackling red cedar . . ." and "visions of that wide fireplace of mud and stones in the snug camp where we spent that first winter . . ." and "spit-tasty, long slabs of choice 'hump' skewered together, four inches thick, brown and 'crumpy' without, red and juicy within, served with sourdough dutch oven biscuits, big and generous and each garnished atop with its shortening—a 'cracklin' of buffalo fat—and a dusting of 'cinnamoned sweetnin.'"[19] Huffman was used to boom-town living—the drafty houses with cold bedrooms and cold parlor corners; enjoying a soddy's warmth, he ignored smoky chimneys and the smell of sweaty bodies and bloody clothes.

The hunting outfit needed shell-loading equipment and a batch of good knives for skinning. And poison to kill bugs that infested the hides as well as poison to bait buffalo carcasses and kill wolves for their hides—an extra income. (One outfit poisoned enough to pave a road through a swamp with their carcasses, creating a "bone road.") And, for the go-getting outfit, some saltpetre and salt to cure meat.

The first Sharps rifle, the Big 50, cost $100 to $150, the second, Old Reliable, about $237 (new price). In addition to one of these, an outfit needed a skinner's wagon or two, if possible tough wagons with iron beds and iron wheels to withstand the rough going. Such wagons, new, cost $600. They needed horses to pull them, or, in rough country, pack mules. They needed at least a fifty-pound keg of powder, and a 400-pound hunk of lead-tin alloy (15 percent tin, 85 percent lead), and 100 to 500 metal cartridge cases (each case they tried to use fifty times before discarding it). Factory-loaded cartridges were hard to obtain; luckily most hunters preferred to load their own cartridges for it cost less, and equally important, they could vary the powder load. Furthermore, factory-loads often jammed or misfired.

How much of a job is it to skin a buffalo? Harry Helgeson, who butchered 3224 government preserve buffalo, thought them harder to skin than cattle for "There are no bubbles or moisture between the hide and meat . . . The hump is . . . hard to skin it is like skinning a bear or hog (like taking rine off bacon) . . . the sides and belly are dry and the hide sticks . . . you can not pelt it, that is pull it off or use a hammer to pound it . . . The buffalo have a ewe neck—and it is very hard to skin without cutting on cows as it is not much thicker than this paper . . . very few butchers can skin a buffalo and do a fast or good job."[20] On the other hand, skinners of the hide-hunting days could have a hide off in fifteen or twenty minutes. Bill Hillman obtained the mythical skinning championship when he skinned seventy carcasses between breakfast and 4 p.m. A more usual experienced skinner averaged twenty to forty hides a day—whereas three greenhorns once took "nearly two days" to remove and peg twenty-four hides. The skinners worked hard, not from tugging to remove the hide, for *they* said it fit loosely on the body and came off readily, but from lifting at the weight of the animal and hide, and working fast while the carcass was warm and the hide came off easily.

A lone skinner had to somehow prop up the carcass to get at its underside, a problem he sometimes solved by getting his shoulder under the beast's front leg and rolling the carcass up onto the spine as far as he could, then jabbing a prod stick onto the ground and slanting it into the carcass just behind the foreshoulder. But two or three skinners working together could roll the carcass far enough to wedge its head under its shoulder, or cut the head off to make a chock, or prop up "the legs that were farthest from the ground." Any method to make the body lie somewhat belly up ready for the skinner's knife; they wanted the whole hide rather than two halves, split along belly and spine, as did the Indians.

Using a razor-sharp, pointed knife, the skinner first slashed under the jaw and then drew his knife the full length of the body to the root of the tail. The next cuts started at each rear foot "running a straight line to the tail." Then a cut from front hooves, over the knees to the brisket. Skelton Glenn claimed such cutting produced a hide more uniform to stretch than the common slashing down the inside of all four legs, but skinners developed such personal methods of skinning that a man could trail any outfit across the prairie by following its skinner's method.

With a crescent-shaped knife, the skinner encircled the neck in front of the ears, and then started removing the hide at the head, peeling to the back of the neck, then down the front and back legs and over the backbone. He walked around to the propped-up side of the buffalo, skinned out those legs and that rib cage and stuffed the bloody hide down under the body; thus when he pulled out the prop the body rolled over and off the hide leaving it ready for loading. He walked around the carcass, spread the hide out, hair side down, folded the leg skins onto the hide, rolled it from head to tail into a roll about three feet wide and "taking hold of this tail would throw it in the wagon the same as a sack of flour." Such a roll weighed about the same as such a sack, for a big bull hide could go eighty-five to 100 pounds; cow hides averaged forty-five to seventy-five pounds. On the days of a big stand, a team and wagon might have to make more than one trip to camp: forty green hides could weigh one and a half tons.

Another way of skinning employed the hide wagon. After the skinner slashed the hide down the center and along the legs, he loosened it at the neck until a rope from a wagon could be tied to it. Then he snubbed the carcass to a stake, or riveted it down by an iron stake through its head, and pulled the hide from the carcass by starting up the team and wagon. Such a method required several men on hand, someone to drive the team and at least two at the carcass with knives at the ready to loosen the hide should it begin to tear. This method left too much flesh on the hide, tore it too often and required too many men. Few outfits with experienced skinners used it, for careful skinning brought top prices.

Drying hides surrounded the hunter's camp like brown weed patches—they called the area "the stake ground." Usually the camp rustler turned hides every four or five days until they dried, in about ten days. He could tell from the rattle they made when he trampled on them if they'd dried sufficiently to turn; they'd then lost about two-thirds of their weight. When cured he turned them over for one night to moisten them enough for folding. If the market price was low, he might "poison" them to hold them for a price rise; at any time, well-cared-for hides commanded more money. Some camps had no stake ground. They figured that "a two full hours of sunshine" would put a glaze on a hide which rebuffed flies, preserving it until it reached market. Skinners for these outfits just tossed the hide onto the prairie, inside toward the sun and went on skinning. At nightfall, before they rolled it, they maybe rubbed a mixture of salt, sulphur and saltpetre along the edges of the hide, an effort to keep insects from entering the roll. They lost a good many hides to bugs and rot.

But even the best outfits sometimes lost hides—to the toughs who drifted about Kansas and Texas stealing hides pegged out and drying. And they sneaked into an outfit's territory to skin animals downed by the other men's bullets. Professional hunters respected another man's rights of discovery, avoided a five-mile area around his camp and tried to hunt in an opposite direction to a neighbor's hunt.

When after eight to ten days a hide had cured, the camp rustler pulled the fifteen or sixteen willow pegs that had held the shrinking hide in place. The drying had produced a "flint" hide. He folded it once, hair side in and lapped it onto a square pile of dried hides, the bend of the hide on the outside, bull, cow, kip hides, each to its own pile. And he watched the weight, for a good hide had to weigh fourteen to twenty-five pounds. When he'd piled them about seven feet high, he threw a big hide over the pile and shoveled dirt upon it to weight it against the constant prairie wind. Another method folded the hair side out, alternating the hides crosswise to the pile to hold it together, then tied all down with rawhide thongs. And still another rolled the hides.

When an outfit had stacked enough hides to fill its wagons, town beckoned; then they baled them, ten to a bale and drove off. Some men stayed away from town only ten days at a time; with luck they might have 500 hides by then—enough to make money for the boss and a spree for them. Some hunters took out several outfits a year. Others, such as the Mooars, stayed with it for months.

In Texas, hunters came upon unnatural herds—buffalo calves only, orphans with pelt not yet fit for the hide yard. Along the Arkansas River, outfits had camped to keep buffalo from drinking, had driven

The artists show much of the hide and bone business in one picture. Paul Frenzeny and Jules Tavernier, *Harper's Weekly*, April 4, 1874. *Courtesy Amon Carter Museum, Fort Worth, Texas.*

them from water by fires at night, then shot them down as the thirst-crazed animals charged in for a drink; these hunters left along the banks "a continuous line of putrescent carcasses" upon which men claimed they could travel jumping from body to body. Everywhere a new sound broke the prairie silence: the buzzing of millions of green-headed flies, the spawn of millions of maggots in the rotting meat. The hunters had "swept away more buffalo than there are cattle in Holland and Belgium."[21]

By 1873, Dodge City hide yards mostly stood empty—the trainloads of hides sent east had depleted the great Kansas herds; hide hunting no longer made a profit. But other herds grazed south of the Arkansas River, herds reserved for Indians. The Mooars, amongst others, rode south to investigate, turned west between the North and South Canadian River and "found the great herd . . . camping at night in the midst of browsing, drowsing thousands . . . For five

days we had ridden through and camped in a mobile sea of living buffalo." On their return, they prepared to go south into Texas; to hunt there they would breach the Medicine Lodge Creek Treaty that gave Indians sole hunting rights here. They visited Fort Dodge to see what the Army might do if they trespassed. The commanding officer said, "Boys, if I were a buffalo hunter I would hunt buffalo where the buffalo are."

Late in September the Mooar outfit crossed the Arkansas into Texas, knowing they moved into dangerous Indian country. By March 1874 hundreds of other hide hunters followed them in spite of the risks. As the new outfits moved in, they passed the ruins of ranchhouses burned in Comanche raids.

In the next three years the great herd thinned under the new hunting, but the volume of hides sold continued to grow and the hunting to attract more people. The year of the big kill, 1876, hunter Joe McCombs killed 4900 (2200 so close together he could see them all); his partners Poe and Jacobs killed 6300 and the Mooars killed 4500. Skelton Glenn saw

> bodies so thick after being skinned, that they would look like logs where a hurricane had passed through a forrest. If they were lying on a hillside, the rays of the sun would make it look like a hundred glass windows. These buffalo would lie in this way until warm weather, drying up, and I have seen them piled fifty or sixty in a pile where the hunter had made a stand. As the skinner commenced on the edge, he would have to roll it out of the way to have room to skin the next, and when finished they would be rolled up as thick as saw logs around a mill. In this way a man could ride over a field and pick out the camps that were making the most money out of the hunt.[22]

The Mooars found Texas Panhandle hunting so good they set up a permanent smokehouse on Deep Creek. They hauled hides and meat the long distance from here to market; John W. Mooar took charge of several wagon trains, hauling for others as well as themselves. He hauled 4000 hides to Denison, Texas, in 1875, eighteen teams of six yokes of oxen, three wagons to a team.

The wagon trains attracted attention at any settlement they passed: big Murphy wagons, wheels seven feet in diameter, bodies painted blue, oxbows and yokes also blue, drawn by Longhorns, their horns painted red. Buffalo tails dangled down all around the load. The biggest of these wagons might hold as many as 500 flint hides, the usual wagon held about 200. In dangerous Indian country, the loads of hides were good forts—sometimes a hollow niche was left in the center where a man with a Big 50 could hold off Indians at 1000 yards.

Many of these hides had been baled in a press "similar to the kind used in early cotton gins before loading." Other hides, loaded in the field for a freighting trip, were battened down ingeniously in the wagon box. Men piled the hides loosely to the top of the box; then they cast a rope over the load, tied the free end to a wagon wheel and started up the team, forcing the hides down and under rows of sharp spikes jutting into the wagon box; by repeating the operation they clamped the hides into a compact, bale-like load.

These wagon trains often belonged to the hide buyers, who began coming out to the Texas camps to bid for hides, as they had in Kansas. In 1877, Joe McCombs sold most of his hides right in camp for $1 a hide. The next year, his best, he again sold in camp the 9700 hides he, Poe and Jacobs had gathered,

for the usual $1 a hide. The buyer had to freight them to market.

In 1876, wagon trains of traders from Kansas moved south, bent on establishing trade towns. Charles Rath located his store south of the Double Mountain Fork of the Brazos. The place became known as Rath City—a town of six adobe and cedar, dirt-floored buildings. Other "cities" shared the business with Rath City. Fort Griffin, an outpost established in 1867 on the Clear Fork of the Brazos River became a supply point for hide hunters in 1874. It did more business than Rath City and the others; its hide yard, piled high with bales, reminded men of the enormous cotton yards farther east. And it had aspirations as a tourist mecca: hotel keepers lied to tenderfeet guests, saying they had no buffalo meat to eat today, but expected some tomorrow—trying to keep them in town extra days.

In 1874, Charlie Myers established Adobe Walls, across from an old adobe-walled fort at White Deer Creek on the Canadian River, a city so nondescript that hunter Seth Hathaway, riding across the prairie, mistook piles of robes nearby for Adobe Walls itself.

The buffalo disappeared from the Texas range about the same time as the Indian. Joe McCombs killed 2200 buffalo in 1877–8, others did almost as well. But when the firing died, the mooing of cattle carried on the eastern breeze; ranchers had moved onto land so recently cleared of buffalo. McCombs killed only 800 buffalo in 1878–9, others took none; some found remnant herds—guns boomed and hopes revived, to die again when only skeletons from previous years lay beyond this year's few carcasses.

Colonel Dodge and most other writers blamed the disappearance of the buffalo on the professional hide hunter of the 1870s and the 1880s. True, this market hunter did kill off the last few millions of buffalo. But hundreds of millions had died before they came, killed since the Spaniards first arrived amongst the estimated thirty to sixty million buffalo on the continent. Perhaps thirty million buffalo remained in 1830, yet by 1870, only forty years later, just four to seven million survived; at least a million buffalo a year had disappeared in these years before the hide hunter; he, from 1870 to 1876 and from 1880 to 1883, killed this usual million-plus a year—depleting the herds as rapidly as earlier hunters and plinkers and people who looked upon them as pests. Dr. Joel Allen, in his monograph of 1876, estimated the pre-hide hunter "annual average destruction" by white and Indian even higher: three to four million for the past thirty or forty years,[23] an annual kill larger than the harvest of the hide hunter. Although the hide hunter went into the shrunken herds and shot every one, wasted many and shot with bloody abandon, he mowed down wild game in an accepted American tradition: his hunting methods scarcely varied from the methods practiced by the majority of American "sportsmen" since colonial times. They had shot game bogged in deep snow, shot swimming deer from canoes, shot hundreds of ducks they couldn't use, abandoned wounded animals, shot game at salt licks and used jack lighting or fire. Furthermore, market hunters had always shot game in huge amounts and wasted much of it. Yet, the hide-hunter felt guilty and made his excuses; the buffalo, unfenceable, a misfit they said, had to go; hide-hunting served the nation by removing the Indian's food supply and subduing him; if he hadn't killed, he said, someone else would have.

But the guilt fell on everyone. Americans killed off the buffalo, all kinds of us slaughtering in our bloody, frontier custom.

The southern herd "disappeared" so rapidly a father who'd promised his children a hunt "before they all played out" found "the end came so suddenly he had no time to act." Hunter John Jacobs went to ranching, disappointed, for "my partner John W. Poe and I expected to be buffalo hunters all our lives." J. Wright Mooar took a few hides to Arizona, then returned to Texas to ranch with brother John. Others, with less capital, turned to cowboying on the same ranges they'd helped to clear—or to horse stealing and cattle rustling. Buffalo wandered here and there, but not enough of them to keep the hide hunting "industry" going. In 1879, an ex-hide hunter sometimes found himself riding line to keep the scattered remnants of buffalo away from the domestic cattle. Men who'd done nothing since 1871 but kill buffalo oiled the Sharps and hung it up. Skinners abandoned their knives: Charles Goodnight and his cowboys found them scattered over the Texas plains, enough to supply the ranch for several years. Everyone did something new—especially the unlucky inventor who showed up in Dodge City in 1876 all set to mass produce buffalo robes with his new process, only to find no hides to tan.

In Fort Griffin, in 1878, cattle raisers held a convention.

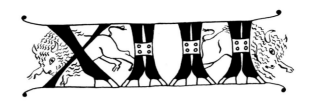

> *"The government was privy to the slaughter*
> *of the buffalo. A man . . . could get all*
> *of the government ammunition he wanted*
> *for nothing—provided he could show*
> *he was going to use it on buffalo."*

FRANK MAYER

GENERALS PHIL SHERIDAN and William Tecumseh Sherman, in charge of the Indian-fightin' Army, commanded soldiers who rode herd on the redskin to keep him on the reservation, to track him down when he wandered from it and punish him. One way of keeping these people home, the generals knew, was to destroy the buffalo. Once gone, the roving tribes would have to conform or starve.

When in 1875 General Sheridan, then Commander of the Military Department of the Southwest, heard that the Texas State Legislature was considering a bill to protect the buffalo, he rode straightway to Austin, Texas. Only six years before at Fort Cobb, Indian Territory, he had spat out an answer to Chief Toch-a-way's claim "Me Toch-a-way, me good Indian" with his famous "The only good Indians I ever saw were dead." Now he chided the joint session of Texas legislators for considering such a foolish bill and suggested, instead, they vote to give unanimous thanks to the buffalo hunters and to provide them each with a medal, a discouraged Indian on one side and a dead buffalo on the other. He went on to say, "Let them kill, skin and sell until the buffalo is exterminated, as it is the only way to bring a lasting peace and allow civilization to advance."[1] Similarly, Colonel Richard Irving Dodge, in 1867 commander at North Platte—who later tried to appear an ardent buffalo conservationist—attempted to quash Sir W. F. Butler's remorse over thirty buffalo slain with, "Kill every buffalo you can. Every buffalo dead is an Indian gone."[2]

Subjugation of the Plains Indians—that's what the Army wanted but couldn't accomplish. They'd tried protecting wagon trains and making the Overland Route safe for stagecoach travel only to find the cavalry chasing an enemy who, unencumbered by supply wagon and caissons, hit and ran, and lived on buffalo. The men in blue, according to a plainsman, "blow the bugle to let the Indians know they are going to sleep. In the morning they blow the bugle to let the Indians know they are going to get up. Between the bugle and their great trains, they manage to keep the red-skins out of sight."[3] By 1868 the troopers had pacified the tribes so little that the Commissioner of Indian Affairs ironically complained that under the present extermination policy the Army was killing about one Indian a month, a rate at which it would finish the job in about 25,000 years. Furthermore, he said, each Indian killed cost the government $1 million; worse still, for every redskin that bit the dust, twenty-five soldiers died. The Commissioner wryly reckoned extermination would cost $300 billion, and 7,500,000

General Miles and his men, in Montana, move through dinner-on-the-hoof. *Frank Leslie's Illustrated Newspaper*, October 18, 1879. *Courtesy The Library Company of Philadelphia.*

American soldiers would have to die if such Indian wars continued.[4] And by 1870 Secretary J. D. Cox of the Department of the Interior agreed—he reported to President Grant that "as a mere question of pecuniary economy," it would be cheaper to feed the Indian "to sleepy surfeiting," while educating his children, than "to carry on a general Indian war for a single year."[5]

Before the Civil War and immediately after it, destroying the buffalo had seemed unnecessary. Then the generals thought their troops to be the equal of any savage fighters, and the politicians in Washington felt that the buffalo should be saved to feed the Indians once they all had been settled on reservations. But now that the boys in blue were losing the Indian wars, Congress and the generals and the Secretary of the Interior—the government—became "privy to the slaughter of the buffalo."

The Army made Sharps and Spencer rifle cartridges "available" if the taker would "swear to shoot it into a buffalo."[6] Furthermore, in 1878, in order to starve Sitting Bull and his band, safely in exile in Canada, the Army used a cordon of Indians, half-breeds and soldiers to fire the grass ahead of the north-moving herds, harass them and keep them from entering Canada and their favorite winter grazing grounds along the Bow River. Not only did they turn them, they slaughtered them, effectively keeping them in place.[7]

This starved the Sioux, but it also starved the Canadian Bloods and incensed the Dominion government. Lord Lorne, Governor General, complained to the U.S. Secretary of State that General Nelson Miles seemed to be holding the buffalo back from returning to Canada. The Governor of Manitoba spoke out more directly, saying that the fires that had burned much of the range ahead of the buffalo had been "started at different points almost simultaneously, as if by some preconstructed arrangement."[8] The United States admitted no such "defoliation."

Canadian buffalo had also been disappearing rapidly, and, as in the United States, the government had taken few steps to protect them. Much of the Red River trade to St. Paul dealt in buffalo robes (a trade which in 1858, one year before a U.S. tax cut it off, amounted to $200,000).[9]

So rapidly did the buffalo decrease once the Canadian West opened to settlement in mid-century (over the Hudson's Bay Company's resistance), that, in the early seventies, a report to the government predicted starvation for the Indian.[10] Winnipeg's *Daily Free Press* pleaded for a protective law, at least during the breeding season, saying the Indian needed to eat buffalo during the time he learned agriculture, arguing that it would be far cheaper to pass a law than to stock the country with cattle for him.[11] Such a law was passed in 1877, a law not to conserve the buffalo, but to help feed the Indian. It forbade the use of buffalo pounds, wanton destruction, killing of buffalo under two years old, and the slaughter of cows during a closed season. But the arrival of Sitting Bull and the Sioux from the United States created a need for more buffalo than this law would allow; Canada repealed the ordinance the next year. Even so the Indian went hungry, partly because the U.S. cordon along the international border turned back buffalo heading north and partly because some Indians chose to sell buffalo meat to Canadian Pacific Railway construction camps.[12]

In the United States, the new buffalo extermination policy was never officially stated by the Army and only hinted at by Secretary of the Interior Columbus Delano, in his annual report of 1873: "I would not seriously regret the total disappearance of the buffalo from our western prairies, in its effect upon the Indians."[13]

Westerners recognized the slaughter for hides as a destroying of the Indian's sustenance: Granville Stuart noted in his journal for 1879–80, "Slaughtering the buffaloes is a government measure to subjugate the Indians."[14] The Army's own Major General W. B. Hazen wrote, "The theory that the buffalo should be killed to deprive the Indians of food is a fallacy, as these people are becoming harmless under a rule of justice."[15]

Nor did everyone in Washington agree with Columbus Delano. In 1871, Territorial Delegate R. C. McCormick of Arizona introduced a bill that made it unlawful for any person to kill a buffalo on the public lands of the United States, except for the purpose of using the meat for food or preserving the robe. The bill also provided that a $100 fine be paid for each buffalo killed. The document was ordered printed; mysteriously, it was never heard of again.

Almost a year later Senator Cornelius Cole of California introduced a resolution that the Committee on Territories be directed to inquire into the expediency of a law to protect the buffalo. Then, two days later, Harry Wilson of Massachusetts again introduced a bill into the Senate restricting the killing of buffalo on public lands. It was referred to the Committee on Territories, which killed it by neglecting to bring it to the floor for debate. Two months later Mr. McCormick of Arizona tried once again to preserve the buffalo.

Congress was unmoved. As the trainloads of hides moved east across the Mississippi, the gentlemen looked the other way. In Cheyenne, that very year of 1872, a shed 175 feet long, sixty feet wide and thirty feet high stood along the Union Pacific tracks, its walls bulging from the hides packed in it. Congress sent no investigating committees.

Congressmen made two more efforts to save the buffalo. On January 5, 1874, Mr. Greenburg Fort of Illinois introduced a bill into the House to prevent the useless slaughter of buffalo. Mr. McCormick of Arizona once again came to the defense.

After debate the House of Representatives decided it could no longer with honor overlook the plight of the buffalo; it passed the bill. Soon after, the Senate passed the same bill and sent it to President Grant for his signature. The President killed it by pocket veto.

Mr. Fort of Illinois made another 1874 effort when he introduced a bill to tax buffalo hides. Nothing came of it. And nothing more was done for two more years, until once again Mr. Fort introduced bills into the House making it illegal to kill buffalo wantonly and providing for a tax on their hides. Both bills died in committee.

Yet, the government could have easily provided for the policing of the kill, not on the hunting grounds, except by restricting certain public lands and patrolling them, but at the points of shipping where government officers would have had the power to license hunting and to stop sales. They also could have stopped the sale of hides taken between June and October (easily recognized by condition of pelt), and the sale of calf hides and cow hides. Any government officer could have monitored the hunting of the professional hide man—everyone knew him and his operation.[16]

1876: The three to four million buffalo that had constituted the southern herd now lay dead.

There was still time to save the northern herd, but Congress made no further move to save the buffalo.

Nor had the state legislatures moved. Colorado and Kansas passed "drastic" hunting laws in 1874—after hunters had exterminated the beast. Texas lawmakers, bemused by Sheridan's Indian-subduing logic, thought it unnecessary to vote any buffalo protection law into the statute books, although in 1887 only eighty "known" buffalo were left in the state. Nor did Kansas protect them. Some states enacted a closed season: Idaho in 1864, Wyoming in 1871, Montana in 1872, Nebraska in 1875, Colorado in 1877, New Mexico in 1880, and North and South Dakota in 1883.[17] But since no one patrolled these buffalo lands and no one controlled the sale of hides, the closed seasons kept few buffalo alive: he disappeared from eastern Montana under the protection of the 1872 law.

After the southern herd disappeared, hunters drifted into Wyoming, the Dakotas and Montana to shoot buffalo in the northern herd, buffalo that had been separated from the southern herd by the disturbing wagon trains on the Oregon Trail and the steam trains on the Union Pacific Railway. The northern hides, soft, deep-furred, as warm and comfy as a feather bed, thick, warm pelts developed to withstand the northern cold, sold for more money than those from Texas and Kansas. Here a man might receive $2.50, $3, even $4 a hide rather than the standard $1 often paid farther south. Here a dead cow was looked upon as $3.50 hard cash, and rival hunters claiming the same dead animal sometimes fought for it. As soon as a hunter or his skinner spread out the skin, he cut his initials in the subcutaneous muscle to guard against mistaking it for his partner's and against theft.

Here the buyers took extra time to grade the robes; each wagon load had to be examined hide by hide. Here buyer and hunter looked for beaver robes, fine and wavy and beaver-colored, for they brought $75 right in Miles City. And they looked for the blue robe (mouse-colored some said), for it brought $16. And also they set aside any black-and-tan robes, for they brought in more than the usual $3.50. Both hunter and buyer hoped to collect a rare, creamy white robe, since it would sell for $200.[18]

Miles City, born in 1876, became the hub of the hide industry, just as Dodge City had in Kansas, for the Northern Pacific Railroad came this far by 1881.

In 1880, numbers of hides had come out of the Missouri-Yellowstone country; 33,000 hides left Bozeman in 1880;[19] 10,000 buffalo were killed for hides in the Judith Basin in winter of 1879–80. These hide hunters had depended on the limited capacity of Yellowstone River steamers to move hides to market:

Most of our citizens saw the big load of buffalo hides that the *C. K. Peck* brought down last season, a load that hid everything about the boat below the roof of the hurricane deck. There were ten thousand hides in that load, and they were all brought out of the Yellowstone on one trip and transferred to the *C. K. Peck*. How such a load could have been piled on the little *Terry* not even the men on the boat appear to know. It hid every part of the boat, barring only the pilot-house and smoke-stacks.[20]

After the arrival of the railroad at Miles City, buffalo hunters increased their kill by at least two-thirds:

One hundred thousand buffalo hides will be shipped out of the Yellowstone country this season. Two firms alone are negotiating for the transportation of twenty-five thousand hides each . . . Reckoning one thousand hides to three car loads, and adding to this fifty cars for the other pelts, it will take at least three hundred and fifty boxcars to carry this stupendous bulk of peltry East to market.[21]

If these hunters were, as some say, more efficient than the Texas hunter, and killed only eleven buffalo for each ten hides marketed, the taking of the one hundred thousand hides removed about ten percent of the adult buffalo of the north (an estimated 1,500,000 animals), a kill equal to the northern herd's annual increase. The coming of the railroad brought more hunters and larger kills and did away with the herd.

Miles City had hide yards, saloons, outfitting stores, whorehouses—just like Dodge. Nearby Fort Keogh and cold weather kept the Indians peaceful, but troops added to the hurly-burly of saloon and sidewalk. Here walked many of the men who'd walked the streets of Dodge: John Cook, Harry Andrews, Hi Bickerdyke, the Frazier brothers, and others. They knew the hide business; they liked the hide price here.

But, to get this price, hunters had to work in the Montana cold because prime price came for prime hides taken between November 15th and December 15th. Mid-January blizzards took some of the gloss away; by mid-February the hide was out of prime. So, top price demanded a hunter learn to cope with Montana below-zero weather. Often the hunter had to skin the animals he shot, for an animal left until a skinner came along froze until the hide stuck. A man kept his hands warm by plunging them into warm buffalo entrails as he worked—another reason for working the carcass while it remained warm. Few men hunted in summer heat; they wanted prime prices for prime hides; hide hunters in Texas had hunted more of the year, sold more hides, but at lower prices. Cold weather helped: no arsenic needed against hide bugs, a rifle barrel heated more slowly. Northern hunting conditions were good simply because of the cold, the "heavy blanket of snow," and "storm-driven" animals. But, of course, often the hides froze board stiff; they had no way to fold them without cracking them or to peg them down into frozen ground; rocks held them down against the wind. In a wagon such hides loaded flat.

The rough country gave good cover and vantage to the hunter. Each morning he might climb a nearby height to spy out a likely herd; coulees and cutbanks often hid him until he reached shooting distance. But

"Hide Wagons on the Whoop-Up Trail in Montana." Glacier Studio, Browning, Montana. *Courtesy Bill Farr, University of Montana.*

if he had to crawl close, he would show plainly against the white snow; he donned flour sacks or canvas-covering as camouflage. And, though hidden, he had to move carefully, since northern buffalo ran off following the slightest startle. They knew the hunters' ways, for Indians here had pushed the hunt for trade robes these fifty years, the Canadian Red River carts had come squeaking twice a year, and, up the rivers, pirogues and river steamboats had spread explorers, trappers, then gold miners across their range. These animals knew enough to git up and git at the trace of man-smell on the wind, but once a man started a stand, the herd milled as stupidly as elsewhere.

The northern hunt was made mostly by professional hunters (they became professionals or froze out), men who knew how to take care of themselves, who understood the buffalo, who learned that here one must skin more carefully: they lost considerable money if they slashed hides or, teamtugging a hide from a carcass, tore it in two; few men used horses for skinning here. These men hunted by the rights of discovery as established earlier. Few farmers lived close enough to come into the herds for after-harvest hunting; few amateur hunters, then, came into the herds looking for winter meat. Few loafers braved the 40° below weather; they preferred to talk of their hide hunting in a cozy saloon.

Those who had no capital but wanted more than wages might take out an outfit for absentee killers, men who stayed east of the Mississippi, tanners mostly, who invested in buffalo killing—sometimes a risky undertaking. One Michigan company hired "hunters" from afar. The hunt over and the "hunters" paid, the company found it had paid for more skins than delivered and many of the delivered skins were spoiled by mishandling.[22]

The hunters here brought in fewer hides than their Kansas and Texas counterparts—maybe 1500 in the short season, but, since only 600 hides could make a showing, they did as well financially. And some made big kills. Doc Augh shot eighty-five in a day, Jim White 121 in two hours and Vic Smith, most "famous" of them all, shot 107 in an hour in one stand—the same year he bragged of killing 5000 in one season (a whopper of a total at these northern prices).

The bad winter of 1880–81 made good hunting for everyone. Snow lay deep in the great triangle formed by the Missouri, Musselshell and Yellowstone Rivers, so deep as to keep the herds from escaping the hunting. The Sioux City *Journal* reported in the spring of '81: "The past severe winter caused the buffalo to bunch themselves in a few valleys where there was pasturage . . . There was no sport about it, simply shooting down the famine-tamed animals as cattle might be shot down in a barn-yard . . . leaving the carcasses to rot."[23]

Everyone moved into the great triangle in 1882: white hide hunters, innumerable Indians, and Métis; all shot for their share of the estimated 250,000 buffalo in this patch of country. From the north came the Cree, the Blackfeet, and the Red River hunters, from the east the Assiniboine and Yanktonai Sioux, from the south the Crow and the white hide hunter.

The final kill of the northern herd degenerated into a compulsive slaughter. The buffalo, unlike their nature, hid in remote coulees, bolted at first sight of man. Seventy-five thousand of them, acting as though in desperation, suddenly crossed the Yellowstone River in 1882 and pushed north through a barrage of gunfire. Evidently the entire herd fell under the onslaught—disappeared as into a hole in the ground—but the optimistic hunters believed thousands of them had just gone north into Canada.

A year later. The fall of 1883. October saw hunting parties outfitting as usual, moving out into the rough lands north of the Yellowstone, guns oiled and ready for the coming butchery. A thousand hunters lined the Canadian border, guns ready to ambush the mythical escapees of last year's slaughter as they returned south. But with the exception of the guns fired at occasional bulls, most of the ponderous barrels fired nary a shot.

The buffalo were all but vanished, but no one believed that it had happened. A last band of 10,000 was discovered in the Dakotas north of the Black Hills, and, before the end of October, hunters decimated it to about 1000 head. Suddenly Sitting Bull and a thousand of his braves left Standing Rock Agency and swept down on the last slaughtering ground. Whites and Indians joined together in one last blood-fest. Vic Smith, famous hunter of the Yellowstone, was part of the wild melee: ". . . when we got through the hunt there was not a hoof left. That wound up the buffalo in the Far West, only a stray bull being seen here and there afterwards."

True.

At James Willard Schultz's Fort Carrol on the Missouri, where 2700 robes had come in last year, only 300 robes came in—and they mostly undesirable bull robes.[24] In St. Paul, which had handled 10,000 hides in 1882–83, "the catch" amounted to but four this year.[25]

And the hide hunters had killed the remaining buffalo in Canada: 200,000 in 1882, 40,000 in 1883, 3000 in 1884, none in 1885.[26] Three years later Canada made it illegal to kill a buffalo: a $200 fine. But, as late as 1897, English "sportsmen" were adding this cost to their Canadian hunting trip and getting their wood buffalo.[27]

Gradually the hunters drifted back to Terry, to Miles City, to Glendive, to Dickinson. They sold their outfits for a few cents on the dollar. They hung around the saloons for awhile, waiting for news of buffalo herds, waiting for the big herds to return from "up north" where all the old hunters swore they were hiding. From time to time they sweated out a rumor of a big herd seen somewhere; each rumor proved false, but because buffalo rumors had always flown about, buffalo herds had always mysteriously disappeared and reappeared, hope of a grand return smoldered on.

Cowboys, riding the newly opened cattle range, found their job complicated by the sudden "increase in the depredations of wolves" upon the cattle herds they guarded. "Wolfers" came in to harvest the wolves. Ex-hunters looked upon this sudden "appearance" of the wolves as indication of hidden buffalo on the increase, and began to plan for more hide-hunting.

But those hunters like Vic Smith, to whom buffalo killing was life, took off to the country surrounding eleven-year-old Yellowstone Park. Once in awhile a few buffalo wandered over the border; if they didn't, a man could always take a chance and go in after one—if the price was right. And the price would very soon be right. The law of supply and demand would skyrocket prices for bull heads suitable for mounting.

The plinker's lust for buffalo blood continued even as the estimated 600 to 1000 remaining skittery buffalo—sole survivors—bolted at the slightest sound.

In Montana, cowboy Ed Carlson ran into a herd of seven, emptied his gun at them, killing one. While he was trying to extract new shells from his cartridge belt an old bull whirled and stopped not twenty-five yards away, "perfectly still, seeming to say in his mute way: 'I am the last of my race; shoot me down.' For a few minutes he stood gazing at me, then whirled and ran after the others . . . That was the last wild buffalo I ever saw on the plains."[28] Carlson's was the typical latter-day experience with "the last wild buffalo I ever saw." The instinct was to reach for a gun instead of a lasso.

And nobody seemed to care: The *Denver Daily News* lightly commented in 1884, "A wild buffalo strayed into Brush a few days ago with some native cattle. He was killed and his carcass sent to Denver." During the same year: a lone bull that wandered near a ranch in the Bad Lands was shot; three men who ran into a herd of 200 "succeeded in killing three of them, and undoubtedly would have slaughtered more had they not run out of ammunition"; a Lieutenant with Princeton's fossil-hunting expedition shot an old solitary bull; the ex-Sheriff of Teton County, Montana, thought he killed the last buffalo in Montana, and was so proud of it he hung the head over the door.

At least one famous hunter went after final trophies. In 1883 Theodore Roosevelt traveled to Medora, North Dakota, to shoot a buffalo before the hide hunter exterminated them. He went home with a head and a robe. Six years later, 1889—when only a few hundred buffalo remained—Roosevelt traveled to the Wisdom River because he "heard that a very few bison were still left." He killed a big bull "in Idaho, just south of the Montana boundary line, and some twenty-five miles west of the line in Wyoming"— more than likely a Yellowstone Park bull that had not noticed the boundary line. Roosevelt said he was glad his guide had no rifle for "it would have been impossible to stop him from firing at such game as bison, nor would he have spared the cows and calves."[29] No bully sportsman, that guide.

Seemingly most people felt about the last few buffalo as a Governor of Maryland had said he felt about ducks—he didn't care about future generations as long as he could duck hunt to his own content during his lifetime. Buffalo on the verge of extinction drew just one more bullet, one like each of Rip Van Winkle's drinks—it didn't count.

According to one tall yarn, the sighting of a herd of buffalo from a Northern Pacific train so excited a passenger, eager to kill before the species had gone, he descended from the train at Belfield, telegraphed friends, and "Howard Eaton's tame buffalo had a narrow escape. Howard says he will have them whitewashed and a lantern with a red light attached to them, and hopes that this will be sufficient to save the lives of his pets."[30]

Commercial hunters still preyed on the buffalo, killing for big money brought on by scarcity. They destroyed a herd of 165 near Jackson's Hole during the winter of 1884–85.[31] Rancher Lee Howard and his cowboys rode into a remnant Texas herd the winter of 1887 and killed fifty-two of them, not for meat, not for pleasure, but, even as time was running out for the buffalo, for profit. His outfit cut forty-two heads from the bodies for mounting. Howard peddled the adult bull heads at $25 apiece, cow heads for only $15. Hide prices had also soared as the supply grew scarce. Howard asked $20 apiece for a few of the poorer buffalo hides, but the prime twenty-eight he sold to the Hudson's Bay Company for $250 each. And Howard found another new market, a market created only by the imminent finish of the species. He sold several of his complete skins to taxidermists, asking $150 for the skin of an adult bull suitable for stuffing. The American Museum of Natural History, having not foreseen the buffalo's demise and now unable to collect specimens in the field, was forced to purchase some of Howard's hides, but from a North Dakota taxidermist.[32]

By 1902 the 635 buffalo alive in 1890 had decreased to an estimated seventy-two in the United States and twenty-five in Canada. (Later several hundred uncounted wood buffalo were discovered in northern Alberta.)

Twenty-five of those in the United States lived within the "protection" of Yellowstone Park, but taxidermists in Livingston, Montana, offered such prices for buffalo heads that poachers endangered the park buffalo: in 1894, $300 for a mounted buffalo head; by 1902, $1000 a head; somewhat up from the $25 to $50 paid when Vic Smith arrived in 1884.[33] At that price the park herd in Lamar Basin could scarcely propagate fast enough to stay ahead of the poachers, and any buffalo found outside the park jeopardized his head and robe. In 1904 somebody killed another "last wild buffalo" near Yellowstone Park.

But about this time, in Pennsylvania, where an estimated million hides had been tanned since 1845, buffalo hides glutted the market; tanners sold bales of unwanted hides to local farmers at $20 a bale, twelve hides to a bale—less than they'd sold for on the range 2000 miles west.[34]

*"Whenever civilized man has met with the larger mammalia
in abundance . . . the temptation to slaughter for the mere sake
of killing seems rarely to be resisted."*

JOEL ALLEN

IN 1884, editors wrote scathingly of the men who had all but exterminated the buffalo, the hide hunters. The editors seemed surprised that the Missouri River Valley held no buffalo where only a couple of years ago a million or two had roamed. They bemoaned the absence of herds along the Platte and the Arkansas and the Cimarron. They spoke of the terrible waste and of the wantonness of those who had worn out guns shooting buffalo for their hides only. They seemed surprised that, in spite of their good intentions, without warning, bad men, behind their backs, had suddenly done away with the buffalo.

But men had been prophesying the buffalo's disappearance for years. As early as 1776, Bernard Romans, a traveler in the United States, worried over their continual destruction for their tongues only. John D. Hunter, raised by Indians, in a book about his experiences spoke his disgust with Manuel Lisa on the Kansas River about 1815, when he saw for the first time the "wide and wanton destruction of game, merely to procure the skins" and the "buffalo carcasses strewed over the ground in a half putrified state."[1]

Game had disappeared so fast along the eastern seaboard that colonial lawmakers had decided to protect it. Georgia's House of Commons had made it illegal to hunt buffalo in certain areas in 1759,[2] a law as effective as the twentieth century's Prohibition Act—the buffalo disappeared from Georgia about 1773. Hunters had killed all the buffalo in Illinois about 1800 and in West Virginia about 1825. They had slaughtered those in Kentucky by 1800 and in Tennessee by 1810. Men settling in eastern Iowa in 1825 found almost no buffalo. The last buffalo living east of the Mississippi were killed off about 1832—by Sioux Indians.

Major Stephen Long's 1819–20 expedition from Pittsburgh to the Rocky Mountains noted that "all the herds of these animals appear to have deserted the country east of Council Bluffs" and found no big herds east of the Little Arkansas' mouth. The report said the nation needed a law to protect the buffalo against mere wantonness. George Catlin, watching and painting the killing along the Missouri in the 1830s, believed that the buffalo would disappear in eight or ten years; Maximilian, observing the west about the same time, wrote of "a very great decrease" in their numbers. In the same year, Josiah Gregg, traveling along the Santa Fe Trail, wrote:

The vast extent of the prairies upon which they now pasture is no argument against the prospect of their total extinction, when we take into consideration the extent of the country from which they have already disappeared . . . they were nearly as abundant east of the Mississippi as they now are upon the western prairies . . . they are rarely seen within two hundred miles of the frontier. Indeed, upon the high plains they have sensibly decreased within the last ten years.[3]

In 1841, John B. Newhall reported none surveyed in Iowa and that "Even the Indians on our border have to go fifteen or twenty days' hunt before they can find this animal."[4] That same year the Osages could find no buffalo on the former prime range near the junction of the Canadian and Arkansas. Their agent reported them traveling farther west for each annual hunt.[5]

In the 1850s, Alexander Ross, writing of the buffalo of the Red River country in Canada, had said, "They are now like a ball between two players. The Americans are driving them north, the British south. The west alone will furnish them a last and temporary retreat."[6] In 1855, Indian Agent John Whitfield reported the Comanches, Kiowas, Kiowa-Apaches, Arapahoes and Cheyennes forced to eat mules and horses because they could find no buffalo. In 1857, the Commissioner of Indian Affairs said that many Indians now lived by plunder because the buffalo were gone.[7] In 1868, General W. F. Raynolds, explorer of Yellowstone country, some of which would become the National Park, said he believed the buffalo would be extinct in "another generation." In 1876, Joel A. Allen, in his monograph "History of the American Bison," concluded that "While the range seems not to have been as yet very materially circumscribed during the last four or five years, the reduction in numbers has been immense, and the vast herds existing there five years since are now represented by only scattered remains."[8]

No American—no editor—could have remained ignorant of the buffalo's continuous extirpation.

(In Russia, the wisent, the European bison, likewise had become reduced to only scattered animals, and in 1852 the Russian Emperor had decreed protection for the animal to stop his extermination. In Europe, just as in North America, man had wasted buffalo. Even Julius Caesar wrote, "They are taken and slain by means of pits dug on purpose . . . They who kill the greatest number, and produce the horns in public as proof, are in high reputation.")[9]

Now that the brown, shaggy shapes no longer stood on the evening horizon, beard blowing in the breeze, homesteaders could no longer visit the buffalo range

in November to gather a frozen wagonload of buffalo humps, thighs and tongues for a winter's eating. The beast that had fed Kentuckian, Kansan and Texan fed few latecomer Nebraskans, Dakotans or Montanans. However, many of them kept warm through the bleak winters by burning buffalo chips and buffalo bones. The bones, they found, burned better than chips (bearing out Sir Richard Burton's contention that wagonmasters had neglected the best fuel, the bone, for the chip). And the homesteader was glad to burn bones to rid his land of them:

> When we got there [Nebraska] buffalo bones was laying around on the ground as thick as cones under a big fir tree, and we had to pick them up, and pile them up, and work around them until we was blamed sick of ever hearing the name buffalo, but we never seen a single live one there in our valley . . . Us children had all helped pick up bones so that Father could plow some sod under for corn and for our house.[10]

Similarly, in Kansas, "Old Buffalo bones was *very thick* all over the upper land of my neighborhood, and so on far away to the West, and were a nuisance to our breaking of the sod."[11]

Early settlers sometimes gathered the bullets found under bone piles and melted them down. Or they braved the rattlesnakes lurking in the skeletons to scavenge the horns that brought $12 to $20 a ton from manufacturers of ornamental hatracks (about their only use, even though manufacturers, taking advantage of the public's interest in anything buffalo, advertised "buffalo horn" buttons and combs, but usually manufactured these from other horn, for they found buffalo horn too brittle and hard to work).

Then bones began to furnish more than pin money—homesteaders found their "first cash crop" in them; the market had expanded. Sugar companies used the fresher, unweathered bones to neutralize the acids produced in sugar refining; fertilizer factories ground the older, cracked, weatherbeaten bones into fertilizer; glue makers used the horns and hoofs; makers of expensive bone china bid for the best bones.

Men began once more to drive their wagons into buffalo land, now to stuff them with bones, the new buffalo bonanza. Railroads built spurs where they'd planned none just to load buffalo bones; now and then they ran out of empty cars to haul bones in; they began to grant favorable shipping rates for this crop to encourage the homesteaders, whose future agricul-

"A Sod House—The Beginning of Better Things. Buffalo Bones in the Foreground."
Courtesy Glenbow Museum, Calgary, Alberta.

tural crops they hoped to haul. Buyers rode parlor cars, stopped off at fresh-sawed towns to contract for the huge ricks of bones which had grown there; homesteaders piled other huge ricks beside right-of-ways long before track-layers arrived, each marking his bones with a painted brand.

The price for dry bones, sun-dried, bare of flesh, averaged $8 a ton (about 8¢ per skeleton); fresh bones sometimes brought $14, ancient bones sometimes $2, and if a man crushed the bones before he sold, he might receive $18. Since the skeleton of one animal only weighed about twenty pounds (skeletons from one hundred animals made up a ton), a rainstorm on a wagonload was a godsend—it might increase the tonnage payments as much as twenty-five percent; a surreptitious overnight soaking of a wagonload in a creek did the same.

Wherever a hide hunter had made his stand, the bones lay as nicely grouped for the bone-picker and his bone wagon as the carcasses had for the skinner and his hide wagon. And around old trading forts, bones lay thick, so grown over with grass a man thought he saw the grey of rabbit ears everywhere pro-

truding above the grass. At Buffalo Gap, Nebraska, settlers of the townsite had to clear away and pile up bones to "get room enough to throw up a few log cabins, and a stagecoach stop and corral."[12]

Those bones that lay on a settler's 160 acres he guarded from other bone-pickers until he could load them himself. On the Dakota plains, he watched out for the Métis, little splinter groups from the Red River colony, still wandering the plains, creaking about in caravans of two-wheel carts, gathering bones— "Camping wherever they worked . . . making a trip to the shipping point when they felt like it." They loaded as many as 1200 pounds of bones in a cart before the caravan moved toward market "like some interminable, wriggling, creeping seamonster . . . hideous noises, which one might imagine coming from such a leviathan would be something like that arising from the greaseless, sun-dried wooden carts . . ."[13] (wags called the carts "Manitoba pianos." You could hear the noise of the ungreased wheels long after they disappeared from sight—each groaned its own noise and waggled "its own individual waggle"). As these people settled farther west, the carts, known as Red

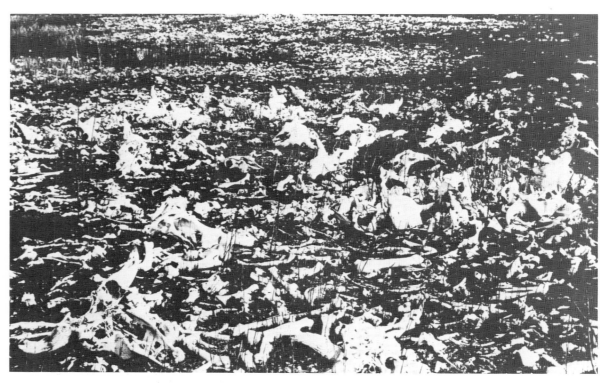

The remains of a hide hunter's "stand"—easy picking for the bone hunter. *Courtesy Glenbow Museum, Calgary, Alberta.*

River Carts, became common along the entire upper Missouri.

These carts had wandered the Canadian and upper Missouri River country since the 1820s (nine carts had once surprised artist Rudolph Kurz by materializing out of the prairie surrounding Fort Union). The twice-a-year buffalo hunt of the Métis in their carts had upset the agricultural routine of Selkirk's Red River Colony, for two thousand to three thousand Métis residents went west to the buffalo herds each spring and fall, just when crops needed attention, seriously depleting the farm labor supply. They hunted to supply the colony and the Hudson's Bay Company with buffalo meat. The hunts, by increasing from the 500 carts of the 1820s, which furnished about forty-five tons of meat, to the 1200 carts of the 1840s, which furnished about 500 tons, outdid the need for meat, and lowered meat prices: for two months' travel and the labor of curing meat, a family realized only about $150. But they buffaloed for adventure's sake more than money, made "a leap in the dark" toward the herds; sometimes they almost starved before they found buffalo. And each year they had to go farther from Pembina, the jumping-off place, until they were making a 600-mile round trip. But only the demise of the buffalo stopped the treks, the twice-yearly camp-outs.

Their latter-day visits with bone loads disrupted one Dakota railroad boom town, stopped traffic while the carts passed the buyer's window, each cart weighed for gross, then to the rick to circle through the streets to weigh tare and receive payment. For three weeks or so after selling, the Métis disturbed the nervous though scornful town; they bought supplies and celebrated, spent their bone money, encamped on the edge of town in a tipi village rimmed by a circle of carts, until one morning, cartwheels squawking, they moved over the horizon onto their prairie home, mysterious and shiftless in the eyes of the honyocker who viewed the expanse of grass as something to be conquered not something to melt into. He promptly went out to his acres to see that the shiftless ones gleaned none of his bones—nor any bones lying close by.

Growing settlements eventually forced these nomads to haul bone 150 miles "over unbroken prairie and around lakes, sloughs, and plowed quarter-sections of settlers, in order to get the pittance their loads might bring." When the bones were gone, their semi-nomadic days of following where the buffalo led—and where their bones whitened—ended. Their women could now join the Indian women who squatted by the corral at the white man's slaughter house attempting to steal beef guts from the half-wild hogs feeding there.

Yet they had had a hand in their own deterioration. Only a few years before, the Canadian Border Survey had found the Métis killing six or eight buffalo a day, taking only the tongues and hump ribs, leaving the rest to waste. The survey picked its way through a "carrion stench" between Frenchman and Milk Rivers, walking through "a life destroying itself."[14]

In spots where the bones lay thick and close to a shipping point, a man had a bonanza. One old fellow piled so many wagonloads along the tracks in Dodge City the locals dubbed him "Old Buffalo Bones." But name-calling couldn't break him of bone piling; he filled 300 railroad cars with bones and retired thinking himself rich. In Colorado, J. R. (Sheep Jim) Lewallen gathered enough bones to buy his first sheep ranch. Freighters out of Dodge City hauling army supplies made the return trip pay by hauling bones local pickers had piled along the way. These freighters drove tandem wagons, a big Studebaker wagon holding five tons in front, a couple of smaller farm wagons behind, filled to the brim and with the pelvic bones arranged about the wagon top to raise the load further. Buffalo bones "was legal tender in Dodge City." Even men who gleaned country where it took five days to gather a wagonload could make enough to buy necessities.

The Great Plains had been called the Great American Desert, but for these few years of bone-picking it became known as Boneland. Earlier, Coronado could have so named it, for bones had whitened valleys when he rode east. And they'd lain along the Platte when the mountain men pushed west. Long before the white man, Indians had named the place where Regina now stands Waskana, or Pile of Bones Creek. Since the dry air of the high plains preserves skeletons for decades (in 1968 a forest ranger picked up a well-preserved skull in the Lost Park region of Colorado), the amount of bones shipped east represented more than the hide hunter kill: the Empire Carbon Works of St. Louis, which estimated it processed seventy percent of the buffalo bones coming east, processed 1,250,000 *tons* of bones.[15] At one hundred animal skeletons per ton, these bones represent 125 million buffalo. Adding the other thirty percent, representing 53,500,000 animals, would produce a total of 178,500,000 buffalo skeletons processed— three to five times the total buffalo thought to inhabit the continent when the Spaniards arrived.

Only the wallows remained on the prairies to remind men of the buffalo—an irritating reminder, as often as not, an alkali bog, too gummy for a plowshare to furrow. The sticky alkali stuff left young Mont Hawthorne's bare feet cracked and burned. One day his mother rubbed linseed oil on them before he went out to follow the plow, but the oil made the stuff ball up until he had to return to the house for his mother to "chisel it off." His father could see some use for such a plague—he saw "how good the stuff would be to put on top of the roof."[16]

Scattered thickets of bones lay in coulees remote from railroads until the country settled. Texans still loaded a bone wagon here and there in 1899, and North Dakota homesteaders drove an occasional bone wagon to railroad siding as late as 1910.

"It was a great help to the settlers," said a Texan. True. In total, men may have made more profit selling bones than selling hides.

"Julian Ralph, in Calgary in 1889, learned that some Indians 'now take their ponies in the springtime and ride away as of old in silence and sadness. "Where are you bound?" some white man inquires. "For the buffalo," is the reply. "But there are no more." "No, we know it." "Then why are you going on such a foolish chase?" "Oh, we always go at this time; maybe we shall find some."'"
DOUGLAS BRANCH

". . . our government was holding out longhorns as bait so's they'd behave theirselves and quit killing whites."
MONT HAWTHORNE

Once the buffalo boom had busted and the ages-old buffalo life had gone, ex-hide hunters went to cowboyin' for thirty dollars a month and keep (furnish your own saddle), and storekeepers made do by peddling barbed wire, shovels and pitchforks to homesteaders. But these—so recently enriched by the buffalo—all, no matter now how poor, how disappointed, made out better than the Indian.

Day after day he sat. Some days he gambled for measly stakes. Some days he stiffly got himself astride his old, knob-kneed buffalo horse and rode to see friends who had no feasts to offer and only worn buffalo robes in sitting places. If he arrived on a lucky day, a friend would sneak a hidden whiskey jug from out of a parfleche and offer it around and around the fireplace until brains numbed and they forgot the boredom of living in the same land moon upon moon, no war parties to join, no dancing, no feasts, no horse-stealing. In the early days of his reservation life, when a man had busted off limits to steal horses, he had sometimes found buffalo, and life had seemed bearable. Now a man on a sneak hunt could, once in a long while, bring a single animal back and sing invitations to a miserable one-buffalo feast.

As late as the early 1900s, newly settled homesteaders were bringing in loads of bones to sell in Glasgow, Montana. Lou Lucke photo. *Courtesy Bill Farr, University of Montana, Missoula.*

A man had nothing to do. He couldn't so much as drag a fire log out of the cottonwood grove; his woman would have scorned to live with such a womanly man. So he watched the women bring in wood to cook scrawny, tasteless government-issue beef, meat he'd not so much as halloed at from behind piskin wall, meat that fell not by arrow in the musk-sour haze of the chase, but by bludgeons in the stink of the white man's slaughterhouse.

When a man itched to move, his women cheerfully threw a few rations into the ramshackle wagon, bundled together lodgepoles and raggedy tipi canvas—no one had warm buffalo-skin lodges now—and hitched the horses, to go visiting friends, maybe only five miles away, an hour's ride. But it meant lodges pitched together, other campfires than one's own, and stories and sharing of food in the old way.

A man knew that the white Indian Agent, the "Major," wanted him to stay home, mind a few cattle, cut hay, do as whites did. But the white man he saw lied and cheated. He'd had a cow taken away by an agent to pay for goods that had never been delivered. He'd seen white men running their cattle on Indian land, against the law. And he disliked the white man's unceremonial brusqueness. He'd called on the major, wanting to talk things over, to spend hours speculat-

ing what to do, but the major had abruptly made a decision and gave an order before the powwow had scarcely started.

Worst of all, the white man seemingly couldn't make up his mind what he wanted to do about the Indian or what the Indian should do. Early on, he'd allowed him to chase the herds of beef brought in, exciting chases of tailing a steer and holding off the kill until the run had warmed the meat enough to make it tasty:

This delivery of beef was one of the best sights I have ever had the pleasure of seeing. The agent's clerk would call out the name of the family that was to have beef and the cowboys would run a longhorn steer out at the gate. Outside of the corral there would be about a hundred warriors, all painted up with war paint and riding his war horse bareback, with a string in the horse's mouth for a bridle, and armed with a Winchester, just as if he were going to war.

When the steer would get about 200 feet from the corral the chief would let out a yell and all of them would make a rush for the animal. Each of them would shoot at the steer. Sometimes they would run him five miles before they could kill him. All of the warriors would rush back and tell the squaws where

Scoffers told Jim Hill his 1907 railroad to the Pacific Coast would haul nothing but buffalo bones. Here is a load for him in Glasgow, Montana. Lou Lucke photo. *Courtesy Bill Farr, University of Montana, Missoula.*

they had left the steer and they would go and skin him and bring the meat back to camp. Then the clerk, on a high board over the gate would call out another family's name and out would come another steer and the yelling and the fun would begin again. I heard that the Indians got to "playing white man" by shooting at some other Indian while the fun was going on and the Indian department changed the plan of delivery.[17]

A man almost believed he chased buffalo once again. Feasting for days. Then those rare good times stopped. The Great White Father commanded the cattle be killed in the white man's way. Butchers came to the agency to fell the steers in stinking sheds to produce cold meat. And the hides disappeared, sent over the hills in wagons. And when the women tried to chop a length of upper gut from the offal piles outside, the white men sent them away.

No buffalo tongue for the Sun Dance; no buffalo dung to burn at the altar fire; no chip to swear the truth upon; no buffalo robe to kneel upon while opening one's medicine bundle; no buffalo heads to use in a bull dance.

Once, a white man, who came to the reservation to draw pictures of Indians and Indian things, had told of buffalo penned up in one of the white man's big cities. Another white man's lie. But a boy who had attended Agency school for a while (a way of learning the secrets of the white man's power) had written a letter to the city telling of their need for holy buffalo things. The proof had come to Agency from the big city: a box of buffalo chips in the mail, the gift of the white man so that once more the sacred buffalo-chip fires might smolder.

Since then the city men had occasionally sent a buffalo robe and a head whenever one of their hidden buffalo died. And once in a great while a tongue arrived. The white man had the Indian's buffalo. He'd killed most of them and hidden the rest, penned them up; perhaps he'd hidden them in a hole in the ground as in the days of Old Man Coyote.

Now if an Indian wanted to call upon the sun he had to wait upon the white man to send him buffalo things . . . .

On July days when the sun shone hot, young men went to the hay field. They used the white man's machine to cut the good grass; they used another machine to pile it; they pitched it onto wagons with spear sticks; they did women's work, but their women didn't sneer.

An old man felt his stomach lurch as he watched

Indians on the hill are awaiting the signal to come down and butcher the cattle killed by the Indian agency employees. *Courtesy Bill Farr, University of Montana.*

Sioux shooting corralled government cattle in 1879 at Standing Rock Agency. Note the man on the right, on the corral, with bow and arrow. W. A. Rogers illustration in *Harper's Weekly*, February 22, 1879. *Courtesy Amon Carter Museum, Fort Worth, Texas.*

them drink milk, whitish, revolting calf's food. No buffalo Indian should drink such stuff; no buffalo Indian should do such work. An old man grunted approval when he heard the words of Washakie, chief of the Shoshones, at the white man's council. The chief, having listened to all of the palaver over the wisdom of reservation life and Indian farming plots, drew himself up and put together one of the shortest Indian speeches ever delivered. He said, "Goddam a potato."

Long after any Indian had seen any wild buffalo, when even the old people had never seen buffalo, tribes yet held to buffalo-impregnated ceremonies. A man used buffalo relics until they wore out and he had to beg new ones from the white men. In 1924, forty years since the buffalo disappeared, Edmund Seymour, President of the American Bison Society, received a penciled plea on tablet paper:

November 23, 1924
Pueblo of Cochiti
Pena Blanca, New Mexico

May Dear Edmund Seymour

I get your letter about to week ago. as you say in you letter about buffalo head and hides and I being wait for you to get too week now I will tell you I dint get any buffalo head no hides so I let you know this you must know this that I dint get any buffalo now is the time to send them down we need them in Christmas to dance with them but you could send them any time. This is all for this time. I send my best regard to you.

Yours Trully,
Louis Ortiz, Governor
Pueblo of Cochiti
Pena Blanca, N.M.

answer soon[18]

But kind-hearted New Yorker, Mr. Seymour, found it difficult to expedite buffalo heads. A month later another letter came to him: ". . . I am always eagerly looking for them . . . In our dances of the Bison dance we use two heads . . . we use our Bison head during Christmas week until after New Year's . . . Well we are practicing dances. . . ."[19] If that year they danced for the Christian Christmas ceremonial, they danced without new buffalo heads, for in mid-January Seymour was still hoping to get heads and hides from a shed at the Moiese Bison Range where they were "practically going to waste" as a possession of the U.S. government.

About this time a butcher at Browning, Montana, on the Blackfeet reservation, thought to profit from the Blackfeet's age-old need for buffalo. He bought a buffalo carcass from the thinning of a government herd and displayed it in his cases to tempt visiting Blackfeet. Not an Indian entered his shop to buy meat, the meat long ago presented to them by Old Man Coyote, meat to be gathered only in sacred ceremonial hunts.[20]

Blackfeet at ancient killing grounds digging buffalo bones to sell in 1943. Fred Williams photo. *Courtesy Glenbow Museum, Calgary, Alberta.*

*". . . when we have fitted the buffalo to its proper sphere, it is
the chief of all ruminants. I will chain him and domesticate a
race of cattle equal to, if not superior to, all ruminants
heretofore known. I will attire myself in clothing made from the
products of the buffalo; even the buttons of my clothes shall be
made of horns and hoofs of that wonderful animal. I will not
rely on the ravens for my food and raiment, and all may rest
assured that I will never suffer from the howling
blizzards, nor for meat go hungry."*
BUFFALO JONES'S VOW

*"I had killed buffalo by the thousands for their skins and had
vowed someday to capture and domesticate enough
to attone for my cussedness."*
BUFFALO JONES

BUFFALO had been a staple of the expanding, young United States democracy for its first hundred years—more than a staple, one of its few luxuries. They had afforded penniless settlers choice cuts of meat: steaks, roasts, liver and kidney. They had provided tongue by the barrelfull to eastern cities. Now we had emptied this seeming inexhaustible, natural larder.

One of the men who vowed to fill it again was C. J. "Buffalo" Jones, ex-hide hunter, who said he vowed his vow in 1886 (in his later days he was a great one for vowing vows that might read well). Jones in his flamboyant way contended that the slaughter for hides had sickened him. He said that as hunter he had sworn off many a time, determined to break his gun over a wagonwheel when he got back to camp, but had put it off. And when next morning guns sounded, he couldn't resist the excitement.

Certainly he was one of the most publicized men to try to perpetuate the buffalo species—C. J. Jones of Kansas, mostly known as Buffalo Jones and sometimes called Colonel. Jones, it appears, would have liked as much fame as Buffalo Bill Cody—and he partially achieved it: Emerson Hough, magazine writer and novelist-to-be who accompanied him to Texas on an expedition to capture buffalo calves, wrote of him, "There is no man in Kansas so well known, perhaps no private citizen better, in the entire United States."[1] Hough knew him in 1887 at a time when he was flush with money made from real estate in the town he fathered, Garden City, Kansas, a time when he had just built a $100,000 marble-faced hotel in the little prairie town (the Buffalo Hotel), and had built a part of the Nickel Plate Railroad, a time when he could write a check for $100,000, a time when he could vote as a member of the state legislature. A long time before he died in poverty. Before he died, Buffalo Jones did far more than the renowned Buffalo Bill toward preserving buffalo.

He loved adventure and notoriety, dreamed impossible dreams, yet attempted to establish a practical, profitable buffalo ranch. By establishing his ranch, he felt he had reformed and was doing penance. It may have salved the Colonel's conscience to believe this, but another buffalo-lover saw a Jones who "had visions of big game hunters coming to his ranch and

Buffalo Jones. Frederic Remington, *Harper's Weekly*,
July 12, 1890. *Courtesy Amon Carter Museum, Fort Worth,
Texas.*

paying him important money to ride and shoot in a buffalo hunt."[2] And a glimpse of his more practical reason may be seen in a phrase about a buffalo calf which almost escaped him: "What should I do? There was a calf worth a thousand dollars, and all that I had to do was catch it."[3]

Whatever his reasons, Buffalo Jones caught sixty-six calves on four different hunts (sixty-six more or less—some say fifty-nine and Jones's different accounts arrive at different totals), trailed them the many miles to his ranch, and raised them to adulthood; he preserved enough buffalo so that, in the 1890s, 500 buffalo living around the world were offspring of the calves raised on his Kansas ranch.[4]

In Emerson Hough's magazine articles about the 1887 calf-capturing trip, Jones's dash and determination measure up to some of his brag.

Hough and his partner, artist A. J. Ricker, bullied their way into this second expedition to the Texas Panhandle. Jones, fearing that such greenhorns might frighten the buffalo away, refused to take them. But when they threatened to trail along on their own, he agreed to sign them on so he could station them out of

the way. Jones, a companion named Ez Carter, and the two men headed south from Garden City.

As they reached the breaks of the South Fork, they stampeded fifty or more buffalo, heads down and humps bobbing, moving far faster than Hough had imagined their seeming clumsiness would allow. The four surprised men piled out of the buggy, scrambled for saddles, calf-hobbles and lassoes.

Jones and Carter readied in Pony Express time, Jones cinching without ever taking his eyes from the rapidly disappearing herd. Hough and Ricker dug out the hobbles, a rope designed by Jones to hold a wild calf without harming him—a large loop in the middle to go over a calf's head and at each end slip nooses to fasten over a calf's hind legs just above the pastern joint.

Jones and Carter snatched what they needed and spurred toward the herd which had turned at a diagonal, meaning they might catch it. Ricker and Hough whipped up their team, in a sweat to keep up. "The wagon jumped over dog-holes, hummocks and sinks, and the springs clashed together at every bound; but we managed to hold on some way,—can't tell you how,—and laid the team flat down in our determination to be in with the crowd." Somehow, in spite of the jouncing and the dust, they saw Buffalo Jones ride into the herd, cut out a cow and calf, twirl his loop about his head and send it over the calf's head. They watched Jones jump from his horse, kneel on the tawny animal, swiftly loop the hobbles about the little fellow and release his lasso all before the mother knew her baby was gone. Jones remounted and galloped on. Writer and artist stopped their wagon near the captive: "He was a comical-looking, round-headed, curly little rascal; we laughed when approaching him. The first thing he did was to utter a hoarse bawl, and charged at us with head down. In doing this, of course the hobble tripped him, and he turned a somersault. Before he could recover we sat down on top of him— the first buffalo calf we had ever seen."

Hobbled or not, lifting the squirming, irritated infant aboard the light wagon developed into a wrestling match, two against one, a match that ended by piling the tent on the struggling calf to pin him to the wagon floor. Then the winded victors rolled after the hunt, urging speed out of their team again while scanning the rough terrain for humps of cinnamon-brown buffalo calf. Before they caught up with Jones and Carter they found and wrestled two more calves into the buggy, one a bull calf big for his age and proportionately feisty.

It was coming on dark. They had to find a camp

Buffalo Jones was part showman and part buffalo savior. Circa 1900. *Courtesy Denver Conservation Center Library.*

A sketch record of some of the incidents of Buffalo Jones's second expedition to the
Texas Panhandle to capture buffalo calves. A. J. Ricker, *The American Field*, 1886.
Courtesy Amon Carter Museum, Fort Worth, Texas.

with water for the blowing horses and a foster mother
or two for the calves, either from the cattle with the
supply wagon behind or from the bunches of half-wild
Texas cattle grazing nearby. They searched separately
until the buggy team with its load of calves nosed out
a trail in the darkness, felt its way down a gentle draw
to a muddy water hole. Hough's halloos brought the
horseback riders. They set up camp, though the air
stank of decomposing bodies of cattle that had died at
the water hole.

Buffalo Jones, with the knowhow learned on his
first calf hunt, constructed a picket line devised so
that the wild things couldn't injure themselves butting and throwing themselves about a snubbing post.
He set up two posts a good distance apart, knotted
three short picket lines sixteen feet apart onto a rope
stretched between the posts, and tied a calf at the end
of each "like a fish on a trot line." The calves had
lots of room to struggle and nothing to hinder them, a
good thing, for they "spent most of their time standing with head down, back humped up, and tail cocked
out, pawing the ground for all the world like an old

bull, and from time to time uttering short, hoarse
bawls."

In spite of everyone's good intentions, the poor
calves got no food or water for twenty-four hours, not
until the supply wagon happened on the campsite the
next evening. Jones had found no range cows. And
the calves had butted away proffered pails of water
although their tongues hung black and swollen from
their mouths and they grunted complainingly.

Upon the arrival of the cattle, the men had to per-
suade the foster mothers to give milk to the calves.
Just in case color might put the calves off, Ez roped a
red cow, as close to buffalo color as any they had. He
hobbled her fore and aft, and with writer Hough's
help wrestled the smallest calf to her, but the cow
kicked, broke the hobble rope and tumbled the calf.
Yet within minutes after the red cow was rehobbled,
the calf, a day's eating to do, learned to gauge her
shiftings and began suckling as if he'd been born to
her. By morning the two had formed a new family,
and the calf acted like a pet raised in a barnyard.

The other two calves couldn't be fooled by short-haired mothers (especially the pure whiteness of one cow bothered them). One calf preferred a beer bottle covered with a rag for a mother, the other adopted a white pail.

A few days later Hough and Ricker were sitting alongside Jones in the wagon seat, jouncing north toward Kansas; the erratic Colonel had called off the expedition, with no more notice than "Pack your bags."

He left fourteen calves tethered in camp to be brought on by those left behind. Typically hasty, Jones pushed home in three days, driving his team as far as it could trot each day. A week and a half afterwards the calves made it to Garden City, seven of them. The other seven had died on the way, one killed when a cowboy had tied it to the tail of a cow to make it trail better. It had cost Jones $1000 to make the trip, about half of the market value of the calves. Ten calves dead, two cows shot (one by Jones for camp meat), perhaps three bulls killed wantonly . . .[5]

Buffalo Jones made three trips to Texas in addition to the one reported by Emerson Hough. The year before, 1886, he had left Kendall, Kansas, on April 24, to capture calves, a venture hastily decided upon. He had come to the Kendall quarry to obtain marble for his hotel in Garden City and had driven past hundreds of cattle destroyed in the winter's snows, fallen with their tails to the storm. The sight had convinced him that the buffalo's ability to endure the prairie climate made the animal a far superior ranch animal to

Domestic cow nursing buffalo calf. E. H. Baynes photo from Frank Bird Linderman Collection. *Courtesy heirs of Frank B. Linderman.*

beef cattle; he decided to go into buffalo raising and went after Texas calves.

He returned to Garden City the middle of May driving fifteen of them.[6] Eight of these he said he had captured in one run, all by himself, saving them from marauding wolves by leaving a piece of his clothing next to each tied calf (the smell would supposedly hold the wolves back for a time). Jones's tall tale runs like this: with the third calf he left his big hat (the first and second had been picked up by the camp wagon, but the wagon was now out of sight), with the fourth his coat, the fifth his vest, the sixth one a boot, the seventh another boot. He roped one more calf, gathered it up, rode hastily back to the seventh which he also loaded onto his horse with him. When he got to the sixth he had all the load he could carry and ahead of him wolves menaced his other captures. Just as he gave up all hope he heard a shot from over the hill, the wagon had joined him in the nick of time to drive off the wolves.[7] When one remembers Hough and Ricker wrestling with each calf to load it, Jones tucking a calf under each arm while riding a horse seems . . . Bunyanesque.

He lost none of these calves to wolves, but four died on the drive to Kansas, sickened on evaporated milk, the only food he had for them (thus his decision to bring milk cows with him the following year).

In 1888, on his third trip, Buffalo Jones captured thirty-seven buffalo calves. He was gone six weeks on this hunt, from the first of May until the middle of June, and spent $1825 gathering the creatures, $500 of which went to Lee Howard, whom Jones discovered capturing calves in the area, as payment to call off his hunt as well as to work for Jones. Jones now had captured fifty-nine head of buffalo.

Buffalo Jones made his last calfnapping expedition to Texas in 1889, and, moreover, tried also to bring back a herd of wild, mature buffalo. Lee Howard again worked for him. Jones brought bloodhounds to catch the scent of hiding buffalo. He also brought carrier pigeons which he released from time to time to carry reports of the expedition back to Garden City, from there wired to the Chicago *Times,* so that the nation might keep up with the details of his trials as buffalo savior.

Later in the month, when they found a herd of twenty-one cows and a bull, they determined to drive them first to camp and then to Kansas. Lee Howard and his men took the bloodhounds to keep the herd under surveillance day and night and push them gradually toward camp. In four days they had the herd near camp and tractable, tractable because they had

"Mr. Jones's Adventure." Frederic Remington, *Harper's Weekly*, July 12, 1890. *Courtesy Amon Carter Museum, Fort Worth, Texas.*

drunk nothing for three days. But they had to abandon the chase: Howard "had put in about 18 hours a day and run them about 3000 miles . . . (their feet) wore out . . . the bottom part was all gone and still they would go and when they got frightened they did not know their feet were sore."[8]

Only seven calves made it all the way to Garden City. Jones now owned sixty-six captured calves.

Others had captured calves long before Jones's efforts (travelers in the West had often seen a few buffalo in settlers' pastures), but Jones received the notoriety because scarcity had aroused public interest. Furthermore, some men had not Jones's luck with calves. George Catlin had helped to capture a dozen calves for shipment to Mr. Chouteau's plantation near St. Louis, but eleven had died on the down river steamboat when it hung up on sandbars far from a milk supply.[9] Old trapper John Y. Nelson, who'd guided Brigham Young to the Great Salt Lake, thought he knew enough about buffalo to raise two calves, but gave up when his kids killed one by peppering it with arrows, and the other got too ornery to have around a family.[10]

In the fall of '79, Vic Smith, who later shot that record number of buffalo in Montana, had a contract to furnish fifty buffalo calves to an eastern firm . . . he to deliver them aboard a Yellowstone River steamer. He and Frank Muzzy, on the banks of the Redwater forty miles north of the Yellowstone, roped all fifty calves in five days. They loaded the fifty on wagons with "racks similar to those in which sheep are hauled, and gave ample room for the calves to move about." They fed the passengers on boiled blue grass, which they drank "eagerly," and lost only one calf on the forty-mile trip to the river.

While waiting for a steamboat they put the forty-nine to pasture. On the sixth morning they woke up to find the pasture fence broken and the calves gone; nearby Gros Ventre Indians had released the prisoners. The men recaptured two; one died, the other Smith sold to a trader at Fort Buford.[11]

But others successfully raised calves. In 1866, twenty years before Buffalo Jones captured his first calf, Charles Goodnight, at the request of his wife, had saved a couple of them from buffalo hunters and had begun to keep a buffalo herd on his Texas ranch, but a partner made off with it. He began a

No man could hold two struggling buffalo calves on horseback in this way. But that's the way he told it. From Inman, *Buffalo Jones: 40 Years of Adventure*, 1899. *Courtesy Amon Carter Museum, Fort Worth, Texas.*

Now that the millions were gone, many ranchers hoped to domesticate the buffalo. E. H. Baynes photo from Frank Bird Linderman Collection. *Courtesy heirs of Frank B. Linderman.*

second herd in 1878. Likewise, six years earlier than Jones's first effort, Scotty Philip and his Indian wife had rounded up forty head of buffalo in the Dakotas and fenced them in.

And in 1873, thirteen years earlier than Jones, brothers William and Charles Alloway and their partner in freighting on the Manitoba plains, James McKay, foresaw the day when buffalo would be gone (they'd just bought 21,000 hides from a brigade of hunters). They resolved to capture some. The brothers joined a hide hunting brigade, herded a milk cow with them, captured three calves on a first trip and three more the following year. By 1877, the Alloways had thirteen buffalo plus three catalo—crossbred to domestic cattle. That year they sold the little herd to Lt. Col. Samuel Bedson of Stony Mountain, Manitoba. He also bought twenty-three head from their partner, James McKay. These buffalo joined a herd begun by Bedson in 1877 when he'd purchased four heifer calves and a bull calf from some Indians. By 1888 Bedson owned 110 head.

In Montana Michel Pablo and Charles Allard had purchased a herd started from calves brought across the Rocky Mountains to the Flathead country in 1873.

Because of all these efforts, by 1900 more plains buffalo lived captive than wild.

Early in 1886, Professor Spencer F. Baird, Secretary of the Smithsonian Institution, decided to send out an expedition to collect specimen hides and skeletons of buffalo—if it could find any animals. He came to this hasty decision because the institution had only one mounted female skin, another unmounted cow skin, no bull or calf skins; and, other than one mounted male skeleton, the only bones in the museum's storerooms were bits and pieces. Equally pressing was the fact that no other institutions in the United States had as much as these incomplete souvenirs. Since the species seemed bound to disappear, "between leaving them to be killed by the care-for-naught cowboys, who would leave them to decay . . . where they fell, and killing them ourselves for the purpose of preserving the remains, there was really no choice." The Smithsonian determined to get enough specimens for themselves and for other institutions. Its chief taxidermist, William T. Hornaday, headed the expedition. Hornaday and two assistants left Washington, D.C. on May 6 on an *exploratory* trip to eastern Montana; they could gather no good hides this late in the season. Fort Keogh, just outside Miles City, provided field transportation, escort, camp equipment, guides and food.

They pitched their tent on Phillips Creek about eighty miles out of Miles City at a spot decided by the six-mule team: it could drag the wagon no farther. They were just on the lip of the last remnant of buffalo country; perhaps thirty-five buffalo used it as a hideout.

From this base camp they rode into the rugged, coulee-cut range to the west, spending each day in the saddle, sometimes camping where night overtook them. These thirty-five buffalo had picked ideal country for their hideaway; it offered thousands of hiding places: dry washes, stumpy hillocks, brush patches, rimrocks and gullies. And each buffalo was far more wary of the hunter than his forebears: he spooked at the slightest untoward movement, he grazed in the most hidden of pastures, he watered with a caution unknown before, he moved constantly. An expert at broken-ground running, he could easily outdistance horses over this badlands terrain.

Though the odds seemed in favor of the buffalo, Hornaday's group soon captured a calf. At camp they had only evaporated milk, and evaporated milk he refused. Hornaday took him to the Phillips ranch eight miles away and put him to suck on one of the milk cows. The ranch he first put up with, then grew to like and lastly tried to take over.

As the men continued their search, they moved through the remnants of the slaughter that had preceded them, buffalo bones by the thousands, skeletons of elk and deer along the river banks, and bear skeletons, too. They gathered eight buffalo skeletons, complete to the smallest bones.

Ten days went by before they saw two old bulls, one of which they killed (although this spring they supposedly would only *locate* buffalo). His splotchy hide they threw away, but they saved his skeleton.

Hornaday now knew buffalo hid here in numbers to warrant a fall hunt. He sent word to Fort Keogh that he was ready to return to Washington. Back at Miles City he took the Northern Pacific east. In the baggage car ahead rode his specimens, including the live buffalo calf, now called Sandy.

In Washington, D.C., Sandy munched the lawn in front of the National Museum at the end of a picket rope (those were simpler days) until one day he charged, pulling Hornaday's assistant off his feet, dragging him through a mud puddle and to the steps of the museum. The museum sent him to a nearby dairy farm, but here he ate too much damp clover and died. His stuffed skin stood in Hornaday's famous bison group at the Smithsonian until the museum dismantled the group and sent it to the University of Montana where it gathers dust in storage.

"The Camp on the Big Porcupine." Note the rough country in which the last of the buffalo hid out. *Cosmopolitan*, October 1887. *Courtesy Amon Carter Museum, Fort Worth, Texas.*

Hornaday returned to Miles City September 27 with seven helpers. They set up camp at a muddy hole on the head of Calf Creek, a location along the high divide that separates the Missouri and Yellowstone drainages, the badlands, where they figured buffalo would hide. They sure hoped so, for so far they'd seen no sign of one.

An element of the rough protective topography undid buffalo instinct: its surface was soft, almost sandy—the buffalo were easily trailed in such stuff. Hornaday and three men followed tracks to a spot where they could see seven plus seven more (the most they would see at once during the expedition) lying on top of a butte about two miles away, completely unaware of approaching danger. The hunters moved closer; all fired at once—and all missed. The beasts stampeded through juniper and sagebrush down the steep sides of the butte and into the furrowed country beyond. But when the gap closed and the big guns boomed again, one man downed two bulls and Hornaday, an expert shot, a cow and a large bull.

In the next days, while Hornaday worked to save the skins from spoiling, the cowboys killed four more buffalo, chasing one old bull twelve miles in order to take him, an enormous old fellow, a real prize. The spent men only had time to dress him out and partially skin the legs before darkness forced them back to temporary camp with Hornaday. But during the night a band of roving Indians, sneaked from some nearby reservation, came one-up on the white man's hunt. They took the hide, all of the edible meat, broke the leg bones for the marrow, and disappeared into the surrounding breaks. But before leaving they smeared red war paint on one side of the head, yellow war paint on the other, and tied a taunting bit of red cloth onto a horn. Hornaday was bitter toward Indians for the rest of his life.

Now the Smithsonian expedition had eight of the twenty buffalo they had come for, and just as with Audubon and others, the hunting fever touched Hornaday. He fretted over having to spend so much time preparing specimens and so little in the chase. Speculation grew about the possibility of killing thirty (they took twenty-three). Hornaday, feeling "deprived of a fair share of the chase," took off for just one more hunt. On this hunt he killed the largest specimen gathered, an old bull, veteran of many hunts who carried four old rifle bullets in his carcass to prove it. (Later, he stood in the foreground in Hornaday's group in the Smithsonian.)

William T. Hornaday making an outline sketch of the dying "prize bull" gathered by his expedition. *Cosmopolitan*, October 1887. *Courtesy Amon Carter Museum, Fort Worth, Texas.*

A strange scientific expedition, this, with a leader more taxidermist than trained zoologist, a man of great enthusiasms who had now become interested in everything to do with buffalo (as he would soon with conservation in general), who would write many articles and books in his enthusiasm for conservation of wildlife (the very next year an article of his began, "At last the game butchers of the great West have stopped killing buffalo. The buffalo are all dead!"),[12] a man who might ignore facts and contradict himself but whose efforts forced much early wildlife legislation. His expanded report of the expedition became a standard reference on buffalo history and habits,[13] although it aroused the ire of Charles Goodnight: "I have just received a book . . . wrote by W. T. Horni-

day. I hope the Doctor will stay clear of hump animals. As he certainly got his wires crossed on the buffalo. . . ."[14]

The group left for Fort Keogh on December 15, driving its overloaded wagons through snow and terrible roads in five days—arriving just twenty-four hours before the beginning of another of the terrible blizzards of 1886–87 that would founder thousands of cattle and ruin most of the cattlemen in the Territory, the winter that inspired Charlie Russell's postcard sketch, "Last of the 5000." The specimens, including deer, coyote, antelope, rabbits, small mammals and birds, as well as buffalo, filled twenty-one big packing cases.

"It is supposed by many that the game in Yellowstone Park is preserved; but reliable accounts assert that it is not."

THE BAD LANDS COWBOY
1884

THE SOUTHERN herd and northern herd disappeared, but a few hundred buffalo wandered unmolested through the sulphur smell of geysers surrounding Yellowstone Lake. This high mountain prairie was too scary for the Indian hunter who saw the steaming mud pots and the spouting waters as signs of evil spirits; he followed no escaping animals here. And this land lay too far from the railroad for the hide hunter, so, although he slaughtered all the buffalo on the lower Yellowstone River, he left several hundred living undisturbed on its headwaters, especially the Pelican Creek and Lamar Valleys.

After 1872 the boundaries of the newly formed Yellowstone Park supposedly protected these for all time. But by 1890 the poachers surrounding the infant park, voracious for the $200 to $500 per head a foray into the park might bring, put them in jeopardy. The poachers especially loved the high country's winters, when deep snow sometimes drove the starving animals across the western park line or trapped them in Pelican Valley, easy victims, heads and hides easily tobogganed out. Everything favored the poachers in winter. The pelt was prime, and snow made the park "fifty times larger": park protection was difficult, even negligible because of understaffing. Things were about

as favorable in the spring. One May, a poacher made it out of the park with two newborn calves crammed into beer boxes on mule back; of course they died of the treatment.

Yet when the poachers brought down park buffalo, they merely followed the example of tourists, local residents, and concessionaires who treated the park as an exclusive shooting range. Many visitors lived off the land. Although the original Yellowstone Park Act had specified that the Secretary of the Interior "shall provide against the wanton destruction of the fish and game found within said park," park regulations permitted hunting for recreation or for use. Hotels loaded their tables with park game. Some visiting dignitaries trophy-hunted as if the government had set aside a private estate for them.

A national park had been boundaried, but as yet the nation little understood what to do with its contents—many people yet scoffed at this notion of private public land, of wild animals *owned* by the public. Much of the formation of the park had come about only as a boundary establishment. The founders felt they needed only to reserve the land and thought little about forests and game.

Congress remained unperturbed by reports of hunters killing game. Congressmen, like all Americans, found it difficult to conceive of not shooting any animal that moved into rifle range. Thus they sat complacently by, ignoring the slaughter of 2000 elk for their skins near Mammoth Hot Springs during the winter of 1874. Eleven years later they paid no attention to Superintendent D. W. Wear's pleas for game laws and his suggestion that they ban all shooting and hunting in the park. In 1881, Harry Yount, resigning as first park game keeper after one year on the job, had suggested that more men be added to protect game as well as suppress fires and enforce other regulations. Congress ignored his suggestions. Earlier, Superintendent Philetus W. Norris (who "protected the wonders [geyser formations] by breaking them off with axe and crowbar, and shipping them by the carload to Washington and elsewhere")[1] had suggested that Congress pay ranchers then living in the park a stipend if they would "domesticate" wild animals on their ranches. Congress did nothing. Norris assumed his administration had stopped the shooting of buffalo, an entirely erroneous assumption as it turned out.

Superintendent Nathaniel Langford thought to oversee the park through giving hotel and other concessions to private citizens, thinking they might do the government's overseeing for it and cut vandalism[2] (hacking of souvenir sinter from geyser cones and chiseling names in the cones) as well as poaching. The concessionaires proved uninterested, so much so that Captain William Ludlow of the United States Army visiting Yellowstone in 1875 reported great destruction of game and continual vandalism (he saw a woman with axe about to split a geyser cone). He suggested protection of the park by the Army; no one but the Secretary of War, who seconded it, heeded his suggestion.[3]

In 1884 Congressmen at last realized that all that made the park unique would be destroyed unless protected; they gave the Army the task of protecting it—and because of this "free" help, promptly halved park appropriations. Administrative headquarters at Mammoth Hot Springs became Fort Yellowstone, and several outposts were established. Captain Mose Harris took over in August 1886.

Captain Harris in his three years as Acting-Superintendent proved a "terror to evil doers." He commanded two Lieutenants and twenty mounted men and later hired one scout (he'd asked for money for three). He used his men to establish a patrol of the boundary and major points of interest. He arrested numerous poachers, ejected squatters, demanded that park guides obtain licenses, expelled flagrant vandals.

He attempted to establish a policy about buffalo

and all park animals. He refused to buy buffalo from a Canadian firm, saying the government in its park intended not to make a collection of domesticated animals, but "to protect the existing game animals so that they may breed in security."[4] His policy for buffalo was ignored in later years and only recently readopted.

Congress thought that troopers would stop the poachers. But as the price for buffalo heads rose, poachers continued to sneak by the scatterings of soldiers. An Acting-Superintendent had only troopers enough to man six wintertime stations about the park, each station occupied by a sergeant and two other soldiers. His men tried to patrol effectively, but, too often, they knew little woodsmanship, understood little about the habits of animals, scarcely knew the part of the park they patrolled, for often their duty lasted only eight to ten months.[5]

The soldier's job was made discouraging because the Army could only keep a poacher in the guardhouse briefly—until the Secretary of the Interior sent orders to release him. It could also confiscate a poacher's equipment, but he bought a cheap rifle (who needed a good one to shoot, point-blank, buffalo floundering in deep snow?) and old, used camping equipment. He smiled as the Army burned the stuff.

Captain Harris set high standards for park protection. His successor, Captain F. A. Boutelle, continued them (especially in his rejection of a plan to put an elevator near the lower falls of the Yellowstone).

Captain George S. Anderson followed Boutelle as Acting-Superintendent in 1891, a man determined to protect all of the park against "wanton destruction" in order to preserve "a public park or pleasuring ground for the benefit and enjoyment of the people"; in him the Yellowstone buffalo found a determined champion. Although the statutes little helped to punish poachers, Captain Anderson devised his own methods of dealing with them. He had the authority to expel poachers; he made expulsion effective punishment. Poachers caught near one border of the park marched, on foot, across the park, accompanied by a mounted trooper, to be expelled across the opposite border.[6]

Three years after Anderson took over, he supported a wintertime expedition into the park. Emerson Hough, the man who had accompanied Buffalo Jones on a calf hunt, Jack Haynes, the outstanding photographer and conservationist, and others would report on winter in "Wonderland" and look for evidence of poaching. As luck would have it, they ran onto the remains of several slaughtered buffalo on Alum Creek; Haynes took pictures of the evidence. Then Captain Anderson, through clever use of his two scouts, provided the capture of a poacher for Emerson Hough to report to the nation.

The Captain and his scouts had suspected that Ed Howell poached buffalo. When they heard he had left Cooke City, on the northern edge of the park, pulling a toboggan load of supplies southward, Scouts Burgess and Troike snowshoed out on a route designed to cross his trail where he came over Specimen Pass—as he'd have to if he intended to get at the buffalo on Pelican Creek.

On March 12, just after sunup, the two scouts intersected the path of the toboggan; turning, they cautiously followed it until they found themselves standing in Howell's empty camp. Fresh ski tracks leading away from the tent showed the direction he'd gone; buffalo heads hanging high in the trees above camp showed what he was up to. The scouts moved after him, following where his ski tracks led, past lodgepole thicket, over rolling ridge, keeping in cover wherever they could. After a long time they heard shots, six of them. Slowly, quietly, they padded across the snow until at last before them, out in a little valley, they saw five black hummocks lying in the snow and a man hunched over one of the hummocks sawing at its head. The scouts stayed hidden in the trees, watching, planning how to capture him. His body was turned toward them, but his head was down and the floppy brim of his hat came down over his eyes.

He didn't see them, but 400 yards of clear snowfield had to be traveled before they could reach him, and at any moment he might raise his head. His rifle leaned against the haunch of one of the dead animals, a little distance away. With it he could outshoot the .38 revolvers carried by the scouts, unless they could get to within handgun distance before he looked up. Burgess decided to run for him, alone (although he had one bad foot, the result of Crow Indians amusing themselves by cutting off some of his toes). Later he told Hough how it was:

> I thought I could maybe get across without Howell seeing me or hearing me, for the wind was blowing very hard. So I started over from cover, going as fast as I could travel. Right square across the way I found a ditch about 10 ft. wide and you know how hard it is to jump with snowshoes on level ground. I had to try it anyhow and some way I got over. I ran up to within 15 ft. of Howell, between him and his gun, before I called to him to throw up his hands, and that was the first he knew of anyone being anywhere in that coun-

try. He kind of stopped and stood stupid like, and I told him to drop his knife. He did that and then I called Troike, and we got ready to come on over to the hotel.[7]

Howell hadn't much getting ready to do: the heads he could be left high in the trees; the newly killed buffalo would rot where they'd fallen. He skied to Lake Hotel, the scouts snowshoed. He wouldn't escape, for he had no gun, and he had no boots for a getaway trip—he'd wrapped his feet and legs in gunnysacking, and fastened on his skis with gunnysack harness. Besides, why escape? "Chipper and gay" about the hotel the next morning, he bragged he'd made $2000 this winter and stood to lose only $26.75 in confiscated equipment.

"Yes, I'm going to take a little walk up to the Post, but I don't think I'll stay there long," he said. ". . . I haven't arranged any plans yet for the future. I may go back into the Park again, later on, and I may not . . . I've been camped over on Pelican since last September."

He seemed to rather enjoy being brought in from out of the lonesome cold: at breakfast he ate twenty-four pancakes and talked constantly between bites, acting as a guest instead of a prisoner.[8]

But the capture of Howell did something to make a law to stop poachers in Yellowstone Park. Emerson Hough immediately wired the news to George Bird Grinnell at the *Forest and Stream* offices. Next day Editor Grinnell was in Washington, D.C. with the news, lobbying for an act already drawn up by Congressman John F. Lacey, one placing the park under the jurisdiction of the courts of Wyoming and forbidding hunting inside the park. Lacey had long pled for such a law, and year after year, the Boone and Crockett Club, the important conservation organization, had fought—against railroads, ranchers, real estate men, miners and hotel keepers who wanted their own way with the public park (they'd continually tried to publicize the park as a remote playground reserved for millionaires).

Hough interviewed every taxidermist in the park's vicinity; each admitted the trade in illegal heads—trade by others, not by him. Hough found at least forty-five "traceable" buffalo had been killed from the "protected herd" of the Yellowstone, with no punishment possible for the killers; Hough wrote: "Kill a Government mule and try what the U.S. Government will do to you." His articles and Haynes's photos played upon the rising, if belated, concern of the public for the buffalo.

With this new evidence before it and public pressure upon it, Congress acted; inside of a month, the National Park Protective Act, making it illegal to kill Yellowstone buffalo, became law, a move so sudden the lobbyists for hotel owners and the like had no time to counter it, a move that poacher Ed Howell took part credit for—"without me you'd have no laws to protect the Park." The new law enacted a fine of $1000 or two years in prison, or both, upon any convicted poacher. At last the Yellowstone Park buffalo herd could graze safely—it seemed.

Yellowstone's wild buffalo, under protection of the 1894 Act, should have increased. They might have if they hadn't come to flee at the whiff of man scent. Winter found them retired into tough country, country where every mouthful of grass had to be excavated from under deep-lying snow. Each spring, scouts found several dead of starvation, sometimes fallen on warm, snowfree geyser slope, one time fallen on frozen Yellowstone Lake where a big bull's muzzling had uncovered only ice.

How many wild buffalo lived in the park? Most Superintendents had guessed about 400, but none had made a count, for the animals bolted and hid so quickly. Captain Anderson sent scouts snowshoeing to the herd in winter to try to count when their brown bodies showed plain against the white. His scouts counted only twenty-five. Twenty-one years of "protection" had resulted in the slaughter of 400 to 600 of the only wild herd (which included, perhaps, a few wood buffalo) remaining in the United States.

About this time Captain Anderson's administration ended. The next several years saw a succession of administrators, too many to be completely effective against poachers, especially when administrators still lacked Congressional support. Even in 1900 Congress earmarked only $5000 for game protection in the park. It went to pay a clerk, to buy hay needed for animals in captivity, to cover incidental expenses and provide for only two scouts when ten were needed. Two scouts could not effectively patrol 3500 square miles of timber, especially in deep snow. During only a part of the winter of 1889–90, Scouts Holt and Morrison covered over 2000 miles on skis "and it was months between times we would be at some of the outlying points."[9] And the patrols became doubly frustrating through shots sounding here and there in the distance and no way to discover the shooter.

Earmarking only $5000 out of $118,000 appropriated for park development meant, according to one critic, that "the project to purchase new stock to infuse fresh blood into the badly inbred and rapidly dwindling herd of bison must be given up." He further contended that this short-sighted policy grew out of the political influence of the Yellowstone Park Transportation Company in Washington: "When the time for the annual appropriation comes around the wheels are again set to work: and with what result? An appropriation of $113,000 for roads, to be maintained by the government and used for the profit of the Transportation Company, and $5000 to protect the game."[10] Not only this, but also the company cut hay and pastured stock on government land—some of the best land for wild game use. This continued hay cutting drove the buffalo from their old home in Hayden Valley—making it even harder for the wild herd, eight cows, five bulls and five calves, to make its way.

The buffalo remained the only decreasing game species in the park.

On July 16, 1902, when Buffalo Jones arrived in the park as Game Warden, the wild herd yet numbered no more than twenty-five or thirty animals.

Buffalo Jones had earlier tried to stir up concern for the park wild buffalo with his suggestion that this herd be moved to Pecos country in New Mexico. Later, he'd traveled to Washington, D.C. and called on the Secretary of the Interior, offering to capture these wild buffalo to save them from "a speedy extermination" by the poachers. He said he planned to corral the Yellowstone Park buffalo, for which he would "accept $200 a month and actual expenses while engaged in capturing and preserving the herd."[11] Though the Assistant Secretary of the Interior approved the idea, the Secretary refused it.

Jones still saw himself as the savior of the buffalo, but at the same time he wanted to make a fortune from them. And he needed a new fortune; the old one was gone: his marble-faced Garden City hotel, his Kansas ranch, his buffalo herd. All he had was his scheming head and his energy. The Yellowstone Park buffalo might help him to a new start.

In 1902, thirty years after the formation of the park, President Roosevelt, by direct presidential action, appointed Buffalo Jones as Game Warden of Yellowstone, with the especial duties of bolstering the bison herd there. Jones stayed in Yellowstone for three hectic years. He rebuilt the bison herd but trod on everyone's toes while doing it, including President Roosevelt's (he made a pest of himself during the President's visit to the park). And he upset the Army. The kind of man who, in Kansas, had hauled passengers across a river free to challenge the high rates at a toll bridge, who could build Finney County, Kansas, a courthouse and give it to the county for a dollar, wasn't the kind of man who could see eye to eye with Major John Pitcher, the Park Superintendent, about buffalo or submit to his folderol about regulations. Nor could the man who had always talked big keep his mouth shut when he had ideas how the park should be run.

Jones chose Mammoth Valley for the buffalo site— an unusual choice to say the least, for they had naturally chosen other sites heretofore. But at that time, Mammoth was the important entrance to the park, and here the most people could visit a buffalo corral.

Since Jones feared that the wild Yellowstone herd was inbred, he brought in new blood. He went to Colonel Goodnight's ranch in Texas to select three bulls from that herd; he may have trailed them cross-country to Yellowstone. Another eighteen cows were purchased from Montana's Allard herd. By late 1902 Jones had established the tame herd in its brand-new corrals and he, to Major Pitcher's dismay, began tending to his further duties as gamekeeper to the Park. Pitcher had hoped that the obstreperous, windy old fellow would leave when he'd established the herd. Jones saw other things to do and went about them in his own flamboyant, heedless way.

The bears of the park already had beome a nuisance, not as highway bandits looking for goodies which would have bolted innumerable stagecoach teams and harassed the touring bicyclists, but as garbage dump raiders and camp robbers. These mischief-makers Jones punished. He roped them, strung them up by a leg and thrashed them with a bean pole while they clawed in every direction. Cruel as the punishment was, it worked; even grizzly bears headed into the tall timber after their spanking. Jones also made it one of his duties to rope and tie bears to remove tin cans wedged onto their feet in garbage raids.[12]

He established a little museum near the corrals. Major Pitcher accused him of here "selling mementoes to tourists and generally prostituting himself for commercial gain and against Park regulations." However, another person who knew Jones at this time, Jack Haynes, park photographer, felt that Jones didn't seem to care if anyone looked at his museum or not.[13] Probably so. Jones hardly seems the memento-selling type; he fitted in as poorly with them as with the army types. But one of the concessionaires saw him as "pompous, opinionated, a thoroughgoing four-flusher"; and the park transportation company routed its coaches to drive by the corrals but scheduled no stop at the museum.[14]

To try to bolster the buffalo herd, Jones built a corral-trap on Pelican Creek to catch some of the wild herd. But Major Pitcher stopped the proposed buffalo drive for fear it might injure the animals. So Jones placed a bull from the new herd in the corral to act as bait, but none of the wild buffalo entered the trap; instead the new bull went off into the hills, tried to join the wild herd, but returned to the corral alone in a few days. When Jones's lone bull wandered out of his corral the next winter to die of starvation, the park scouts saw it as a needless death—the old buffalo keeper could have prevented it by closing the gate, corraling the bull where feed had been stacked.

Later Scout Peter Holte skied with Jones on a calf-capturing trip and wrote an account of the trip designed to show up the old man's ineptness as a buffalo handler. They captured two calves, no thanks to Jones's skiing. He had wobbled downhill on skis after a third calf, upended in a sagebrush and threshed there while the calf escaped. Holte, though hating to lose the calf, enjoyed the old man's failure . . . earlier Jones had responded to Holte's dual calf capture with "he was sorry he had not been there as he would have caught some grown ones."

They put the calves on toboggans and slid them to Lake Hotel. There the calves refused to feed on the canned milk Jones claimed they liked—although he'd killed four calves with it in Texas in 1886. The scouts dragged the calves to the stable and saw to it the cow fed the calves while Jones stayed inside nursing snow-blinded eyes.

In a few days they tobogganed the calves to the new herd at Mammoth where a domestic cow mothered them.[15]

Buffalo Jones stayed three years in the park, three years that wore on Major Pitcher's nerves. Once the Major wrote to him, "whenever I desire or need your advice or assistance concerning matters pertaining to the Park, I will inform you of the fact."[16] But Jones had the support of the Secretary of the Interior. When, in the summer of 1905, he complained of the Army's niggardliness in assigning scouts to help him carry out his duties, the Secretary of the Interior placed him in direct charge of all the game in the park. Yet, that September, Jones resigned to enter another buffalo speculation in the Kaibab country of northern Arizona. He'd recently been on leave much of the time.

The tame, corralled herd of twenty-one had increased to forty-four.

The year after Jones left, this herd was moved from the exposed situation which Jones had chosen for it to a site that buffalo preferred near the mouth of Rose Creek in the Lamar Valley. Major Pitcher branded each one "U.S."[17]

The wild roving herd also began to increase, but interest in its welfare lagged for the tame herd increased to fifty-seven animals in 1906, 121 in 1910 and 147 animals in 1911 (they turned it out two hours daily to graze, but it refused to go wild). Outbreaks of hemorrhagic septicemia killed numbers of this herd's young animals in 1911, but, after vaccination, the herd thrived to the point where several "surplus" calves were castrated in 1918. In 1925 the Park began slaughtering these steers for market. In 1928 the herd numbered 886, and the Park had, over the years, shipped 101 buffalo to zoos and seventy to become the nuclei of other herds.[18] Yet poaching continued. In 1922 Dan Beard felt it impossible to ever save the park's wild life.[19] As late as 1925, hunters killed forty buffalo in Gallatin Valley just outside the park.[20]

"Buffalo cannot be handled or sold like dry goods."
HOWARD EATON

*". . . buffalo breeding is as good an investment
as real estate."*
CHARLES ALLARD

*"GENUINE NORTH AMERICAN BISON
. . . Buy a pair for Ranch or Farm . . .
We supply Buffalo for Zoos, Parks, Circuses and Barbecues."*
PHILIP BUFFALO RANCH

BY 1906, buffalo owners and buyers were shipping buffalo so frequently some of them scampered up and down loading chutes more often than their domestic cousins, the Herefords, who usually rode a train only once, a final ride to the Chicago stockyards. During the years between 1880 and 1920 buffalo migrated as folklore would have had them—by boxcar: north from the Goodnight herd to Montana, south to the 101 Ranch, west from Jones's Kansas herd to Monterey, California, where no modern buffalo had ever lived, east from his herd to New Hampshire and the Austin Corbin Game Preserve. And some emigrated across the Atlantic to an English estate (countrified buffalo, panicked by the New York dock's electric lights, broke away and lumbered about the shed for an hour before capture; landlubber buffalo at first lurched about in seasickness during the stormy crossing). Other buffalo spent much of their lives riding the cars with Buffalo Bill Cody's Wild West Show. The big beasts habituated themselves to barnstorming or ocean voyages (they were drenched with saltwater spray on most of the trip to England) as well as they had adapted to varying climates, topography and elevations of North America.

About 1900, buffalo living in privately-owned herds seemed to assure a buffalo future. The Philip South Dakota herd contained about 300 animals. J. E. Dooley's herd on Antelope Island in the Great Salt Lake numbered thirty-five; Charles Goodnight owned 200; the 101 Ranch ran thirty-six head; showman Pawnee Bill Lillie kept fifty to sixty on his Oklahoma ranch; Austin Corbin's game preserve enclosed a herd of 136; J. W. Gilbert ran some on his Nebraska ranch as did Wallis Huidekoper in Montana. In zoos and parks little buffalo families stood in pens no bigger than an ordinary wallow, panting, eyes glazed, stupid. The Atcheson, Topeka and Santa Fe Railroad kept a few at Bismarck Grove, Kansas. Dick Rock kept a few near Henry's Lake, Idaho (he enjoyed teasing them; one day a bull gored him to death when he carelessly turned his back). Larger than all of these, the biggest herd in the United States—buffalo still living wild on Montana's Flathead Indian Reservation—was the Pablo-Allard herd of 440 animals. But all of these herds added up to only slightly more than 1000 plains buffalo alive in the United States. Perhaps another 100 lived in Europe.

The buffalo owners expected the herds and the business to expand. Michel Pablo told Kootenai Brown "he saw where he could sell his buffalo to parks and museums and make a good thing of them." And his partner, Charles Allard, in an 1896 magazine article, wrote that the buffalo business was "as good an investment as real estate," for hides sold at $100 apiece and mounted heads at $200 to $500. He and Pablo evidently wanted to corner the market: although their buffalo numbered "about 140 now, and by the next fall there will be fully 200 of them . . . we need them all at present. We receive letters every day from museums, parks, and shows, wanting them in all quantities and though we might dispose of them singly, we have no pairs to sell."[1] Selling no pairs meant selling no breeding stock to start rival herds. Likewise, Scotty Philip claimed he "never sold a cow."

Pablo and Allard had a big advantage over all other buffalo raisers—free pasture. Thousands of acres of Flathead Reservation land, almost unused by others, free to them as half-Indians married each to an Indian woman. They thought they had the perfect place to raise catalo as well as buffalo—Wild Horse Island in Flathead Lake. The men reckoned without the strong buffalo-nature of the crossbreeds—a half-mile swim was nothing to them; they often appeared dripping wet on the mainland to destroy gardens and scare gardeners. When Jones wanted them back to start the Arizona venture, Pablo happily sold them.

But he kept his buffalo, for the business thrived: he sold a few at a time, perhaps 150 altogether over several years. No need worry about buffalo surviving anymore.

Or so it seemed.

But Austin Corbin died and his family felt that most of the buffalo could no longer be supported on the New Hampshire Blue Mountain Game Preserve, along with other disappearing American game animals. This herd, the heirs found, cost about $30 a head to feed during the winter: a calf in his first winter ate a half ton of hay, the following winter he ate a ton and then increased his intake a half ton a year until mature when he ate three tons per winter. So anxious to move from under this cost were the Corbin heirs, they sold eight to a taxidermist and several bunches to small zoological parks ("a fate worse than death" Hornaday called the zoo sales).[2] Eventually they reduced the herd to a permanent twenty-five members. Likewise, after Scotty Philip died, his sons wanted to sell the herd. And when Charles Allard died, half of the Pablo-Allard herd was sold here and there. Then the United States decided to open the Flathead Indian Reservation to homesteaders; Michel Pablo would soon have no place to raise buffalo.

War Cloud, the enormous bull of Austin Corbin's New Hampshire herd, circa 1908. Photo by E. H. Baynes. From the Frank Bird Linderman Collection. *Courtesy heirs of Frank B. Linderman.*

In 1904 a select few could still hunt buffalo—on the Scotty Philip ranch. South Dakota Governor Herud is one of the men to the right roasting the body-warm heart. Al Lucke photo. *Courtesy Bill Farr, University of Montana.*

The buffalo once again stood endangered.

Pablo had to find other land or start shooting. At first he tried for a township or so of land in public domain, hoping that the federal government would see his herd as a national heritage, but the government, short-sighted as ever about buffalo, seemed to assume that dots on a U.S. map locating private buffalo herds meant buffalo saved. Pablo then offered to sell the herd to the government, but something went wrong. Gossips whispered that Pablo's Salish wife refused to sell buffalo to a government that had done her people so much wrong; other rumormongers said that Howard Eaton had proffered the herd for Pablo but had received no solid government offer in return. The government owned fifty-seven tame and thirty wild buffalo in Yellowstone Park, and would soon stock the 8000 acres of the Wichita Game Preserve with more buffalo. It wanted no more.

In 1906, as the time drew near for fences to crisscross the reservation, Pablo went to Canada to try to lease cheap land for his buffalo. But Howard Douglas, Superintendent of Rocky Mountain Park at Banff, suggested that Canada buy the buffalo instead. The Minister of the Interior agreed. Pablo, now in his seventies, knew this as the chance to get out of the buffalo novelty business. He agreed to sell his herd at $250 a head and went home to begin loading buffalo.

Before Michel Pablo could denude the Flathead hills of buffalo, other men, eastern conservationists, began clothing them with the familiar raisin-brown shapes again. These persons, members joined together in the American Bison Society, had helped to per-suade Congress to buy 13,000 acres of Flathead Reservation land for a National Bison Range (bison they said when they wrote a title, buffalo they said when they wrote each other). Some Montanans hoped that those Bison Society members who stopped by Pablo's loading chutes had come to Montana to interfere with the shipment of Pablo's herd from the United States to Canada. Quite the opposite. They, like many other Americans, wished these hundreds might stay here, but they, unlike other Americans who cried that the sale must be stopped, applauded Canada's preservation. The Bison Society meant to save buffalo, not argue about who saved them.

First of all it meant to establish government reserves because private owners might send herds to the slaughterhouse whenever the price of heads dropped or the novelty of seeing buffalo from their windows palled. The society knew that earlier private plans to establish buffalo preserves had gone awry: in 1876, Charles Trasker, a conservation-minded Englishman, had purchased several thousand acres from Texas for a buffalo park. He had chosen the land well, a ten-mile-long valley, skirted by high bluffs, watered by a good stream. He had planned to wall up the one open end of the valley and to keep his buffalo preserved. Unfortunately, he went broke building fine buildings; and he took so long building them the buffalo in Texas had all but disappeared.[3]

Men and women had begun meeting as conservation groups now that the passenger pigeon no longer flew, deer and elk grazed only in the remotest hideaways, and buffalo lived mostly in pastures. The Boone and Crockett Club and the Campfire Club had been fighting against the market hunter who sold wild game to meat markets and fancy restaurants. They saw the Lacey Law enacted. They convinced rifle and ammunition manufacturers that game must be protected if they meant to sell guns and shells to future hunters—that it would become more profitable to cater to sportsmen than market hunters. But since these conservationists hadn't a single-minded devotion to the preservation of buffalo, some men, members of both these clubs, became convinced that they must form a special conservation group devoted to saving him alone.

One of the first men to propose a buffalo-saving group, Ernest Harold Baynes, had, before he became a buffalo watcher, earned a living lecturing as a bird-watcher. But after seeing his first buffalo on Austin Corbin's Blue Mountain Game Preserve in 1904, he became a believer in super-buffalo and spent hour upon hour with the herd.

Baynes trained two of Corbin's calves to the yoke, an education which locals described as "Baynes hitches 'em up, and they take him where they damned please." But at a fair, Baynes raced a buffalo a half mile to win over a steer. And, even as new-fangled tractors worked, he dreamed of a day when men might plow with buffalo oxen.

Many of his hours went into combing and carding buffalo wool, for he, like Goodnight and Jones, dreamed of a day when men might don buffalo-wool trousers. He sent batches of buffalo wool to woolen mills. Their reports convinced him that buffalo woolen goods could be manufactured and marketed. Others had developed a similar interest in buffalo wool. "Arizona Bill" Grasher saved the wool picked up from an Arizona herd for New York's Museum of Natural History; a Yellowstone Park naturalist asked for particulars of Baynes's experiments (he wanted to make ranger mackinaws out of the wool); the United States De-

Michel's Salish wife, who, rumor has it, so hated the United States she kept Michel from selling their herd to it. More likely, the U.S. bid too low. *Courtesy University of Montana Archives, Missoula.*

partment of Agriculture tested the wool for wearability. The Reed City (Michigan) Woolen Mills made up blankets for Charles Goodnight from wool he'd sent them, but had to add karakul wool to obtain a longer fibre. The Bison Society considered gaining publicity by gathering wool, weaving it, and tailoring it into a suit for The President of the United States.[4]

Baynes, as lecturer, felt that people would pay to hear about the plight of the buffalo and the possibilities of buffalo domestication, so he traveled his former bird-talk circuit, lecturing, showing pictures of the yoke of buffalo and exhibiting samples of buffalo cloth.

After delivering the lecture in New York City before the Campfire Club he talked to its President, William Hornaday, and Hornaday agreed to act as president of a buffalo-saving organization, should one form. He, now head of the New York Zoological Park, allowed a first meeting of such a group to be held in the lion house of the park. Only fourteen of the 200 invited persons met, but they created the American Bison Society there within hearing of the roars of the big cats. The men elected Hornaday as President.

Hornaday could make things hum. In addition to leading the Smithsonian expedition, he'd been a zoological collector in Borneo, Malay, South America and the West Indies, shooting lions and tigers and jaguars for museums in the United States. Later, after gathering the buffalo specimens in Montana, he'd mounted a buffalo family for exhibit at the Smithsonian, presenting them in an entirely new way—standing together in lifelike postures in real soil, at a wallow; heretofore museum animals had been stuffed to indicate just the general shape of the living body and had been exhibited standing on a plank rather than in a "real" place. More recently, as Director of the New York Zoological Park, he had delighted park visitors by eliminating many cages and by recreating natural environments in which animals moved as if at home. He wrote books by doing a chapter every Sunday— "sixteen more Sundays and I'll be done." He was the practical organizer, the man who could deal with red tape: "I ignored it, and in due course of nature the man who gave the order apparently forgot it."

Hornaday could make Baynes's dream society come true, although they didn't get along—Hornaday detested him as an "illiterate Jackass," who, he said, never raised a dollar for the Bison Society, but gave his 113 buffalo lectures for personal profit. What irritated Hornaday and other members was, evidently, "The way he goes around saying how he saved the

bison . . . nobody else is on the map. I don't mind his saying he started the Bison Society." The society ignored the fact that on his lecture tour, Baynes, on his own, visited all of the major herds of the West and induced promises of live buffalo gifts from each, and that his many articles, although written for income, had created an awareness of the society and its work.

Hornaday had, in 1905, before the formation of the Bison Society, agreed to send twelve of the Zoological Park's buffalo to the new 8000-acre Wichita National Forest Reserve, as a gift to the United States to establish a national herd. No one else had ever thought to *give* buffalo to the government—Philip and Pablo had wanted to *sell*; the gift surprised Congress into appropriating, without a dissenting vote, $15,000 to erect buildings and to fence the new range. The United States would now own at least ninety-nine buffalo, counting the Yellowstone Park herd. Hornaday felt that Americans needed more than these two herds if their great-grandchildren were to enjoy living buffalo. He and the society felt the species could not propagate itself "for centuries" within the confines of zoos, it needed open range. He meant to see to it that government-owned buffalo would graze on nine more public ranges; ten herds could scarcely be swept away by disease or war, tornado or fire. (Perhaps not well understood by prospective donors was his intent of only seven herds as exhibition herds. The three others would operate as commercial herds.)

These Bostonians and New Yorkers of the Bison Society marked the map with possible places for government herds. They considered ranges in New York, New Hampshire and Illinois, but decided that none of these areas held the public interest as did the Flathead country of Montana where Pablo had successfully raised buffalo. Dr. Morton Elrod at the University of Montana, a member of the Bison Society's advisory board, found 13,000 acres of land above the Flathead River, not the land the Pablo buffalo had grazed but near to it, land where good water flowed, trees provided shade and protection from storms, land not potted with prospect holes that would have to be filled in. Especially important he thought was that this land lay closer to the railroad than Pablo's—"a visitor may step off the train at Ravalli and in five minutes be in the range."[5]

Hornaday proposed that the Bison Society purchase buffalo as another gift to the United States. Montana's Senator Joseph M. Dixon pushed through Congress a bill authorizing the purchase of the land (Flathead tribal funds gained $30,000 from land sold

These men hoped to train a buffalo team. Most such efforts ended when calves became willful adults. E. H. Baynes photo from Frank Bird Linderman Collection. *Courtesy heirs of Frank B. Linderman.*

at $1.50 to $7.00 per acre). The Bison Society set about finding people who would contribute $10,000 to buy buffalo.

The $10,000 found its way into the Bison Society treasury in spite of tight fists and some know-it-all newspaper editors who attacked the plan. The Kansas City *Journal* poked fun at the society, saying it couldn't find any buffalo to save because they were all gone. An Indianapolis paper said, "Why Boston people should take an interest in the buffalo and why any intelligent person should care for the preservation of these moth-eaten, ungainly beasts . . . are conundrums no one answered."[6]

Fiery-tempered, pugnacious, opinionated, emotional, Hornaday carried out any job all the way—even to inspecting daily all of the exhibits in the New York Zoo. When he first saw the buffalo nickel he damned it "as a sad failure as a work of art—the buffalo head droops and it looks as if it had spent its life in a small enclosure." Later in life he saw to it that plumage from egrets and other birds could no longer be imported into the United States to adorn ladies' hats, thus saving these birds from extinction. At another time he took part in the Alaska Game Bill fight, objecting to a

situation where "For $40 any saloon loafer can get a 'hunter's license' to kill . . . and sell the meat . . . let's pound that bill and it's backers to pulp!" Still later he refused an offered $25,000 a year by rifle manufacturers if he would stop his fight against automatic guns used by hunters. As Edmund Seymour wrote of Hornaday, "He is the King Pin of us all."[7]

When Treasurer Clark Williams totted up the contributions to the Bison Society's fund for the Montana herd, he found $565.50 more than the $10,000 needed. Most contributions had borne postmarks of cities east of the Mississippi River, country in which buffalo had ceased to roam 150 years earlier; twenty-one ladies of Boston, who surely had yet to see a buffalo on the range, had mailed in $500. On the other hand, all of the citizens of Montana, some of whom had banked money from killing buffalo, some of whom stood to bank money from a herd established in the state, mailed in only $366. Shameful though this showing seems, the envelopes from Montana had contained more money than the envelopes from all of the other hide-hunter states combined. Oklahoma, Wyoming (its only contributor was Howard Eaton) and Nebraska had raked up only $100 for the buffalo

Michel Pablo who sold his buffalo herd to Canada—as much of it as he could round up. *Courtesy Montana Historical Society, Helena.*

between them; Kansas and Texas, where the slaughter had been the worst, had sent in nary a dollar, nor had South Dakota and North Dakota. Nor can one find the names of Buffalo Bill or Buffalo Jones on the list of donors. Nor of the railroads that hauled the hides; nor of the leather companies that tanned them.

On October 17, 1909, thirty-seven head of buffalo began exploring the piney ridges above Jocko Creek and the Flathead River and began pawing out the wallows that today still serve as dust baths. And Game Warden Hodges began making their care "the sole business of his life." He'd worked with cattle in Colorado, but never with buffalo—but he'd stood at the top of the Civil Service examinations. And he proved a worker, but, "as a writer of letters, he is 'the limit,'" Hornaday found; when he asked for information about the herd he received "ten or twenty lines." But the man had no time for letter writing: in one year he did "$4500 worth of improving on the Range." And

he had his difficulties: "the Indians Cut my fence a gain in January, I hapened a long a bout the time they was cutting it and i Smoked them Up a litle and they havent bothered me since, it was not my fault that There Were not a red Hide hanging on the Fence i done my best, if i hadof had my 30.30 some of the red whelps woudnot have gone to camp, they hav not Interfeared with the Park since."[8]

The Bison Society paid $10,200 for thirty-four of the thirty-seven buffalo from the nearby Conrad herd (some people felt they should have bought Pablo buffalo). Two of the three other buffalo Mrs. Conrad donated, the third came from Charles Goodnight—just one because his other gift buffalo had died while waiting on the Conrad ranch. Other promised buffalo were coming, except for those from James J. Hill, the railroad maker, who wrote to say he'd butchered his because they'd become such a nuisance.

The United States now owned 151 animals: ninety-five in Yellowstone Park, twenty on the Wichita Preserve and these thirty-seven on Moiese. A buffalo census prepared by the Bison Society in 1910 showed 2108 buffalo alive in North America, 1076 in Canada and 1032 in the United States.[9]

To prepare for his Canada shipment, Michel Pablo spent the winter of 1906–07 building a corral on his range, three sides logs, one side a cliff, to hold the bunches as he brought them in. Yet, come spring, he found that cows with calves refused to be herded, and bulls, frisky on new green grass, ran cantankerously in any direction (cowboylike he tried to run them from horseback rather than quietly footherd them). And those animals he was able to chase into the corral escaped, once by climbing up and over the cliff, once, after a fourth side of plank and log replaced the cliff, by prying planks off. At the end of two months, Pablo's $100,000 seemed likely to stay in Canada.

Then Joe Allard, son of his former partner, offered to round up the beasts for $2000. Pablo accepted. Allard hired seventy-five of the best horsemen for miles around and put all of them to chasing a small group of a dozen or so animals at a time (about six men per buffalo). Allard succeeded in running buffalo into the new corral—twelve at a time. In July, Pablo could count 215 of them plodding within the railings, enough to fill a train at about ten beasts to a boxcar. He'd planned to drive the herd to the railroad; now he knew he couldn't. He hauled them railward six at a time, two each in especially constructed cage wagons, three tandem wagons hauled by ten to sixteen horses.

But like children reluctant to leave mother, the buffalo refused to board the train, refused to run up the chute—especially the bulls (cows they could load by moving their calves in ahead of them—they'd follow). Pablo ordered each bull lassoed, and slowly, in a tug-of-war between the buffalo at the loop end of the rope and all of the men who could grab a handhold at the other end, each stubborn animal was dragged up the incline and into a car. The men tugged all day to load sixteen animals. Too slow. Teams of horses replaced the tugging men and the loading went faster, but because of the ruckus inside the car, sometimes they could force only eight animals into it (the ruckus once toppled helpers from a car's roof. And once a bump catapulted three corral sitters into the buffalo melee below—from which they as quickly catapulted themselves up the corral boards again). At last a twenty-car train steamed off the siding onto the main line, 215 buffalo headed for Canada. The train had to stop several hours in Helena to repair stock cars damaged by the inmates.

Three days later 300 spectators greeted the train as it arrived at Lamont, Alberta. It took two days to unload the critters (although they gave little trouble, being mostly interested in a drink). The buffalo stayed in this pasture for a few months until the Wainwright Preserve, near Battle River, east of Edmonton, was ready for them, enclosed by seventy-four miles of woven wire fence. Not as big as the Flathead Reservation, but space enough for a buffalo to have a good walk before he had to turn around.

Pablo and his cowboys went back to the Montana hills for more buffalo. They chased them for three months before a second batch of 180 animals rode the rails north.

Pablo had filled the Canadian order and ridded himself of a lot of buffalo, yet, in October, when he rode about the reservation, he found he could count almost 200 buffalo on this land from which he'd just removed 395. Another calf crop might increase his herd to almost pre-Canada size. Time to start shooting it seemed, but when the Canadians heard the news they told him to continue shipping buffalo, all he could round up.

But now he chased the wiliest and toughest of his herd, those that had outrun his cowboys so far. By snowfall they'd rounded up not a buffalo. Pablo and his men mounted again in April, chased buffalo until mid-July, then gave up. He shipped none of these wise-to-the-chase buffalo in 1908.

That autumn Pablo built an enormous buffalo trap—one that Conquistador Zaldívar and his men attempting to corral 10,000 buffalo could have used. Leading to this corral he built a V-shaped funnel, each leg several miles long, strung with barbed wire and decorated with rags to flutter scarily in the wind (even as Indians at piskins had fluttered hides at the beasts). He built log booms to keep the buffalo from swimming down the Flathead River and escaping, as they had been doing, and he constructed smaller corrals here and there about the buffalo's range, places where small groups might be held for the wagons, where if the corral broke he'd not lose all the animals, as he had previously.

This year, 1909, writers came to cover the last contest between wild buffalo and men; Charlie Russell, the famous cowboy artist, sketched and rode in the chase; cowboys' wives came wearing "skirts . . . of buff duck, divided . . . bright coloured sweaters, buckskin gauntlets, with bead trimmings, and rakish-looking sombrero hats." Onlookers came as if to a Wild West Show. But this last great roundup made a Wild West Show look like an old ladies' riding club.

The big bulls, infuriated by the constant harassment, began to charge in earnest and without showing the usual warning kink of the tail. A bull knocked Johnny Decker's horse down, pinning him underneath; as the buffalo gored the horse, Pablo and Decker's brother shot the buffalo twelve times; he shook his head, jumped over horse and rider, broke through the corral and escaped. At another time Decker stayed atop his horse while an enraged bull carried both of them 300 yards on his horns before he stumbled and dropped his double load. A photographer, engrossed in focusing under his black cloth, found himself surrounded by buffalo and swung himself onto a tree branch while the animals charged below him, humps grazing his feet, hoofs clicking against his camera and tripod as they jumped them. (Another photographer, Norman Luxton, had his camera smashed when a pony rolled on it; he taped it together, and took the most well-known pictures of the roundup.) Twenty-five enraged buffalo had to be shot, some just in time to save the life of man or horse.

In July, after weeks of hairbreadth escapes, Pablo had a trainload of 190 buffalo for Canada. But the daily performances of a real life Wild West Show seemed to have worn out him and his men. From July to October they could bring in only 28 of the 150 they hoped to capture.

In all of 1910 Pablo shipped only sixty-eight buffalo, in 1911 only seven, in 1912 only seven. Al-

Hustling a Pablo buffalo toward a boxcar and a long ride from Ravalli, Montana to Wainwright, Alberta. *Courtesy University of Montana Archives, Missoula.*

Few of the buffalo went up the chute so willingly. *Courtesy University of Montana Archives, Missoula.*

Most buffalo engaged in a tug-of-war with men on the opposite side of the boxcar.
Courtesy University of Montana Archives, Missoula.

Newly arrived Pablo buffalo graze in Canada, watched by their new owners. *Courtesy Glenbow Museum, Calgary, Alberta.*

though most of the Montana herd now lived in Alberta, 695 of them, Pablo still lived in a quicksand of buffalo: seventy-five of them remained. And, as settlers moved onto the reservation, he found himself liable for damage his *betes noires* might wreak.

Finally, he killed those buffalo who continually made nuisances of themselves and allowed friends who yearned for one more buffalo hunt to shoot some of them. Strangers allowed as how they'd like a chance at buffalo; Pablo said he'd give them a public hunt at $250 a buffalo. Then, Montanans, their consciences at last aroused from the sleep not even the booming of the hide hunter's guns had disturbed, saw to it that the Montana Attorney-General stopped such commerce in buffalo bodies. He declared that, with the opening of the reservation to settlers, wild animals were under protection of the state game laws. Pablo could neither kill them nor ship them to Canada; he relinquished his claim to them legally, surely with some sigh of relief.

Before Pablo gave up, the Bison Society had unloaded the thirty-seven buffalo within the fenced range near his pasture. The new herd roamed here, protected from the seventy-five wild Pablo buffalo grunting nearby. The Bison Range couldn't let them through the fence even after Pablo and Canada had relinquished them, for the State of Montana claimed them—though it had no way to protect them. The seventy-five buffalo disappeared to poachers just outside the fence of a range designed to protect buffalo, disappeared at a time when those outside the fence outnumbered those inside the fence.

Canada paid Michel Pablo $170,000 in all. So he, the last man to chase the wild buffalo, became the only man to fulfill the dream of 400 years—making a fortune from raising buffalo.

The plight of Pablo's buffalo-raising neighbor in the Flathead country, Alicia Conrad, reveals a more typical predicament of the buffalo lover trying to preserve the animal but with no free range for its pasture, trying to find a market for surplus animals, raising buffalo both as a labor of love and for money enough to keep the herd solvent.

Alicia's husband had bought a nucleus herd in 1902, before he died, part of the dispersal of Allard's herd. Mrs. Conrad preserved the herd until "advancing years and consequent loss of my robust health" forced her to give up the buffalo upon which she had lavished so much of her life.

Her interest shows in her correspondence. Over the years she tried (unsuccessfully as it turned out) to

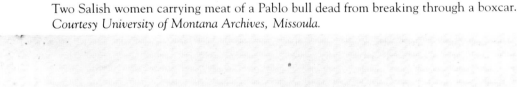

Two Salish women carrying meat of a Pablo bull dead from breaking through a boxcar.
Courtesy University of Montana Archives, Missoula.

Note the Christmas decorations in this butcher shop: Buffalo for Christmas dinner was once an American tradition. Above the buffalo's head stands the author's father, at one of his first jobs.

trade bulls with other owners of purebred stock, to keep her herd from inbreeding—a desire that grew out of her reading of books and pamphlets on animal breeding and of her knowledge of herds from correspondence with the Bison Society (it warned buyers to beware of animals from mixed herds). After the outbreak of hemorrhagic septicemia in the Yellowstone herd, she gathered information from experts and had her herd vaccinated. Her concern for the herd's well-being led to a rule that no photographers or buyers could disturb it in the spring when the cows were with calves. She refused to ship animals in midwinter cold. Her care developed animals considered by M. S. Garretson as of "the best and purest blood" in the world.

But in order to maintain the herd, it had to pay its way. She, as all buffalo growers of the time, depended heavily on the national custom of buffalo for Christ-

mas dinner. In November of 1919, for instance, she wrote 274 letters to bankers in thirteen states asking them to recommend butchers with good credit ratings. Then followed 164 letters and twenty-three telegrams to the butchers offering and dickering for buffalo, butchered or live and crated: some shops liked to receive the animals crated and alive to "drive around principle streets" and to display on the sidewalk in front of the shop before butchering.

But the Christmas market failed to thin her herd, usually consisting of fifty to seventy animals, as necessary; she had to write to other markets. Many of her letters went to Howard Eaton, buffalo broker, of Wolf, Wyoming, even though his commission would cut into her profit. They exchanged letters from 1903 to 1920, hers usually in response to his overly optimistic letters describing purely speculative opportunities: "Think I can use about a carload of buffs if the deal goes

Buffalo cow and calf. Photo taken at the Alicia Conrad ranch, near Kalispell, Montana, by E. H. Baynes on an inspection trip for the American Bison Society. Photo from the Frank Bird Linderman Collection. *Courtesy heirs of Frank B. Linderman.*

through"; "any order for ½ car or more, will bring me back at once"; "I believe I can dispose of all your surplus Buffs this year"; "I'm trying hard to sell a lot of Buffs for the St. Louis fair"; "will I think, be able to sell 15 or 20 this spring . . . can also buy from Mr. Pablo, but your bunch is so close to RR that if not too high, I'd rather buy from you"; "If I made pymt of $100—as forfeit, would the bunch be held for me until about April"; "I was unable to close the deal for the 10 Buffs—*thro' no fault* but money market."

Eaton's letters to Alicia Conrad reveal the highly speculative nature of the buffalo business in those interim days; he *had* to wheel and deal to manipulate the novelty market in buffs: "these people cannot be rushed, or they are apt to drop the notion of buying . . . I write 6 hours daily—much of the time about Buffs . . . to people who wish to buy, or think of buying, or want information for friends who *may* buy Buffs . . . you have to give some latitude to prospective buyers . . . it takes *lots* of *letters* and *time* to close most sales." He, as he said, was "not in it for glory, but for cash," and he had to watch the details: "I get *horse rates* [from the railroads], if Buffs are reduced to *horse valuation* . . . have to figure closely on this deal—

Have to ship over 2000 miles. . . . If head is skin'd out as I suppose, I'd let it dry a few days, until a cold snap comes, when it can go *for* freight. . . . If I cannot do so (deal with you), I'll send farther East for heifer, and can buy an 18 mos Bull of A1 stock—Park raised for a little less than your price."

Speculating as usual, Eaton thought he discovered a new market in supplying buffalo or buffalo hides to Indians: "Am trying to sell the *old bull* Buff you wrote about to a rich Indian for medicine. . . . If you have a photo of him (or one with as good a roll [sic] and beard.) please send same to me. . . . If you kill any Buffs between *now* and Xmas, please quote me price . . . the *long hair* on top and sides of hump is especially desired by the Indians, and they will not buy a hide if cut short."[10]

The buffalo herds indeed existed precariously in such a situation, through no fault of the buffalo owners, but through the shifting novelty market. By 1919, neither she nor Eaton could find many buyers for live buffalo; Eaton found sales only in old bull hides "with scalp and tail on—what were called *Head and Tail Robes*"—the meat, just as in the hide hunting days, went to waste.

This speculative, get-rich-quick market, that had sometimes led even the ordinary man to invest in a robe from Mrs. Conrad on the supposition it would increase in value, had disappeared with the growth of private herds and the establishment of government herds.

In order to preserve her herd Mrs. Conrad advertised heads for sale in magazines designed to reach the well-to-do homemaker, offering heads to grace the den wall. She attempted to smooth out the problems of the trade. Expressmen pulled out head hair by the handfuls because they used the hair as a handle, she solved this by wrapping the heads in burlap; when a dealer complained of hair falling from a head, she advised him that "treatises on the subject" advised never to comb a mounted buffalo head.

In 1919, she could no longer afford to expend the necessary energy. And she felt, "I have personally done my share toward propagating and preserving this species of noble animal." She found no buyer for three discouraging years; then, in 1922, the Gibson Brothers, meat packers at Spokane, bought the herd to be kept on their ranch at Yakima ("not to be slaughtered or dispersed"), ninety animals for $15,000, about $166 each.

The herd left her ranch, but, as she had feared, the new generation showed little of her "interest and sentimental feeling." Six months later it was up to her to make the report of herd disposal to the Bison Society, for all its letters to the Gibson Company had brought no answers—"it would appear as if they do not care to have any communications with our Society."[11]

Boosters in many western states had begun to covet a government-supported herd such as the Moiese National Bison Range herd, for it could mean tourists scattering money nearby. South Dakota felt a herd would add to its Black Hills, but the Bison Society found that possible squabbles over the rights to mining claims made the hills untenable for a permanent buffalo herd. It suggested the Wind Cave National Park as a good range if a few adjoining water holes were purchased. Its report stated, "The citizens of Rapid City and Hot Springs are both anxious that the Game Reserve be located in their vicinity."

With the prospect of a national herd in South Dakota, George Philip saw a way of moving out from under his herd, now that buffalo business had soured. But in 1912 Congress appropriated $26,000 for fencing South Dakota land and for buying South Dakota water holes but no money for buying South Dakota buffalo. In November 1913, fourteen New York buffalo arrived at Wind Cave Park.

Eleven months before the shipment to South Dakota, the Bison Society had released six buffalo into a fenced pasture in Nebraska's Niobrara Game Preserve, buffalo given to the Society by J. W. Gilbert, a Nebraskan who'd stipulated that his gift must not leave the state. The society had raised $2500 for fencing, mostly through the work of T. S. Palmer in Washington, D.C.[12]

The United States now owned five buffalo herds— enough herds, advised Hornaday (the North American 1911 census stood at 2760, captive and wild). He praised W. F. Hooper, the new President of the Bison Society, for establishing the Wind Cave herd but suggested that with the "future of the American Bison quite . . . secured, the society should perhaps do what they can to help protect the Prong-horned antelope."[13] To his disgust, the Bison Society went ahead with his original plan to establish ten government herds.

In 1916, the society agreed to help the Forest Service obtain pureblood buffalo for a game preserve in the Pisgah National Forest, North Carolina. Austin Corbin, Jr. would donate six buffalo if the society would crate and ship them. M. S. Garretson, Secretary of the Bison Society, accompanied them.

Garretson was the man for handling animals, since he'd left his New Jersey home early and spent years cowboying in the West, then returned east to run a riding academy. Interested in everything western, he became a charter member of the Bison Society and was made its secretary in 1921 at the instigation of the new president, Edmund Seymour (himself a western buff who'd spent eight years cowboying and had witnessed the hide slaughter in Montana; but now, at his bank president's desk at 45 Wall Street, he lived the western life vicariously through correspondence with westerners and his conservation work). Seymour had found Garretson methodical, orderly, and able to write a good letter. The society couldn't pay Garretson for his services, but managed $100 at Christmas to pay expenses, and eventually Hornaday found him a job as curator of the Heads and Horns Building in Bronx Park. For more than twenty years he corresponded with any buffalo lover who cared to write. He wrote a pamphlet about buffalo which many schools used, a pamphlet which grew into his book of 1938, *The American Bison*. He fired off buffalo lore to any author needing background material.

He and Seymour worked together as secretary and president for over twenty years. Both saw to much of the establishment of an Alaskan buffalo herd in the 1930s. They both continued to write to anyone inquiring about buffalo, wrote as secretary and president—and almost the only active members—of the now minuscule Bison Society.

Four of the Pisgah buffalo died in 1920. The Bison Society shipped three more, but by 1925 these had died, leaving only three buffalo wandering the Pisgah. These three still lived lonely in the pasture in 1928 when Secretary Garretson wrote to President Seymour:

> I suppose we might just as well wipe the Pisgah herd off the map since the Government cares so little for them . . . The great trouble is, the Gov. usually develops a sudden and acute attack of economy or something when it comes to spending anything for the preservation of Wild Life and the care and attention it has bestowed on such herds as has been presented to the people, does not lend much encouragement for future donations. . . . I know that I have scratched the Gov. pretty sharp from ears to tail but . . . When a man or a horse tries to put something over on me, I don't forget it when I start to ride 'em.[14]

Garretson praised the Canadian way of caring for buffalo and advised Seymour that if our government continued to mishandle the animals the society had donated, the society should demand control of any further herds donated to the government.

Bison Society feelings were sore not only because the Pisgah herd had failed, but also because in Montana local conservationists had wangled elk onto the Moiese range—now 500 elk cropped its grass before buffalo could get at it; the range was being depleted, the buffalo were suffering.

Seymour and the Bison Society fought during World War I against ranchers who contended that the war-time shortage of mutton and beef meant wild game in the National Parks and the Game Reserves should be slaughtered and their grazing lands populated by sheep and cattle—another scheme to wrest away park lands from the public. In Montana, ranchers pressed the Missoula Defense board to open the Moiese Range to them. Seymour, apprised of this, appealed to Washington. T. S. Palmer replied, "We have more schemes for killing 'surplus' buffalo, elk and other game than I care to remember. . . . It is premature to consider canning buffalo unless we wish to can the herds for good and all." He advised Seymour, "Stay where you are rather than wanting to sign up in govt. Need your conservation work—to head off schemes to kill the buffalo on one pretext or another." Frederick C. Walcott of the Food Administration wrote the Bison Society to assure "the protection of wild life from hysterical slaughter." He regarded game as a breeding reserve just as he did domestic stock. But in war-time San Francisco, the zoo keepers slaughtered buffalo to feed the bears.[15]

After the war the national worry over the buffalo continued, although the buffalo census stood at 12,521. In 1923, Secretary Garretson, in reply to letters concerning three buffalo bulls about to be slaughtered by private owners in South Dakota, wrote, "They are not *beginning* to slaughter the buffalo, they have never *ceased* slaughtering them . . . that's why the Bison Society was formed. . . ."[16]

*"... [The catalo] will become very popular and valuable
for the western ranges."*
CHARLES GOODNIGHT

*"They might be put down as typical of American life ...
They are the perfect animal for the plains
of North America."*
BUFFALO JONES

O N FRIDAY, July 31, 1964, the *Lethbridge Herald* bore a headline "CATTALO EXPERIMENT ENDING   HERD TO BE SLAUGHTERED SHORTLY." The butchering of this herd in the next month ended a fifty-year Canadian experiment that had tried to cross buffalo and cattle to produce a meat animal with the hardiness to live in northern Canada. The butchering also ended the many dreams of producing magnificent catalo herds raised on the land once lorded over by their part-grandfathers. But the Canadian catalo disappeared not because they starved in Arctic blizzard, not because men disliked their meat. No, they were hardy and tasty. The Canadian government killed off the new breed because ranchers didn't need them: Hereford and Angus breeds had proved tough enough for northern plains winters.

A photograph accompanying the newspaper story shows two men clipping catalo hair samples to test for cold hardiness; the Canadians had crossbred to develop a warm, buffalo-hair winter coat on the catalo as well as to retain the cow's small, thus frost-protected, udder. Below this photograph is another showing what the caption says are four catalo bulls; uncaptioned I would have thought one a Polled Hereford, the others

also of domestic breeds. Where's the hump that early crossbreeders hoped to plant on the back of domestic cattle to profit from pounds of extra-paying choice cuts? Where's the long warm hair? These aren't the catalo that Texan Charles Goodnight tried to bring forth in the late nineteenth century. These aren't the catalo that Kansan Buffalo Jones dreamed of when he coined the word back in the 1880s, although he first spelled it cattelo and, later, decided the word should retain only three letters for each family—catalo.

Perhaps Buffalo Jones's catalo existed mostly in his dreams. True, he grazed catalo at his Garden City ranch but it's doubtful if many of those he exhibited here were born of his buffalo. He'd gone to Colorado in 1883 to see his first catalo and had come home scheming to crossbreed if he could produce such 1800-pound carriers of meat as he saw there. For this he caught Texas calves. He thought to produce a catalo adapted to differing climates, one-quarter buffalo for Texas and the South, one-half for Colorado and Kansas and three-quarter buffalo for farther north.[1] He claimed that catalo outdid any beef animal in hardiness and meat production, but when he wrote about crossbreeding he shied away from facts; although he wrote most persuasively and lovingly of the beast, it appears his fame arose as much from his way with language as his way with buffalo.

In 1887, typically slam-bang, he turned young buffalo bulls in with his Galloway cows, hoping for a hybrid calf crop—a wild hope, for these were scarcely bulls, they were the two-year-olds and yearlings he'd captured as calves on the Staked Plains in 1886. No calves resulted. The next year, 1888, he reported eighty or ninety pregnant cows—but only produced two live calves. Worse, thirty of the cows had died giving birth or before. But he cruelly kept on "experimenting." To him, at this time, catalo only resulted from a buffalo father and a domestic mother. He believed larger domestic cows would survive birth more successfully, ignoring the fact that hybrid calves are smaller at birth than either bisontine or taurine calves; when they continued to die, he went on breeding. In his haste, he had little other choice: a domestic bull stayed aloof from shaggy, wild-smelling buffalo cows.

He now had two hybrid heifers (a hybrid is a 50/50 cross) that could bear no calves until two or three years old—and possibly, as hybrids, might prove sterile. Rather than wait he bought Sam Bedson's Canadian herd of eighty-three animals and with it acquired twenty crossbreeds.

Jones outbid the Canadian government for Bedson's herd, paying about $300 a head ($25,000 for the herd), and then hurried to ship it out of the country because of a rumor the Dominion might prohibit its "only herd" from leaving the country.[2] (Hardly its only herd. Lord Strathcona had purchased twenty-seven of Bedson's buffalo, given five to Winnipeg and the balance to Banff National Park, and wild buffalo lived in northern Alberta.) He now had a herd of 135, but sold twenty-four to J. E. Dooley for his herd on Antelope Island in Utah's Great Salt Lake.

Jones believed his new stock could produce catalo—a word to him that meant, now, the offspring of parents each with buffalo and domestic cattle blood in their veins (others thought of any hybrid as a catalo). The only catalo of this definition grazing on his ranch were those he had brought there from Canada, although his own stock had, this same year, produced two more hybrid heifers. In a few years his calves might produce a catalo mixture.

But, as a victim of the recession of the early 1890s, he had to sell his herd five years after he bought it, in 1893, to Charles Allard and Michel Pablo in Montana. Jones, then, bred catalo for only six years or so, hardly enough time to allow him to become the catalo

expert newspaper and magazine stories made him out to be, stories that held him up as second only to Buffalo Bill as an expert upon things western—especially buffalo things. Jones didn't deserve his reputation as a catalo breeder; his bad luck cut off his breeding experiments. Buffalo Jones saved the buffalo whose blood flows in many of the herds living in the United States today but crossbred few catalo.

In his brief experimentation, he ran up against the major difficulties of crossing a buffalo bull and a domestic cow. First, too many domestic cows die; no cattleman can stay in business losing a third of his calf-bearers each season. Second, surviving cows often abort bull calves or bear them dead. Third, any live bull calf often proves sterile. Others experienced these difficulties: Charles Allard gave up trying to raise catalo on Flathead Lake's Wild Horse Island, because he lost too many cows. About the same time in New Jersey, Rutherford Stuyvesant gave it up when nineteen of his Galloway cows died calving.[3] P. E. McKilip in Kansas had quit after ten years, for the same reason.[4] Consequently, since cattlemen need a large calf crop (and a fertile one) to stay in business, western newspapers often discouraged catalo experimentation.

The reverse cross, a buffalo cow with a domestic bull, has killed fewer cows and produced more fertile bull calves, but, in nineteenth-century experiments, domestic bulls usually met up with cows smelling of the wild and stayed away from them.

Earlier crossbreeders reported little of such breeding difficulties. Robert Wycliffe of Lexington, Kentucky, wrote Audubon in 1843 of his experiments. After purchasing, in 1813, two buffalo cows from a man who'd brought them from the Upper Missouri, he bred them to domestic bulls. He found the heifers fertile, but remained unsure if the "half-buffalo bull will reproduce again." He developed some catalo striped like a zebra (in fact the coloration of catalo often runs to an "undesirable" brindle striping). Crossbreeding efforts had permeated much of the country east of the Mississippi throughout the eighteenth century. In 1750, Peter Kalm wrote that in his travels he'd met people who raised buffalo they'd captured in Carolina and southern Pennsylvania. Kentuckians kept cattle they claimed had descended from buffalo, animals that had the black horns and hooves and some of the buffalo hump, though they sported the varicolor markings of domestic cattle. Likewise, Albert Gallatin wrote of domesticated buffalo in Virginia and of a fertile "mixed breed . . . quite common in 1784 in some of the northern counties of Virginia. . . . From a want of fresh supply of the wild animal, they have merged

Frederic Remington's drawings of Buffalo Jones's catalo. *Harper's Weekly,* July 12, 1890.
Courtesy Amon Carter Museum, Fort Worth, Texas.

into the common kind. They were no favorites as they yielded less milk." But, in the 1880s, one hundred years later, a Nebraskan claimed fourteen quarts a day from one cow and that "almost all the cheese is made of buffalo milk" in his area. Also, James P. Swain of Bronxville, New York, found that his catalo, a cross with Jerseys, gave milk with twenty-seven percent, almost-colorless cream. His catalo allowed a boy to handle them and stood calmly for milking. (Farmers preferred as milkers catalo cows with less than half buffalo blood.)[5]

Some early crosses may have come about because of natural intermingling of cattle and buffalo (some people have contended cattle loved to run off with the wild herds): artist Kurz heard "there are sometimes crossbreeds that are said to be very large splendid fellows" in the herds near Fort Union, Colonel Dodge saw some in the Republican River country about 1874, and Buffalo Bill Cody exhibited some creatures in 1888 he called catalo, captured, he claimed, near Zacatecas, Mexico. But, such crossings seem rare. Charles Goodnight claimed they didn't occur in the wild state. They are rare in the domesticated state: Montana's Spokane Ranch, which has run cattle and buffalo together for over twenty years, has experienced no natural crossings.[6]

Charles Goodnight raised buffalo and catalo on his Texas ranch. He hung on to his money longer than Buffalo Jones; he could afford to lose cows and raise infertile bulls year after year in crossbreeding experiments.

He captured six buffalo in 1866 to raise on his Elk Creek ranch—although he could see wild herds on any hillside. But the friend he left them with sold them "and never even gave me a part of the money." Ten years later he laid out another ranch in the Texas Panhandle country. The hide hunters were then clearcutting his acres of buffalo, and his wife begged him once again to put a few on the ranch, before the country was bare of them. Goodnight roped two calves, hauled them to the ranch and turned the little fellows in to suckle Texas cows—who kicked them when they tried. The calves soon learned to put off suckling until Goodnight came to the corral to lambast any kicker with a stick.

Later he roped seven calves, bought a calf (one of the last roped in New Mexico) and three more were given to him. The herd increased; he maintained it at 200 to 250 head. The buffalo roamed their own pasture, a part of his 50,000 acres. He castrated many calves for he believed fights among fertile bulls cut down the impregnating of cows, and that old, fertile bulls became fence-breakers. By 1886 he could say he'd raised buffalo "in a small way . . . for the past ten years, but without giving any particular attention to it."

In 1882 one of his cowboys discovered a hybrid heifer in with the cattle, the daughter of the fence-jumping buffalo bull, Old Sikes, and one of the Texas cows—Goodnight's first catalo, or cattelow as he at first liked to spell it. A rare happening, a natural crossbreeding on the range, but Old Sikes had been raised with Texas cows and served them readily. From then on Goodnight bred some cattelow on his place in the hope that he would produce a scientific wonder: a crossbreed that any western rancher could raise on his range in competition with purebred beef cattle.

In this crossbreeding he used hardy Polled Angus. He wanted to save the buffalo's hump for he knew that selling more meat per animal—good roast and steak—would attract any stockmen; he claimed that his cattelow dressed out sixty-six percent meat, an average of 150 pounds more than ordinary cattle. Not only this. He said a mature cattelow, before butchering, gained faster and weighed more than a comparable mature range cow.[7] And Goodnight kept hoping that his cattelow would some day develop the extra buffalo rib to be covered with further cuts of high-priced meat.

When Goodnight, riding about his buffalo herd, stopped to admire one of his cattelow, maybe the zebra-striped animal, the talk of the countryside, he saw an animal that would pass on all of the wondrous buffalo qualities. He saw a superbeast that required little salt, ate no locoweed, shrugged off diseases that cattle suffered from and fattened on foods cattle only sniffed at. He looked at a beast that ate farther into the seed-rich base of bunch grass because of its extra incisors, and one that would live longer and bear calves longer than her domestic sister in the adjoining pasture. And as he rode, he watched for signs of the superior brains (the buffalo brain is about one-third larger than the cattle brain) he claimed his cattelow had inherited from buffalo: he believed they wouldn't drift in front of a blizzard, wouldn't let the heel flies get at their heels (they tucked them under when they lay down), wouldn't lie down facing uphill making it impossible for them to get to their feet again—all stupid things he saw his cattle do. As he watched a cattelow mother, he was sure he saw a better mother than a domestic mother. In his mind, the buffalo's superbeast qualities had replaced many of the characteristics of his Polled Angus—although some offspring were hornless like the Angus. Goodnight tasted better flavor when cattelow meat lay on his tongue; buffalo grease, he claimed, never bothered a man's stomach; his favorite "elixir" was a mixture of buffalo extract and whiskey.

Goodnight kept watch over each pregnant domestic cow, yet he couldn't discover why she brought forth mostly dead or aborted cattelow bull calves. He kept watch over any successfully born hybrid cattelow bull calf, yet he couldn't discover why the calf often grew up sterile. He claimed that his cattelow bulls from cows of three-quarters buffalo blood and a Polled Angus bull were fertile,[8] but other, more scientific experimenters have found this not true. In his later years he wrote many letters to the American Bison Society about his "experiments," even furnished an article to a breeder's magazine—although he complained of such a journal, "its articles are so cumberous and filled with phrases, and go off into such immense details without the common sense part, that I have not been able to gain much from it." But years of observation had taught him that to cross buffalo and cattle successfully, he had to use domestic bulls to impregnate buffalo cows, and to do this he had to raise them together from birth, to allow the bulls to become accustomed to the shaggy, fearsome cows. Under this method he claimed to have produced cattelow to the thirty-second cross,[9] but, to William Hornaday, he had produced only a herd of "a hopeless mixture of impure blood."

Goodnight kept on with his buffalo and his cattelow into his old age. When, in 1910, at seventy-five, he found himself almost broke, he yet believed that the incorporated "Goodnight American Buffalo Ranch Company" would, at its rate of increase, be worth a million dollars in ten years. He intended the company to "devote much time in cattle breeding from the cattalos" (he'd changed his spelling).[10] But his ranch went down and his fortune. Yet he continued his buffalo interests: he saw to it that the Taos Pueblo had hides and tallow for ceremonials, and, though poor himself, gave a starter herd to it.

Goodnight had provided buffalo for the nation to enjoy; today's Yellowstone Park herd as well as the National Bison Range herd carry the blood of his buffalo.

In 1894, far to the north of the Goodnight Ranch, in Bobcaygeon, Ontario, a wealthy lumber man, Mossom Boyd, began crossing buffalo and various cattle breeds—Polled Angus, Hereford, West Highland, Sussex and Devon, as well as scrub cattle—"to learn which sort would yield the choicest fur."[11] He wanted

an animal for the far north. He understood breeding in the way Colonel Goodnight did: he knew that hybrids born of the first cross of two species usually grew larger and stronger than either parent; he believed that to produce a crossbred animal with certain characteristics—meatiest hump or choicest fur—he should use the male of the species containing these for the first cross and then experiment by crossing any fertile hybrid with purebreds or other crossbreeds in hopes of consistently reproducing the traits he wanted.

Mossom Boyd differed from Charles Goodnight and Buffalo Jones in that his mind ordered things better. He filled his reports to the American Breeder's Association with charts and photographs and lists of observations. He noted that the mature hybrid offspring of a domestic cow and a buffalo bull showed certain dominant buffalo characteristics—"altogether . . . finer looking animals than the bison": it retained the buffalo brown—but brindled; it wore a buffalo hump; it lost, somewhat, the slinky buffalo hips yet wore the short buffalo tail; its hair grew longer than cattle's and it wore this long hair all year since it shed no patches in the spring. And when the hybrid animal spoke he grunted—he'd lost the moo.[12]

Like Goodnight and Jones, Boyd publicized his belief that his crossbreeds were superior to range cattle and that they would become a future range animal raised for their fur as well as for their meat.

But by 1908 he only *hoped* that a fertile catalo bull might develop "in one or two crosses"; five years later his quarter-blood bull had fathered only five calves—he was "more or less fertile"—and, of his twenty-four hybrid cows, only three produced calves regularly. He had decided that male hybrid calves so often were born dead because during pregnancy the mother produced "an abnormal secretion of amniotic fluid"—which later the Canadian government experiment proved true.[13] Only his eighth-blood and quarter-blood cows could be depended upon to calve. In 1914, after twenty years of breeding, he was far from being able to show a new beef and fur animal.

That year he died, and his remaining twenty crossbred animals were sold to the Canadian government; seven catalo cows, one catalo bull, nine hybrid cows and three hybrid bulls went to Wainwright Park, Canada's new buffalo preserve, to begin the catalo experiment.

On a wintry day in 1905 Buffalo Jones once again swung down from the train in Washington, D.C. In the baggage coach ahead lay things he'd brought to show President Theodore Roosevelt. Jones felt that

Teddy, part-time westerner, would be delighted to watch the reels of motion pictures he'd shot of wild animals in Yellowstone Park and to run his hands over the big catalo robe, described in a Washington newspaper as "a glossy blackish brown with hair not quite as long as a bear's." Just as he'd figured, the films and the robe got him into the White House and gave him a chance to explain his Grand Canyon catalo project to the President. He wanted to place buffalo and cattle on the Kaibab, the vast land above the north rim of the Grand Canyon, there to raise catalo in marketable amounts.

Soon after this chat, the United States gave Jones permission to fence a portion of the Kaibab public lands. Later in the year the President proclaimed this Kaibab region the Grand Canyon National Game Preserve.

Jimmy Owens, once with Jones in Yellowstone Park, earlier with Goodnight in Texas, and now appointed gamekeeper on the Kaibab, had been watching over a few buffalo he and Jones owned as partners. Men in Fredonia, Arizona, impressed with Jones's supposed buffalo knowhow and his governmental backing, joined his company, put up money to buy Galloway cows to cross with buffalo, as well as a Persian sheep that Jones somehow intended to cross with deer. Jones and his company made a contract with the U.S. Government—went partners with it—the government to receive a percentage of the increase and to furnish some animals (two Yellowstone Park bulls eventually arrived on the Kaibab).[14] For this Arizona herd, Jones retrieved some of his former buffalo.

Once again Jones tried breeding catalo using Galloway cattle. On a visit to Washington he noised it about that although his hybrids and quarter breeds were sterile, his one-eighth breeds had proved potent—which he surely knew to be incorrect. Of course the Grand Canyon Company produced no fertile catalo bulls.

And other projects occupied his mind. Since 1900 he'd been trying to convince the government that it should place buffalo on a reserve in the extreme southwest corner of New Mexico. In that year he'd managed to have a bill introduced in Congress to form a 3300-acre reserve there and populate it with 150 buffalo. Jones said this herd would double every four years, and promised the government that in twenty-four years it would have 6000 buffalo (which would have vastly overgrazed the land). Luckily nothing ever came of the bill. He also tried to get Congress to move its Yellowstone Park herd to this warmer area—although when he talked of catalo hides in Washington, he bragged that the cold of the Grand Canyon produced the best hides.

When Jones's Arizona catalo proved sterile and his Persian sheep refused to mate with deer, the warmer climates beckoned even more. One day he rounded up those buffalo he figured were his, perhaps fifty head, and pushed out for Las Vegas, New Mexico: as the Forest Service put it, ". . . one day we heard the whole bunch had been moved . . . nothing done, but we scolded him by letter . . . Jones got tired of his end of it and the first we knew the best part of the herd was down in Garden City, Kansas."[15] That's a long way from where Jones's daughter said he kept the herd—Las Vegas and then Portales, New Mexico. After a year or so he sold them to a man in San Antonio, ridding himself for the last time of buffalo.[16]

In 1919 he died moneyless in Kansas City. He'd spent his last days trying to promote a "patented water elevator" he'd designed that he hoped would "save the world from starvation." He claimed to "syphon" water to a higher level which "physics tells . . . is impossible, but what do I care for physics . . . My plant is running in secret."[17] During these years he wrote long letters to the Bison Society's Edmund Seymour claiming that he, not Charles Goodnight, had first developed the catalo, and he urged this spelling of the word on the society. Seymour wrote regularly—he told Hornaday he had a "tender spot" for the old man—in fact he had seen to it that the society made Jones an honorary member and paid his $25 fee and presented him as speaker at an annual society banquet. He pled for Jones's "one t" spelling of catalo, saying it looked better and was easier to write. And he stood as mediator between the two old men, Goodnight and Jones, in their letter-writing quarrel over who first bred catalo.

Before receiving Mossom Boyd's catalo, the Canadian Department of Agriculture had double-fenced about 4000 acres of the Wainwright preserve in Alberta for the catalo experiment and had crisscrossed this enclosure with other fences to separate various crossbreeds. All seemed to be in readiness for Boyd's catalo, but the Department hadn't reckoned that oversize hybrids carried so much of buffalo speed and orneriness. When the Wainwright hands tried to get Mossom Boyd's big bull, Quinto Porto, snubbed down to give the veterinarian a chance to look him over, he "took a yen for the open spaces . . . taking a few posts and some Page wire with him . . . the snubbing post, wire gate and two cowboys hanging onto the end of the lariat." The department had to rebuild its corrals, and the Wainwright cowboys had to learn how to handle ill-tempered hybrids that could outrun and outstay their horses.[18]

But the Hybrid Station, as it was known, had more immediate success with building new corrals and handling animals than it did with producing a breed of catalo. Quinto Porto failed to father any calves. Two buffalo bulls were then brought through the double fences, but they ignored the catalo, stood morosely in far corners or wandered the fence line trying to get back to their own herd. After three years of hoping the bulls would get over their homesickness, the department sent them home again. Mossom Boyd's herd had produced no calves. Now the cowboys brought buffalo bull calves through the fence to grow up with catalo.

Eventually the bulls grew up and fathered calves through domestic cows, but Goodnight, Jones or Boyd could have foretold what would happen. Too many cows died abirthing, too many cows aborted bull calves, too many bull calves proved sterile, too many bull calves died. Here the experiment could have ended, for no domestic bull had yet enough overcome his aversion to a buffalo cow to mate with one.

Then, in 1935, the Canadians brought in sixty buffalo heifers to grow up with domestic bulls. In 1937, these began to bear hybrid calves, but not until they became grandmothers, in 1941, did a completely fertile catalo bull develop. Unfortunately he could scarcely be called a catalo: his blood ran thirty-one parts domestic animal and one part buffalo. In 1956, the herd was closed at 100 head for it had sufficient catalo bulls and cows. The experimenters found fertility equal to and sometimes better than ordinary beef animals. They tested the meat and found it compared equally to Hereford meat, but the carcass retained something of the buffalo's narrow hips, undesirable in a beef animal. Unlike the claims of earlier breeders, the Canadians found catalo calves, when fed, did not put on beef as rapidly as domestic calves.[19]

The Canadians had determined several reasons for infertility in catalo bulls. One major reason: the buffalo bull had developed a small, thick-skinned, hairy scrotum that held its testes close to the body for warmth in cold climates. Such warmth interfered with spermatogenesis of sperm containing domestic cattle chromosomes; only the 31/32 crossing dropped the testes low enough in the scrotum to produce a temperature that allowed spermatogenesis of domestic sperm. Thus the assured fertility of this slim cross.[20]

The experiment ended; the catalo were slaughtered. Fifty years of crossbreeding ended without officially establishing a catalo breed of beef cattle. But the new breed can always be established if and when ranchers farther north decide they need the cold-hardy characteristics.

Today some ranchers owning buffalo herds still hope to cross their buffalo and their domestic cattle to produce superbeast; most every ranching community boasts a man earnestly attempting to produce him. Consequently, travelers in the West do see, rarely, a giant outcropping in the grass, bovine in shape but too large for any cattle—a big, Roman-nosed catalo. But vast catalo herds, capable of producing more beef per animal than any domestic herds, still roam only the pastures of the imagination, as far from reality as when Buffalo Jones wrote to Edmund Seymour "if I had plenty of money like you Wall St. fellows have, I would develop one of the most valuable Domestic Bovines in existence."

*"I cannot think of much of anything but the possibility of
doing something great
with the buffaloes for humanity."*
MARY GOODNIGHT

*"We had prime buffalo at a banquet . . .
believe me, it got a lot more favorable comment than the
pheasant they also served."*
L.R. HOUCK

CHARLES GOODNIGHT knew as much about buffalo as anybody, but he was sentimental about them, saw them always as superbeast. Buffalo tallow, Goodnight claimed, was medicinal. In 1916, he sent batches of it to the Bison Society's President Seymour in New York (so much that Seymour complained, "What in 'thunder' will I do with this buffalo fat?"). Seymour sent some to Dr. Robert T. Morris, Madison Avenue physician, to have its supposed medicinal benefits assayed. Morris answered that he couldn't experiment until he knew what it was. "Tell me what is in the bottle and I can charge somebody twenty-five dollars for finding out if I have hurt him by using it." Another doctor commented that Buffalo Balm's viscosity would be good for automobile gears. On the other hand, Goodnight received a request for another twenty pounds of the stuff from Dr. H. J. Tillotson of Los Angeles, who said he had used it on rectal cases and the privates with "great benefits." Goodnight wrote Seymour later in the year of other qualities of tallow: it was a fine preservative—when used with mince the unrefrigerated mixture remained edible for over a year.[1]

Buffalo home remedies had been praised by others before Goodnight. Early prairie travelers thought they could detect improvement in sick men who could keep down a pint of water mixed with a gill of buffalo gall, saying that it braced the nerves, restored the appetite, helped digestion, cured an ulcerated stomach, and would "snatch others from the very threshold of a certain grave"—although its use at first might be "noisome" and might make some vomit or have a "gentle laxative effect." One man claimed he drank six full gills of liquid buffalo fat drippings, for "the stomach never rebels against buffalo fat."

The Goodnights saw such wonders in buffalo. Charles told Seymour that tuberculosis among Indians had "thribbled since they have no buffalo." And in 1916 wrote about their "discovery" of buffalo soap:

> . . . It is not soap at all but so made. . . . Now we take this soap and mix it with water and it makes a compound with far reaching qualities. It has no taste and smell of soap and has qualities unknown to us. . . . I put two applications on a corn and it absolutely stopped soreness. . . . I am satisfied it will relieve rheumatism. By all means have it tried on infant paralysis. Try it for tuberculosis. I do believe it will work. It is harmless. We do not know what we have found. Help me hunt it out. I believe it stands a fair chance to become the discovery of the age.[2]

And Mary wrote, "you tell your doctors for me that I have been working over the soap for six or eight weeks [!] and know whereof I speak."

In addition to the medicinal qualities of the buffalo soap, Goodnight claimed it could be used to clean oil paints, to clean "silver and book of all description," as a "disinfectant" or to "kill insects." He'd found a supersoap from the superbeast—a concoction the King and the Duke might have brewed on Huck's raft.

Goodnight clipped "superior" wool from the buffalo and made it into blankets "superior" to the ordinary sheepswool product. He saw a great medicine in these blankets, too, for they sparked in the dark, not as phosphorous but as electricity, for "some claim they can feel the shock." (He believed that buffalo "carry more electricity than any animal known.") A beast with electric wool was, Goodnight felt, worthy of experiment by Edison or endowment by Carnegie. But these gentlemen proved uninterested in beastiology.

Earlier plainsmen had seen buffalo everywhere doing buffalo things, and had heard tales of buffalo doings. Jim Bridger told a story of buffalo herds in the Salt Lake valley being killed by seventy feet of snow falling on them in seventy days, preserving them until spring. Then Bridger tumbled them into the Salt Lake and had enough pickled buffalo to last him and the whole nation for years. And that's why no one found buffalo near Salt Lake.[3]

Another tall one deals with a man incarcerated by holdup men in a flour barrel. Buffalo began playfully rolling the barrel about and one buffalo's tail slipped through the bunghole—which the victim grabbed: "a thrilling ride, you say? . . . My nerves were worn to a frazzle and so was the buffalo's tail, when I finally succeeded in driving him into Three Forks a couple of hours later." Citizens there shot the beast "before I could get it through their thick heads . . . I wouldn't have that noble animal shot . . ." But he kept the hide as proof of his tale of the tail.[4]

The whole buffalo frontier, like Goodnight, fabricated lore about superbeast to explain his doings, folklore describing a latter-day unicorn.

Men had watched him rub and wallow. They'd seen trees debarked and prairie boulders polished from his rubbing. They knew his strength. They told how he, because of his rubbing and butting and pawing, had cleared the prairies of trees from the Mississippi to the Rockies.

Plainsmen knew enough of the beasts existed to clear these acres, for they "calklated" that exactly 17,000,000 of them grazed that broad area. Exactly—

for plainsmen figured this to be the exact amount necessary to replace the annual kill with calves—exactly.

These 68,000,000 cloven hooves were said never to crush an unnecessary blade of the prairie grass (which had sprung up in place of the trees), because the beasts traveled in single file, each hoof "stepping in the exact print" of those before him. The beasts so insisted on single file procedures, says legend, that each marched according to his place in line, and when they left a rendezvous they "departed in single file according to the exact order of their arrival." If the lead buffalo wallowed, all wallowed, somewhat as pelicans flap their wings in follow-the-leader fashion. If superbeast ran, the herd "always" formed a V-shape and "kept their formation behind their file leader."

How such a daintily stepping creature could be the same natural engineer that scuffed out the buffalo trails, choosing always the easiest grade, isn't clear. Yet those who saw the buffalo as superbeast swore he did, claiming the "best roads to Onondargo, from all parts are the buffalo trails," and that buffalo had chosen one 200-mile trail as well as a surveyor; claiming many of the early railroads followed buffalo trails and that on the B & O, between Grafton and Parkersburg, West Virginia, "in two instances the trail runs exactly over tunnels"; claiming that "the Union Pacific up the valley of the Platte follows buffalo trails practically all the way from Omaha into the Rocky Mountains." Such overenthusiasm for buffalo know-how overlooks the fact that deer also feel out an easy grade, elk find natural passes, but men credit them with no superskills. And, as for the trails supposedly following the Platte, Peter Burnett complained of traveling along this river because buffalo trails ran at right angles to the river.

The beast has no built-in Abney level.

Such a mythological creature, a rival of Bunyan's Blue Ox, was not imperiled by winter's snow, for he was "known" to burrow under the snow and there in snug tunnels graze at his ease and comfort while the blizzard howled overhead. In similar Bunyanesque fashion, if any Blue Calf was wounded, Blue Ma and Blue Auntie always came back after him, through the hails of lead, and, supporting between them whichever end was incapacitated, helped the child off the field. So said Buffalo Jones, who also claimed Blue Ma would horn a lariat from her roped calf to free it.

Another recurrent folktale says that superbisons, when hunted on the open prairie, always ran to the left "in the direction of the sun"—left, to a man facing north. They did, not because they were addicted to left-hand turning but because right-handed hunters came at them from the right in order to be in a natural shooting position, to the right of the animal; this hunter naturally milled the herd to the left—in the direction of the sun.

Numerous mythologies were fitted to the superbeast image. Canadians and Americans saw Pablo's herd, arrived in Canada, charge out of the railway cars onto the Alberta prairie and pick out grass-grown trails and wallows disused for twenty-five years—unerringly. Seton, the naturalist, wrote that a herd always tended to work back to its birth place and, if the herd was wiped out, this birthplace pasture "remained vacant for years." Others thought that cows "seek the same place each year to drop their calves." Garretson in his book about buffalo claimed that wild buffalo die rather quickly when their legs are tied, evidently basing a general law on one instance reported by Buffalo Jones. Jones himself claimed that buffalo never trot but either gallop or walk. Some men said swimming cows carried calves on their backs. Other men believed in a small breed of white buffalo living near Great Bear Lake River. Some men believed that the buffalo always stampeded for the nearest timber during a hail storm, no matter if trees grew miles away. Others vowed that buffalo stayed close by Indians, but moved out when they smelled white man. One man could see a signal of change of direction "pass gradually through the herd" in response to "a moderate bowing . . . of the leader's neck." Others believed that buffalo, like the elephant, never forgot "an injury or a friend." And some claimed that his hump was a water reservoir.

Buffalo hunters believed that the bulls looked out for the herd—after all, when hunters chased a herd they always found the bulls to the rear, protecting, it seemed, with "a gallantry to the fair sex," the cows and calves ahead. Actually, cows outran bulls. Such biased observers as Buffalo Jones saw devotion in the buffalo "family" because they hadn't sense enough to run from a hunter-killed carcass—"a pathetic sight," he wrote, to see a family grieving at the side of a dead mother "until the last one could easily be slain." Some men claimed that bulls protected newborn calves— "the bulls keep scattered round the prairie . . . charge furiously at anything that approaches." Impossible. Bulls, separated from cows during the winter, join cow herds after calves are born. During the summer, hunters approaching a herd watched what they called "sentinel bulls"—grazing at the edge of the herd. Supposedly they grazed there as sentinels; seemingly,

however, they grazed there because they preferred to stay away from the cows and their calves.

Some white men attributed the buffalo's final disappearance to mystical behavior suitable to a superbeast: they were hiding; they'd gone north to Canada en masse; they were "seen" in 1887 swimming the Missouri River near Painted Woods, North Dakota, years after they were gone. A man wrote the American Bison Society in 1938, asking for information about the "1872 migration of the American Bison to Canada, where they perished in Baffin Bay region amid the unyielding beauty of snowdrifts and ice flows." He wanted pictures of it!

Persistent folktales obscure the founding of the Pablo-Allard herd in the Flathead Valley. The standard story, the one that the Department of the Interior repeats in information folders, is the one about a Pend d'Oreille Indian, Walking Coyote, who, in 1872 or '73, brought four bison calves across the mountains to the Flathead Valley after capturing them on the Marias River. Eleven years later, he owned thirteen; he sold ten of them to Michel Pablo and Charles Allard for $250 a head.

Folklorish embellishments add color to this story— but little else. A trader on the Marias River, Charles Aubrey, told a Hiawathian tale in which he suggested to Sam Short Coyote that to make amends to his Flathead tribesmen and the mission fathers for his bigamous second marriage, now ended, "he rope some buffalo calves now nearly a year old—hobble them and keep them with my milch cows. . . . he could then drive them across the mountains by the Cadotte Pass, and give them as a peace offering to the fathers at the mission."[5] According to Aubrey, Sam captured seven head of buffalo and started over the mountains heading west into the sunset.

But old timer Kootenai Brown, friend of Pablo, wrote that the nucleus herd from "the Sweetgrass Hills" was given to a Roman Catholic priest and that it was raised at a convent for Indian children, where the animals became "tame enough for the children to play with."[6]

And Enos Michel Conkey, a Flathead, said:

> We do not know what you say about this Indian man (Running Coyote) you say brought in some buffalo calves. What we do know is that four calves were brought back with a buffalo hunting party by a fifteen year old boy named Hawk Blanket. The calves' mother had been killed and he did not like to see them left to starve or to be killed by wolves.[7]

Although running buffalo tended to go around any obstruction anyway, the rifles firing must have comforted the men. "A Buffalo Stampede; Splitting the Herd." Frederic Remington, 1893. *Courtesy Glenbow Museum, Calgary, Alberta.*

Conkey also said that later Sam Wells, the boy's father, claimed the calves, raised buffalo until he had fifty head which he sold to Pablo-Allard.

Directly opposed to all of this hearsay is the straightforward narrative of Helen Howard who credited the U.S. Indian Agent to the Flatheads, Peter Ronan, with starting the Flathead buffalo herd.[8] And an examination of Ronan's reports reveals that in 1878 he suggested to the Indians that they drive some buffalo over the mountains. He stated that they drove two cows and a bull from near Fort Shaw through Cadotte Pass. He further stated that the three buffalo had increased to twenty-seven and were owned by two cattle owners. He also stated that he had suggested that the United States buy the herd and propagate buffalo to feed the reservation.[9]

This straightforward report from a man of undoubted integrity seems a logical explanation of how a nucleus herd reached the Flathead.

Myth tellers yarned about the all-destroying buffalo stampede, something that seems never to have trampled anyone or destroyed any wagon train, although "their great humps that rolled at one like millions of iron hoops, bounding in the air at every little obstacle encountered" scared a man, or the stench and "the rolling motion of the herd" nauseated him. Stampede yarns told by professional Western Adventurers, the Buffalo Bills, and Buffalo Jacks, and Buffalo Joneses, were designed to enhance their bravado. Buffalo Jones wrote of the stampede as "this moment when the heart fluttered at the roots . . . the living cataract . . . woe unto any and all living creatures that chanced to be in its pathway . . . To flee from their wrath would have been the height of folly." But those who'd actually stood in front of the stampeding herd reported little danger. L. C. Fouquet, standing before "herd after herd running into the wind" felt "as if they would run over us, however they dodged us everytime at the most skarish moment."[10] George Brown, hide hunter, "never saw the time when they would not give the way for a wagon or a horseman." He once stood in front of a running group but they gave him "plenty of room and I never had any fear of being run over."[11] A camp cook lost on the prairies awoke at night to find a herd running right at him, but "by his shouting and action they swerved and passed him without injury."[12] James Willard Schultz, hiding behind a wagon from a stampede coming down through a Blackfeet encampment, saw them "threading their way between the lodges, nimbly jumping from side to side to avoid them, kicking out wickedly at them as they passed." After the herd had passed "no one had been hurt, not a lodge had been overturned."[13] Men crossing the plains in wagon trains felt that the main danger of a buffalo stampede came from the stampede of their mules and oxen to join the herd. The running herds were less compact than imagined; the beasts were more agile than imagined. Furthermore, they were easily turned by firing shots.

Today, as a person watches the Moiese herd switch and turn, dodging horseback riders, corral gates, and footmen, he can see buffalo are wary of anything in their path and tend to run around it rather than over it. They seem not the most dangerous animal in North America as Ernest Thompson Seton believed.

Charlie Russell based his yarn "Broke Buffalo" on another bit of widely told folklore—the superbuffalo's twice yearly migration. Charlie has it that:

> There used to be a man on the Yellerstone . . . that catches a pair of yearling buffalo. He handles them humpback cows till they're plumb gentle. . . . One day he decides to put them in a yoke. . . . Next spring a neighbor talks him into breaking sod with them. It's springtime and they don't mind going north . . . but he can't turn them. They started north and that's where they's going . . . when he quits the handles they's still plowing north. . . . If he could find a country with seasons no longer than his field, they'd do for driving team. If he was fixed so he could spend his winters in Mexico and his summers in Canada, they'd be just the thing.[14]

Mythical buffalo; mythical migration. Folklore told to account for the beast's strange absences, to account for the thousands of buffalo all moving in one direction. Such movement seemed similar to the seasonal migrations of birds. Buffalo grazed in Texas in the winter and buffalo grazed in Montana in the summer; to the believer in superbeast, they must be the same buffalo. Others saw a spawning tide in them. A railroad conductor thought all the herds going south died there—he'd seen none going north; some plainsmen believed that those going north were making a one-way journey to breed. Travelers across the Great Plains noted hundreds of buffalo trails leading north

or south, obvious signs of migration, thought they—ignoring the fact that major rivers on the plains run east and west so that buffalo coming to water traveled north or south. Men contended that running buffalo always ran south; one man believed it so avidly he claimed that a bull killed in Jackson's Hole in 1891 was the same bull his father wounded north of there in 1888—it has headed south and, he said, "they had the habit of migrating south."

These men failed to realize that buffalo moved erratically within a range familiar to them, much as do other large mammals; northern buffalo stayed in the north, southern buffalo in the south. Buffalo have no inherent instinct to migrate long distances north or south such as is present in some birds—the bronze cuckoo, for instance, that can fly its great traditional route though raised away from its own kind. Tales of buffalo migration are folklore.

Artist George Catlin, writing of his 1834 Missouri River trip, believed in another piece of buffalo hocus-pocus rather than in common sense. He reported that while at a fur post at the mouth of the Teton, he had captured several buffalo calves by separating a calf from its mother, then covering its eyes with his hands and blowing up its nostrils—"a known custom of the country . . . after which I have, with my hunting companions, rode several miles into encampment with the little prisoner busily following the heels of my horse the whole way."[15]

Catlin didn't know the calf would have followed him without the hocus-pocus with the nostrils and the laying on of hands. Calves pestered numerous travelers by adopting them and trailing along behind. But he had seen it work with his own eyes; he swore to it—"I am now willing to bear testimony to the fact." Twelve years later Audubon repeated the myth. Fifty-five years later W. F. Hornaday solemnly reprinted it in his 1887 report to the Smithsonian Institution, the report that for decades was the bible of buffalo behavior. In 1956, a Canadian rewriter presented it once again. The trappers on the Teton, pulling Catlin's leg, stretched more legs than his.

To those who believe in superbuffalo, no meat is like his, in all ways superior to beef. Colonel Goodnight tasted superior meat when he bit into a buffalo rib; so did Buffalo Jones—but they had meat to sell. Yet others, with no market in mind, testified to the wonderful flavor of buffalo meat. "I still think buffalo meat the sweetest meat in the world," said Peter Burnett, remembering his journey to Oregon. Such comments reveal more about the quality of nineteenth-century beef than the quality of buffalo meat. A quarter of buffalo is in no way as palatable as a quarter of today's purebred ranch beef. Buffalo tongue and choice cuts are perhaps tastier and more tender (the cuts frontiersmen most often ate) but the other cuts are inferior, and the stew meat is almost inedible—stringy, tough, unpleasant on the tongue. A few such meals and a man understands why mountain men and Indians took mostly choice meat from the carcass.

But the supermeat myth continues, promoted today by the National Buffalo Association, private raisers of buffalo for the market. L. R. Houck, its president, proclaimed that:

> Young buffalo . . . make a tremendous market. The trouble with consumer taste for buffalo in past years has been that the usual source at barbecues and special dinners was an old herd cull. But get a young buffalo in its prime, and, let me tell you, you won't find any meat better. A T-bone—and you get one more from a buffalo carcass—is tremendous.

T-bones, yes; chuck roast, no.

The Buffalo Association repeats other old myths in the same newspaper story:

> Buffalo enthusiasts claim buffalo range better than domestic cattle and are not bothered by extreme heat or cold. They say they are a greater converter of feed than domestic animals.
>
> "They'll put on five pounds a day on less consumption of feed than a domestic steer," Houck says. "And the butchered carcass will dress out with more usable meat than the usual 50 to 60 per cent in a domestic steer."[16]

Here's a ring of the professional folklore of Buffalo Jones, Charles Goodnight, Pablo and Allard, and Pawnee Bill, a folklore designed to increase the marketable value of commercial herds.

Buffalo folklore continues. A forester told me the Buffalo Jones Arizona catalo experiment failed because cattle couldn't give birth to humped buffalo calves—but a calf has no hump at birth. A writer claims that since buffalo grazed into the prevailing winds, they moved in a circle 300 miles in diameter, causing one herd to summer where the other had wintered. Recently an old-timer claimed in his reminiscences that every buffalo in the world today is a descendant of seven calves captured by Buffalo Jones in Texas in the 1880s.

Not so.

*"It thrilled me no end to read of those intrepid archers risking
their lives against those ferocious, bucket-fed buffalo."*
DENVER POST

*"The bison of America are not . . . on the verge of extinction . . .
the American Bison Society . . . have done so well . . .
that last year 1,400 surplus buffalo had to be killed.
It would almost seem that they have overshot their mark . . .
it is rather a tough fate for a member of a proud breed,
who thought he was being saved from extinction,
to find himself being slaughtered to make
room for others coming in."*
ROBERT BENCHLEY

IN 1923, letters began filling the IN basket on the desk of Horace Albright, Superintendent of Yellowstone Park. Now that 600 buffalo lived in the Park—600 that had to be fed in the winter or starve—Albright announced that the Park had buffalo to give away. The letters in his basket came from people who thought they'd enjoy a buffalo as a pet. A little girl's letter asked for a "cute, gentle little buffalo to play with," a mother and father asked for a buffalo to amuse their children who had tired of playing with cats and dogs. One man complained that he had to cancel his order for a pair of buffalo because his wife "is afraid the buffaloes might hurt the children." Other people complained that the buffalo they received were too big—they'd wanted a smaller size. Albright refused many requests, explaining to people that buffalo didn't belong in back yards.[1]

Their size and wildness had always made buffalo undesirable as pets. Owners had captured them as calves, played with them while their butting couldn't hurt, scampered out of their way as horns began to sprout, but penned the full-size pet or slaughtered him. In the 1870s, the sutler at Fort Hays had kept a calf that learned the cute trick of drinking beer. But as a not-so-cute, drunken two-year-old he could clear out the Officer's Club in one alcoholic charge, and, from the top of the billiard table, dare anyone to return. Sometimes he staggered part way upstairs only to lose his nerve and have to be blindfolded and backed down the steps. As his horns curved and pointed the Club game grew more Pamplonian; fortunately he soon died a dissolute death.

Wagon trains along the Platte picked up orphaned calves as pets, a trouble to feed but a pleasure to tease. The calves tagged along during the day, then chased amongst the children, bucked and raced about the encampment circle in the dusk, butting at favorite targets. The two pets of the 1834 Nathaniel Wyeth train chose John K. Townsend, the famous naturalist, to bedevil.

Most every frontier fort mingled a few buffalo with its milk cows. Keepers of stage stations along the Overland Route penned some to play with until a barbecue date was set; Mounties at Fort Walsh, Canada, broke the boredom of outpost life by keeping buffalo pets. In the 1840s, Uncle Dick Wootton captured about forty head near Bent's Fort on the Santa Fe Trail and put them up for sale; when no buyers arrived, he drove them east along the Trail, all the way to Independence. Farmers on the frontier often captured calves to take a stab at buffalo raising. In Iowa, in

Rose Wentworth's famous buffalo, the Calgary Stampede, 1912. Note the nose rings. The "trained" buffalo were led rather than driven along the parade route. *Courtesy Glenbow Museum, Calgary, Alberta.*

1847, some of them hauled crated calves captured in northern Iowa to a pasture near Vinton. Another Iowa herd, raised from captured calves, lived forty years near Merrimac.[2]

Most buffalo-raisers considered the beast domesticated if he would stay in pasture. For a beast to hitch to wagon or plow, they broke domestic oxen, rather than wasting their few spare moments breaking intractable buffalo. But those who had more time occasionally trained and yoked buffalo. In Texas some of the ciboleros, the Mexican horseback hunters, came north across the Rio Grande in wagons drawn by mixed oxen and buffalo teams. And in Montana, in 1878, robe trader Andrew Garcia was visited by six squawking Red River carts, one drawn by "four buffalo hooked up to his cart; buffalo was not so hard to domesticate if they were captured when calves—and to capture them was no hard job."[3] Uncle Dick Wootton claimed three pairs of his herd would work as yoked teams. And, as we've seen, Buffalo Jones and Ernest Baynes each claimed they drove a buffalo team. More recently, in Alberta, the Calgary Brewery buffalo team appeared in holiday parades drawing a festooned chariot; in South Dakota, a Pierre buffalo team raced horses and usually won. Trainers, wishing to astound the world, have convinced buffalo to walk on their knees, climb ramps, dance in circles—even to climb a

ramp and dive into a water tank. Buffalo learn tricks; they're not "incapable of being trained or domesticated," the popular assumption of most old-time westerners about buffalo, but they scarcely become domestic stock. Nor backyard pets.

If backyards could have contained pet buffalo, Park Superintendent Albright could have given away enough animals to keep the Yellowstone herd at a size the park could feed. But with backyards out of the question, with few ranchers yet interested in buffalo raising, with zoos and park compounds stuffed with buffalo, Albright had to begin slaughtering them to keep the herd from starving. The meat he sold at cost or donated to Indian tribes.

Similarly, in 1921, Canada announced that it had had to slaughter 1000 of the Wainwright herd to avoid overpopulating the range. And, in 1924, the Moiese Bison Range announced the impending slaughter of 200–300 buffalo. In the fifteen years since the formation of the Bison Society, buffalo had filled their available grazing space.

The United States and Canadian governments now had to learn to butcher animals and market meat, a thing governments knew little about. They tended to kill those pesky old bulls—get them out of the herd and onto the butcher's block. Tough old bull meat in the butcher shop angered such private buffalo growers as Spokane meat packer O. D. Gibson, the buyer of the Conrad herd, who complained to the Bison Society that the government's butchering methods were "killing the industry."[4] He also objected to government pricing of its buffalo meat well below a price he could sell at (apparently one reason the government could sell its tough meat).

Canada, through the 1920s, made most surplus buffalo carcasses into pemmican that fur companies still demanded for trade or sale to trappers of the far north. The government made up the mixture into ten, twenty, thirty, and fifty pound packs and sold it for 30¢ a pound. During the depression years both the United States and Canada delivered surplus buffalo meat to agencies which fed the hungry.

Of course surplus buffalo meant only that the ranges could feed no more animals, not that too many buffalo existed, not that the buffalo was saved. Consequently, people who had so recently worried about the fate of the buffalo, who had sent checks to the Bison Society to save the animal, objected to the killing. They began to write W. T. Hornaday to ask if this slaughter was right; Hornaday complained he didn't know how to answer these people.

He could have pointed out that no bison range system could possibly hold all of the progeny of the established herds. The Moiese herd in its first years seemed to be doubling every three years. Hornaday could have shown that if this reserve preserved only the offspring from the original thirty-seven, at a doubling every three years, it would have had to find room for over 150 million buffalo by 1971—more than the number roving the continent about 1492.

The Bison Society kept pushing the government into forming more bison ranges to hold excess live buffalo; carcasses could come later. Buffalo traveled to Alaska to live in the wilds again. Crow and Sioux Indians managed to finagle herds for their reservations, although the Sioux, who also managed the herd by marketing the culls, after eleven years ran out of markets for poor meat and asked that the buffalo be replaced by Herefords. South Dakota's Custer State Park began a herd next to the Wind Cave herd. And a new herd began in Platte National Park. The buffalo seemed likely to survive.

In 1924, seventy-two head of buffalo scrabbled for grass in Arizona's overgrazed, drouth-ridden Houserock Valley. The Forest Service complained "they were a perfect nuisance to everyone in that region"; local ranchers fenced off the water holes and buffalo calves died for lack of water. Uncle Jimmy Owens claimed fifty-four of them—what he had left from the herd he'd owned with Buffalo Jones. He wanted to sell them. Uncle Jimmy had long ago resigned from his job as gamekeeper of the Kaibab and had gone to hunting mountain lions at $100 for each dead cat . . . and had matted a wall of his barn with the nailed-down paws of lions he'd killed. But now he owed a man $1200 and his old muscles no longer wanted to follow cougar spoor nor keep after a buffalo herd. He wrote the Game Department of Arizona, saying it could buy his buffalo herd "after the movie people get theirs—if they ever do." The remaining buffalo in Houserock belonged to the Grand Canyon Cattle Company; they shipped them to their holdings in Old Mexico.

The Arizona Fish and Game people hankered after Uncle Jimmy's buffalo for they wanted to manage a hunter's herd. They asked the state legislature to buy the herd for Arizona, but it, like Congress in Washington, refused to spend money for saving buffalo. So the Department outmaneuvered the politicians; it "got busy and traded with Uncle Jimmy on the installment plan," paid him $125 a month from money available in its own funds.[5] The herd became theirs in 1927.

The department had meant to hunt the herd only after 200 animals lived on its range, but that very fall seventeen hunters paid $2.50 each to kill seventeen buffalo. And in 1929 the state allowed ten more hunters to cull the herd of ten old buffalo. Like the Kansas railroad excursionists of the 1870s, these hunters wanted a close shot and a big buffalo head, a big robe, a 2000 pound weight to brag about. Their shots effectively cleansed the herd of old fellows who would soon collapse anyway, old fellows who stood quietly for the shooter. Trophies they provided; sport they did not.

Almost every year from 1927 to 1973 gun-pointers helped Arizona to cull its herd. The state charged a "hunter" $40 to crop buffalo from its two buffalo ranches, the Houserock plus the newer Raymond Ranch. For his $40 a "hunter" got the head, the hide and one quarter of the meat. If he wanted more meat he could buy it from the state. Fifty to one hundred riflemen and archers who liked the thrill similar to shooting milk cows in the barnyard went "buffalo-hunting" each year.

Most buffalo lovers judged Canadian methods of raising buffalo superior to ours. When they read reports from the Wainwright range, they saw figures of tremendous herd increase: 1911, 918 buffalo; 1916, 2396 buffalo; 1920, 5000 buffalo. Consequently, Canadians could slaughter buffalo and cause less outcry amongst conservationists than could United States buffalo herders—a kill of 1000 at Wainwright in 1921 seemed sensible rather than wasteful. The discovery of wild wood buffalo living in the Great Slave Lake region made Canada seem even more the buffalo's savior. Especially when, in 1922, Canada formed Wood Buffalo Park, an enormous new buffalo reserve of 17,000 square miles, to contain these remnants of the wild herd.

But many buffalo lovers turned against Canadian methods when in 1925 Canada announced that it would ship surplus Wainwright animals—plains buffalo—north by train and by river boat to live with Wood Buffalo Park animals—wood buffalo—in the new reserve. Most zoologists objected to the mixing of the subspecies, for they felt that the two, living together, would interbreed and destroy the fewer wood buffalo as a separate subspecies. And buffalo lovers objected to plains buffalo invading the land which wood buffalo had ranged since before Samuel Hearne had first seen them in the 1700s . . . perhaps 170,000 had lived in this north country then. Yet conservationists, zoologists and buffalo lovers admitted Wainwright could hold no more than 5000 buffalo. And 1800 calves a year at Wainwright made almost 1800 deaths necessary—or a new reserve. The question: did the plains animal have to share the woods animal's reserve?

Canadians felt that they knew a bit about raising buffalo. They had been caring for government herds since 1879 when Lord Strathcona had presented some to the government at Banff National Park. They had made laws against killing wood buffalo as early as 1877 and in 1893 had instructed the Mounties to protect them. In 1907 they had sent special Mountie patrols through the country and had appointed special constables to keep an eye on men traveling amongst the buffalo.[6]

By 1925, Canadians owned some 8000 buffalo, more than any other country; they had become buffalo experts.

The American Bison Society stood aside from the furor over plains buffalo moving to wood buffalo territory because Seymour and Hornaday believed, in spite of zoologists, that the two subspecies showed no appreciable differences, and because it felt Canada wanted none of its advice: Garretson wrote, "Canada dislikes to credit the Bison Society for anything it has done towards saving the buffalo, because from their point it was Canada, and Canada alone that prevented their extermination";[7] the Canadians *had* done some chortling: "In short Canada has saved the buf-

falo . . . He's more majestic than ever . . . with thousands to choose from, a 2100 lb. specimen was the largest American museum expeditions were able to secure."[8]

Scientists remained adamant on separation of the subspecies. Canadian zoologists, led by William Rowan at the University of Alberta, wrote many letters opposing the government plan. American zoologists passed a resolution condemning the proposed action. Canadian J. H. Fleming suggested, "It would be better to shoot all the Wood Buffalo and put them in museums than to have their blood contaminated."[9]

The Canadian government, however, had to disperse the Wainwright herd: it had overstocked on buffalo by buying the entire Pablo herd. People had begun to fuss about using valuable agricultural land for buffalo, and officials were "at their wits end what to do with their increase."[10]

Politicians seldom listen to the advice of scientists whether the problem be one of pure air or of pure bison subspecies. At the end of 1925 the Canadian government announced it had shipped 1634 plains buffalo to Wood Buffalo Park. In the next two years it shipped 5039 more plains buffalo by train and river boat to the new park.

Wood buffalo began disappearing as a subspecies almost immediately. Hugh Raup, after an investigation in 1933, said that the wood buffalo "is probably disappearing" and that possibly only the hybrids could survive. J. Dewey Soper spent much time wandering Wood Buffalo Park studying the herds. He wrote in 1941, "At the present time it is relatively rare to meet an unquestioned athabascae." He thought perhaps only ten to fifteen percent of the animals in the park had pure wood buffalo blood.[11] In the 1940s, tuberculosis appeared in a number of animals; in the 1960s, biologists noted its incidence decreased the farther animals lived from "the site of introduction of the Wainwright animals."[12] For a number of years most everyone considered the wood buffalo absorbed into the plains buffalo strain, but in 1957 several Wood Buffalo Park officers, flying a census route, spotted a big black herd in a remote part of the park, a herd seventy-five miles from any other buffalo and separated from these others by impassable muskeg. It proved to be a pureblood herd.[13] The park has kept it separated from other herds ever since.

In Yellowstone Park in the 1920s Superintendent Horace Albright arranged a buffalo stampede each year, an extravaganza complete with Indians, cowboys, stagecoaches and frightened buffalo. Once again

A photo taken when Yellowstone Park administrators thought of the park herd as a show herd and put it through its paces for visiting notables. E. H. Baynes photo from Frank Bird Linderman collection. *Courtesy heirs of Frank B. Linderman.*

Americans (a few) could experience the novelty of buffalo herds in motion, not herds upon herds until they blackened the earth from horizon to horizon, but humps and horns enough to astonish an eye used to only one or two animals in a zoo, enough bodies to fill a photograph from edge to edge. Consequently, motion picture photographers filmed this event and later used the stampede in the movie *The Thundering Herd*. In Canada, as part of a big chase contracted for by a motion picture studio (at a fee large enough to more than cover the cost of the Pablo herd), buffalo died for the camera; Indians apparently killed them; actually the buffalo fell killed by the bullets of crack rifle shots hidden off camera.

Albright's perfect tourist attraction followed the precept that shows featuring buffalo would always bring out a crowd. In 1868 Joseph McCoy had brought three buffalo to Chicago as a part of the Wild West show which advertised his Abilene, Kansas, stockyard. Galloping buffalo had filled Buffalo Bill's main tent with dust; he dared not tour without them, even to Europe.

Earlier showmen had presented bloodier spectacles. In Richmond, Virginia, an 1818 paper carried this advertisement:

RARE SPORT AT THE EAGLE HOTEL

The public are respectfully informed that a GRAND BATTLE will be fought on Thursday, the 24th inst. in the yard of the Eagle Hotel, between the BUF-FALOE, and eight or ten of the best dogs that can be procured in this City. They will be turned loose in a Circus, prepared expressly for the purpose, when the spectators will be gratified with a view (from the Porticos) of the surprizing strength, activity, and ferocity, of the Buffaloe.[14]

Almost 100 years later, men were still promoting buffalo-baiting. In 1906, three Americans representing the Philip Buffalo Ranch of South Dakota, brought two buffalo to the Plaza de Toros in Juarez, Mexico.

When the big, eight-year-old buffalo was about center ring, the bull gates opened and a glossy, red bull thrust himself into the arena at a fighting gallop, head up searching for something to gore, blowing his breath in bursts. He saw the buffalo standing placidly; he galloped into a quartering position, paused and charged at this animal's flank, nearer and nearer. In a moment a horn would be deep in buffalo flesh. Then—thunk—bull's head met buffalo's head in the place buffalo's flank had been. The three Americanos chortled; they'd known all along what the crowd and the fighting bull hadn't: a buffalo pivots on his front legs, thus easily protects his flanks.

The buffalo bumped heads with three fighting bulls before, bored with this bumping of heads, he lay down for a nap while his three adversaries careered around the ring looking for an escape hole. The crowd cheered.[15]

But people grew to dislike buffalo-baiting. Even showman Pawnee Bill Lillie, about to sell buffalo to a Mexican, upon learning that he intended to put them in the bull ring, refused the sale. And naturalists ob-

jected to exhibiting government buffalo in Wild West stampedes. Toward the end of the 1920s, buffalo in Yellowstone Park and government preserves began to live unharried by showmen.

Today, herds such as the Moiese herds are rounded up once a year for inoculation and branding—and picture-takers abound. But the Yellowstone Park herd lives unmolested. And a completely wild Utah herd roams the Henry Mountains, having moved to them from the nearby desert after its transplant there from Yellowstone Park. Once a year hunters harvest it; it lives much as buffalo have always lived in North America.

Buffalo and Spanish bull about to meet in arena. One of the many instances of a show-man pulling in a crowd by pitting buffalo against animal; one man brought a lion in! Photo by James Scotty Philip. *Courtesy South Dakota State Historical Society.*

TODAY, not many people force buffalo to stampede. Private owners hold them quiet to retain poundage. Government protectors hold them free from pursuit (except for the annual roundup), in the mistaken belief that a life unharassed by man comprises the true, natural buffalo state.

Thus most visitors to western herds see none of the swift, bobbing flow of the herd at full gallop, nor feel the remnant rumble of the once thundering herd, nor wonder at the effortless gallop of the bull, rocking along as if coasting, yet outdistancing the straining gallop of the horse. Rarely do these tourists see him easily trot his 1800 pounds up a steep hillside, as light on his toes as a deer; mostly tourists see cowlike placidity—easy cropping of grass or lazy chewing of cud, unless they happen upon the activity of rutting season. But during the October roundup at the Moiese Bison Range in Montana one can feel the power, see the speed and grace in the ungainly looking buffalo. Then the cowhands from nearby arrive to halloo the herd of almost 400 into the corrals and through the chutes for branding, weighing and brucellosis shots.

Standing above a pen containing a snorting seven-year-old bull fresh from the scary rattling of cans on long poles, jumpy from the shocks of the electric prod, one comprehends the respect a wolf had for those hind legs as a powerful kick from one splits a 2 × 10, one comprehends the respect the grizzly bear had for those horns when the energy from a twelve-inch charge sways the upright logs supporting the catwalk underneath you and gouges long splinters from the boards.

The beasts thread a maze of chutes to the squeeze press and to the scales for yearly weigh-in; some fight the process once again, some trot through like a rat retraveling a well-learned maze. But today at Moiese no beast turns into a chute that leads to the slaughterhouse, as he might have only a few years ago, for now ranchers want live buffalo to add to existing herds or to start new herds. Moiese and other ranges auction the animals alive through sealed bid. In recent years they have butchered no buffalo to thin the herds.

In 1964, only twenty-five to thirty animals left the Moiese Range alive, in 1967, fifty-five animals left, in 1974, seventy. And, in 1974, a three-year-old bull brought the top price of $750; the herd price averaged $476.92, up from the 1967 average of $413.[1] In 1964, the Moiese preserve dealt in buffalo leftovers at only

$18 a robe and $5 a skull; in 1969, when it sold only live animals, it sold a bull's head and cape suitable for mounting at $201.[2]

Some families, loading their first buffalo onto the pickup, look askance at the new box that shakes under the thumping of its contents. "Strong enough?" a man asks about his plywood construction. The government man nods, "Fine. What gives us fits are horse trailers. Never hold 'em." Other men load a dozen into big two-and-a-half ton trucks, never mind the thumping in there, and drive off assuredly toward Oregon, or Colorado or Wyoming to herds already numbering in the hundreds.

Today, more than 175 such men raise buffalo and belong to the National Buffalo Association. They have a lot of pride and interest in their animals— enough so that fifty percent of them (an unusually large percent) took the time to answer a questionnaire inquiring into their problems. . .

The herds graze healthily in New York and Florida as well as in Wyoming, in California as well as in Texas; only a herd in Hawaii seems unwell. The profit in buffalo raising is good, for the price fluctuates far less than the price for beef. And the demand increases each year: today's 175 association owners (up ninety since 1967) raise about 25,000 buffalo (up 15,000 since 1967);[3] they sell to an ever-increasing market— a market now buying buffalo for starter herds as well as for slaughter. Enough buffalo exist today in the West to make it a home where the buffalo yet roam—somewhat—jumping fences and eluding pursuers, arriving from points unknown, appearing in the old magic way: "I just woke up one morning and there he was in the pasture," complained a Montana man, who wanted to be rid of a "full of mean" buffalo locked in his corral and "nothing but trouble since he wandered in."

The private herds thrive on both western ranches and eastern farms, although they demand much more attention in the East than the West. For one thing, parasites abound in the smaller, much-used eastern pastures, parasites that don't harm cattle but can kill buffalo. Since western ranches allow buffalo to roam more freely, they concentrate less in one area and the parasites have less chance to thrive. Yet even in the eastern pastures men find buffalo relatively disease-free and able to thrive on native grasses. (The herd in Florida does best roaming the palmettos, choosing its own food rather than being fed.) In the West, men find buffalo disease-free except for brucellosis, probably contracted from cattle.

Most western owners find buffalo easier to care for than cattle, but some eastern owners warn that extra work and expense result from building and caring for the extra-strong pens and fences. And they mention the effort of worming and parasite control, work that westerners may not need to schedule. Westerners say that buffalo prove less accident-prone than domestic cattle, but some easterners say they prove equally prone, admitting, however, their buffalo live confined, sometimes crowded in pens, each animal watching for dominant animals, causing them to "move very fast and they are far more afraid of each other than they are of man"—consequently a number of gorings and collisions with walls and machinery occur. And in the close quarters of the eastern farm they fight more than cattle.

In order to handle such an unruly bunch, some eastern owners have used the old carrot-on-a-stick maneuver: they feed buffalo not so much as a dietary necessity but as a way of moving them where they want them. After learning a feeding routine they'll congregate at a feeding ground and readily follow the feed truck to another location, even to a distant pasture. Otherwise the herd often proves difficult to move.

Westerners, able to let their buffalo roam freely, find them more able to care for themselves than cattle, especially in the winter. Where there's adequate feed they live as of old, nuzzling aside the snow to crop the underlying grass, often making it until spring without hay. And ranchers believe they show the legendary instinctive way of heading into the blizzard, showing no tendency to drift with the wind and smother themselves in a packed bunch against a fence corner as do sheep or cattle. They sometimes run during bitter cold, evidently exercising to warm themselves. A buffalo-raiser in eastern Montana, where tough winters often kill domestic cattle, found that "our losses due to bad winters have been nil." A Nebraskan, noting he has never seen ice build up over a buffalo's eyes and nose, as it does in cattle, suspects the animals have extra blood supply there.

Ranchers find buffalo don't bloat in an alfalfa field or poison themselves eating noxious weeds or bad hay as do cattle. And they find also that the buffalo not only choose to eat rough foods that cattle pass by, but, since they enjoy rough country, they use more of a range, especially its far corners, than do cattle. They also believe buffalo range farther from the water hole than cattle.[4] Some ranchers object to the wallows depleting the range, while others put up with it because its dust creates a natural insect control that saves the cost and time of spraying.

Owners of buffalo seem to raise them as much for their affection for and interest in them as for profit. An Oklahoman raises buffalo so that his grandchildren may know the nature of the famous American animal; an Indiana couple began raising them twenty years ago because they worried over their scarcity. Some owners keep notes on them, study them with the hope that whatever they learn may help others; some pamper them. One eight-year-old bull lives as a pet, comes when he's called, allows his lady owner to ride him or nap stretched out on him while he chews his cud. Other owners, mindful of the fact they have wild beasts here, never turn their backs on them and keep a watch over the friendliest cow for, although she hooks a horn in play at a friend, she will hook in seriousness if the friend goes between her and her newborn calf.

But their very wildness seems part of their appeal, since, even though trained from babyhood, their inborn traits differ from those of domestic cows. A three-month-old buffalo calf may come when called for a goody, but at two years old he may become enraged when that goody doesn't appear each time the trainer appears. Experienced buffalo trainers avoid this by feeding goodies only from a bucket; if the two-year-old sees no bucket he expects no goody. And no matter the degree of domestication, those who work with them find they blow and snort and charge, trying a bluff on anyone, stranger or friend. Some people, content that each is "quite a bluffer," walk about their herds—even jog through them. The lady who naps on her pet bull bluffs her bluffer—when he runs at her she runs at him. But one owner warns, "Most people get in trouble when they try to make pets of them." A herd shows its wild traits when it finds enemies about the farm: they "pay no attention to the cattle, but seem to really dislike the hogs on two occasions I have had them break the fence & kill several hogs, really mutilate them. I have also known them to kill porcupines that were unfortunate enough to get in the pasture." When they run, the old, wild sure-footedness allows them skillfully to avoid gopher holes. One herd showed a wild concern for three newly purchased calves. It chased the little creatures until it cornered them for a good inspection and an all-over tongue-lapping. And—a glimpse of the old gregariousness: "One got separated by a fence one day so he jumped in our lake swam across, the whole herd ran to the edge of lake greeted him then all stampeded like a celebration."

Pastured buffalo readily notice strangers or an unusual gathering of people and move toward the strange-ness to investigate, a help to restaurants and places that raise them as attractions, a hindrance to those who would like to get some work done but find curious buffalo "looking over their shoulder." Such curiosity also leads buffalo to investigate land beyond the fence if they can. The Florida herd now and then investigates a nearby golf course, the unfenced Catalina Island herd sometimes closes the local airport. Consequently, a beginner in buffalo raising writes, "One thing we know, they won't stay home."

Yet most raisers seem to have little trouble keeping the traditional rover at home. One man keeps them within the ordinary fencing he would use for cattle and observes "they never reach through for grass on the other side" as cattle do. Raisers need not build fences overly high, contrary to government practice. For the most part the big critters seem not to charge through or jump over lightweight and low barriers unless a fence separates two groups. Then the gregarious instinct takes over; they have to join those others, and down goes the fence.

As we might expect, the buffalo owner's affection for him still gives rise to a little loving folklore, showing foremost in beliefs such as the buffalo is "a hell of a lot smarter than cattle" and "they are smarter than man," plus a raft of superbeast claims: buffalo deplete the range less than domestic cows because they have a "softer bite," the herd always mercy-kills an old, diseased or crippled animal, buffalo never founder themselves on bad feed. One man swears buffalo dance during electric storms, executing steps similar to those in Indian buffalo dances.

A majority of these buffalo raisers believe that buffalo meat tastes better than beef (one man hasn't "butchered a beef in four years"), although some admit they eat only the corn-fattened product. About thirty percent of the growers say they eat none of the stuff (one raiser of twenty years' experience finds it too dark and coarse). One man warns that buffalo meat should roast slowly—ten hours at 250 degrees to avoid dryness. Another feels it's best as leftovers.

As to the old-time traditional beliefs about buffalo, today's owners disagree. In considering the buffalo's famed going-a-long-time-with-no-drink, about half of the owners believe he uses less water than cattle and half believe he uses as much. When questioned about the buffalo's supposed poor eyesight, far more believe he sees well than poorly: he recognizes vehicles and people, sees men at a good distance, and "can see a gate open pretty easily." Of course, as they admit, easterners observe a lot of unnaturally small buffalo groups in small pastures, while a few westerners see little of their big groups because of the large range, so eastern and western conclusions may conflict. Furthermore, most herds are small: the average herd contains only twenty-eight animals and more than half contain less than twenty. Moreover about half of the buffalo owners have raised buffalo only five years or less. We still may have more buffalo folklore than accurate buffalo information.

Only a few owners attempt to raise catalo; these know of the Canadian results but hope that some alchemy of this magical superbeast will yet bypass anatomical structure. They, too, have become enraptured with buffalo wandering about their place: "I love my buffalo" is a constant refrain in letters from buffalo owners.

No owner seems to follow a set theory about raising buffalo as a meat animal. Some say buffalo seem to fatten about the same as cattle, but respond less to force-feeding in a feed lot than do cattle, although they may do better than cattle when fed only hay during the winter. But one owner feels a buffalo can't be fattened, one says he fattens only after he's three years old and his hump well-formed, another says he needs at least 180 days to fatten—twice as long as a domestic beef—while still another warns that over ninety days of fattening may cause the meat to lose its buffalo quality, thus losing its distinct specialty appeal. For the most part today's buffalo do well on their traditional grass, but careful owners feed pregnant cows just before birth and feed the bulls especially well during the rut. Some care pays off: most owners report eighty-five to one hundred percent of their cows bearing calves each year.

Buffalo raisers seldom castrate calves to gain more meat; castrating a buffalo seems, to one owner, to make his legs grow longer but not increase his meatier parts. Another raiser believed that "the shock of castration keeps a buffalo bull [steer?] from ever totally developing."

The marketing of buffalo today remains as it was 120 years ago—finding specialty buyers. Most raisers of small herds find local specialty markets—Elks banquets, private buyers of quartered or halved carcasses for locker meat, and restaurants—all they can handle.[4] (The high prices have attracted modern rustlers who cart off live buffalo in trucks. In 1962 they made off with forty head of the Wind Cave herd.)[5]

The market has become so good that one cattle grower has begun changing from raising only Angus to only buffalo. He claims they bring more money, have less disease, and are better for people to eat (the meat contains less cholesterol and less fat, and people al-

lergic to beef can often safely eat it). But, growers warn that buffalo slaughtering costs run higher than those for domestic beef, transporting them to market costs more, as does finding one's own market.

Today, a raiser or two may find a small market in selling buffalo blood as a basis for medical serum, but many raisers have found a larger market in catering to the bloodthirstiness of plinkers who like to shoot at sure-thing targets, who will pay for a walk in the pasture to shoot down a buffalo as he stands chewing his cud. A plinker can have his choice of laying him low in a midwestern pasture or on a western range (the difficulty of western shooting can be seen in one ranch's brochure—an airplane parked within 100 feet of buffalo).

And, just as 100 years ago, the urge to plink at buffalo rises in the casual passerby. One Canadian, investigating why his placid herd had turned irritable, found their bodies filled with .22 pellets from the rifles of passing plinkers who felt the urge of the old North American shoot-at-'em tradition.[6]

Today, in parks and reserves, a bull often stands quietly for photographers—unless the man holding the black box annoys him. Then sometimes his temper breaks, his tail knots and he charges. A few years ago in Thermopolis, Wyoming, one gored and broke the bones of a man who had thrown rocks at him to awaken him and make him stand pretty for his picture. A year or two later, a man walked into the same herd and tapped a bull on the head. The bull tagged him as he turned his back to walk away. In Yellowstone Park in 1971, a bull killed a picture taker, charging to remove himself from a circle of tourists.

Today, on government ranges buffalo live long lives protected by fences and by law, protected from disease by immunization shots, protected from starving in the snow by winter feeding, but they yet fall through the ice to drown and starve in icy weather with food not more than a day's walk away. In Canada's Wood Buffalo Park the old, the sick and the young die under wolf attack. The hunter there faces difficulty in the tuberculosis that infects the herd. He has to know how to recognize tuberculosis lesions in a carcass or run the risk of contracting the disease himself. Anthrax, tuberculosis, wolves, hunters and accidents all keep this herd of the far north from overreaching the capacity of the range.

Today, letters once again fill the IN basket of the Superintendent of Yellowstone Park, but these letters request no buffalo pets, they demand that he round up and test the herd for brucellosis, and, if he discovers any infected animals, destroy them. The letters come from nearby ranchers, from the Montana Stockgrowers' Association, and from veterinarians. These haters of the park and its use of range for other than livestock pay little attention to Mary Meagher, Park Biologist and buffalo expert, arguing that patrolling the park borders can reduce the danger of infecting nearby cattle to zero, or to her plea that their program would destroy "the Yellowstone bison as a free-ranging wild population with unique esthetic and scientific values." Economics before esthetic value any old day to a stockman's association. The fact that no brucellosis has developed in the cattle herds near the park in the last ten years sways the cattleman not at all. Nor the argument by the President of the National Buffalo Association: "It's never been proved that bison have the same strain of brucellosis as is found in cattle." (No one knows whether buffalo caught the infection when cattle invaded their range or if they suffered it endemically before cattle arrived.) The stockmen go along with a veterinarian who *feels* bison do transmit brucellosis to cattle.[7]

Any buffalo wandering beyond the boundaries of Yellowstone Park risks never recrossing the boundary back to safety. The ranchers might shoot him. And, also, poaching buffalo makes a once-in-a-lifetime story; cowboys in bars outside the park border, after a few beers, allow as how they know a little about such poaching—all done by some other fellow, of course.

The annual buffalo roundup at Moiese seems like a fiesta in the October sunshine. Families come to lunch in the pleasant grove along the creek and share their potato chips with a pet deer as he stands at their table. Cowhands, too old to chase the buffalo, walk the catwalks of the corral with long rattler-poles and lean out to rattle the old beer cans wired to them near a recalcitrant buffalo's ear. Or they help at the scales, telling a one-horned buffalo, "Easy now, easy. That's how you lost that horn, turning around in the chute." One sees some of the same faces each year amongst the onlookers, those for whom buffalo watching is as good as circus watching. And always those with clipboards, notebooks or cameras: free-lance writers, camera crews for TV, professors, reporters, Job Corps classes, public school classes. The crowd outnumbers the buffalo and slows the work. But no worker seems anxious. It's a buffalo ceremony in the October sunshine.

Here, today, Salish Indian children stand, wide eyes watching the snorting and pawing and dust-throwing of the corraled buffalo, then file off the viewing platform, down the steps and into their big bus to return to school; they're on a field trip to see real live buffalo. Once in awhile a blanketed grandma comes along, wrinkled and bent, and stares at the buffalo as if thinking back to buffalo hunts. But old as she is, she could scarcely have followed the hunt. Perhaps she remembers buffalo stories her grandmother told her, perhaps she prays the old buffalo prayers her grandfather taught her, prayers suited to a life long gone.

Canadian Blackfeet selling souvenir buffalo horns to tourists. *Courtesy Public Archives of Canada.*

NOTES

CHAPTER I

Sources of quotations heading the chapter:

Louis Hennepin, *A New Discovery of a Vast Country in America*, ed. Reuben Gold Thwaites, 2 vols. (Chicago: A. C. McClurg & Company, 1903), 1:46.

Sir George Simpson, *An Overland Journey Around the World* (Philadelphia: Lee and Blanchard, 1847), p. 55.

John McDougall, *Pathfinding on Plain and Prairie*, p. 248, as cited in Frank Gilbert Roe, *The North American Buffalo* (Toronto: University of Toronto Press, 1951), p. 384.

1. Henry Kelsey, *The Kelsey Papers* (Ottawa: Public Archives of Canada, F. A. Ackland, Printer, 1929), p. 15.

2. Zebulon Pike, *Arkansaw Journal*, ed. Stephen Harding Hart and Archer Butler Hulbert (Denver: The Stewart Commission of Colorado College and the Denver Public Library, 1932), p. 96.

3. Robert S. Bliss, "The Journal of Robert S. Bliss," *Utah Historical Quarterly* 4 (July 1931):72.

4. James Josiah Webb, *Adventures in the Santa Fe Trade, 1844–47*, ed. Ralph Bieber (Glendale, California: Arthur H. Clark Company, 1931), p. 162.

5. George Catlin, *North American Indians*, 2 vols. (Edinburgh: John Grant, 1926), 2:109.

6. Hennepin, *A New Discovery*, 1:90–92.

7. Martha Ferguson McKeown, *Them Was the Days* (Lincoln: University of Nebraska Press, 1961), p. 111.

8. Max Miller, *Shinny on Your Own Side* (Garden City: Doubleday, 1958), p. 161.

9. Henry Leavitt Ellsworth, *Washington Irving on the Prairie*, ed. Barbara D. Simison and Stanley T. Williams (New York: American Book Company, 1937), pp. 62–63.

10. Alexander Henry (the elder), *Travels and Adventures in Canada and Indian Territories between the Years 1760 and 1776* (New York: I. Riley, 1909), p. 119.

11. "Diary of an Emigrant of 1845," *Washington Historical Quarterly* 1–2 (1906–1908): 143.

12. John Steele, "Extracts from the Journal of John Steele," *Utah Historical Quarterly* 6 (1933): 8.

13. Robert W. Richmond and Robert W. Mardock, ed., *A Nation Moving West* (Lincoln: University of Nebraska Press, 1966), p. 313.

14. Clarence B. Bagley, "Along the Oregon Trail in 1852," *Motor Travel* 15 (February 1924): 11–12.

15. Lorenzo D. Young, "Diary of Lorenzo D. Young," *Utah Historical Quarterly* 14 (1946): 160.

16. Charles Larpenteur, *Forty Years a Fur Trader on the Upper Missouri*, ed. Elliott Coues, 2 vols. (New York: Francis P. Harper, 1908), 1:154.

17. Alexander Henry, *The Manuscript Journals of Alexander Henry and of David Thompson, 1799–1814*, ed. Elliott Coues, 2 vols. (Minneapolis: Ross and Haines, 1965), 1:314.

18. Edwin James, "An Account of an Expedition from Pittsburgh to the Rocky Mountains," *Early Western Travels*, ed. R. G. Thwaites, 32 vols. (Cleveland: The Arthur H. Clark Co., 1905), 15:315.

19. Henry J. Helgeson to Mr. Blakeless, 1 January 1956, Montana Historical Society files, Helena, Montana.

20. Edwin Way Teale, *Autumn in America*, pp. 150–51, quoted in Porter G. Perrin, *Writer's Guide and Index to English*, third edition (New York: Scott, Foresman and Co., 1959), p. 141.

21. Walter McClintock, *The Old North Trail* (London: Macmillan and Co., Limited, 1900), p. 363.

22. Catlin, *North American Indians*, 1:282.

23. H. Arnold Bennett, "The Mystery of the Iowa Buffalo," *Iowa Journal of History* 32 (1934): 60.

24. J. Dewey Soper, "History, Range and Home Life of the Northern Bison," *Ecological Monographs* 11 (October 1941): 378.

25. Catlin, *North American Indians*, 1:282.

26. Tom McHugh, "Social Behavior of the American Buffalo (Bison bison bison)," *New York Zoological Society Pamphlet* 43 (31 March 1958): 37.

27. "An Indian Girl's Story of a Trading Expedition to the Southwest about 1841," ed. Winona Adams, *Frontier and Midland* 10 (1930): 345.

28. John C. Jacobs, "The Last of the Buffalo," *World's Work* 17 (January 1909): 11,100.

29. James Chambers, "Fort Sarpy Journal," *Contributions to the Historical Society of Montana*, vol. 10 (Helena: Naegele Printing Co., 1940), p. 177.

30. Paul Kane, *Paul Kane's Frontier, Including Wanderings of an Artist Among the Indians of North America*, ed. J. Russell Harper (Austin and London: The University of Texas Press, 1971), p. 60.

31. James Willard Schultz, *My Life as an Indian* (Boston and New York: Houghton Mifflin Company, 1906), p. 323.

32. Peter Koch, "Life at Musselshell in 1869 and 1870," *Contributions to the Historical Society of Montana*, vol. 2 (Helena: Naegele Printing Co., 1896), p. 7.

33. Bayard H. Paine, *Pioneers, Indians and Buffaloes* (Curtis, Nebraska: The Curtis Enterprises, 1935), pp. 153–54.

34. Fortescu Cuming, *Cuming's Tour to the Western Country, 1807–1809* (Cleveland: Arthur H. Clark Co., 1904), pp. 175–78.

35. Edward Douglas Branch, *The Hunting of the Buffalo* (New York and London: D. Appleton and Co., 1929), pp. 21–22.

36. John McDougall, *Saddle, Sled, and Snowshoe: Pioneering on the Saskatchewan in the Sixties* (Cincinnati: Jennings and Graham, 1896), p. 250.

37. Joel Allen, "History of the American Bison," *Ninth Annual Report of the United States Geological and Geographic Survey of the Territories, 1875* (Washington: Government Printing Office, 1877), p. 506.

38. Vicente de Zaldívar, report in *Spanish Exploration in the Southwest, 1542–1706*, ed. H. E. Bolton (New York: Charles Scribner's Sons, 1916), pp. 228–29.

39. Washington Irving, *A Tour on the Prairies*, ed. John Francis McDermott (Norman: University of Oklahoma Press, 1944), p. 177.

40. William Marshall Anderson, "Anderson's Narrative of a Ride to the Rocky Mountains in 1834," *Frontier and Midland* 19 (Autumn 1938): 55.

41. Fernando del Bosque, "Diary of Fernando del Bosque," *Spanish Exploration in the Southwest, 1542–1706*, ed. H. E. Bolton (New York: Charles Scribner's Sons, 1916), p. 298.

42. Allen, "History of the American Bison," p. 523.

43. Ibid.

44. Ibid., p. 479.

45. George P. Winship, ed., *The Journey of Coronado, 1540–1542* (New York: A. Lovell and Company, 1922), p. 237.

46. Zaldívar, report, pp. 225–26.

47. Frederick C. Chabot, *With the Makers of San Antonio* (San Antonio: Artes Graficas, 1937), pp. 155–56.

48. Frank Gilbert Roe, *The North American Buffalo* (Toronto: University of Toronto Press, 1951), pp. 96, 216, 681–84; Allen, "History of the American Bison," p. 475.

49. Mitford M. Mathews, *A Dictionary of Americanisms* (Chicago: University of Chicago Press, 1951), p. 205.

50. Martin S. Garretson, *The American Bison; the Story of its Extermination as a Wild Species and its Restoration Under Federal Protection* (New York: New York Zoological Society, 1938), p. 10.

51. Garrick Mallery, "Picture Writing of the American Indians," *Tenth Annual Report of the Bureau of Ethnology to the Secretary of the Smithsonian Institution, 1888–89* (Washington: Government Printing Office, 1893), pp. 25–822.

52. H. M. T. Powell, *The Santa Fe Trail to California, 1849–1852, The Journal and Drawings of H. M. T. Powell*, ed. Douglas S. Watson and R. Grabhorn (San Francisco: The Book Club of California, 1931), p. 31.

53. Mari Sandoz, *The Buffalo Hunters; the Story of the Hide Men* (New York: Hastings House, 1954), p. 83.

CHAPTER II

Sources of quotations heading the chapter:

George P. Hammond and Agapito Rey, ed., *The Rediscovery of New Mexico, 1580–1594* (Albuquerque: The University of New Mexico Press, 1966), p. 87.

George W. Brown, "Life and Adventures of George W. Brown," ed. William E. Connelley, *Collections of the Kansas State Historical Society* 17 (1926–28): 115.

1. Young, "Diary of," p. 158.

2. John Palliser, *The Journals, Detailed Reports and Observations Relative to the Exploration by Captain Palliser* (London: George Edward Eyre and William Spottiswoode, 1863), p. 148.

3. Henry, *The Manuscript Journals of*, 2:62.

4. Gene Christman, "The Mountain Bison," *The American West* 8 (May 1971): 47.

5. George A. Custer, *My Life on the Plains*, ed. Milo Milton Quaife (New York: The Citadel Press, 1962), pp. 13 and 15.

6. W. E. Webb, *Buffalo Land* (Cincinnati and Chicago: E. Hanneford and Co.; San Francisco: F. Dewing and Co., 1872), p. 291.

7. E. T. Seton, "American Bison or Buffalo," *Scribner's Magazine* 40 (October 1906): 401–02.

8. McHugh, "Social Behavior of Buffalo," p. 7.

9. *Santa Fe Daily New Mexican*, 3 April 1869.

10. Brown, "Life and Adventures," p. 98.

11. Durward Allen, *Our Wildlife Legacy* (New York: Funk and Wagnall's, 1954), p. 70.

12. Edward Harris, *Up the Missouri with Audubon, the Journal of Edward Harris*, ed. John Francis McDermott (Norman: University of Oklahoma Press, 1951), p. 96 and pp. 141–42.

13. Henry, *The Manuscript Journals of*, 1:46.

14. Henry J. Helgeson to Mr. Blakeless, 1 January 1956.

15. McHugh, "Social Behavior," p. 22.

16. Kane, *Paul Kane's Frontier*, p. 143.

17. McHugh, "Social Behavior," p. 35.

18. William Albert Fuller, "The Biology and Management of the Bison of Wood Buffalo National Park," *Wildlife Management Bulletin*, Series 1 (Ottawa: Canadian Wildlife Service, 1966), p. 35.

19. Meriwether Lewis and William Clark, *Original Journals of the Lewis and Clark Expedition, 1804–1806*, ed. Reuben Gold Thwaites, 8 vols. (New York: Dodd and Mead Company, 1904), 1:212.

20. Henry, *The Manuscript Journals of*, 1:136.

21. Tom McHugh, *The Time of the Buffalo* (New York: Alfred A. Knopf, 1972), p. 149.

22. Young, "Diary of," p. 157; John Crook, "John Crook's Journal," *Utah Historical Quarterly* 6 (April 1933): 55.

23. Allen, "History of Bison," p. 472.

24. James Willard Schultz, *Blackfeet and Buffalo*, ed. Keith C. Seele (Norman: University of Oklahoma Press, 1962), p. 169.

25. Soper, "History of Northern Bison," p. 398.

26. Lewis and Clark, *Original Journals of*, 1:58.

27. Richard Owen Hickman, "'Dick's Works'; An Overland Journey to California in 1852," ed. Paul Phillips, *The Frontier* 9 (March 1929): 246.

28. Isaac Cowie, *The Company of Adventurers* (Toronto: W. Briggs, 1913), p. 433.

29. George Andrew Gordon, "Recollections of George Andrew Gordon," *Collections of the Kansas State Historical Society* 16 (1923–25): 499.

30. Young, "Diary of," p. 157.

31. "Montana Lou" Grill, "Buffalo Hunting," *Philipsburg Mail* (Montana). (Clipping in Montana folder, Missoula Public Library; no date or page given.)

32. J. L. Hill, *The Passing of the Indian and Buffalo* (Long Beach: George W. Moyle Publishing Co., no date), p. 32.

33. Pedro de Castañeda, "The Narrative of the Expedition of Coronado, by Pedro de Castañeda," *Spanish Explorers in the Southern United States, 1528–1543*, ed. Frederick W.

Hodge and H. T. Lewis (New York: Charles Scribner's Sons, 1907), p. 254.

34. Franklin L. Stone, "Extracts from the Diaries and Letters of Franklin L. Stone," *The Frontier and Midland* 12 (November 1931–May 1932): 379.

35. Lewis and Clark, *Original Journals of*, 1:153.

36. Jacob Fowler, *The Journal of Jacob Fowler*, ed. Elliott Coues (New York: Francis P. Harper, 1898), pp. 156–57.

37. Powell, *The Santa Fe Trail*, p. 38.

38. Horace Greeley, *An Overland Journey from New York to San Francisco in the Summer of 1859*, ed. Charles Duncan (New York: Alfred A. Knopf, 1964), pp. 72–3.

39. Thomas J. Farnham, "Travels in the Great Western Prairies," *Early Western Travels*, ed. Reuben Gold Thwaites, 32 vols. (Cleveland: A. H. Clark Co., 1906), 28:96.

40. Hill, *The Passing of Buffalo*, p. 32.

41. Frank Gilbert Roe, "The Numbers of the Buffalo," *Proceedings and Transactions of the Royal Society of Canada* (1937), pp. 171–203.

42. Noah Brooks, "The Plains Across," *The Century Magazine* 43 (April 1902): 57.

43. Anderson, "Anderson's Narrative," p. 57.

44. Seton, "American Bison," p. 386.

45. McHugh, *The Time of the Buffalo*, pp. 16–17.

46. Roe, *North American Buffalo*, p. 707.

47. Christman, "The Mountain Bison," p. 44.

48. Francis D. Haines, "The Westward Limits of the Buffalo," *Pacific Northwest Quarterly* 31 (1940): 394.

49. N. S. Shaler, *Nature and Man in America* (New York: C. Scribner's Sons, 1891), pp. 183–84.

50. Soper, "History of Northern Bison," pp. 344 ff.

51. James Evetts Haley, *Charles Goodnight* (Norman: University of Oklahoma Press, 1949), p. 443.

52. Henry J. Helgeson to Mr. Blakeless, 1 January 1956.

53. Harris, *Up the Missouri*, pp. 71–72.

54. Lewis and Clark, *Original Journals of*, 2:329.

55. Ibid.

56. "Saving the Buffalo," *The Beaver* (June 1948), p. 11.

57. John McDonnell, *Les Bourgeois de la Compagnie*, 1:294, quoted in Roe, *North American Buffalo*, p. 168.

58. Henry, *The Manuscript Journals of*, 1:175–178.

59. Alexander Philip Maximilian, Prince of Wied, "Travels in the Interior of North America, 1830–1834," *Early Western Travels*, ed. Reuben Gold Thwaites, 32 vols. (Cleveland: The A. H. Clark Co., 1906), 22:382.

60. Norbert Welsh, *The Last Buffalo Hunter*, as told to Mary Weeks (New York: T. Nelson and Sons, 1939), pp. 105–10.

61. Henry, *The Manuscript Journals of*, 1:253–54.

62. Fuller, "The Biology and Management of Bison," p. 38.

63. Mari Sandoz, *Love Song to the Plains* (Lincoln: University of Nebraska Press, 1966), p. 97.

64. A. E. Cameron, "Notes on Buffalo: Anatomy, Pathological Conditions, and Parasites," *Veterinary Journal* 79

(1923): 333; A. E. Cameron, "Some Further Notes on Buffalo," *Veterinary Journal* 80 (1924): 413–17.

65. McHugh, "Social Behavior of Buffalo," p. 28.

66. Edward R. Warren, "Altitude Limits of Bison," *Journal of Mammology* 8 (February 1927): 105–108.

67. Allen, "History of American Bison," p. 467.

68. Henry J. Helgeson to Virginia Walton, 28 August 1955, Montana Historical Society Files, Helena, Montana.

69. Henry Inman, *Buffalo Jones' Adventures on the Plains* (Lincoln: University of Nebraska Press, 1970), p. 209.

70. H. H. Damon to Martin S. Garretson, no date, American Bison Society Files, Conservation Library Center, Denver.

71. Brooks, "The Plains Across," p. 811.

72. McHugh, "Social Behavior of Buffalo," p. 8.

73. "Travels with General Oglethorpe," *Colonial Travels*, pp. 219–20, quoted in Roe, *North American Buffalo*, p. 243.

74. Seton, "The American Bison," p. 402.

75. Clark B. Stocking to Edmund Seymour, 8 March 1917, American Bison Society files, Conservation Library Center, Denver.

76. W. T. Hornaday, "Discovery, Life History, and Extermination of American Bison," *Report of National Museum, 1887* (Washington: Government Printing Office, 1889), p. 540.

77. Haley, *Charles Goodnight*, p. 441.

CHAPTER III

Source of quotation heading the chapter:

Louis A. Brennan, *No Stone Unturned* (New York: Random House, 1959), p. 152.

1. Loren C. Eiseley, "The Paleo Indians: Their Survival and Diffusion," *New Interpretations of Aboriginal American Culture*, ed. Betty J. Meggers and Clifford Evans (Washington: The Anthropological Society of Washington, 1955), pp. 1–11.

2. Jesse D. Jennings, *Prehistory of North America* (New York: McGraw-Hill Book Company, 1968), p. 72.

3. Morris F. Skinner and Ove C. Kaisen, "The Fossil Bison of Alaska and Preliminary Revision of the Genus," *Bulletin American Museum of Natural History* 89 (1947): 125–256.

4. Russell D. Guthrie, "Bison Evolution and Zoogeography in North America During the Pleistocene," *The Quarterly Review of Biology* 45 (March 1970): 1–15.

CHAPTER IV

Sources of quotations heading the chapter:

Hennepin, *A New Discovery*, 1:48.
Henry, *The Manuscript Journals of*, 1:170.

1. Dale F. Lott, "Sexual and Aggressive Behavior of American Bison (Bison Bison)," mimeographed, p. 19.

2. Ibid., p. 20.

3. Brooks, "The Plains Across," p. 809.

4. Schultz, *My Life as an Indian*, p. 61.

5. Mallery, "Picture Writing," p. 323.

6. Allen, "History of American Bison," p. 512.

7. P. E. McKillip, "A Story of the Buffalo," *The Westerners Brand Book* (Los Angeles: 1949–50), pp. 137–40.

8. Olive K. Dixon, *The Life of Billy Dixon* (Dallas: P. L. Turner, 1927), p. 70.

9. Henry J. Helgeson to Mr. Blakeless, 1 January 1956.

10. Henry, *The Manuscript Journals of*, 1:167 and 273.

11. Schultz, *My Life as an Indian*, p. 169.

CHAPTER V

Source of quotation heading the chapter:

Joe Ben Wheat, "A Paleo Indian Bison Kill," *Scientific American* 216 (January 1967): 50.

1. Joe Ben Wheat, "A Paleo Indian Bison Kill," *Scientific American* 216 (January 1967): 49–52.

2. Louis A. Brennan, *No Stone Unturned* (New York: Random House, 1959), p. 195.

3. Richard B. Lee and Irven De Vore, ed., *Man the Hunter* (Chicago: Aldine Publishing Co., 1968), pp. 85–89.

4. Stuart W. Conner, "Prehistoric Man in the Yellowstone Valley," *Red Man's West*, ed. Michael Kennedy and Stuart Conner (New York: Hastings House, 1965), p. 4.

5. Waldo R. Wedel, "Environment and Native Subsistence Economies in the Central Great Plains," *Smithsonian Miscellaneous Collections*, vol. 101 (Washington: Smithsonian Institution, 1941): 9.

6. Lewis Henry Morgan, *Lewis Henry Morgan, The Indian Journals 1859–62*, ed. Leslie A. White and Clyde Walton (Ann Arbor: The University of Michigan Press, 1959), p. 207, n. 64.

7. Haines, "The Westward Limits," pp. 396–397.

8. Álvar Núñez Cabeza de Vaca, "Narrative of Cabeza de Vaca," in *Spanish Explorers in the Southern United States, 1528–1543*, ed. F. W. Hodge and H. T. Lewis (New York: Charles Scribner's Sons, 1907), pp. 99–105.

9. Castañeda, "The Narrative of," p. 363.

10. Bolton, *Spanish Exploration*, p. 230.

11. Castañeda, "The Narrative of," p. 334.

12. Cabeza de Vaca, "Narrative of," p. 114.

13. Bolton, *Spanish Exploration*, pp. 154, 173, 174, 184.

14. Castañeda, "The Narrative of," p. 362.

15. Zaldívar, report, p. 230.

16. Fray Alonso de Benavides, "Memorial to His Holiness, Pope Urban VIII, Our Lord . . . on February 12, 1634," *Fray Alonso Benavides' Revised Memorial of 1634*, ed. Frederick Webb Hodge, George P. Hammond and Agapito Rey (Albuquerque: The University of New Mexico Press, 1945), p. 39.

17. "A Buffalo and Elk Hunt in 1842 by Hal—A Daco-

tah," *The Land Lies Open*, ed. Theodore Christian Blegen (Minneapolis: University of Minnesota Press, 1949), p. 24.

18. Sebastian Râle, "Relation of Sebastian Râle," *The Jesuit Relations and Allied Documents, 1610–1791*, ed. Reuben Gold Thwaites, 73 vols. (Cleveland: Arthur W. Clark Co., 1900), 47:169.

19. Julien Binneteau, "Relation, January, 1769," *The Jesuit Relations*, 65:75.

20. Hennepin, *A New Discovery*, 1:242.

21. Ibid.

22. McDougall, *Saddle, Sled and Snowshoe*, pp. 23–24.

23. Duncan M'Gillivray, *The Journal of Duncan M'Gillivray of the Northwest Company*, Introduction, notes and appendix by Arthur S. Morton (Toronto: The Macmillan Company of Canada, Ltd., 1929), p. 47.

24. George Bird Grinnell, *The Cheyenne Indians, Their History and Ways of Life* (vol. 2, New Haven: Yale University Press, 1924; vol. 1, New York: Cooper Square Publishers, 1962), 1:26.

25. Kelsey, *The Kelsey Papers*, p. 13.

26. James Josiah Webb, *Adventures in Santa Fe Trade*, p. 167.

27. John C. Ewers, *The Blackfeet, Raiders of the Northwestern Plains* (Norman: University of Oklahoma Press, 1958), p. 148.

28. Antony Hendry, "The Journals of Antony Hendry," ed. Lawrence Burpee, *Proceedings and Transactions of the Royal Society of Canada*, 3rd series, 1 (1907): 333.

29. M'Gillivray, *The Journal of*, p. 44.

30. Henry, *The Manuscript Journals of*, 2:725.

31. Carling Malouf, "Cultural Connections Between the Prehistoric Inhabitants of the Upper Missouri and Columbia River Systems" (Ph.D. dissertation, Columbia University, 1956), p. 87.

32. Richard G. Forbis, "A Stratified Buffalo Kill in Alberta," in "Symposium on Buffalo Jumps," ed. Malouf and Conner, Montana Archaeological Society Memoir No. 1 (May 1962, mimeographed), p. 44.

33. Haines, *The Buffalo*, p. 69.

34. Henry Inman, *The Old Santa Fe Trail* (New York: The Macmillan Co., 1898), p. 203.

35. Malouf, "Cultural Connections Between Inhabitants," p. 83.

36. William N. Moyers, "A Story of Southern Illinois," *Journal of the Illinois State Historical Society* 24:32.

37. H. P. Lewis, "Buffalo Kills in Montana," p. 22. In files of University of Montana Library.

38. "Symposium on Buffalo Jumps," p. 44.

39. Ibid., p. 41.

40. Barnum Brown, "The Buffalo Drive: An Echo of a Western Romance," *Natural History* 32 (January–February 1932): 80.

41. W. F. Butler, *The Wild North Land* (New York: A. S. Barnes & Co., 1904), pp. 207–08.

42. John Long, "Voyages and Travels, 1768–1782," *Early Western Travels*, ed. R. G. Thwaites, 32 vols. (Cleveland: The Arthur H. Clark Co., 1904), 1:133.

CHAPTER VI

Sources of quotations heading the chapter:

Waldo R. Wedel, "Culture Sequence in the Central Great Plains," *Smithsonian Miscellaneous Collections*, vol. 100 (Washington: Smithsonian Institution, 1940): 327.

Clark Wissler, "The Influence of the Horse in the Development of Plains Culture," *The American Anthropologist* 16 (1914): 18.

1. J. Frank Dobie, *The Mustangs* (New York: Bantam Books, 1958), p. 27.

2. Hendry, "The Journal of," 1:328 and 335.

3. Waldo R. Wedel, "Culture Sequence in the Central Great Plains," *Smithsonian Miscellaneous Collections*, vol. 100 (Washington: Smithsonian Institution, 1940): 327.

4. Ely Moore, "A Buffalo Hunt with the Miamis in 1854," *Collections of the Kansas State Historical Society* 10 (1907–08): 405–07.

5. John C. Ewers, "Were the Blackfoot Rich in Horses?" *American Anthropologist* 45 (1943): 607; Ewers, *The Blackfeet*, p. 95.

6. Maximilian, "Travels in America," 22:351.

7. Pike, *Arkansaw Journal*, p. 71.

8. John F. Firresty, *War Path and Bivouac* (Lincoln: University of Nebraska Press, 1966), p. 121.

9. Roe, *North American Buffalo*, pp. 663–64.

10. Matthew Cocking, *The Journal of Matthew Cocking*, p. 111, quoted by Roe, *North American Buffalo*, p. 638.

11. Welsh, *The Last Buffalo Hunter*, p. 44.

12. Stanley Vestal, "Sitting Bull's Maiden Speech," *The Frontier* 12 (March 1932): 269.

13. Moreton Frewen, *Milton Mowbray and Other Memories* (London: Herbert Jenkins, Ltd., 1924), p. 163.

14. Kane, *Wanderings of an Artist*, p. 60.

15. Richard Irving Dodge, *The Plains of the Great West* (New York: Archer House, 1959), p. 129.

16. M. T. McCreight, *Buffalo Bone Days* (Sykesville, Pennsylvania: Nupp Printing Company, 1939), p. 18.

17. Judge A. McG. Bede to Edmund Seymour, 29 October 1919, American Bison Society files, Conservation Library Center, Denver.

18. Edwin Thompson Denig, "Indian Tribes of the Upper Missouri," *Bureau of American Ethnology Forty-sixth Annual Report, 1928–1929* (Washington: Government Printing Office, 1930), p. 531.

19. Catlin, *North American Indians*, 1:225.

20. Vestal, "Sitting Bull's Speech," p. 270.

21. Fowler, *The Journal of Jacob Fowler*, p. 62.

22. Melvin R. Gilmore, "Indian Tribal Boundary Lines and Monuments," *Indian Notes* 5 (1928): 59; Gilmore, "Some Indian Ideas of Property," *Indian Notes* 5 (1928): 140.

23. George Bird Grinnell, *Pawnee, Blackfoot, and Cheyenne* (New York: Charles Scribner's Sons, 1961), p. 278.

24. Thomas L. Riggs, "The Last Buffalo Hunt," *Independent* 63 (4 July 1907): 32; Maximilian, "Travels in North America," 23:293–94; John Work, *The Journal of John*

Work, ed. William S. Lewis and Paul C. Philips (Cleveland: Arthur H. Clark Co., 1923), p. 121.

25. Claude E. Schaeffer, "The Bison Drive of the Blackfeet Indians," in "Symposium on Buffalo Jumps," p. 28.

26. John Joseph Mathews, *The Osages, Children of the Middle Waters* (Norman: University of Oklahoma Press, 1961), p. 306; Mildred P. Mayhall, *The Kiowas* (Norman: University of Oklahoma Press, 1962), p. 28.

27. Branch, *The Hunting of the Buffalo,* pp. 44–45; Grinnell, *The Cheyenne Indians,* 1:258; Schultz, *My Life as an Indian,* p. 207.

28. Denig, "Indian Tribes," p. 535.

29. Thomas B. Marquis, *Wooden Leg, A Warrior Who Fought Custer* (Lincoln: University of Nebraska Press, 1967), p. 88.

30. Morgan, *The Indian Journals,* p. 99.

31. Frank B. Linderman, *American, The Life Story of a Great Indian* (New York: The John Day Co., 1931), p. 17.

32. Farnham, "Travels in Prairies," 28:85–87.

33. Frank H. Mayer and Charles B. Roth, *The Buffalo Harvest* (Denver: Sage Books, 1958), p. 32.

34. Frank Gilbert Roe, *The Indian and the Horse* (Norman: University of Oklahoma Press, 1962), pp. 357 and 362; Denig, "Indian Tribes," p. 531.

35. Denig, "Indian Tribes," p. 466.

36. John R. Barrows, "Life in Montana in 1880," *The Frontier* 8 (November 1927): 38.

37. Josiah Gregg, *The Commerce of the Prairies,* ed. Max L. Moorhead (Norman: University of Oklahoma Press, 1954), p. 201.

38. Linderman, *American,* pp. 106–07.

CHAPTER VII

Source of first quotation heading the chapter:

George E. Hyde, *Life of George Bent,* ed. Savoie Lottinville (Norman: University of Oklahoma Press, 1968), p. 199.

1. Schultz, *Blackfeet and Buffalo,* p. 312.

2. Ibid., p. 54.

3. C. M. Russell, "Early Days on the Buffalo Range," *Recreation* (April 1897), p. 227.

4. Gregg, *Commerce of the Prairies,* pp. 188–89.

5. J. Lee Humfreville, *Twenty Years Among Our Hostile Indians* (New York: Hunter & Co., Publishers, 1899), p. 439.

6. M'Gillivray, *The Journal of,* pp. 28–29.

7. Schultz, *Blackfeet and Buffalo,* p. 352; James Willard Schultz, *Apauk, Caller of Buffalo* (Boston and New York: Houghton Mifflin Co., 1916), p. 103.

8. Work, *The Journal of,* pp. 85–133.

9. Chambers, "The Fort Sarpy Journal," p. 178.

10. Nicholas Point, *Wilderness Kingdom, Indian Life in the Rocky Mountains: 1840–1847* (New York, Chicago, San Francisco: Holt, Rinehart and Winston, 1967), p. 123.

11. Alexander Mackenzie, *Voyages from Montreal on the River St. Lawrence Through the Continent of North America* (Toronto: The Radisson Society of Canada, Ltd., 1927), 1:cxiv.

12. Morgan, *The Indian Journals,* p. 124.

13. Francois Chardon, *Chardon's Journal of Fort Clark, 1834–39,* ed. Annie Heloise Abel (Pierre: 1932), p. 176.

14. Albert-Alexandre Pourtalès, *On the Western Tour with Washington Irving, The Journals and Letters of Count de Pourtalès,* ed. George Spaulding, trans. Seymour Feiler (Norman: University of Oklahoma Press, 1968), p. 70.

15. Catlin, *North American Indians,* 1:284.

16. Harris, *Up the Missouri,* pp. 147–49.

17. R. B. Marcy, *Marcy and the Gold Seekers,* ed. Grant Foreman (Norman: University of Oklahoma Press, 1939), p. 262.

18. Russell, "Early Days on the Buffalo Range," p. 229.

19. Alfred Powers, ed., *Buffalo Adventures on the Western Plains* (Portland, Oregon: Binford and Mort, 1945), pp. 25 and 33; G. B. Grinnell, "Last of the Buffalo," *Scribner's Magazine* 12 (September 1892): 285.

20. Russell, "Early Days on the Buffalo Range," p. 229.

21. Ellsworth, *Washington Irving on the Prairie,* p. 103.

22. Ibid., pp. 104–05.

23. Humfreville, *Twenty Years Among Indians,* p. 441.

24. Marcy, *Marcy and Seekers,* p. 257.

25. Mayer and Roth, *Buffalo Harvest,* p. 32.

26. Catlin, *North American Indians,* 1:227.

27. Riggs, "The Last Buffalo Hunt," p. 32.

CHAPTER VIII

Source of quotation heading the chapter:

Sir Richard Burton, *The Look of the West* (Lincoln: University of Nebraska Press, 1966), p. 64.

1. Allen, *Our Wildlife Legacy,* p. 10.

2. Tom Rivington, "Letters from Tom Rivington," *Frontier and Midland* 13 (November 1932–May 1933): 62.

3. Ibid., p. 63.

4. John C. Ewers, *Indian Life on the Upper Missouri* (Norman: University of Oklahoma Press, 1968), p. 172.

5. Henry (the elder), *Travels and Adventures,* p. 312.

6. Henry, *The Manuscript Journals of,* 2:725.

7. Work, *The Journal of,* p. 118.

8. Marquis, *Wooden Leg,* p. 35.

9. Thomas H. LeForge, *Memoirs of a White Crow Indian,* as told by Thomas B. Marquis (New York and London: The Century Co., 1928), p. 171.

10. Elias J. Marsh, "Journal of Elias J. Marsh," *South Dakota Historical Review* 1–2 (October 1935–July 1937): 102.

11. Hennepin, *A New Discovery,* 1:149.

12. Andrew Garcia, *Tough Trip Through Paradise,* ed. Bennett H. Stein (Boston: Houghton Mifflin Co., 1967), p. 359.

13. Hornaday, "Discovery and Extermination of Bison," p. 449.

14. Henry, *The Manuscript Journals of,* 1:175.

15. Chambers, "The Fort Sarpy Journal," pp. 105–06.

16. Fowler, *The Journal of,* p. 62.

17. Wheat, "A Paleo Indian Bison Kill," p. 52.

18. Schultz, *Blackfeet and Buffalo,* pp. 322–331.

19. Patrick Gass, *Journal of the Lewis and Clark Expedition* (Minneapolis: Ross & Haines, 1958), p. 307.

20. Tribes varied in tanning methods. For various accounts see: Grinnell, *The Cheyenne Indians,* 1:213–217; Rudolph Kurz, "Journal of Rudolph Kurz," ed. J. N. B. Hewitt, *Bureau of American Ethnology, Bulletin No. 115* (Washington: Government Printing Office, 1937), p. 261; Henry Boller, *Among the Indians, Four Years on the Upper Missouri, 1858–1862* (Lincoln: University of Nebraska Press, 1872), pp. 304–05; Robert Lowie, *Indians of the Plains* (Garden City: Doubleday and Co., The Natural History Press, 1963), p. 67; Alice C. Fletcher and Francis LaFlesche, *The Omaha Tribe* (New York: The Johnson Reprint Corporation, 1970), pp. 342–45.

21. Robert H. Lowie, *The Crow Indians* (New York: Farrar & Rinehart, Inc., 1935), p. 77.

CHAPTER IX

Source of quotation heading the chapter:
Alice C. Fletcher, "Giving Thanks," *Journal of American Folklore* 13 (July–September 1900): 263.

1. H. M. Wormington, *Ancient Man In North America* (Denver: Denver Museum of Natural History, 1957), pp. 84 and 127–28.

2. Schultz, *My Life as an Indian,* p. 85.

3. Chardon, *Chardon's Journal,* p. 63.

CHAPTER X

Source of quotation heading the chapter:
James Willard Schultz, *My Life as an Indian,* p. 60.

1. Harold A. Innis, *The Fur Trade in Canada* (New Haven: Yale University Press, 1962), p. 216.

2. Lewis and Clark, *Original Journals of,* 2:306–07.

3. R. O. Merriman, "The Bison and the Fur Trade," *Queen's Quarterly* (July–September 1926), pp. 83–84.

4. M'Gillivray, *The Journal of,* p. xlviii.

5. Innis, *Fur Trade,* pp. 132 and 143.

6. W. F. Butler, *The Great Lone Land* (London: Sampson, Low, Marston, Low & Searle, 1872), pp. 153–54.

7. Viscount Milton and W. B. Cheadle, *The North-West Passage by Land,* p. 53, cited by Roe, *North American Buffalo,* p. 605.

8. Merriman, "Bison and Fur Trade," p. 84.

9. Ibid., p. 90.

10. Ibid., p. 85.

11. Henry, *The Manuscript Journals of,* 2:616.

12. Merriman, "Bison and Fur Trade," p. 84.

13. Ibid., p. 86.

14. Henry, *The Manuscript Journals of,* 1:273; Merriman, "Bison and Fur Trade," p. 86.

15. Henry (the elder), *Travels and Adventures,* p. 312.

16. Alice M. Johnson, ed., *Saskatchewan Journals and Correspondence* (London: The Hudson's Bay Record Society, 1967), p. 118.

17. M'Gillivray, *The Journal of,* p. 49.

18. Henry, *The Manuscript Journals of,* 2:548–49.

19. Johnson, *Saskatchewan Journals,* p. 133.

20. M'Gillivray, *The Journal of,* p. 47.

21. Merriman, "Bison and Fur Trade," pp. 88–94.

22. John Perry Pritchett, *The Red River Valley, 1811–1849* (New Haven: Yale University Press, 1942), p. 128.

23. Wayne Gard, *The Great Buffalo Hunt* (New York: Alfred A. Knopf, 1959), p. 48.

24. Merriman, "Bison and Fur Trade," p. 87.

25. Hiram Chittenden, *The American Fur Trade of the Far West,* 3 vols. (New York: The Press of the Pioneers, Inc., 1935), 2:950; Chardon, *Chardon's Journal,* pp. 32, 70, 118.

26. Kenneth Gordon Davies, ed., *Letters from Hudson Bay, 1703–40* (London: Hudson's Bay Record Society, 1965), pp. 60 and 67.

27. Roe, *North American Buffalo,* p. 247.

28. Maximilian, "Travels in America," 23:264.

29. Adolphus Wislizenus, *A Journey to the Rocky Mountains in the Year 1839* (St. Louis: Missouri Historical Society, 1912), p. 58.

30. Theodore R. Davis, "The Buffalo Range," *Harper's Magazine* 38 (January 1869): 162.

31. Morgan, *The Indian Journals,* p. 157.

32. Chittenden, *American Fur Trade,* 2:950; H. A. Trexler, "The Buffalo Range of the Northwest," *Mississippi Valley Historical Review* 7 (March 1921): 355.

33. Gard, *Great Buffalo Hunt,* p. 57; Garretson, *American Bison,* p. 97.

34. Gard, *Great Buffalo Hunt,* p. 48.

35. "The Fort Benton Journal," *Contributions to the Historical Society of Montana,* vol. 10 (Helena: Naegele Printing Co., 1940), p. 61.

36. Kurz, "Journal of," p. 271.

37. Chardon, *Chardon's Journal,* p. 54.

38. Ibid., note 226, p. 243.

39. John Owen, *The Journal and Letters of John Owen,* 2 vols., ed. Seymour Dunbar, notes by Paul Philips (New York: Edward Eberstadt, 1927), 1:181.

40. Lewis and Clark, *Original Journals,* 1:306.

41. Larpenteur, *Forty Years a Fur Trader,* pp. 191–92.

42. Chardon, *Chardon's Journal,* note 74, pp. 222–23.

43. Schultz, *My Life as an Indian,* pp. 277–78.

44. Garcia, *Tough Trip Through Paradise,* p. 202.

45. Ibid., pp. 121 and 204.

46. Kurz, "Journal of," p. 155.

47. Oscar Lewis, "The Effects of White Contact Upon Blackfoot Culture," *Monographs of the American Ethnological Society, No. 6* (1942), pp. 35–36.

48. Ewers, *The Blackfeet*, p. 95.

49. Ibid., pp. 258–59.

50. Kurz, "Journal of," p. 261.

51. Ibid., pp. 250–51.

52. Merriman, "Bison and Fur Trade," p. 91.

53. Ibid., p. 92.

54. Schultz, *My Life as an Indian*, p. 386.

55. Garcia, *Tough Trip Through Paradise*, p. 228.

56. Ibid., p. 151.

57. Samuel Hearne, *Coppermine Journey*, ed. Farley Mowat (Boston: Little, Brown and Co., 1958), p. 44.

CHAPTER XI

Sources of quotations heading the chapter:

A. R. Ross, "Hunting Buffalo in the Seventies," *Colorado Magazine* 23 (March 1946): 85.

McKillip, "A Story of the Buffalo," p. 137.

Greeley, *An Overland Journey*, p. 73.

John Minto, "Reminiscences of Honorable John Minto, Pioneer of 1844," *The Quarterly of the Oregon Historical Society* 2 (March 1901–December 1902): 146–47.

1. George D. Brewerton, "In the Buffalo Country," *Harper's* (September 1862), p. 447.

2. Wislizenus, *Journey to Rocky Mountains*, pp. 44–45.

3. Ibid.

4. Anderson, "Anderson's Narrative," p. 55.

5. Morgan, *Indian Journals*, p. 193.

6. Charles Dickens, *American Notes* (Greenwich, Connecticut: Fawcett Publications, Inc., 1961), p. 192.

7. A. J. Vaughn, letter, *Contributions to the Historical Society of Montana*, vol. 10 (Helena: Naegele Printing Co., 1940), p. 192.

8. William Clark Kennerly, "My Hunting Trip to the Rockies in 1843," *Colorado Magazine* 22–23 (1945): 36.

9. Overton Johnson and William H. Winter, *Route Across the Rocky Mountains with a Description of Oregon and California*, reprinted in *Oregon Historical Quarterly* 7 (1906): 79.

10. Lewis H. Garrard, *Wah-To-Yah and the Taos Trail*, ed. Ralph P. Bieber (Glendale, California: Arthur H. Clark Co., 1938), p. 198.

11. Webb, *Adventures in Santa Fe Trade*, p. 48.

12. Kurz, "Journal of," pp. 141–42.

13. Pat T. Tucker, "Buffalo in the Judith Basin, 1883," *Frontier* 9 (March 1929): 226.

14. John McDonald of Garth, cited by Arthur S. Morton, editor, *The Journal of Duncan M'Gillivray*, p. xlvii; Zenas Leonard, *Adventures of Zenas Leonard, Fur Trader, 1821–1836*, ed. W. F. Wagner (Cleveland: The Burrows Brothers, 1904), p. 74.

15. M'Gillivray, *The Journal of*, p. 67.

16. Bustamente, "Declaration of Bustamente," p. 148.

17. Juan Dominguez de Mendoza, "Itinerary of Juan Dominguez de Mendoza," *Spanish Exploration in the South-west*, ed. Herbert Eugene Bolton (New York: Charles Scribner's Sons, 1916), pp. 339–41.

18. Hill, *The Passing of the Buffalo*, p. 30.

19. George F. Ruxton, *Adventures in Mexico and the Rocky Mountains* (London: J. Murray, 1847), p. 267.

20. Minto, "Reminiscences of Minto," pp. 155–56.

21. Burton, *The Look of the West*, pp. 60–61.

22. Blegen, *The Land Lies Open*, pp. 52–53.

23. Don Juan de Oñate, "Letter Written by Don Juan de Oñate," *Spanish Exploration in the Southwest*, ed. Herbert Eugene Bolton (New York: Charles Scribner's Sons, 1916), p. 255; Dickens, *American Notes*, p. 209; Anderson, "Anderson's Narrative," p. 57; Rivington, "Letters from Tom Rivington," p. 65.

24. E. N. Andrews, "A Buffalo Hunt by Rail," *Kansas Magazine* 3 (May 1873): 450–58; "Lively Scene on an American Prairie," *Frank Leslie's Illustrated Newspaper*, 28 November 1868, pp. 173–74.

25. Theodore G. Grieder, "The Influence of the American Bison or Buffalo on Westward Expansion" (M.S. thesis, University of Iowa, 1928), p. 34; Lester H. School to M. S. Garretson, 19 June 1935, American Bison Society papers, Conservation Center Library, Denver, Colorado.

26. Paine, *Pioneers, Indians and Buffaloes*, p. 68; Catlin, *North American Indians*, 2:53–54.

27. Henry, *The Manuscript Journals of*, 1:167.

28. E. Richard Shipp, "Doc Carver—Buffalo Hunter," *Northwest Tribune* (Stevensville, Montana), 13 October 1927. (Newspaper clipping, Buffalo file, Missoula Public Library, Missoula, Montana.)

29. James, "An Account of an Expedition from Pittsburgh to the Rocky Mountains," p. 241.

CHAPTER XII

Sources of quotations heading the chapter:

Granville Stuart, *Forty Years on the Frontier*, 2:104.

Mayer and Roth, *The Buffalo Harvest*, p. 32.

1. Ledillon Patrick, "French Buried Treasure in Southern Illinois," *Illinois History* 11 (October 1957): 21.

2. Archer Butler Hulbert, *Forty-Niners* (Boston: Little, Brown and Co., 1932), p. 102; Dagmar Mariager, "Hunting the Bison," *Overland Monthly* (August 1889), p. 196.

3. Davis, "The Buffalo Range," p. 163.

4. Hornaday, "Discovery and Extermination of Bison," p. 444.

5. Mayer and Roth, *The Buffalo Harvest*, pp. 61–62.

6. W. Skelton Glenn, "The Recollections of W. S. Glenn, Buffalo Hunter," *Panhandle-Plains Historical Review* 22 (1949): 19–22.

7. J. Evetts Haley, *The XIT Ranch of Texas and the Early Days of the Llano Estacado* (Norman: University of Oklahoma Press, 1953), p. 22.

8. Glenn, "The Recollections of," pp. 34–37.

9. Mayer and Roth, *The Buffalo Harvest*, pp. 53–54.

10. Ibid., p. 35.
11. Glenn, "The Recollections of," p. 22.
12. "Buffalo Which Roamed West Aided Reds to Withstand Whites," *Spokesman-Review* (Spokane, Washington), 29 May 1921, p. 2.
13. Ibid.
14. Brown, "Life and Adventures of," p. 121.
15. J. Wright Mooar, "Buffalo Days," as told to James Winford Hunt, *Holland's* 52 (May 1933): 11.
16. Seth Hathaway, "The Adventures of a Buffalo Hunter," *Frontier Times* 9 (December 1931): 111.
17. Mayer and Roth, *The Buffalo Harvest*, p. 64.
18. Stuart N. Lake, "The Buffalo Hunters," *Saturday Evening Post* (25 October 1930), pp. 12–13.
19. Mark H. Brown and William R. Felton, *The Frontier Years* (New York: Holt and Co., 1955), p. 67.
20. Henry J. Helgeson to Mr. Blakeless, 1 January 1956.
21. Allen, "History of Bison," p. 557.
22. Glenn, "The Recollections of," pp. 24–25.
23. Joel A. Allen, "The North American Bison and Its Extermination," *Pennsylvania Monthly* 7 (March 1876): 219.

CHAPTER XIII

Source of quotation heading the chapter:
William Henry Hutchinson, "Hides, Hams and Tongues," *Westerners Brand Book (Denver Annual)* 6 (1950–1951): 210.

1. John R. Cook, *The Border and the Buffalo* (Topeka, Kansas: Crane and Co., 1907), pp. 113–14.
2. Butler, *The Great Lone Land*, p. 241.
3. Robert Taft, *Artists and Illustrators of the Old West* (New York: Bonanza Books, 1953), p. 68.
4. Fayette Avery McKenzie, *The Indian in Relation to the White Population of the United States* (Columbus: by the author, 1908), pp. 12–13.
5. Ibid.
6. F. J. Clifford, "A Note on Bison Hunting: A Few Were Saved," *Oregon Historical Quarterly* 52 (March 1951): 262.
7. Frank Gilbert Roe, "The Extermination of the Buffalo in Western Canada," *Canadian Historical Review* 15 (1934): 16–17.
8. Joseph Kinsey Howard, *Strange Empire* (New York: William Morrow and Co., 1952), pp. 292–93.
9. Harold E. Briggs, *Frontiers of the Northwest* (New York: Appleton-Century Co., 1940), p. 132.
10. "Buffalo in Canada," *Scarlet and Gold*, Parts 1–6 (1921), p. 28.
11. *Daily Free Press* (Winnipeg), 16 October 1876.
12. "Buffalo in Canada," p. 28.
13. Branch, *Hunting of Buffalo*, p. 176.
14. Granville Stuart, *Forty Years on the Frontier*, 2 vols., ed. Paul C. Phillips (Cleveland: Arthur H. Clark Co., 1925), 1:104.
15. Branch, *Hunting of Buffalo*, p. 179.
16. Allen, "The Bison and its Extermination," p. 219.
17. Theodore S. Palmer, "Chronology and Index of the More Important Events in American Game Protection," *U.S. Department of Agriculture, Biological Survey Bulletin Number 41* (Washington: Government Printing Office, 1912), p. 18.
18. Sandoz, *Buffalo Hunters*, p. 348.
19. Briggs, *Frontiers of the Northwest*, p. 166.
20. Hornaday, "Discovery and Extermination of Bison," p. 503.
21. Ibid.
22. Dan R. Conway, *Northwest Tribune* (Stevensville, Montana), February 1927. (Clipping in Montana History folder, Missoula Public Library, Missoula, Montana).
23. Hornaday, "Discovery and Extermination of Bison," p. 503.
24. Schultz, *My Life as an Indian*, p. 393.
25. *Bad Lands Cowboy* (Little Missouri, Medora P.O., Dakota), 20 November 1884, p. 4.
26. "Buffalo in Canada," p. 25.
27. Thomas Johnson, "Natural History. The Canadian Northwest," *Forest and Stream* 49 (23 October 1897): 323.
28. Hill, *The Passing of the Indian*, p. 37.
29. Theodore Roosevelt, *The Wilderness Hunter* (New York and London: G. P. Putnam's Sons, 1893), p. 249.
30. *Bad Lands Cowboy*, 20 November 1884, p. 1, col. 5.
31. Clifford, "A Note on Bison Hunting," p. 261.
32. Hornaday, "Discovery and Extermination of Bison," p. 502.
33. Ibid., p. 521; Theodore Roosevelt and George Bird Grinnell, ed., *Hunting in Many Lands* (New York: Forest and Stream Publishing Co., 1895), p. 400; Garretson, *The American Bison*, p. 197; *Forest and Stream* (14 April 1894), p. 309.
34. Henry Wharton Shoemaker, *A Pennsylvania Bison Hunt* (Middleburg, Pennsylvania: The Middleburg Post Press, 1915), p. 44.

CHAPTER XIV

Source of quotation heading the chapter:
Allen, "History of the American Bison," p. 558.

1. John D. Hunter, *Manners and Customs of Several Indian Tribes Located West of the Mississippi* (Minneapolis: Ross and Haines, 1957), p. 94.
2. John H. Goff, "The Buffalo in Georgia," *The Georgia Review* 11 (Spring 1957): 27.
3. Gregg, *Commerce on the Prairies*, p. 370.
4. Bennett, "The Mystery of the Iowa Buffalo," pp. 60–73.
5. Ernest Wallace and E. Adamson Hoebel, *The Comanches* (Norman: University of Oklahoma Press, 1952), p. 63.
6. Alexander Ross, *The Red River Settlement* (Minneapolis: Ross and Haines, Inc., 1957), p. 267.
7. Wallace and Hoebel, *The Comanches*, p. 64.

8. Allen, "History of Bison," p. 561.

9. Benjamin Draper, "Where the Buffalo Roamed," *Pacific Discovery* (March–April 1958), p. 14.

10. McKeown, *Them Was the Days*, p. 110.

11. L. C. Fouquet, "Buffalo Days," *Collections of the Kansas State Historical Society* 16 (1923–1925): 347.

12. McKeown, *Them Was the Days*, p. 190.

13. M. I. McCreight, *Buffalo Bone Days* (Sykesville, Pennsylvania: Nupp Printing Co., 1939), p. 39.

14. Wallace Stegner, *Wolf Willow* (New York: The Viking Press, 1955), p. 95.

15. McCreight, *Buffalo Bone Days*, p. 39.

16. McKeown, *Them Was the Days*, p. 111.

17. James C. Shaw, *Pioneering in Texas and Wyoming* (Orin, Wyoming: by the author, 1931), pp. 32–33.

18. Louis Ortiz to Edmund Seymour, 23 November 1924, American Bison Society files, Conservation Center Library, Denver, Colorado.

19. Ibid., 22 December 1924.

20. Clifford, "A Note on Bison Hunting," p. 264.

CHAPTER XV

Sources of quotations heading the chapter:

Inman, *Buffalo Jones' Adventure*, p. 50.

C. J. Jones to Edmund Seymour, 8 April 1917, American Bison Society files, Conservation Center Library, Denver, Colorado.

1. Inman, *Buffalo Jones' Adventure*, p. 113.

2. "Saving the Buffalo," *The Beaver* (June 1948), pp. 10–13.

3. Inman, *Buffalo Jones' Adventure*, p. 209.

4. Ibid., p. 265.

5. Emerson Hough, "The Last of the Buffalo," *The American Field* 26 (3 July–21 August 1886), pp. 5 ff.

6. Inman, *Buffalo Jones' Adventure*, pp. 66–81.

7. Ibid., pp. 78–79.

8. Lee Howard, "An Attempt to Capture Buffalo Alive in Present Oklahoma in the late 1880's," *Kansas Historical Quarterly* 17 (August 1949): 238–39.

9. Catlin, *North American Indians*, 1: 287–88.

10. John Y. Nelson, *Fifty Years on the Trail* (Norman: University of Oklahoma Press, 1963), pp. 261–62.

11. Vic Smith, "Roping Buffalo Calves," *Recreation* (May 1896), pp. 365–66.

12. W. T. Hornaday, "The Passing of the Buffalo," *Cosmopolitan* (October 1887), p. 85.

13. Hornaday, "Discovery and Extermination of Bison," pp. 367–548.

14. Charles Goodnight to Edmund Seymour, 4 January 1923, American Bison Society files, Conservation Center Library, Denver, Colorado.

CHAPTER XVI

Source of quotation heading the chapter:

Bad Lands Cowboy (Little Missouri, Medora P.O., Dakota), July 18, 1884, p. 2.

1. George S. Anderson, "Protection of Yellowstone Park Game," *Hunting in Many Lands*, ed. Theodore Roosevelt and George Bird Grinnell (Forest and Stream Publishing Co., 1895), p. 381.

2. H. Duane Hampton, *How the U.S. Cavalry Saved Our National Parks* (Bloomington: Indiana University Press, 1971), pp. 34–39.

3. Ibid., pp. 40–41.

4. Ibid., p. 91.

5. L. R. Freeman, "Protect the Game in Yellowstone Park," *Recreation* (June 1900), p. 426.

6. Hampton, *How Cavalry Saved Parks*, p. 111.

7. Emerson Hough, "Yellowstone Park Game Exploration," *Forest and Stream* (March–August 1894), p. 378.

8. Ibid.

9. Freeman, "Protect the Game," p. 426.

10. Ibid., p. 427.

11. Inman, *Buffalo Jones' Adventure*, p. 263.

12. Robert Easton and Mackenzie Brown, *Lord of Beasts* (Tucson: University of Arizona Press, 1961), pp. 127 and 264.

13. Ibid., pp. 121–25.

14. Interview with Frank Stevens at Three Forks Rest Home, Three Forks, Montana, 23 August 1965.

15. Peter Holte, "Catching Buffalo Calves," *Forest and Stream* (17 September 1910), pp. 448–50; (24 September 1910), pp. 488–90.

16. Easton and Brown, *Lord of Beasts*, p. 125.

17. Wayne B. Alcorn and Curtis H. Skinner, "History of the Bison in Yellowstone Park" (File No. 715–03, Chief Ranger's Office, Yellowstone Park), mimeographed.

18. Victor H. Cahalane, "Restoration of Wild Bison," *Transactions of the North American Wildlife Conference* 9 (1944): 135–137.

19. Dan Beard to Edmund Seymour, September 1921, American Bison Society files, Conservation Center Library, Denver, Colorado.

20. Martin S. Garretson to Dick Adams, 1 July 1925, American Bison Society files, Conservation Center Library, Denver, Colorado.

CHAPTER XVII

Sources of quotations heading the chapter:

Howard Eaton to Alicia Conrad, 7 February 1907, Conrad file, Archives, University of Montana Library, Missoula, Montana.

Charles Allard, "Breeding Buffaloes," *Self-Culture* (May 1895), pp. 81–82.

Letterhead, Philip Buffalo Ranch, South Dakota, circa 1910.

All quotations from letters come from the American

Bison Society papers now in the Conservation Center Library, Denver Public Library unless attributed to other sources.

1. Charles Allard, "Breeding Buffaloes," *Self-Culture* (May 1895), p. 81.

2. E. H. Baynes, "A Great Buffalo Herd in Winter Quarters," *Suburban Life* (February 1906), p. 55; Austin Corbin to Edmund Seymour, 20 September 1918.

3. Don H. Biggers, "Buffalo Butchery in Texas Was a National Calamity," *Farm and Ranch* (14 November 1925), p. 29.

4. Ray E. Grasher (Arizona Bill) to Edmund Seymour, 2 June 1919; E. H. Baynes to Edmund Seymour, 26 June 1920; Edmund Seymour to T. S. Palmer, 23 May 1917.

5. Morton J. Elrod, "The Flathead Buffalo Range: A Report to the American Bison Society," *Report of the American Bison Society* (New York: American Bison Society, 1908), pp. 15–49.

6. James Dolph, "The American Bison Society: Preserver of the American Buffalo and Pioneer in Wildlife Conservation" (M.S. thesis, University of Denver, 1965), p. 81.

7. Ibid., p. 80.

8. A. W. Hodges to W. J. Spurzem, 28 November 1910.

9. Census table, *Report of the American Bison Society* (New York: American Bison Society, 1910), pp. 31–32.

10. Selected letters from the Conrad file, Archives, University of Montana Library, Missoula, Montana.

11. Alicia Conrad to William T. Hornaday, 25 April 1919.

12. Ernest Harold Baynes, "Pessimism Concerning Buffaloes," in Conrad file, Archives, University of Montana Library.

13. W. T. Hornaday to G. A. Smith, 10 October 1918.

14. M. S. Garretson to Edmund Seymour, 28 January 1928.

15. T. S. Palmer to Edmund Seymour, 24 August 1917; 21 August 1917; 17 October 1917; F. C. Walcott to W. T. Hornaday, 11 December 1917; W. T. Hornaday to Edmund Seymour, 15 December 1917.

16. Martin S. Garretson to Editor of the New York *Times*, 2 March 1923.

CHAPTER XVIII

Sources of quotations heading the chapter:

Charles Goodnight to W. O. Wharton, 4 November 1910.

C. J. Jones, "Buffalo Breeding," *Farmer's Review* (22 August 1888), p. 534.

All letters referred to are in the American Bison Society papers now in the Conservation Center Library, Denver Public Library unless attributed to other sources.

1. C. J. Jones, "Buffalo Breeding," *Farmer's Review* (22 August 1888), p. 534.

2. Inman, *Buffalo Jones' Adventure*, pp. 238–39.

3. W. T. Hornaday, *Wild Life Conservation in Theory and Practice* (New Haven: Yale University Press, 1914), p. 207.

4. McKillip, "Story of the Buffalo," p. 141.

5. Martin S. Garretson, "The Catalo," *Report of the American Bison Society, 1917–1918* (New York: American Bison Society, 1918), pp. 30 ff.; Allen, "The Bison and Its Extermination," p. 222; Allen, "History of Bison," p. 587.

6. Interview with Frank McDowell, Spokane Ranch, Big Hole Valley, Montana, 9 October 1972.

7. Charles Goodnight, "My Experience with Bison Hybrids," *The Journal of Heredity* 5 (May 1914): 199.

8. Ibid.

9. Edmund Seymour to T. S. Palmer, 17 May 1917.

10. Charles Goodnight to Edmund Seymour, 12 November 1917; Charles Goodnight to W. O. Wharton, 4 November 1910; H. A. Fleming to W. O. Wharton, 14 November 1910.

11. M. M. Boyd, "A Short Account of an Experiment in Crossing the American Bison with Domestic Cattle," *American Breeder's Association Annual Report* 4 (1908): 324.

12. Ibid., p. 325.

13. Ibid., p. 328.

14. "Report on the Grand Canyon Buffalo Herd (1924)," American Bison Society files, Conservation Center Library, Denver, Colorado; Easton and Brown, *Lord of Beasts*, pp. 133–34, 140–41.

15. Will C. Barnes to W. T. Hornaday, 7 November 1922.

16. C. J. Jones to Edmund Seymour, 8 April 1910; *History of Finney County, Kansas* (Garden City, Kansas: Finney County Historical Society, 1950), p. 109.

17. C. J. Jones to Edmund Seymour, 20 May 1917.

18. E. J. Cotton, "Hybrids," *Canadian Cattlemen* (November 1949), p. 13; E. J. Cotton, "The Cattalo—Last Chapter," *Canadian Cattlemen* (October 1964), p. 9.

19. V. S. Logan and P. E. Sylvestre, *Hybridization of Domestic Beef Cattle and Buffalo* (Ottawa: Department of Agriculture, 1950), p. 4.

20. Ibid., p. 3; H. F. Peters, "Experimental Hybridization of Domestic Cattle and American Bison" (Manyberries, Canada: Canada Agricultural Experimental Farm, 1964), pp. 326–32.

CHAPTER XIX

Sources of quotations heading the chapter:

Mary Goodnight to Edmund Seymour, 30 September 1916.

L. R. Houck quoted by Associated Press in the *Missoulian* (Montana), 24 November 1967.

All letters referred to are in the American Bison Society papers now in the Conservation Center Library, Denver Public Library unless attributed to other sources.

1. Edmund Seymour to Mr. Bronson, 13 December

1916; Dr. Robert Morris to Edmund Seymour, 27 September 1916; Dr. Joseph Root to Edmund Seymour, 9 September 1916; Dr. H. J. Tillotson to Charles Goodnight, 22 April 1918; Charles Goodnight to Edmund Seymour, 4 December 1916; 31 August 1916.

2. Charles Goodnight to Edmund Seymour, 31 August 1916.

3. Hubert Howe Bancroft, *History of Nevada, Colorado and Wyoming* (San Francisco: H. L. Bancroft and Co., 1890), pp. 3–4.

4. Honora De Busk Smith, "Cowboy Lore in Colorado," *Southwestern Lore* 9 (1931): 34–37.

5. Charles Aubrey, "The Edmonton Buffalo Herd," *Forest and Stream* (6 July 1907), pp. 11–12.

6. Kootenai Brown, "Recollections of Kootenai Brown," in files of the Historical Society of Montana, Helena, Montana.

7. Clifford, "A Note on Bison Hunting," p. 263.

8. Helen Addison Howard, *Northwest Trail Blazers* (Caldwell, Idaho: Caxton Printers, 1963), pp. 222–23.

9. Peter Ronan, "Report of the Flathead Agency, August 16, 1888," *Report of the Secretary of the Interior*, Vol. 2 (Washington: Government Printing Office, 1888), p. 158.

10. Fouquet, "Buffalo Days," p. 344.

11. Brown, "Life and Adventures," p. 127.

12. Alfred Jacob Miller, *The West of Alfred Jacob Miller*, ed. Marvin C. Ross (Norman: University of Oklahoma Press, 1968), p. 141.

13. Schultz, *My Life as an Indian*, p. 209.

14. C. M. Russell, "Broke Buffalo," *Trails Plowed Under* (New York: Doubleday and Co., 1953), pp. 145–47.

15. Catlin, *North American Indians*, 1:287–88.

16. L. R. Houck, quoted by Associated Press in *Missoulian* (Montana), 24 November 1967.

CHAPTER XX

Sources of quotations heading the chapter:

The *Denver Post*, March 2, 1947, quoted by Mitford M. Mathews, *A Dictionary of Americanisms*, p. 205.

Robert Benchley, *From Bed to Worse, or Comforting Thoughts About the Bison* (New York: Harper and Brothers, 1934), pp. 50–51.

All letters referred to are in the American Bison Society papers now in the Conservation Center Library, Denver Public Library unless attributed to other sources.

1. Horace Albright and Frank J. Taylor, *Oh, Ranger!* (Palo Alto: Stanford University Press, 1928), pp. 50–52.

2. L. H. Pammel, "Buffalo in Iowa," *Annals of Iowa* 18 (October 1930): 415 and 418.

3. Garcia, *Tough Trip Through Paradise*, p. 225.

4. O. D. Gibson to M. S. Garretson, 12 October 1928.

5. W. T. Hornaday to Edmund Seymour, 18 January 1917; James T. (Uncle Jimmy) Owens to G. M. Willard, 2 February 1924; E. C. Hatch to George W. P. Hunt, 28 January 1924; G. M. Willard to Edmund Seymour, 5 February 1924; D. E. Pittis to Edmund Seymour, 15 October 1927; G. M. Willard to Edmund Seymour, 3 January 1924.

6. Hugh M. Raup, "Range Conditions in the Wood Buffalo Park of Western Canada with Notes on the History of the Wood Bison," *American Committee for International Wild Life Protection* 1 (1933): 13–14.

7. Note initialled M.S.G. in Bison Society files.

8. F. H. Kitto, "The Survival of the American Bison in Canada," *Geographical Journal* 63 (1924): 437.

9. J. H. Fleming to Francis Harper, 3 April 1925.

10. W. T. Hornaday to Mr. Rush, 5 November 1917.

11. Raup, *Range Conditions*, pp. 18–19; Soper, "History of the Northern Bison," pp. 375–76.

12. William Albert Fuller, "The Biology and Management of the Bison of Wood Buffalo National Park," *Wildlife Management Bulletin* 1 (1962): 31.

13. "Wood Buffalo Rescue Plan," *Red Deer Advocate* (Red Deer, Alberta), 17 January 1961; "Plan Will Protect Rare Wood Buffalo," *Edmonton Journal*, 19 January 1961.

14. "Sports of the South!!" *The Clarion and Tennessee State Gazette*, 29 January 1819.

15. George Philip, "South Dakota Buffaloes versus Mexican Bulls," *South Dakota Historical Review* 2 (1937): 51–72.

CHAPTER XXI

Sources of quotations heading the chapter:

Great Falls Tribune.

National Buffalo Association member.

1. "Bison Range Bids Bountiful," *Missoulian* (Montana), 15 September 1974.

2. "Sale of Hides Nets $1,050.50," *Missoulian*, 14 March 1970.

3. Steve Moore, "Buffalo Market Bulletin," *Missoulian*, 11 April 1974.

4. All of this information gleaned from a questionnaire sent to all members of the National Buffalo Association.

5. "Last Buffalo Hunt Is for Rustlers," *Albertan* (Calgary), 21 March 1962.

6. Henry Stelfox, "Buffalo at Rocky Mountain House," *Canadian Cattlemen* (March 1958), p. 25.

7. Homer Bigart, "Ranchers Claim Park Bison Pose Health Threat to Cattle," *New York Times News Service*, no date.

SELECTED BIBLIOGRAPHY

BOOKS

Adair, Cornelia. *My Diary August 30th to November 5, 1874.* Austin and London: University of Texas Press, 1965.

Albright, Horace, and Taylor, Frank J. *Oh, Ranger!* Palo Alto: Stanford University Press, 1928.

Allen, Durward L. *Our Wildlife Legacy.* New York: Funk and Wagnall's, 1954.

Anderson, George S. "Protection of Yellowstone Park Game." In *Hunting in Many Lands.* Edited by Theodore Roosevelt and George Bird Grinnell. New York: Forest and Stream Publishing Co., 1895, pp. 377–400.

Bad Heart Bull, Amos. *A Pictorial History of the Oglala Sioux.* Text by Helen Blish, introduction by Mari Sandoz. Lincoln: University of Nebraska Press, 1967.

Baillie-Grohman, W. A. *Camps in the Rockies.* London: 1882.

Bancroft, Hubert Howe. *History of Nevada, Colorado, and Wyoming.* Vol. 25. San Francisco: H. L. Bancroft and Company, 1890.

Beal, Merrill D. *The Story of Man in Yellowstone.* Caldwell, Idaho: The Caxton Printers, Ltd., 1949.

Benavides, Fray Alfonso de. "Memorial to His Holiness, Pope Urban VIII, Our Lord . . . on February 12, 1634." In *Fray Alonso Benavides' Revised Memorial of 1634.* Edited by Frederick Webb Hodge, George P. Hammond, Agapito Rey. Albuquerque: The University of New Mexico Press, 1945.

Benchley, Robert. *From Bed to Worse, or Comforting Thoughts About the Bison.* New York: Harper and Brothers, 1934.

Biggers, Dan Hampton. *Pictures of the Past.* Colorado, Texas: Colorado Spokesman, and Ennis, Texas: Biggers Printing Office, 1902.

Binneteau, Julien. "Relation, January, 1769." In *The Jesuit Relations and Allied Documents, 1610–1791.* 73 vols. Edited by Reuben Gold Thwaites. Vol. 65. Cleveland: The Burrows Brothers Co, 1896–1901.

Blegen, Theodore Christian. *The Land Lies Open.* Minneapolis: University of Minnesota Press, 1949.

Boller, Henry A. *Among the Indians, Four Years on the Upper Missouri, 1858–1862.* Lincoln: University of Nebraska Press, 1972.

Bolton, H. E., ed. *Spanish Exploration in the Southwest, 1542–1706.* New York: Charles Scribner's Sons, 1916.

Bosque, Fernando del. "Diary of Fernando del Bosque." In *Spanish Exploration in the Southwest.* Edited by Herbert Eugene Bolton. New York: Charles Scribner's Sons, 1916, pp. 291–309.

Bowers, Alfred W. *Mandan Social and Ceremonial Organization.* Chicago: The University of Chicago Press, 1950.

Branch, Douglas. "Buffalo Lore and Boudin Blanc." In *Rainbow in the Morning.* Edited by J. Frank Dobie. Hatboro, Pennsylvania: Folklore Associates, Inc., 1965, pp. 126–136.

Branch, Douglas. *The Hunting of the Buffalo.* New York and London: D. Appleton and Co., 1929.

Brennan, Louis. *No Stone Unturned.* New York: Random House, 1959.

Briggs, Harold. *Frontiers of the Northwest; a History of the Upper Missouri Valley.* New York: Appleton-Century, 1940.

Brininstool, E. A. *Fighting Red Cloud's Warriors.* Columbus: The Hunter-Trader-Trapper Co., 1926.

Brown, Mark H., and Felton, William R. *The Frontier Years, L. A. Huffman, Photographer of the Plains.* New York: Holt and Co., 1955.

Burdick, Usher Lloyd. *Tales from Buffalo Land; The Story of Fort Buford.* Baltimore: Wirth Brothers, 1940.

Burton, Sir Richard. *The Look of the West 1860.* Lincoln: University of Nebraska Press, 1966.

Bustamente, Pedro de. "Declaration of Pedro de Bustamente." In *Spanish Exploration in the Southwest.* Edited by Herbert Eugene Bolton. New York: Charles Scribner's Sons, 1916, pp. 142–49.

Butler, W. F. *The Great Lone Land.* London: Sampson, Low, Marston, Low & Searle, 1872.

Butler, W. F. *The Wild North Land.* New York: A. S. Barnes & Co., 1904.

Cabeza de Vaca, Álvar Núñez. "Narrative of Cabeza de Vaca." In *Spanish Explorers in the Southern United States, 1528–1543.* Edited by F. W. Hodge and H. T. Lewis. New York: Charles Scribner's Sons, 1907, pp. 1–123.

Castañeda, Pedro de. "The Narrative of the Expedition of Coronado, by Pedro de Castañeda." In *Spanish Explorers in the Southern United States, 1528–1543.* Edited by Frederick W. Hodge. New York: Charles Scribner's Sons, 1907, pp. 1–123.

Catlin, George. *North American Indians.* 2 vols. Edinburgh: John Grant, 1926.

Catlin, George. *O-Kee-Pa, A Religious Ceremony and Other Customs of the Mandans.* Edited by John C. Ewers. New Haven and London: Yale University Press, 1967.

Chambers, James. "Fort Sarpy Journal, 1855–1856." In *Contributions to the Historical Society of Montana.* Vol. 10. Helena: Naegele Printing Co., 1940, pp. 100–187.

Chardon, Francois A. *Chardon's Journal of Fort Clark, 1834–1839.* Edited by Annie Heloise Abel. Pierre, South Dakota, 1932.

Chittenden, Hiram Martin. *The American Fur Trade of the Far West.* 2 vols. New York: The Press of the Pioneers, Inc., 1935.

Collins, Henry H., Jr. *1951 Census of American Bison.* Bronxville: The Blue Heron Press, 1952.

Collins, Henry H., Jr. *The Unvanquished Buffalo.* Bronxville: The Blue Heron Press, 1952.

Coman, Katherine. *Economic Beginnings of the Far West.* 2 vols. New York: Macmillan Co., 1912.

Conard, Howard Louis. *"Uncle Dick" Wootton.* Chicago: W. E. Dibble, 1890.

Conner, Stuart W. "Prehistoric Man in the Yellowstone Valley." In *Red Man's West.* Edited by Michael Kennedy and Stuart Conner. New York: Hastings House, 1965.

Cook, John R. *The Border and the Buffalo.* Topeka: Crane and Co., 1907.

Cook, Joseph H. *Fifty Years on the Frontier.* New Haven: Yale University Press, 1923.

Cowie, Isaac. *The Company of Adventurers.* Toronto: W. Briggs, 1913.

Cuming, Fortescu. *Cuming's Tour to the Western Country, 1807–1809.* Cleveland: The A. H. Clark Co., 1904.

Custer, Elizabeth B. *Tenting on the Plains.* New York: Charles L. Webster & Company, 1887.

Custer, George A. *My Life on the Plains.* Edited by Milo Milton Quaife. New York: The Citadel Press, 1962.

Dary, David. *The Buffalo Book.* Chicago: The Swallow Press, Inc., 1974.

Davidson, G. C. *The North West Company.* Berkeley: University of California Press, 1918.

Davies, Kenneth Gordon. *Letters from Hudson Bay, 1703–40.* London: Hudson's Bay Record Society, 1965.

Dewees, W. B. *Letters from an Early Settler of Texas.* Louisville: Morton and Griswold, 1852.

Dickens, Charles. *American Notes.* Greenwich, Connecticut: Fawcett Publications, Inc., 1961.

Dixon, Olive K. *The Life of Billy Dixon.* Dallas: P. L. Turner, 1927.

Dobie, J. Frank. *The Longhorns.* New York: Grosset and Dunlap, 1941.

Dobie, J. Frank. *The Mustangs.* New York: Bantam Books, 1958.

Dodge, Richard Irving. *Our Wild Indians: Thirty-three Years' Personal Experience Among the Red Men of the Great West.* Hartford, Connecticut: A. D. Worthington and Company, 1890.

Dodge, Richard Irving. *The Plains of the Great West.* New York: Archer House, 1959.

Dusenberry, Verne. *The Montana Cree, A Study in Religious Persistence.* Stockholm: Almquist and Wiksell, 1962.

Easton, Robert, and Brown, Mackenzie. *Lord of Beasts.* Tucson: University of Arizona Press, 1961.

Ellsworth, Henry Leavitt. *Washington Irving on the Prairie.* Edited by Stanley T. Williams and Barbara D. Simison. New York: The American Book Co., 1937.

Ewers, John C. *The Blackfeet, Raiders of the Northwestern Plains.* Norman: University of Oklahoma Press, 1958.

Ewers, John C. *Indian Life on the Upper Missouri.* Norman: University of Oklahoma Press, 1968.

Farnham, Thomas J. "Travels in the Great Western Prairies, 1839." In *Early Western Travels.* 32 vols. Edited by R. G. Thwaites. Cleveland: A. H. Clark Co., 1906. Vols. 28–29.

Finley, G. F., and Greig, Robert. *Cattle Breeding.* Edinburgh: Tweeddale Court, and London: 33 Paternoster Row, 1925.

Firresty, John F. *War Path and Bivouac.* Lincoln: University of Nebraska Press, 1966.

Fletcher, Alice C., and LaFlesche, Francis. *The Omaha Tribe.* New York: The Johnson Reprint Corporation, 1970.

Foreman, Grant. *Indian Removal.* Norman: University of

Oklahoma Press, 1953.

"The Fort Benton Journal." In *Contributions to the Historical Society of Montana.* Vol. 10. Helena: Naegele Printing Co., 1940, pp. 1–99.

Fowler, Jacob. *The Journal of Jacob Fowler.* Edited by Elliott Coues. New York: Francis P. Harper, 1898.

Frewen, Moreton. *Milton Mowbray and Other Memories.* London: Herbert Jenkins, Ltd., 1924.

Garcia, Andrew. *Tough Trip Through Paradise.* Edited by Bennett H. Stein. Boston: Houghton Mifflin Co., 1967.

Gard, Wayne. *The Great Buffalo Hunt.* New York: Alfred A. Knopf, 1959.

Garrard, Lewis H. *Wah-To-Yah and the Taos Trail.* Edited by Ralph P. Bieber. Glendale: Arthur H. Clark Co., 1938.

Garretson, Martin S. *The American Bison.* New York: The New York Zoological Society, 1938.

Gass, Patrick. *Journal of the Lewis and Clark Expedition.* Minneapolis: Ross & Haines, 1958.

Greeley, Horace. *An Overland Journey from New York to San Francisco in the Summer of 1859.* Edited by Charles T. Duncan. New York: Alfred A. Knopf, 1964.

Gregg, Josiah. *The Commerce of the Prairies.* Edited by Milo Milton Quaife. Lincoln: University of Nebraska Press, 1967.

Grinnell, George Bird. *Blackfoot Lodge Tales.* New York: Charles Scribner's Sons, 1923.

Grinnell, George Bird. *By Cheyenne Campfires.* New Haven and London: Yale University Press, 1926 & 1962.

Grinnell, George Bird. *The Cheyenne Indians, Their History and Ways of Life.* Vol. 2, New Haven: Yale University Press, 1924; Vol. 1, New York: Cooper Square Publishers, 1962.

Grinnell, George Bird. *Pawnee, Blackfoot, and Cheyenne.* New York: Charles Scribner's Sons, 1961.

Grinnell, George Bird. *Pawnee Hero Stories and Folk Tales.* New York: Charles Scribner's Sons, 1920.

Haines, Francis. *The Buffalo.* New York: Thomas Y. Crowell Co., 1970.

Haley, James Evetts. *Charles Goodnight.* Norman: University of Oklahoma Press, 1949.

Haley, James Evetts. *The XIT Ranch of Texas and the Early Days of the Llano Estacado.* Norman: University of Oklahoma Press, 1953.

Hamilton, W. T. *My Sixty Years on the Plains.* New York: Forest and Stream Publishing Co., 1905.

Hammond, George P., and Rey, Agapito. *The Rediscovery of New Mexico, 1580–1594.* Albuquerque: The University of New Mexico Press, 1966.

Hampton, H. Duane. *How the U.S. Cavalry Saved Our National Parks.* Bloomington: Indiana University Press, 1971.

Harris, Edward. *Up the Missouri with Audubon, the Journal of Edward Harris.* Edited by John Francis McDermott. Norman: University of Oklahoma Press, 1951.

Hearne, Samuel. *Coppermine Journey.* Edited by Farley Mowatt. Boston: Little, Brown and Company, 1958.

Hebard, Grace. *Washakie.* Cleveland: The Arthur H. Clark Co., 1930.

Hendry, Antony. "The Journal of Antony Hendry." Edited by Lawrence Burpee. *Proceedings and Transactions of the Royal Society of Canada.* 3d. Series, 1 (1907): 307–54.

Hennepin, Louis. *A New Discovery of a Vast Country in America.* 2 vols. Edited by Reuben Gold Thwaites. Chicago: A. C. McClurg & Co., 1903.

Henry, Alexander. *The Manuscript Journals of Alexander Henry and of David Thompson, 1799–1814.* 2 vols. Edited by Elliott Coues. Minneapolis: Ross and Haines, 1965.

Henry, Alexander (the elder). *Travels and Adventures in Canada and Indian Territories between the Years 1760 and 1776.* New York: I. Riley, 1909.

Hill, J. L. *The Passing of the Indian and Buffalo.* Long Beach: George W. Moyle Publishing Co., 1917.

Hodder, Frank H. *Audubon's Western Journal.* Cleveland: A. H. Clark Co., 1906.

Hodge, Frederick Webb, ed. "Handbook of American Indians North of Mexico." *Bureau of American Ethnology Bulletin No. 30.* 2 vols. Washington: Government Printing Office, 1907–1910.

Hodge, F. W., and Lewis, H. T. *Spanish Explorers in the Southern United States, 1528–1543.* New York: Charles Scribner's Sons, 1907.

Horgan, Paul. *Great River, the Rio Grande in North American History.* 2 vols. New York: Rinehart and Company, Inc., 1954.

Hornaday, William Temple. *Wild Life Conservation in Theory and Practice.* New Haven: Yale University Press, 1914.

Howard, Helen Addison. *Northwest Trail Blazers.* Caldwell, Idaho: Caxton Printers, 1963.

Howard, Joseph Kinsey. *Strange Empire.* New York: William Morrow and Company, 1952.

Hulbert, Archer Butler. *Forty-Niners.* Boston: Little, Brown and Company, 1932.

Hulbert, Archer Butler. *Historic Highways of America.* Cleveland: Arthur H. Clark Co., 1902.

Humfreville, J. Lee. *Twenty Years Among Our Hostile Indians.* New York: Hunter & Co., 1899.

Hunter, John D. *Manners and Customs of Several Indian Tribes Located West of the Mississippi.* Minneapolis: Ross and Haines, 1957.

Hyde, George E. *Life of George Bent.* Edited by Savoie Lottinville. Norman: University of Oklahoma Press, 1968.

Inman, Henry. *Buffalo Jones' Adventures on the Plains.* Lincoln: University of Nebraska Press, 1970.

Inman, Henry. *The Old Santa Fe Trail.* New York: The Macmillan Co., 1898.

Innis, Harold A. *The Fur Trade in Canada.* New Haven: Yale University Press, 1962.

Irving, Washington. *A Tour on the Prairies.* Edited by John Francis McDermott. Norman: University of Oklahoma Press, 1956.

James, Edwin. "An Account of an Expedition from Pittsburgh to the Rocky Mountains in the Years 1819, 1820." In *Early Western Travels.* 32 vols. Edited by R. G. Thwaites. Cleveland: The Arthur H. Clark Co., 1905. Vols. 14–17.

Jennings, Jesse D. *Prehistory of North America*. New York: McGraw-Hill Book Co., 1968.

Johnson, Alice M., ed. *Saskatchewan Journals and Correspondence*. London: The Hudson's Bay Record Society, 1967.

Judson, Katherine B. *Myths and Legends of the Great Plains*. Chicago: A. C. McClurg and Co., 1913.

Kane, Paul. *Paul Kane's Frontier*. Edited by J. Russell Harper. Austin and London: The University of Texas Press, 1971.

Kelsey, Henry. *The Kelsey Papers*. Ottawa: F. A. Ackland, Printer, 1929.

Kennedy, Michael, and Conner, Stuart, editors. *The Red Man's West*. New York: Hastings House, 1965.

Kersey, Ralph. *Buffalo Jones*. Garden City, Kansas: The Elliott Printers, 1958.

King, Henry C. "An Old-Time Buffalo Chase." In *Field and Stream Treasury*. Edited by Hugh Grey and Ross McCluskey. New York: Henry Holt and Co., 1955.

Kirkpatrick, James. "A Reminiscence of John Bozeman." In *Frontier Omnibus*. Edited by John Hakola. Missoula, Montana: University of Montana Press, 1962, pp. 255–61.

Koch, Peter. "Life at Musselshell in 1869 and 1870." In *Contributions to the Historical Society of Montana*. Vol. 2. Helena: Naegele Printing Co., 1896, pp. 292–303.

Larpenteur, Charles. *Forty Years a Fur Trader on the Upper Missouri*. Edited by Elliott Coues. 2 vols. New York: Francis P. Harper, 1908.

Lee, C. H. *Long Ago in the Red River Valley*. St. Paul: 1880.

Lee, Richard, and DeVore, Irven, editors. *Man the Hunter*. Chicago: Aldine Publishing Co., 1968.

LeForge, Thomas H. *Memoirs of a White Crow Indian*. As told by Thomas B. Marquis. New York and London: The Century Co., 1928.

Leonard, Zenas. *Adventures of Zenas Leonard, Fur Trader and Trapper*. Edited by W. F. Wagner. Cleveland: The Burrows Brothers Co., 1904.

Lewis, Meriwether, and Clark, William. *Original Journals of the Lewis and Clark Expedition*. 8 vols. Edited by Reuben Gold Thwaites. New York: Dodd and Mead Co., 1904.

Linderman, Frank B. *American, the Life Story of a Great Indian*. New York: The John Day Co., 1931.

Linderman, Frank B. *Red Mother*. New York: The John Day Co., 1932.

Llewellyn, K. N., and Hobell, E. Adamson. *The Cheyenne Way*. Norman: University of Oklahoma Press, 1941.

Long, John. "Voyages and Travels, 1768–1782." In *Early Western Travels*. 32 vols. Edited by R. G. Thwaites. Cleveland: The Arthur H. Clark Co., 1904.

Lowie, Robert H. *The Crow Indians*. New York: Farrar & Rinehart, Inc., 1935.

Lowie, Robert H. *Indians of the Plains*. Garden City, New York: The Natural History Press (Doubleday and Co.), 1963.

Luxton, Norman. *The Last of the Buffalo*. Cincinnati: Tom Jones, 1909.

Lydekker, R. *The Ox and Its Kindred*. London: Methuen and Co., 1912.

McClintock, Walter. *The Old North Trail*. London: Macmillan and Co., 1900.

McCreight, M. I. *Buffalo Bone Days*. Sykesville, Pennsylvania: Nupp Printing Co., 1939.

McDonald, Jerry N. *North American Bison*. Berkeley: University of California Press, 1981.

McDougall, John. *Saddle, Sled and Snowshoe; Pioneering on the Saskatchewan in the Sixties*. Cincinnati: Jennings & Graham, 1896.

M'Gillivray, Duncan. *The Journal of Duncan M'Gillivray of the Northwest Company*. Introduction, Notes and Appendix by Arthur S. Morton. Toronto: The Macmillan Co., Ltd., 1929.

McHugh, Tom. *The Time of the Buffalo*. New York: Alfred A. Knopf, 1972.

McIntire, James. *Early Days in Texas*. Kansas City: McIntire Publishing Co., 1902.

Mackenzie, Alexander. *Voyages from Montreal on the River St. Lawrence through the Continent of North America*. Toronto: The Radisson Society of Canada, Ltd., 1927.

McKenzie, Fayette Avery. *The Indian in Relation to the White Population of the United States*. Columbus: by the author, 1908.

McKeown, Martha Ferguson. *Them Was the Days*. Lincoln: University of Nebraska Press, 1961.

Marcy, R. B. *Marcy & the Gold Seekers*. Edited by Grant Foreman. Norman: University of Oklahoma Press, 1939.

Marquis, Thomas B. *Wooden Leg, A Warrior Who Fought Custer*. Lincoln: University of Nebraska Press, 1967.

Marsh, James H. *The Fur Trade*. Don Mills, Ontario: The Macmillan Co., 1973.

Mathews, John Joseph. *The Osages, Children of the Middle Waters*. Norman: University of Oklahoma Press, 1961.

Mathews, Mitford M. *A Dictionary of Americanisms*. Chicago: University of Chicago Press, 1951, p. 205.

Maximilian, Prince of Wied. "Travels in the Interior of North America, 1833–1834." In *Early Western Travels*. 32 vols. Edited by R. G. Thwaites. Cleveland: The A. H. Clark Co., 1902. Vols. 22–25.

Mayer, Frank H., and Roth, Charles B. *The Buffalo Harvest*. Denver: Sage Books, 1958.

Mayhall, Mildred P. *The Kiowas*. Norman: University of Oklahoma Press, 1962.

Mendoza, Juan Dominguez de. "Itinerary of Juan Dominguez de Mendoza." In *Spanish Exploration in the Southwest*. Edited by Herbert Eugene Bolton. New York: Charles Scribner's Sons, 1916, pp. 339–341.

Miller, Alfred Jacob. *The West of Alfred Jacob Miller (1837)*. With an account of the artist by Marvin C. Ross. Norman: University of Oklahoma Press, 1968.

Miller, Max. *Shinny on Your Own Side*. Garden City, New York: Doubleday, 1958.

Morgan, Dale L. *Jedediah Smith and the Opening of the West*. Lincoln: University of Nebraska Press, 1969.

Morgan, Lewis Henry. *The Indian Journals, 1859–62*. Edited and introduction by Leslie A. White. Ann Arbor:

University of Michigan Press, 1959.

Morice, A. G. *History of the Northern Interior of British Columbia*. Toronto: William Briggs, 1904.

Nasatir, A. P., ed. *Before Lewis and Clark; Documents Illustrating the History of the Missouri, 1785–1804*. 2 vols. St. Louis: St. Louis Historical Documents Foundation, 1952.

Nelson, John Y. *Fifty Years on the Trail*. Norman: University of Oklahoma Press, 1963.

Oñate, Don Juan de. "Letter Written by Don Juan de Oñate." In *Spanish Exploration in the Southwest*. Edited by Herbert Eugene Bolton. New York: Charles Scribner's Sons, 1916, pp. 212–222.

Osborn, Henry Fairfield. *The Age of Mammals*. New York: The Macmillan Co., 1910.

Osgood, E. S. *The Day of the Cattleman*. Minneapolis: The University of Minnesota Press, 1929.

Owen, John. *The Journal and Letters of Major John Owen*. 2 vols. Edited by Seymour Dunbar, notes by Paul Phillips. New York: Edward Eberstadt, 1927.

Paine, Bayard H. *Pioneers, Indians and Buffaloes*. Curtis, Nebraska: The Curtis Enterprises, 1935.

Palliser, John. *The Journals, Detailed Reports and Observations Relative to the Exploration by Captain Palliser*. London: George Edward Eyre and William Spottiswoode, 1863.

Park, Ed. *The World of the Bison*. Philadelphia and New York: J. B. Lippincott Co., 1969.

Parker, Samuel. *Journal of an Exploring Tour Beyond the Rocky Mountains*. Ithaca, New York: Andrews, Woodruff, & Gauntlet, 1844.

Phillips, Paul C. *The Fur Trade*. Norman: University of Oklahoma Press, 1961.

Pike, Zebulon. *Arkansaw Journal*. Edited by Stephen Harding Hart and Archer Butler Hulbert. Denver: The Stewart Commission of Colorado College and The Denver Public Library, 1932.

Point, Nicholas. *Wilderness Kingdom, Indian Life in the Rocky Mountains: 1840–1847*. Translated by Joseph P. Donnelly. New York, Chicago and San Francisco: Holt, Rinehart and Winston, 1967.

Pourtalès, Albert-Alexandre. *On the Western Tour with Washington Irving, The Journals and Letters of Count de Pourtalès*. Edited by George F. Spaulding, translated by Seymour Feiler. Norman: University of Oklahoma Press, 1968.

Powell, H. M. T. *The Santa Fe Trail to California, 1849–1852, The Journal and Drawings of H. M. T. Powell*. Edited by Douglas S. Watson and R. Grabhorn. San Francisco: The Book Club of California, 1931.

Powers, Alfred, ed. *Buffalo Adventures on the Western Plains*. Portland, Oregon: Binford and Mort, 1945.

Pritchett, John Perry. *The Red River Valley, 1833–1849*. New Haven: Yale University Press, 1942.

Râle, Sebastian. "Relation of Sebastian Râle." In *The Jesuit Relations and Allied Documents, 1610–1791*. 73 vols. Edited by Reuben Gold Thwaites. Cleveland: Arthur W. Clark Co., 1896–1901. Vol. 47.

Richmond, Robert Z., and Mardock, Robert W., editors. *A Nation Moving West*. Lincoln: University of Nebraska Press, 1966.

Roe, Frank Gilbert. *The Indian and the Horse*. Norman: University of Oklahoma Press, 1962.

Roe, Frank Gilbert. *The North American Buffalo*. Toronto: University of Toronto Press, 1951.

Roosevelt, Theodore. *Hunting in Many Lands*. New York: Forest and Stream Publishing Co., 1895.

Roosevelt, Theodore. *The Wilderness Hunter*. New York and London: G. F. Putnam's Sons, 1893.

Ross, Alexander. *The Red River Settlement*. Minneapolis: Ross and Haines, Inc., 1957.

Ruede, Howard. *Sod House Days*. Edited by John Ise. New York: Cooper Square Publishers, Inc., 1966.

Russell, C. M. *Trails Plowed Under*. New York: Doubleday and Company, 1953.

Ruxton, George F. *Adventures in Mexico and the Rocky Mountains*. London: John Murray, Albemarle Street, 1847.

Ruxton, George F. *Life in the Far West*. Edited by LeRoy R. Hafen. Norman: University of Oklahoma Press, 1951.

Sandoz, Mari. *Buffalo Hunters; the Story of the Hide Men*. New York: Hastings House, 1954.

Sandoz, Mari. *Love Song to the Plains*. Lincoln: University of Nebraska Press, 1966.

Santleben, August. *A Texas Pioneer: Early Staging and Overland Freighting Days on the Frontiers of Texas and Mexico*. Edited by I. D. Affleck. New York: The Nesle Publishing Co., 1910.

Schultz, James Willard. *Apauk, Caller of Buffalo*. Boston and New York: Houghton Mifflin Co., 1916.

Schultz, James Willard. *Blackfeet and Buffalo*. Edited by Keith C. Steele. Norman: University of Oklahoma Press, 1962.

Schultz, James Willard. *My Life as an Indian*. Boston and New York: Houghton Mifflin Co., 1906.

Seger, John H. *Early Days Among the Cheyenne and Arapahoe Indians*. Edited by Stanley Vestal. Norman: University of Oklahoma Press, 1934.

Shaler, N. S. *Nature and Man in America*. New York: Scribner's Sons, 1891.

Shaw, James C. *Pioneering in Texas and Wyoming*. Orin, Wyoming: by the author, 1931.

Shoemaker, Henry Wharton. *A Pennsylvania Bison Hunt*. Middleburg, Pennsylvania: The Middleburg Post Press, 1915.

Simpson, George. *An Overland Journey Round the World*. Philadelphia: Lee and Blanchard, 1847.

Smet, Pierre Jean de. *Letters and Sketches with a Narrative of a Year's Residence among the Indian Tribes of the Rocky Mountains*. Philadelphia: M. Fithian, 1843.

Southesk, James Carnegie, Earl of. *Saskatchewan and the Rocky Mountains*. Rutland, Vermont: C. E. Tuttle Co., 1969.

Stands in Timber, John, and Liberty, Margot. *Cheyenne Memories*. Assisted by Robert M. Utley. New Haven and

London: Yale University Press, 1967.

Steele, S. B. *Forty Years in Canada*. New York: Dodd, Mead and Co., 1915.

Stegner, Wallace. *Wolf Willow*. New York: The Viking Press, 1955.

Stuart, Granville. *Forty Years on the Frontier*. 2 vols. Edited by Paul C. Phillips. Cleveland: Arthur H. Clark Co., 1925.

Sutley, Zack T. *The Last Frontier*. New York: Macmillan Co., 1930.

Taft, Robert. *Artists and Illustrators of the Old West*. New York: Bonanza Books, 1953.

Taylor, Joseph Henry. *Sketches of Frontier and Indian Life on the Upper Missouri and Great Plains*. Washburn, North Dakota: by the author, 1895.

Teale, Edwin Way. Cited in Porter G. Perrin, *Writer's Guide and Index to English*. New York: Scott, Foresman and Company, 1959, p. 151.

Thomson, Frank. *Last Buffalo of the Black Hills*. Printed by the author, 1968.

Tixier, Victor. *Tixier's Travels on the Osage Prairie*. Edited by John Francis McDermott and J. Albert Salvan. Norman: University of Oklahoma Press, 1940.

Toponce, Alexander. *Reminiscences of Alexander Toponce*. Ogden, Utah: Mrs. Katie Toponce, 1923.

Trefethen, James B. *Crusade for Wildlife*. Harrisburg, Pennsylvania: The Stackpole Company, 1961.

Trenholm, Virginia Cole, and Carley, Maurine. *The Shoshonis, Sentinels of the Rockies*. Norman: University of Oklahoma Press, 1964.

Tucker, Patrick T. *Riding the High Country*. Edited by Grace Stone Coates. Caldwell, Idaho: The Caxton Printers, Ltd., 1933.

Utley, Robert M. *The Last Days of the Sioux Nation*. New Haven and London: Yale University Press, 1963.

Vaughn, A. J. "Letter, 15 July 1856." In *Contributions to the Historical Society of Montana*. Vol. 10. Helena: Naegele Printing Co., 1940, p. 192.

Vernam, Glenn. *Man on Horseback*. Lincoln: University of Nebraska Press, 1972.

Vestal, Stanley. *Mountain Men*. Boston: Houghton Mifflin Co., 1937.

Wallace, Ernest, and Hoebel, E. Adamson. *The Commanches*. Norman: University of Oklahoma Press, 1952.

Webb, James Josiah. *Adventures in the Santa Fe Trade, 1844–47*. Edited by Ralph P. Bieber. Glendale, California: Arthur H. Clark Co., 1931.

Webb, Walter P. *The Great Plains*. Boston: Houghton Mifflin Co., 1951.

Webb, William Edward. *Buffalo Land*. Philadelphia: Hubbard Bros., 1872.

Wedel, Waldo R. *Prehistoric Man on the Great Plains*. Norman: Oklahoma University Press, 1961.

Welsh, Norbert. *The Last Buffalo Hunter*. By Mary Weeks as told to her by Norbert Welsh. New York: T. Nelson and Sons, 1939.

Wheeler, Homer W. *Buffalo Days*. Indianapolis: Bobbs-

Merrill Co., 1923.

Whitehead, Charles E. "Game Laws." In *Hunting in Many Lands*. Edited by Theodore Roosevelt and George B. Grinnell. New York: Forest and Stream Publishing Co., 1895.

Winship, George P., editor. *The Journey of Coronado, 1540–1542*. New York: A. Lovell & Co., 1922.

Wislizenus, Adolphus. *A Journey to the Rocky Mountains in the Year 1839*. St. Louis: Missouri Historical Society, 1912.

Wissler, Clark. *The American Indian*. New York: D. C. Murtrie, 1917.

Wood, Louis W. *The Red River Colony*. Toronto: Glasgow, Brook and Co., 1922.

Work, John. *The Journal of John Work*. Edited by William S. Lewis and Paul C. Phillips. Cleveland: The Arthur H. Clark Co., 1923.

Wormington, H. M. *Ancient Man in North America*. Denver: Denver Museum of Natural History, 1957.

Wyman, Walker D. *The Wild Horse of the West*. Lincoln: University of Nebraska Press, 1967.

Zaldívar, Vicente de. Report in *Spanish Exploration in the Southwest*. Edited by Herbert Eugene Bolton. New York: Charles Scribner's Sons, 1916, pp. 223–232.

PERIODICALS

Adams, Jane Ford. "What are Buffalo Horn Buttons?" *National Button Bulletin* 11 (September 1952): 299–302.

Adams, Winona, editor. "An Indian Girl's Story of a Trading Expedition to the Southwest About 1841." *Frontier and Midland* 10 (1930): 338–51.

Allard, Charles. "Breeding Buffaloes." *Self-Culture*, May 1895, pp. 81–82.

Allen, W. A. "The Buffalo Range." *Forest and Stream*, 23 December 1880, p. 411.

Anderson, William Marshall. "Anderson's Narrative of a Ride to the Rocky Mountains in 1834." Edited by Albert J. Partoll. *Frontier and Midland* 19 (Autumn 1938): 54–63.

Andrews, E. N. "A Buffalo Hunt by Rail." *Kansas Magazine* 3 (May 1873): 450–58.

Aubrey, Charles. "The Edmonton Buffalo Herd." *Forest and Stream*, July 1907, pp. 11–12.

Aubrey, Charles. "Memories of an Old Buffalo Hunter." *Forest and Stream*, 25 July 1908, pp. 133–34; 1 August 1908, pp. 173–74; 8 August 1908, pp. 216–17.

Bagley, Clarence B. "Along the Oregon Trail in 1852." *Motor Travel* 15 (January–February 1924): 11–12.

Barnes, Will C. "The Bison of House Rock Valley." *Nature Magazine*, 10 October 1927, pp. 216–21.

Barnes, Will C. "Longhorns and Buffaloes." *The Breeder's Gazette* 30 (November 1916): 1020.

Barrows, John R. "A Wisconsin Youth in Montana." *The Frontier* 8 (November 1927): 38–59.

Baynes, E. H. "A Great Buffalo Herd in Winter Quarters." *Suburban Life*, February 1906, p. 55.

Baynes, E. H. "Fight to Save the Buffalo." *Country Life*,

January 1908, pp. 295–98.

Baynes, E. H. "In the Name of the American Bison." *Harper's Weekly*, 24 March 1906, pp. 404–06.

Baynes, E. H. "Largest Herd of Bison in the World." *Country Calendar*, July 1905, pp. 262–65.

"Big Game Destruction." *Forest and Stream*, 11 May 1882, p. 289.

Biggers, Dan H. "Buffalo Butchery in Texas Was a National Calamity." *Farm and Ranch*, 14 November 1925, pp. 28–29.

Blanco, Cabia. "A Buffalo Hunt with the Comanches." *Forest and Stream*, 7 January 1905, pp. 2 and 5; 21 January 1905, pp. 46–47; 28 January 1905, pp. 67–68; 4 February 1905, p. 86; 11 February 1905, pp. 110–111.

Booth, Margaret, editor. "Dinwiddie Journal." *Frontier and Midland* 8 (March 1928): 115–30.

Bradley-Birt, F. B. "Concerning Buffaloes." *Cornhill*, March 1917, pp. 367–74.

Brewerton, George D. "In the Buffalo Country." *Harpers*, September 1862, pp. 447–466.

Brooks, Noah. "The Plains Across." *The Century Magazine*, April 1902, pp. 803–820.

Brown, Barnum. "The Buffalo Drive: An Echo of a Western Romance." *Natural History* 32 (January–February 1932): 75–82.

"Buffalo By-Names." *Pony Express Courier* 1 (January 1935): 31.

"The Buffalo Hunt." *Harper's Weekly*, 6 July 1867, p. 426.

"Buffalo in Canada." *Scarlet and Gold*, 1921, pp. 25–29.

Burhans. "The Last Buffalo Roundup in Colorado." *Mid-Pacific Magazine*, August 1919.

Christie, Robert. "I Rode the Buffalo Roundup." *Saturday Evening Post*, 12 May 1951, pp. 158–60.

Christy, Miller. "The Last of the Buffaloes." *The Field*, 10 November 1888, pp. 697–699.

Cotton, Bud. "The Cattalo—Last Chapter." *Canadian Cattlemen*, October 1964, pp. 8–9, 38–40.

Cotton, E. J. "Hybrids." *Canadian Cattlemen*, November 1949, pp. 12–13 and 36–37.

Crabb, E. D. "Buffalo Bullfight." *Scientific American Supplement* 84 (8 September 1917): 148.

Cumming, C. F. G. "Destruction of American Buffalo." *Good Words* 25 (1882–1886): 388.

Davis, Theodore H. "The Buffalo Range." *Harper's Magazine*, January 1869, pp. 147–63.

DeVoto, Bernard. "The West; A Plundered Province." *Harpers*, August 1934, pp. 355–364.

Draper, Benjamin. "Where the Buffalo Roamed." *Pacific Discovery*, March–April 1950, pp. 14–27.

Earles, Mrs. David. "Interview." By Maurice Howe. *Frontier and Midland* 17 (Winter 1937): 145–48.

East, Ben. "Big Buffalo Hunt." *Outdoor Life*, October 1958, p. 34.

"Extermination of Buffalo." *Scientific American* 73 (23 November 1895): 330.

"Extermination." *Scientific American* 82 (6 January 1900): 8.

"Extracts from a Journal Kept in the Spring of 1835." *American Turf Register and Sporting Magazine*, February 1836, pp. 263–68; March 1836, pp. 310–14.

Farley, Tom. "Bull vs Buffalo." *Sports Afield*, January 1934.

"A Final Buffalo Hunt." *Science*, 11 June 1886, pp. 520–21.

Forest and Stream, 14 April 1894, p. 309.

Freeman, L. R. "Protect the Game in Yellowstone Park." *Recreation*, June 1900, pp. 425–27.

Gage, E. W. "Buffalo Roundup at Wainwright." *Travel*, December 1935, pp. 33–34.

Gard, Wayne. "On the Buffalo Range." *Texas Parade*, November 1954, pp. 41–43.

Gard, Wayne. "Where Buffalo Roamed." *Progressive Farmer* (Texas edition), August 1953, p. 18.

"Great Naturalist." *World's Work*, December 1905, p. 7017.

Grinnell, G. B. "Last of the Buffalo." *Scribner's Magazine*, September 1892, pp. 267–286.

Hartung, A. M. "They Tried to Produce a New Kind of Cow." *Western Livestock Journal* 34 (1948): 118–19.

Hathaway, Seth. "The Adventures of a Buffalo Hunter." *Frontier Times*, December 1931, pp. 105–12 and 129–35.

Hawley, S. "New National Bison Herd." *Country Life*, March 1914, p. 136.

Hedlin, Ralph. "The Buffalo as a Northern Resource." *The Beaver*, Summer 1960, pp. 24–28.

Hickman, Richard Owen. "Dick's Works." Edited by Paul C. Phillips. *Frontier* 9 (March 1929): 242–60.

Holder, C. F. "Crime of a Century." *Scientific American*, December 1899, pp. 378–79.

Holte, Peter. "Catching Buffalo Calves." *Forest and Stream*, 17 September 1910, pp. 448–50; 24 September 1910, pp. 488–90.

Hornaday, William T. "The Passing of the Buffalo." *Cosmopolitan*, October 1887, pp. 85–231.

Hough, Emerson. "The Last of the Buffalo." *The American Field*, 3 July–21 August 1886, pp. 5–173.

Hough, Emerson. "Yellowstone Park Game Exploration." *Forest and Stream*, March–August 1894.

Hough, Emerson. "The Survivors." *Saturday Evening Post*, 11 December 1920, pp. 12 ff.

"How the True Cattalo is Bred." *Scientific American* 133 (August 1925): 89.

Hunter, J. Marvin, Sr. "John W. Mooar, Successful Pioneer." *Frontier Times*, September 1952, pp. 331–37.

"Hybridization of Domestic Cattle and Buffalo." *The Cattleman*, November 1942, pp. 69–77.

Inman, H. "Last of the Buffalo." *Harper's Weekly*, 12 July 1890, pp. 536–39.

Jacobs, John Cloud. "The Last of the Buffalo." *World's Work*, January 1909, pp. 11,098–11,100.

Jarman, Rufus. "Buffaloes Are His Business." *True*, April 1964, p. 35.

Johnson, Thomas. "Natural History. The Canadian Northwest." Letter from Fort Saskatchewan, N. W. T., to Editor, *Forest and Stream*, 23 October 1897, p. 323.

Jones, Charles Jesse. "My Buffalo Experiments." *Indepen-*

dent, 7 June 1906, pp. 1351–1355.

Jones, Charles Jesse. "Buffalo Breeding." *Farmer's Review*, 22 August 1888, p. 534.

Jones, C. J. "Passing of the Buffalo." *Overland*, August 1907, pp. 157–62.

Kauffman, Harlan B. "Hunting the Buffalo." *Overland Monthly*, August 1915, pp. 165–70.

Kilgore, Bruce. "Forty Years of Defending Parks." *National Parks*, 33: 40–46.

Lake, Stuart N. "The Buffalo Hunters." *Saturday Evening Post*, 25 October 1930, pp. 12–13 and 83–85.

"Last of the Buffaloes." *The Field, the Country Gentleman*, 10 November 1888, p. 697.

Laut, Agnes C. "Where Buffaloes are Kings." *Independent and Weekly Review*, 23 April 1921, pp. 433–34.

Laut, Agnes C. "The World's Largest Buffalo Herd." *Travel*, July 1929, pp. 12–16.

Lillie, Gordon W. (Pawnee Bill). "Restoring the Bison to the Western Plains." *Cosmopolitan*, October 1905, pp. 651–54.

Logan, Herschel C. "Royal Buffalo Hunt." *American Rifleman*, October 1952, pp. 37–42.

McDee, M. "Buffalo in Canada." *Canadian Magazine*, September 1919, pp. 351–58.

McKay, W. Henry. "Last Buffalo." *Canadian Cattlemen* 11–12 (1948–49): 22.

McLaren, A. "A Texas Buffalo Herd." *Outdoor Life* 26 (1910): 375–378.

MacTavish, N. "Last Great Roundup of Buffaloes." *Canadian Magazine* 33 (October 1909): 482–91; 34 (November 1909): 25–35.

Mariager, Dagmar. "Hunting the Bison." *Overland Monthly*, August 1889, pp. 190–196.

Mengarini, Gregory. "Mengarini's Narrative of the Rockies." Edited by Albert J. Partoll. *Frontier and Midland* 18 (Spring 1938): 211–14.

Montagnes, J. "Add Bisons to Cattle and You Have Cattalo." *National Livestock Producers* 25 (1947): 16.

Montagnes, J. "Cattalo, the New Quadruped." *Countryman* 34 (1946): 285.

Mooar, J. Wright. "Buffalo Days." As told to James Winford Hunt. *Holland's*, January 1933, pp. 13 and 24; February 1933, pp. 10 and 44; March 1933, pp. 8, 24, and 28; April 1933, pp. 5 and 22; May 1933, pp. 11, 12, and 24; July 1933, pp. 10 and 30.

Murphy, R. "Tales of the Buffalo." *Saturday Evening Post*, 14 June 1952, p. 47.

"My First Buffalo Hunt." *Leisure Hour*, 26 August 1865, pp. 529–31.

"National Zoological Park Has White Bison Bull." *Science*, n.s. 88 (November 1938): 307.

Nelson, J. "How Practical Are Cattalo? (Buffalos and domestic cattle have been long crossbred)." *American Feed and Grain Dealer* 30 (1946): 8–9, 24, 42.

Nordyke, Lewis. "The Great Buffalo Roundup of 1945." *Saturday Evening Post*, 16 June 1945, pp. 14–15, 37–39.

Oldys, Henry. "Poaching in the Yellowstone Park." *Forest and Stream*, 15 February 1908, p. 255.

"The Passing of the Wood Bison." [By a Canadian Zoologist.] *Canadian Forum* 5 (1925): 301–05.

Pitcher, John. "National Park Game." *Forest and Stream*, January 1905, pp. 64–69.

"Putnam Letters. 1846–1852." *The Frontier* 9 (November 1928): 56.

R. L. "Present Condition of American Bison and Seal Herds." *Nature*, 3 November 1910, pp. 12–13.

"Revival of the Bison." *Scientific American Supplement*, 29 October 1914, pp. 24103–04.

Richardson, D. S. "Last Buffalo." *Overland*, n.s. 54 (1909): 455.

Riggs, Thomas L. "The Last Buffalo Hunt." *Independent*, 4 July 1907, pp. 24–38.

Riley, Smith. "Buffalo—A Verb." *Nature Magazine*, April 1934, pp. 185–86.

Rister, Carl Coke. "Indians As Buffalo Hunters." *Cattleman*, August 1928, pp. 17–19.

Rivington, Tom. "Letters from Tom Rivington." Edited by Grace Hebard. *Frontier and Midland* 13 (November 1932–May 1933): 148–157.

Roosevelt, Theodore. "Buffalo Hunting." *St. Nicholas*, December 1889, pp. 136–143.

Rowan, William. "Canada's Buffalo." *Country Life* 66 (1929): 358.

Rumley, Charles. "Diary: From St. Louis to Portland, 1862." Edited by Helen Addison Howard. *Frontier and Midland* 19 (1939): 140–200.

Russel, Hamlin. "The Story of the Buffalo." *Harper's Monthly Magazine*, April 1893, pp. 795–98.

Russell, C. M. "Early Days on the Buffalo Range." *Recreation*, April 1897, pp. 227–29.

Satterthwaite, Franklin. "The Western Outlook for Sportsmen." *Harper's New Monthly Magazine*, May 1889, pp. 873–88.

"Saving the Buffalo." *The Beaver*, June 1948, pp. 10–13.

Seton, E. T. "American Bison or Buffalo." *Scribner's Magazine*, October 1906, pp. 385–405.

Sheperd, George. "First Range Cattle (A Buffalo Biography)." *Canadian Cattlemen*, March 1939, p. 152.

Shufeldt, R. W. "The American Buffalo." *Forest and Stream*, 14 June 1888, pp. 4–5.

Smith, H. H. "Want a Buffalo?" *Colliers*, 12 August 1944, p. 28.

Smith, Vic. "Roping Buffalo Calves." *Recreation*, May 1896, pp. 365–66.

"Spectator Visits a Bison Herd." *Outlook*, 28 April 1906, pp. 931–38.

Steffens, C. G. "Running the Last Buffalo." *Canadian Cattlemen*, January 1956, p. 6; February 1956, p. 26.

Stelfox, Henry. "Buffalo at Rocky Mountain House." *Canadian Cattlemen*, March 1958, pp. 8 and 25.

Stone, Franklin L. "Extracts from the Diaries and Letters of Franklin L. Stone." Edited by Lulu Stone. *Frontier and*

Midland 12 (November 1931–May 1932): 375–80.

Thompson, A. W. "Last of the Buffalo in Texas." *Cattle-man*, April 1930, pp. 29–31.

Tucker, Pat T. "Buffalo in the Judith Basin, 1883." *The Frontier* 9 (March 1929): 226–227.

Tucker, Pat T. "The Long Horns." *The Frontier* 11 (March 1931): 282–84.

Upham, Hiram D. "Upham Letters from the Upper Missouri, 1865." Edited by P. C. Phillips. *Frontier and Midland* 13 (November 1932–May 1933): 311–17.

Vestal, Stanley. "Sitting Bull's Maiden Speech." *The Frontier* 12 (March 1932): 269–70.

Wallace, Lew. "A Buffalo Hunt in Northern Mexico." *Scribner's Monthly*, March 1879, p. 713.

Walsh, G. E. "Story of the Buffalo." *Scientific American*, 20 February 1897, p. 119.

Webb, W. P. "A Texas Buffalo Hunt with Original Photographs." *Holland's*, October 1927, pp. 10–11, 101–02.

Wheat, Joe Ben. "A Paleo Indian Bison Kill." *Scientific American*, January 1967, pp. 44–52.

JOURNALS of HISTORY

Bennett, H. Arnold. "The Mystery of the Iowa Buffalo." *Iowa Journal of History* 32 (1934): 60–73.

Bigler, Henry W. "Extracts from the Journal of Henry W. Bigler." *Utah Historical Quarterly* 5 (April 1932): 35–64.

Bliss, Robert S. "The Journal of Robert S. Bliss." *Utah Historical Quarterly* 4 (July 1931): 67–96.

Boardman, John. "The Journal of John Boardman." *Utah Historical Quarterly* 2 (1929): 19–21.

Brown, George W. "Life and Adventures of George W. Brown." Edited by William E. Connelly. *Collections of the Kansas State Historical Society* 17 (1926–28): 98–134.

Bryant, Thomas Julien. "Harry S. Yount." *Annals of Wyoming* 3 (1925): 164–175.

Burlingame, Merrill G. "Buffalo in Trade and Commerce." *North Dakota Historical Quarterly* 3 (1929): 262–91.

Burnett, Peter Hardiman. "Recollections and Opinions of an Old Pioneer." *Oregon Historical Society Quarterly* 5 (March 1904): 64–97.

Cabe, Ernest, Jr. "A Sketch of the Life of James Hamilton Cator." *Panhandle-Plains Historical Review* 6 (1923): 13–23.

Cahill, Luke. "An Indian Campaign and Hunting with Buffalo Bill." *Colorado Magazine* 4 (August 1927): 125–35.

Christman, Gene. "The Mountain Bison." *The American West* 8 (May 1971): 44–47.

Clifford, F. J. "A Note on Bison Hunting: A Few Were Saved." *Oregon Historical Quarterly* 52 (March 1951): 254–64.

Cosgrove, Hugh. "Reminiscences of Hugh Cosgrove." *Oregon Historical Quarterly* 1 (1900): 256–69.

Crook, John. "John Crook's Journal." *Utah Historical Quarterly* 6 (April 1933): 51–62.

Davis, Thomas M. "Building the Burlington Through Nebraska." *Nebraska History* 30 (1949): 317–47.

Dean, Cora. "Early Fur Trading in the Red River Valley, from the Journals of Alexander Henry, Jr." *Collections, State Historical Society of North Dakota* 3 (1910): 350–68.

De Girardin, E. "A Trip to the Bad Lands in 1849." Translated by S. M. Stockdale. *South Dakota Historical Review* 1 (1936): 51–78.

Dougherty, Lewis B. "Experiences of Lewis Birsell Dougherty on the Oregon Trail." Edited by Ethel M. Withers. *Missouri Historical Review* 24 (1930): 359–78; 25 (1931): 102–15, 306–21, 474–89.

Espinosa, J. Manuel. "Journal of the Vargas Expedition into Colorado, 1694." *Colorado Magazine* 16 (May 1933): 81–90.

Fouquet, L. C. "Buffalo Days." *Collections of the Kansas State Historical Society* 16 (1923–1925): 341–352.

Gilmore, Melvin R. "Indian Tribal Boundary Lines and Monuments." *Indian Notes* 5 (1928): 59.

Gilmore, Melvin R. "Some Indian Ideas of Property." *Indian Notes* 5 (1928): 137–44.

Glenn, W. Skelton. "The Recollections of W. S. Glenn, Buffalo Hunter." Edited by Rex W. Strickland. *Panhandle-Plains Historical Review* 22 (1949): 15–64.

Goff, John. "The Buffalo in Georgia." *The Georgia Review* 11 (Spring 1957): 19–28.

Goodman, A. T. "Buffalo in Ohio." *Western Reserve Historical Society Tract* (January 1877), pp. 1–2.

Gordon, George Andrew. "Recollections of George Andrew Gordon." *Collections of the Kansas State Historical Society* 16 (1923–25): 497–504.

Hafen, LeRoy R. "Fort Jackson and the Early Fur Trade on the South Platte." *Colorado Magazine* 5 (February 1928): 9–18.

Hastings, Loren B. "Diary of Loren B. Hastings." *Oregon Pioneer Association Transactions* (1923), pp. 12–26.

Holden, W. C. "The Buffalo of the Plains Area." *West Texas Historical Association Year Book* 2 (June 1926): 8–17.

Holden, W. C. "Robert Cyrus Parrack, Buffalo Hunter and Fence Cutter." *West Texas Historical Association Year Book* 21 (1945): 29–49.

Hough, John A. "Early Western Experiences." *Colorado Magazine* 17 (1940): 101–12.

Howard, Lee. "An Attempt to Capture Buffalo Alive in Present Oklahoma in the Late 1880s." *Kansas Historical Quarterly* 17 (August 1949): 233–42.

Howells, John Ewing. "Diary of an Emigrant of 1845." *Washington Historical Quarterly* 1 (October 1906): 138–58.

Hutchinson, William Henry. "Hides, Hams and Tongues." *Westerners Brand Book, Denver Annual* (1950–1951), pp. 208–17.

Jepson, Glenn L. "Ancient Buffalo Hunters of Northwestern Wyoming." *Southwest Lore* 19 (September 1953): 19–25.

Johnson, Overton, and Winters, William H. "Route Across the Rocky Mountains with a Description of Oregon and California." *Oregon Historical Quarterly* 7 (1906): 62–104, 163–210, 291–327.

Kennerly, William Clark. "My Hunting Trip to the Rockies

in 1843." As told to Bessie K. Russell. *Colorado Magazine* 22–23 (1945): 23–38.

Kidder, John. "Montana Miracle: It Saved the Buffalo." *Montana, the Magazine of Western History* 15 (Spring 1965): 32–67.

Kincaid, Naomi. "Rath City." *West Texas Historical Association Year Book* 24 (1948): 40–46.

Kingston, C. S. "Buffalo in the Pacific Northwest." *Washington Historical Quarterly* 23 (July 1932): 163.

McCombs, Joe S. "On the Cattle Trail and the Buffalo Range." Edited by Ben G. Grant and J. H. Webb. *West Texas Historical Association Year Book* 11 (1935): 93–101.

McKillip, P. E. "A Story of the Buffalo." *The Westerners Brand Book, Los Angeles* (1949–50), pp. 137–50.

Marsh, Elias J. "Journal of Elias J. Marsh." *South Dakota Historical Review* 1–2 (October 1935–July 1937): 79–127.

Maynard, David. "Diary of David S. Maynard." *Washington Historical Quarterly* 1 (1906): 50–62.

Mechem, Kirke. "Home on the Range." *Kansas Historical Quarterly* 17 (November 1949): 313–39.

Merriam, John C. "The Migrations of the Buffalo." *American Antiquarian and Oriental Journal* 29 (November–December 1907): 333–38.

Merriman, R. O. "The Bison and the Fur Trade." *Queen's Quarterly*, July–September 1926, pp. 78–96.

Minto, John. "Reminiscences of Honorable John Minto, Pioneer of 1844." Edited by H. S. Lyman. *The Quarterly of the Oregon Historical Society* 2 (March 1901–December 1901): 119–234.

Mooar, J. Wright. "The First Buffalo Hunting on the Panhandle." *West Texas Historical Association Year Book* 6 (1930): 109–11.

Mooar, J. Wright. "Frontier Experiences." *West Texas Historical Association Year Book* 4 (1928): 89–92.

Moore, Ely. "A Buffalo Hunt with the Miamis in 1854." *Collections of the Kansas State Historical Society* 10 (1907–1908): 402–09.

Moyers, William N. "A Story of Southern Illinois." *Journal of the Illinois State Historical Society* 24 (1931): 26–104.

Nesmith, James W. "Diary of Emigration of 1843." *Oregon Historical Society Quarterly* 7 (1906): 329–59.

Newby, William T. "William T. Newby's Diary of the Emigration of 1843." Edited by Harry N. M. Winton. *Oregon Historical Society Quarterly* 40 (1939): 219–42.

Pammel, L. H. "Buffalo in Iowa." *Annals of Iowa* 17 (October 1930): 403–34.

Patrick, Ledillon. "French Buried Treasure in Southern Illinois." *Illinois History* 11 (October 1957): 21.

Philip, George. "South Dakota Buffaloes versus Mexican Bulls." *South Dakota Historical Review* 2 (1937): 51–72.

Ramsay, Alexander. "Alexander Ramsay's Gold Rush Diary of 1849." *Pacific History Review* 18 (1949): 437–68.

Records, Ralph W. "At the End of the Texas Trail: Range Riding and Ranching, 1878." *West Texas Historical Association Year Book* 19 (1943): 109–20.

Riddell, Francis A. "The Recent Occurrence of Bison in Northeastern California." *American Antiquity* 18 (October 1952): 168–69.

Rister, Carl Coke. "The Significance of the Destruction of the Buffalo in the Southwest." *Southwestern Historical Quarterly* 33 (July 1929): 34–49.

Roe, Frank Gilbert. "The Extermination of the Buffalo in Western Canada." *Canadian Historical Review* 15 (1934): 1–23.

Ross, A. R. "Hunting Buffalo in the Seventies." *Colorado Magazine* 23 (March 1946): 84–87.

Russell, Elizabeth Everitt. "Hunting Buffalo in the Early Forties." *Journal of American History* 18 (1924): 137–48.

Schultz, C. Bertrand. "Some Artifacts Sites of Early Man in the Great Plains and Adjacent Areas." *American Antiquity* 8 (January 1943): 242–48.

Smith, E. Willard "With Fur Traders in Colorado, 1839–40—The Journal of E. Willard Smith." Edited by LeRoy R. Hafen. *Colorado Magazine* 27 (July 1950): 161–88.

Smith, Honora DeBusk. "Cowboy Lore in Colorado." *Southwestern Lore* 9 (1931): 27–44.

Steele, John. "Extracts from the Journal of John Steele." *Utah Historical Quarterly* 6 (1933): 3–28.

Stevenson, C. Stanley. "Buffalo East of the Missouri in South Dakota." *South Dakota Historical Collections* 9 (1918): 376–392.

Sublette, William L. "Fragmentary Journal of William L. Sublette." *Mississippi Valley Historical Review* 6 (1919): 99–110.

Tallmadge, Frank. "Buffalo Hunting with Custer." *Cavalry Journal* 38 (January 1929): 6–10.

Thomas, Chauncey. "Butchering Buffalo." *Colorado Magazine* 5 (April 1930): 41–54.

Trexler, H. A. "The Buffalo Range of the Northeast." *Mississippi Valley Historical Review* 7 (March 1921): 348–62.

Young, Lorenzo. "Diary of Lorenzo D. Young." *Utah Historical Quarterly* 14 (1946): 133–71.

GOVERNMENT and SCIENTIFIC REPORTS

Allen, Joel. "The American Bisons, Living and Extinct." *Memorial Museum of Comparative Zoology* 4:1–246.

Allen, Joel. "History of the American Bison." *Ninth Annual Report of the United States Geological and Geographic Survey of the Territories, 1875*. Washington: Government Printing Office, 1877, pp. 443–587.

Allen, Joel. "How Long the Buffaloes Remained in Illinois." *American Field* 22 (9 August 1884): 128.

Allen, Joel. "The North American Bison and Its Extermination." *Pennsylvania Monthly* 7 (March 1876): 214–24.

Allen, Joel. "The Northern Range of the Bison." *American Naturalist* 11 (1877): 624.

Allen, Joel. "Note on the Wood Bison." *Bulletin, American Museum of Natural History* 13 (1900): 63–67.

Anderson, R. M. "Wood Buffalo Park, N. W. T." *Annual Report, Division of Biology*. Toronto: National Museum of Canada, 1927, pp. 17–19.

Arrington Report. Phoenix, Arizona: Arizona Game and Fish Department, 1934.

Bandelier, A. F. "Report of an Archaeological Tour in Mexico in 1881." *Papers of the Archaeological Institute of America,* 1884.

Boyd, M. M. "A Short Account of an Experiment in Crossing the American Bison with Domestic Cattle." *American Breeder's Association Annual Report* 4 (1908): 324–31.

Boyd, Mossom M. "Crossing Bison and Cattalo." *Journal of Heredity,* May 1914, pp. 187–97.

Bringing Back the Buffalo. Ottawa: Department of Interior, 1926. 4 pp.

Bushnell, David. "The Various Uses of Buffalo Hair by the North American Indians." *American Anthropologist* 2 (1909): 401–425.

Cahalane, Victor H. "Restoration of Wild Bison." *Transactions of the North American Wildlife Conference* 9 (1944): 135–43.

Cameron, A. E. "Notes on Buffalo Anatomy, Pathological Conditions, and Parasites." *Veterinary Journal* 79 (1923): 331–36.

Cameron, A. E. "Some Further Notes on Buffalo." *Veterinary Journal* 80 (1924): 413–17.

Culbertson, Thaddeus. "Journal of an Expedition to the Mauvaises Terres and the Upper Missouri in 1850." Edited by John Francis McDermott. *Bureau of American Ethnology Bulletin 147.* Washington: Government Printing Office, 1952. 164 pp.

Deakin, A., Muir, G. W., and Smith, A. G. "Hybridization of Domestic Cattle, Bison and Yak." *Report of the Wainwright Experiment, No. 479.* Department of Agriculture, Canada, 1935. 30 pp.

Deakin, A., Muir, G. W., Smith, A. G., and MacLellan, A. S. "Hybridization of Domestic Cattle and Buffalo (Bison Americanus)." *Progress Report of the Wainwright Experiment.* Department of Agriculture, Canada, 1935–1941. 10 pp.

Denig, Edwin Thompson. "Indian Tribes of the Upper Missouri." Edited by J. N. B. Hewitt. *Bureau of American Ethnology Forty-Sixth Annual Report (1928–1929).* Washington: Government Printing Office, 1930, pp. 375–654.

Dorsey, George A., and Kroeber, A. L. "Traditions of the Arapaho." *Field Columbian Museum Publication 81.* Chicago: 1903.

Eiseley, Loren C. "The Paleo Indians: Their Survival and Diffusion." *New Interpretations of Aboriginal American Culture.* Ed. Betty J. Meggers and Clifford Evans. Washington: The Anthropological Society of Washington, 1955, pp. 1–11.

Eiseley, Loren, and Schultz, C. Bertrand. "Paleontological Evidence for the Antiquity of the Scottsbluff Bison Quarry and its Associated Artifacts." *American Anthropologist* 37 (1935): 306–319.

Elrod, Morton J. "The Flathead Buffalo Range." *Report of the American Bison Society.* New York, 1908, pp. 15–49.

Emory, W. H. "Notes on a Military Reconnaissance from Fort Leavenworth in Missouri to San Diego in California." *Senate Executive Document,* 30th Congress, 2nd Session, III, No. 7, p. 14.

Ewers, John C. "The Last Bison Drives of the Blackfoot Indians." *Journal of the Washington Academy of Sciences* 39 (November 1949): 355–60.

Ewers, John C. "Were the Blackfoot Rich in Horses?" *American Anthropologist* 45 (1943): 602–10.

Fletcher, Alice. "Giving Thanks: A Pawnee Ceremony." *The Journal of American Folklore* 13 (July–September 1900): 261–66.

Fryxell, F. M. "The Former Range of the Bison in the Rocky Mountains." *Journal of Mammology* 9 (May 1928): 129–39.

Fuller, William Albert. "The Biology and Management of the Bison of Wood Buffalo National Park." *Wildlife Management Bulletin* 1 (1962): 1–52.

Garretson, Martin S. *A Short History of the American Bison Society.* New York: American Bison Society, 1927.

Garretson, Martin S. "The Cattalo." *Report of American Bison Society, 1917–1918.* New York, 1918, pp. 30 ff.

Gilbert, E. W. "Animal Life and Exploration of Western America." *Scottish Geographic Magazine* 47 (1931): 19–28.

Goodnight, Charles. "My Experience with Bison Hybrids." *The Journal of Heredity* 5 (May 1914): 197–99.

Goodwin, George C. "Buffalo Hunt, 1935." *Natural History* 36 (1935): 156–64.

Graham, Maxwell. *Canada's Wild Buffalo.* Ottawa: Department of the Interior, 1923. 17 pp.

Gray, Annie P. *Mammalian Hybrids: A Checklist with Bibliography.* Commonwealth Agricultural Bureau, 1954.

Grinnell, George B. "Tenure of Land Among the Indians." *American Anthropologist* 9 (January 1907): 1–11.

Guthrie, Russell D. "Bison Evolution and Zoogeography in North America During the Pleistocene." *The Quarterly Review of Biology* 45 (March 1970): 1–15.

Guthrie, Russell D. "Pelage of Fossil Bison—a New Osteological Index." *Journal of Mammology* 47 (1966): 725–27.

Haines, Francis. "The Northward Spread of Horses Among the Plains Indians." *American Anthropologist* 40 (1938): 429–37.

Haines, Francis. "Where did the Plains Indians Get Their Horses?" *American Anthropologist* 40 (1938): 112–17.

Hall, R. H. "A Buffalo Robe Biography." *The Museum Journal* [University of Pennsylvania] 17 (1926): 5–35.

Hammer, R. S. "The Canadian Bison-Cattle Cross." *Proceedings of the Scottish Cattle Breeding Conference.* Edited by G. F. Finley. Edinburgh: Oliver and Boyd, 1925. Chapter 23.

Heller, E. "The Big Game Animals of Yellowstone National Park." *Roosevelt Wild Life Bulletin* 2 (1925): 405–67.

Hornaday, W. T. "Discovery, Life History, and Extermination of American Bison." *Report of the National Museum,*

1887. Washington: Government Printing Office, 1889, pp. 367–548.

Hough, W. "The Bison as a Factor in Ancient American Culture History." *Scientific Monthly* 30 (August 1925): 89.

Johnson, Charles W. "Protein as a Factor in the Distribution of the American Bison." *Geographical Review* 41 (1951): 330–31.

Jones, C. J. "Breeding Cattalo." *American Breeder's Association Annual Report* 3 (1907): 161.

Kitto, F. H. "The Survival of the American Bison in Canada." *Geographical Journal* 63 (1924): 431–37.

Kroeber, A. L. "Cheyenne Tales." *The Journal of American Folklore* 13 (July–September 1900): 161–190.

Kurz, Rudolph F. "Journal of Rudolph Friedrich Kurz: An Account of His Experiences Among Fur Traders and American Indians During the Years 1846 to 1852." Edited by J. N. B. Hewitt. *Bureau of American Ethnology Bulletin No. 115*. Washington: Government Printing Office, 1937, pp. 1–382.

Larson, Floyd. "The Role of Bison in Maintaining the Short Grass Plains." *Ecology* 21 (April 1940): 113–21.

"The Last Wild Buffalo." *American Game Protective Association Bulletin* 13 (1924): 4–6.

Leopold, Aldo. "Wildlife in American Culture." *Journal of Wildlife Management* 7 (1943): 1–6.

Lewis, Oscar. "The Effects of White Contact Upon Blackfoot Culture." *Monographs of the American Ethnological Society, No. 6* (1942), pp. 34–42.

Logan, V. S., and Sylvestre, P. E. *Hybridization of Domestic Beef Cattle and Buffalo*. Ottawa: Department of Agriculture, 1940.

Loring, J. Alden. *Report on Certain Lands in South Dakota Suitable for a Buffalo and Game Reserve*. New York: American Bison Society, 1911.

Loring, J. Alden. *The Wichita Buffalo Range, a Report to the New York Zoological Society*. New York: Tenth Annual Report of the New York Zoological Society, 1906.

Lowie, Robert H. "Myths and Traditions of the Crow Indians." *Anthropological Papers of the American Museum of Natural History*. Vol. 25. New York: American Museum Press, 1922.

MacGregor, R. "The Domestic Buffalo." *Veterinary Record* 53 (1941): 443–50.

McHugh, Tom. "Social Behavior of the American Buffalo (Bison Bison Bison)." *Zoologica* 43 (March 1958).

Mallery, Garrick. "Picture Writing of the American Indians." *Tenth Annual Report of the Bureau of Ethnology*. Washington: Government Printing Office, 1893, pp. 25–822.

Meagher, Mary. "Yellowstone's Bison, a Unique Wild Heritage." *The Environmental Journal*, May 1974, pp. 9–14.

Merriam, C. Hart. "The Bison in Northeastern California." *Journal of Mammology* 7 (1926): 211–14.

Muller-Beck, Hansjurgen. "Paleohunter in America: Origins and Diffusion." *Science* 152 (27 May 1966): 1191–1210.

Nelson, E. W. "Recent Efforts to Break Down Game Protective Laws." *Bulletin, American Game Protective Association* 7 (1918): 26–27.

Palmer, Theodore S. "Chronology and Index of the More Important Events in American Game Protection, 1776–1911." *U.S. Department of Agriculture, Biological Survey Bulletin No. 41*. Washington: Government Printing Office, 1912.

Palmer, T. S. "Game as a Natural Resource." *Bulletin No. 1049, U.S. Department of Agriculture*. Washington: Government Printing Office, 1922.

Peters, H. F. *Experimental Hybridization of Domestic Cattle and American Bison*. Manyberries, Canada: Canada Agricultural Experimental Farm, 1964.

Raup, Hugh M. "Range Conditions in the Wood Buffalo Park of Western Canada with Notes on the History of the Wood Bison." *American Committee for International Wild Life Protection* 1 (1933): 1–52.

Raynolds, W. F. "Report on the Exploration of the Yellowstone and the Country Drained by the River." *Senate Executive Document 77*, 40th Congress, 1st Session.

Reports of American Bison Society. New York: American Bison Society, 1905–1930.

Roe, Frank Gilbert. "The Numbers of the Buffalo." *Proceedings and Transactions of the Royal Society of Canada* (1937), pp. 171–203.

Ronan, Peter. "Report of the Flathead Agency, August 16, 1888." *Report of the Secretary of the Interior*. Vol. 2, pp. 155–58. Washington: Government Printing Office, 1888.

Rush, W. M. "Bang's Disease in the Yellowstone National Park Buffalo and Elk Herds." *Journal of Mammology* 13 (1932): 371–72.

Ruth, Clara. "Preserves and Ranges Maintained for Buffalo and other Big Game." *U.S. Bureau Biological Survey, Wildlife Restoration and Management Leaflet 95*. Washington: Government Printing Office, 1939. 20 pp.

Scott, Hugh Lenox. "Notes on the Kado, or Sun Dance of the Kiowa." *American Anthropologist* 13 (July–September 1911): 345–79.

Seibert, F. V. "Some Notes on Canada's So-called Wood Buffalo." *Canadian Field Naturalist* 39: 204–06.

Simms, S. C. "Traditions of the Crows." *Publication 85, Anthropological Series*. Vol. 2. Chicago: Field Columbian Museum, 1903.

Skinner, Morris F., and Kaisen, Ove C. "The Fossil Bison of Alaska and Preliminary Revision of the Genus." *Bulletin of the American Museum of Natural History* 89 (1947): 125–256.

Skinner, M. P. "The Hoofed Animals of Yellowstone." *American Museum Journal* 16 (1916): 86–95.

Soper, J. Dewey. "History, Range, and Home Life of the Northern Bison." *Ecological Monographs* 11 (October 1941): 347–412.

Strong, William Duncan. "From History to Prehistory in the Northern Great Plains." *Smithsonian Miscellaneous*

Collections. Vol. 100. Washington: Smithsonian Institution, 1940.

Strong, William Duncan. "The Plains Culture in the Light of Archeology." *American Anthropologist* 35 (1933): 271–87.

Sylvestre, P. E., Logan, V. S., and Muir, G. W. "Hybridization of Domestic Cattle and the Bison." Canadian Department of Agriculture, 1948. Mimeographed. 7 pp.

Taylor, Walter P. "The Buffalo." *Monthly Bulletin of the Texas Game, Fish and Oyster Commission* 4 (January 1941): 2–8.

Turney-High, Harry. "The Diffusion of the Horse to the Flatheads." *Man* 35 (December 1935): 183–85.

United States Department of the Interior. *Management of Buffalo Herds*. Washington: Government Printing Office, 1955.

Warren, Edward R. "Altitude Limit of Bison." *Journal of Mammology* 8 (February 1927): 102–09.

Wedel, Waldo R. "Culture Sequence in the Central Great Plains." *Smithsonian Miscellaneous Collections*. Vol. 100. Washington: Smithsonian Institution, 1940, pp. 291–352.

Wedel, Waldo R. "Environment and Native Subsistence Economies in the Central Great Plains." *Smithsonian Miscellaneous Collections*. Vol. 101. Washington: Smithsonian Institution, 1941.

Wissler, Clark. "The Influence of the Horse in the Development of Plains Culture." *American Anthropologist* 16 (1914): 1–25.

Yount, Harry. "Report of the Gamekeeper." *Fifth Annual Report of the Superintendent of Yellowstone Park*. Washington: Government Printing Office, 1881, pp. 62–63.

NEWSPAPERS

Ariza, John Francis. "The Buffalo Finds His Haven at Last." *New York Times Magazine*, 30 September 1928, p. 8.

Bad Lands Cowboy (Little Missouri, Medora P.O., Dakota), 18 July 1884, p. 2; 20 November 1884, pp. 1 and 4.

"Bear Gulch to Yellowstone Lake in 1867." *Montana Post* (Virginia City), 31 August 1867, p. 6.

Bigart, Homer. "Ranchers Claim Park Bison Pose Health Threat to Cattle." *New York Times* News Service, no date.

"Bison Range Bids Bountiful." *Missoulian* (Montana), 15 September 1974.

"Buffalo Which Roamed West Aided Reds to Withstand Whites." *Spokesman-Review* (Spokane), 29 May 1921, p. 2.

"'Cattalo' Cross Doesn't Work Out." *The Modern Farmer* (Winnipeg), 28 August 1958.

"Cattalo Experiment Ending." *The Lethbridge Herald* (Alberta), 31 July 1964.

Coates, Grace Stone. "Three Forks Man Recalls Smithsonian Buffalo Hunt for National Museum." *Billings Gazette* (Montana), 29 September 1948.

Conway, Dan R. *Northwest Tribune* (Stevensville, Montana), February 1927. (Clipping in Montana History folder, Missoula Public Library, Missoula, Montana.)

Daily Free Press (Winnipeg), 16 October 1876.

Daily New Mexican (Santa Fe), 3 April 1869.

Forssen, John A. "Today's Market Can't Match Big Buffalo Sale of Half Century Ago." *Missoulian* (Montana), 5 January 1958.

Grill, "Montana Lou." "Buffalo Hunting." *Philipsburg Mail* (Montana). (Undated clipping in Montana History folder, Missoula Public Library, Missoula, Montana.)

Jeffersonian Republican (Missouri), 20 July 1833, p. 2.

"Last Buffalo Hunt Is For Rustlers." *Albertan* (Calgary), 21 March 1962.

Lethbridge Herald (Alberta), 1 July 1964.

"Lively Scene on an American Prairie—A Buffalo Hunt by Steam." *Frank Leslie's Illustrated Newspaper*, 28 November 1868, pp. 173–74.

Missoulian (Montana), 28 June, 1 July, 11 October 1909.

Moore, Steve. "Buffalo Market Bullish." *Missoulian* (Montana), 11 August 1974.

"Plan Will Protect Rare Wood Buffalo." *Edmonton Journal*, 19 January 1961.

"Protection of the Buffalo." *Daily Free Press* (Winnipeg), 16 October 1876.

"Sale of Hides Nets $1050.50." *Missoulian* (Montana), 14 March 1970.

Shipp, E. Richard. "Doc Carver—Buffalo Hunter." *Northwest Tribune* (Stevensville, Montana), 13 October 1927.

"Sports of the South!!" *The Clarion and Tennessee Gazette*, 29 January 1819, p. 3.

Sullivan, Mark. "Census of Buffalo." *Boston Evening Transcript*, 10 October 1890.

"U.S. Buffalo Making a Big Comeback." *Missoulian* (Montana), 24 November 1967.

Victoria Advocate (Texas), 23 August 1879, p. 2.

Voorhees, Luke. "Perils and Trials of the Early Stage Coach." *Sunday State Leader* (Cheyenne, Wyoming), 15 July 1917.

Willson, Roscoe G. "How the Buffalo Came to Arizona." *Arizona Republic* (Phoenix), 16 October, 23 October 1960.

Wilson, A. W. "Old Time Buffalo Hunter Recalls the Days When the Thundering Herd Dominated the Plains." *Kalispell Times* (Montana), 30 April 1931.

"Wood Buffalo Rescue Plan." *Red Deer Advocate* (Alberta), 17 January 1961.

UNPUBLISHED WRITINGS

Alcorn, Wayne B., and Skinner, Curtis H. "History of the Bison in Yellowstone," File No. 715-03, Chief Ranger's Office, Yellowstone Park. Mimeographed.

Alvis, Barry Newton. "Settlement and Economic Development of Union County, New Mexico." M.A. thesis, University of Colorado, 1934.

"American Bison in Yellowstone Park. Yellowstone Nature Notes." March 1, 1928, pp. 3–5.

Andrews, Anne Margaret. "The Economic Value of the Buffalo." M.A. thesis, University of Southern California, 1942.

Brown, Kootenai. "Recollections of Kootenai Brown." Files of Historical Society of Montana, Helena.

Dolph, James A. "The American Bison Society: Preserver of the American Buffalo and Pioneer in Wildlife Conservation." M.S. thesis, University of Denver, 1965.

Dowling, Alice B. "The Significance of the Destruction of the American Bison in the Southwest." M.A. thesis, University of Oklahoma, 1932.

Forbis, Richard G. "A Stratified Buffalo Kill in Alberta." In "Symposium on Buffalo Jumps." Edited by Carling Malouf and Stuart Conner. Montana Archaeological Society Memoir No. 1, May 1962. Mimeographed.

Grieder, Theodore G. "The Influence of the American Bison or Buffalo on Westward Expansion." M.A. thesis, University of Iowa, 1928.

Kidd, Kenneth E. "Blackfoot Ethnography." M.S. thesis, University of Toronto, 1937.

Lewis, H. P. "Buffalo Kills in Montana." Files in University of Montana library.

Lindsley, Chester A. "The Chronology of Yellowstone National Park, 1806 to 1939." Files of Yellowstone National Park Library.

Lott, Dale F. "Sexual and Aggressive Behavior of American Bison (Bison Bison)." In my files. Mimeographed.

Malouf, Carling. "Cultural Connections Between the Prehistoric Inhabitants of the Upper Missouri and Columbia Rivers Systems." Ph.D. dissertation, Columbia University, 1956.

Malouf, Carling, and Conner, Stuart, editors. "Symposium on Buffalo Jumps. Montana Archaeological Society, Memoir No. 1," May, 1962. University of Montana Library. Mimeographed.

Merriman, R. O. "The American Bison as a Source of Food: A Factor in Canadian Economic History." M.S. thesis, Queen's University, 1925.

"Report on the Grand Canyon Buffalo Herd (1924)." In American Bison Society files, Conservation Center Library, Denver, Colorado.

Schaeffer, Claude E. "The Bison Drive of the Blackfeet." Museum of the Plains Indians, Browning, Montana.

Seymour, Edmund. "The American Bison." In American Bison Society papers, Conservation Center Library, Denver.

"Summary of History of Yellowstone Buffalo Herd." In Yellowstone Park Library, File No. 59973584.

LETTERS in AMERICAN BISON SOCIETY PAPERS

Barnes, Will C., Assistant Forester, U.S. Forest Service, to W. T. Hornaday, 7 November 1922.

Baynes, E. H. to Edmund Seymour, 26 June 1920.

Beard, Dan to Edmund Seymour, September 1921.

Bede, Judge A. McG. to Edmund Seymour, 29 October 1919.

Corbin, Austin to Edmund Seymour, 20 September 1918.

Damon, H. H. to Martin Garretson. No date.

Fleming, H. A. to W. O. Wharton, 14 November 1910.

Fleming, J. H. to Francis Harper, 3 April 1925.

Garretson, Martin S. Note initialed MSG.

Garretson, M. S. to Editor of New York Times, 2 March 1923.

Garretson, Martin S. to Edmund Seymour, 28 January 1928.

Garretson, Martin S. to Dick Adams, 1 July 1925.

Gibson, O. D. to M. S. Garretson, 12 October 1928.

Goodnight, Charles to Edmund Seymour, 31 August 1916.

Goodnight, Charles to Edmund Seymour, 4 December 1916.

Goodnight, Charles to Edmund Seymour, 12 November 1917.

Goodnight, Charles to Edmund Seymour, 4 January 1923.

Goodnight, Charles to W. O. Wharton, 4 November 1910.

Goodnight, Mary to Edmund Seymour, 30 September 1916.

Grasher, Ray E. (Arizona Bill), to Edmund Seymour, 2 June 1919.

Hatch, E. C. to George W. P. Hunt, Governor of Arizona, 28 January 1924.

Hodges, A. R. to W. J. Spurzen, 28 November 1910.

Hornaday, W. T. to Mr. Rush, 5 November 1917.

Hornaday, W. T. to Edmund Seymour, 18 January 1917.

Hornaday, W. T. to Edmund Seymour, 15 December 1917.

Hornaday, W. T. to G. A. Smith, 10 October 1918.

Jones, C. J. to Edmund Seymour, 8 April 1917.

Jones, C. J. to Edmund Seymour, 24 February 1917.

Jones, C. J. to Edmund Seymour, 20 May 1917.

Jones, C. J. to Edmund Seymour, 8 April 1910.

Morris, Robert T., Dr., to Edmund Seymour, 27 September 1916.

Ortiz, Louis to Edmund Seymour, 23 November 1924.

Ortiz, Louis to Edmund Seymour, 22 December 1924.

Owens, J. T. (Uncle Jimmy) to G. M. Willard, 2 February 1924.

Palmer, T. S. to Edmund Seymour, 21 August 1917.

Palmer, T. S. to Edmund Seymour, 24 August 1917.

Palmer, T. S. to Edmund Seymour, 17 October 1917.

Pittis, D. E. to Edmund Seymour, 15 October 1927.

Root, Joseph, Dr., to Edmund Seymour, 9 September 1916.

School, Lester H. to M. S. Garretson, 19 June 1935.

Seymour, Edmund to Mr. Bronson, 13 December 1916.

Seymour, Edmund to T. S. Palmer, 17 May 1917.

Seymour, Edmund to T. S. Palmer, 23 May 1917.

Stocking, Clark to Edmund Seymour, 8 March 1917.

Tillotson, H. J., Dr., to Charles Goodnight, 22 April 1918.

Willard, G. M. to Edmund Seymour, 3 January 1924.

Willard, G. M. to Edmund Seymour, 5 February 1924.

LETTERS IN OTHER COLLECTIONS

Eaton, Howard to Alicia Conrad, 7 February 1907. (Conrad papers, Archives, University of Montana Library.)

Helgeson, Henry J. to Virginia Walton, 28 August 1955; to Mr. Blakeless, 1 January 1956. (Montana Historical Society Library, Helena, Montana.)

Luxton, Norman to Mr. McCoy, 2 October 1961. (Norman K. Luxton papers, Glenbow Foundation Library, Calgary, Alberta.)

INTERVIEWS

McDowell, Frank. Interviewed at Spokane Ranch, Big Hole Valley, Montana, 9 October 1972.

Stevens, Frank. Interviewed at Three Forks Rest Home, Three Forks, Montana, 23 August 1965.

INDEX

HEADS, HIDES & HORNS
has been designed
by
WHITEHEAD & WHITEHEAD
set in Goudy Old Style by G&S TYPESETTERS
printed and bound by EDWARDS BROTHERS, *Ann Arbor*
calligraphy by BARBARA WHITEHEAD
1985